INFORMATION TECHNOLOGY PROJECT MANAGEMENT

Providing Measurable Organizational Value

Jack T. Marchewka

Northern Illinois University

www.wiley.com/college/marchewka

Acquisitions Editor   *Beth Lang Golub*
Assistant Editor   *Lorraina Raccuia*
Marketing Manager   *Gitti Lindner*
Managing Editor   *Lari Bishop*
Associate Production Manager   *Kelly Tavares*
Production Editor   *Sarah Wolfman-Robichaud*
Photo Researcher   *Shoshanna Turek*
Illustration Editor   *Benjamin Reece*
Cover Design   *Jennifer Fisher*
Cover Image   *Lester Lefkowitz/Corbis*

This book was set in Times by Leyh Publishing LLC and printed and bound by R.R. Donnelley & Sons. The cover was printed by Phoenix Printing.

This book is printed on acid free paper.

ISBN: 0-471-39203-0

Printed in the United States of America

10 9 8 7 6 5 4 3 2 1

This project is dedicated to the memory of my mother, Josephine.
And also to Beth, Bill, Tim, Kellie Ann, Matt, and my father, Ted.
Thanks for all of your support.

BRIEF CONTENTS

CONTENTS

CHAPTER 2   Conceptualizing and Initializing the IT Project   23

CHAPTER 11   **Managing Organizational Change, Resistance, and Conflict   256**

CHAPTER 12   **Project Implementation, Closure, and Evaluation   281**

PREFACE

Welcome to *Information Technology Project Management—Providing Measurable Organizational Value*. This book was written to help people understand the processes, tools, techniques, and areas of knowledge needed to successfully manage information technology (IT) projects.

The idea of project management has been around for a long, long time. In fact, it was around before the great pyramids of Egypt were created. Today, project management has emerged as its own field, supported by a body of knowledge and research across many disciplines. Although still relatively new, the fields of Management Information Systems (MIS) and Software Engineering have their own bodies of knowledge that include various tools, techniques, and methods supported by a continually growing base of research.

Unfortunately, the track record for IT projects has not been as successful as one might expect, although the situation appears to be improving. One reason for this improvement has been a greater focus on a project management approach to support the activities required to develop and deliver information systems. Just as building a system is more than sitting down in front of a computer and writing code, project management is more than just creating fancy charts or diagrams using one of the more popular project management software packages.

We can, however, build a system that is a technical success but an organizational failure. Information systems—the products of IT projects—are planned organizational change. Information technology is an enabler for new products, services, and processes that can change existing relationships between an organization and its customers or suppliers, as well as among the people within the organization.

This change can represent a threat to many groups. Therefore, people may not always be receptive to a new information system, regardless of how well it was built or how up-to-date the technology, tools, and techniques. On the other hand, people in an organization may rightfully resist an information system that does not function properly or meet their envisioned needs. Therefore, we must take an approach that does not consider the technical side over the organizational side or vice versa. Attention to both the technical and organizational sides of IT projects must be balanced in order to deliver a successful project.

But what is a successful project? Many people and authors define project success in terms of the project being completed on time and within budget. I will not argue that completing a project by its intended deadline and within its allocated resources is not important. I will, however, argue that on time and on-budget are important, but not necessarily sufficient conditions for project success. For example, would a project that was expected to be completed within six months and cost no more than $1 million be considered unsuccessful if the project required an extra day or an extra dollar to complete?

You may think this is trivial, but at exactly what point in terms of schedule or budget does the project become unsuccessful?

We can also turn things around and ask whether finishing the project early and under-budget makes the project successful. Of course any organization would like to spend less money and have its system delivered early, but what if the system does not perform as required? More specifically, what value will the organization receive by spending six months and $1 million on this particular project? Therefore, an organization expects to receive some kind of organizational value from the implemented system when it makes an IT investment.

As you will see throughout this text, a project's measurable organizational value, or MOV, defines a project's value to the organization and becomes the project's measure of success. Moreover, a project's MOV also provides a foundation for integrating project management and IT concepts, tools, and techniques, as well as for various decisions that are made from the project's conceptualization to its closure.

APPROACH

In writing this book, I have tried to create a balance between concept and application. Many project management books tend to cover a broad set of topics with little practical application. Others tend to focus on the tools and techniques, but fall short in showing how everything ties together.

This book was written with the student in mind. Many years ago—more than I would care to admit—when I was a student, one of my instructors said that the problem with many textbooks was that they were written by professors for other professors. That statement stuck with me over the years. When I began writing this text, I wanted to be sure that it was written with the student in mind.

Learning and understanding how to apply new concepts, tools, and techniques can be challenging enough without being made more complex by obscure writing. As you will find out, learning concepts is relatively easy when compared to putting them into good practice. This book is intended for both undergraduate and graduate students. While it has no specific prerequisites, you should have at least an introductory class in information systems or programming under your belt. You should find that the concepts of IT project management will compliment courses in systems analysis and design.

Those of you who are undergraduates will not be thrust into the role of a project manager immediately after graduation. My goal is to help prepare you for the next several progressions of your career. For example, your first assignment may be to work on a project as a programmer or analyst. The knowledge that you will gain from this text will give you a good idea of how your work fits into the big picture so that you can be a more valuable project team member. More challenging and interesting assignments and opportunities for advancement will follow as you continue to gain more knowledge and experience. Eventually, this may lead to a leadership role where your knowledge and experience will be put to the optimal test.

On the other hand, you may have already acquired some experience and now find yourself in the role of a project manager. This text will provide you not only with the big picture, but also with a foundation for applying directly the tools, processes, and methods to support the management and delivery of a successful IT project.

This book follows a generic Information Technology Project Methodology (ITPM). Most students who read this book will never have been on a real IT project. I have written this book based on a flexible methodology that attempts to bridge the questions: How do I get started?, What do I do next?, How do we know when we're finished? This methodology provides a structure for understanding how projects are initiated, conceptualized, planned, carried out, terminated, and evaluated. This methodology will take you through the different phases of the project life cycle and introduce the concepts and tools that are appropriate for each specific phase or stage of the project. In addition, you will find the methodology and central theme of this text is that IT projects should provide measurable value to organizations.

The text provides an integrated approach to IT project management. It incorporates the nine areas outlined in the Project Management Institute's Project Management Body of Knowledge (PMBOK). The concepts associated with information systems management and software engineering when integrated with PMBOK provide an important base of knowledge that builds a foundation for IT project management. This integration helps to distinguish IT projects from other types of projects such as construction or engineering.

The text also integrates a knowledge management approach. The area of knowledge management is an area of growing interest and development. Knowledge management is a systematic process for acquiring, creating, synthesizing, sharing, and using information, insights, and experiences to create business value. Here, the concept of learning cycles provides a unique approach for defining and creating new knowledge in terms of lessons learned. These lessons learned can be stored in a repository and made available throughout the organization. Best practices can be developed from the lessons learned and integrated or made a part of an organization's IT project methodology. Over time, the generic ITPM introduced in this text can evolve and become a valuable asset to an organization as it becomes aligned with the organization's culture and business. In turn, this evolving process will provide the organization with increased capability and maturity that hopefully will increase the likelihood of successful projects.

CHAPTER OVERVIEWS

The material in each chapter provides a logical flow in terms of the phases and processes required to plan and manage an IT project. The text begins with a call for a better way to manage IT projects and then focuses on the deliverables and processes required to initiate a project. Once a decision to approve and fund an IT project is made, the project must be planned at a detailed level to determine the project's schedule and budget. The planning and subsequent execution of the project's plan are supported by the project management and information technology bodies of knowledge.

- *Chapter 1: The Nature of Information Technology Projects* describes the software crisis and the context of IT project management. This includes defining what a project is and the discipline of project management. The concepts of the project life cycle and systems development life cycle are also introduced.

- *Chapter 2: Conceptualizing and Initializing the IT Project* introduces an Information Technology Project Management Methodology (ITPM) and the concept of measurable organizational value (MOV), which will provide a foundation for this text. In addition, the first phase of this methodology, conceptualizing and initializing the project, and the first deliverable of this methodology, the business case, are described and discussed.

- *Chapter 3: Developing the Project Charter and Baseline Project Plan* introduces project integration management and a project planning framework to support the development of the project plan.

- *Chapter 4: The Human Side of Project Management* describes the formal and informal organization so that the project manager and team can conduct a stakeholder analysis to better understand the organizational landscape. Project team selection and the roles of the project manager are discussed, as is the concept of learning cycles to support a knowledge management approach to IT project management.

- *Chapter 5: Defining and Managing Project Scope* introduces and describes the project management knowledge area called project scope management. The project's scope defines what the project team will and will not deliver to the project sponsor or client. Scope management processes also ensure that the project's scope is properly defined and that controls are in place in order to manage scope throughout the project.

- *Chapter 6: The Work Breakdown Structure and Project Estimation* describes the project management tool called the work breakdown structure (WBS), which breaks up the project's scope into work packages that include specific deliverables and milestones. Several traditional project estimation approaches will be introduced, as will several software engineering techniques and metrics for software estimation.

- *Chapter 7: The Project Schedule and Budget* introduces several project management tools, including Gantt charts, activity on the node (AON), critical path analysis, program evaluation and review technique (PERT), and precedence diagramming, that can be used to develop the project schedule. A project budget can then be developed based upon the activities defined in the WBS, the project schedule, and the cost of the resources assigned or required.

- *Chapter 8: Managing Project Risk* describes the concept of risk management and introduces a framework for defining and understanding the integrative nature of risks associated with an IT project. Several qualitative and quantitative approaches and tools will be introduced for analyzing and assessing risks so that appropriate risk strategies can be formulated.

- *Chapter 9: Project Communication, Tracking, and Reporting* focuses on developing a communication plan for reporting the project's progress to various project stakeholders. This chapter includes an introduction to the concept of earned value and a system of project metrics to monitor and control the project.

- *Chapter 10: IT Project Quality Management* provides a brief history of the quality movement, the people involved, and their philosophies and teachings as an underpinning to support the project quality objective. Several quality systems to support IT project quality will also be discussed. These include the International Standards Organization (ISO), TickIT, Six Sigma, and the Capability Maturity Model (CMM). Together, the concepts, teachings, philosophies, and quality system approaches provide a basis for developing the IT project quality plan.

- *Chapter 11: Managing Organizational Change, Resistance, and Conflict* describes the nature and impact of change associated with the delivery of an information system on the people within an organization. Several organizational change theories will be introduced so that a change management plan can be formulated and executed in order to ease the transition from the current system to the system that will be implemented.

- *Chapter 12: Project Implementation, Closure, and Evaluation* describes the tactical approaches for installing and delivering the project's product—the information system. In addition, the processes for bringing closure to the project and evaluating the project team and the project's MOV are discussed.

- *Appendix A: An Introduction to Function Point Analysis* provides a more detailed discussion on counting function points than is provided in Chapter 6.

ORGANIZATION AND SUPPORT

The beginning of each chapter includes an opening vignette or story that describes a particular situation faced by a project manager and team undertaking an IT project. This scenario will set the stage for the concepts and tools introduced in the chapter and make the learning of the material more meaningful. From a student's perspective, this will attempt to answer the "so what?" and "why do I have to know this?" questions that should be addressed.

For many chapters there is a Web-based practicum that includes a set of integrated hands-on case assignments. The case assignments allow the student to play the role of a project team member who has been hired by a newly formed consulting firm. The Web site provides all the background for the company. The cases lead the student through the various stages of planning an IT project for a client. They include several deliverables such as the project charter, project plan, scope management plan, risk plan, and implementation plan, and they require the student to apply the concepts and techniques covered in the book.

More specifically, each case assignment will include both a hands-on and a critical thinking component. For example, the hands-on component of the case assignment may ask students to develop a project plan using Microsoft Project. However, the student would then be asked to answer questions about how specific concepts discussed in the book relate to the hands-on component. The hands-on component allows students to develop a particular skill, while the critical thinking component allows them to reflect upon how their actions may affect the project in different ways.

The supporting Web site for the Web-based project management community will host a discussion or chat area that allows students, instructors, project management experts, and even the author to discuss and share ideas from around the world.

In addition, the Web site will host various student support materials. For example, it links to various IT and project management-related Web sites and articles to support the material included in the text. A trial version of Microsoft Project 2002 has also been included with the text.

An instructor's manual, test bank, and presentation slides are available. A section of the Web site has been partitioned just for instructors to support the sharing of teaching ideas and experiences.

ACKNOWLEDGEMENTS

I would like to thank my editor Beth Lang Golub, Lorraina Raccuia, and Jennifer Battista of John Wiley & Sons, and Lari Bishop and Shoshanna Turek of Leyh Publishing for all of their hard work. I would also thank all of the reviewers for their insightful and helpful comments.

Patricia A. McQuaid   *California Polytechnic State University*
John M. Kohlmeier   *DePaul University*
Dennis Adams   *University of Houston*
Anthony R. Hendrickson   *Iowa State University*
Chelley Vician   *Michigan Technological University*
Rajiv Sabherwal   *University of Missouri–St. Louis*
Mark Nissen   *Naval Postgraduate School*
Gurpreet S. Dhillon   *University of Nevada, Las Vegas*
Bel G. Raggad   *Pace University*
Dale Perrin, Ph.D.   *University of Phoenix*
Laurie J. Kirsch   *University of Pittsburgh*
Dr. Laura L. Hall   *University of Texas at El Paso*
Ann Banks Pidduck   *University of Waterloo*

ABOUT THE AUTHOR

Jack T. Marchewka is an associate professor, the Barsema Professor of Management Information Systems, and the director of the Business Information Technology Transfer Center (BITTC) at Northern Illinois University. He received his Ph.D. from Georgia State University's department of Computer Information Systems in 1994 and was a former faculty member at Kennesaw State University. Prior to entering academia, Dr. Marchewka was a vice president of MIS for a healthcare company in Atlanta, Georgia.

Dr. Marchewka has taught a number of courses at both the undergraduate and graduate levels and has been a guest lecturer at the Rotterdam School of Management, Erasmus University in the Netherlands. His current research interests include IT project management, electronic commerce, knowledge management, and organizational security and business continuity. His articles have appeared in journals such as *Information Resources Management Journal, Information Technology & People, Journal of International Information Management,* and *Journal of Informatics Education and Research.*

Jack Marchewka is also an instrument-rated commercial pilot, who enjoys his family, flying, golf, guitars, good BBQ, riding his motorcycle, and a good laugh.

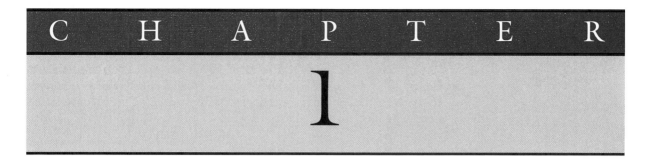

The Nature of Information Technology Projects

CHAPTER OBJECTIVES

Chapter 1 provides an overview of information technology project management (ITPM). After studying this chapter, you should understand and be able to:

- Describe the software crisis and how the often dismal track record for information technology (IT) projects provides a motivation for changing how we view and manage IT projects.
- Explain the socio-technical, project management, and knowledge management approaches that support ITPM.
- Define what an IT project is and describe its attributes.
- Define the discipline called project management.
- Describe the role and impact IT projects have on an organization.
- Identify the different roles and interests of project stakeholders.
- Describe the project life cycle, the systems development life cycle, and their relationship.
- Identify the Project Management Body of Knowledge (PMBOK) and its core knowledge areas.

GLOBAL TECHNOLOGY SOLUTIONS

Tim Williams placed the phone gently back in its cradle. He sat for a moment, not sure whether he felt excitement or sheer terror. Or, could it be he was feeling both? Kellie Matthews, his partner in Global Technology Solutions (GTS), had just told Tim that Husky Air, a business air charter company, was very interested in having them develop an information system. This was the moment Tim had been waiting for—

their first client! Before Husky Air will sign a contract, however, they need to know what GTS will deliver, how much it will cost, and when the project will be completed.

As the project's manager, Tim knows that getting this contract is important. Husky Air would be the company's first and, so far, only client. Tim also understands that a successful project could lead to other work with Husky Air. Moreover, a verbal or written recommendation would provide additional credibility to help GTS get its foot in the door with other potential clients.

While working together in the information services department at a large company, Tim and Kellie decided that a small, independent consulting firm could be successful developing smaller IT-based systems. The lure of being their own bosses and the potential for financial and personal rewards were too great to resist. Tim and Kellie cashed in their stock options, and GTS was born. They decided that Kellie would develop new business and manage the day-to-day operations of GTS, while Tim would deliver and manage the projects. New employees with specific skill sets would be hired as needed to support particular projects.

Although both Tim and Kellie had worked in IT for several years, neither of them had ever managed a consulting project before. Aside from the questions posed by Husky Air (What will you deliver? How much will it cost? How long will it take?), Tim felt a bit overwhelmed because he knew the success or failure of this project would have an immediate impact on the viability of the new firm.

Things to Think About:

1. If you were in Tim's shoes, what feelings do you think you would experience?
2. What questions would you have?
3. What might help reduce your anxiety and uncertainty as an inexperienced project manager?
4. Where do you begin a new project?

INTRODUCTION

The new millennium provides a vantage point from which to look back at our past and ahead to our future. Many people at the end of the century emptied their bank accounts, stockpiled food and water, and even went so far as to head for the hills for fear that computers would crash and civilization would fall into mass confusion. Fortunately, the reported Y2K computer-related problems were few and not especially critical. Was the problem hyped? Not really. Was there really a problem? Yes! Many companies spent millions of dollars to change and test the dates in their computer systems so the passing of January 1, 2000 would have no effect. Just ask one of the many IT professionals who worked hard and long on a Y2K project. You may even know, or be, one of those people.

What made the Y2K problem fascinating was that just about everyone was in this together and the project had an immovable deadline. As a result, the field of information technology received a great deal of attention in the media and the boardroom. Even though it was shortsightedness that created the problem, the few reported Y2K problems prompted some to believe this was the IT profession's shining hour. Moreover, the risks and costs associated with the Y2K problem captured the attention of senior management. As a result, people at different levels, including senior management, and in different functional areas became more involved with and interested in information technology. The good news is that the world of IT moved from the back office to the boardroom. The bad news is that IT may be doomed to repeat past mistakes.

After Y2K, it appeared that companies now had the time and money to start on their IT projects that had been on hold. Electronic commerce and the integration of enterprise resource planning (ERP) packages were at the top of the IT project list for many organizations. The demand for skilled IT professionals and project managers to head up these new initiatives had never been stronger. It seemed as though recruiters couldn't hire experienced professionals and university graduates fast enough to meet the demand.

Unfortunately, this golden time for IT did not last. The tragic events of September 2001 had a profound impact on the world and the global economy. As a result, many organizations were forced to make some difficult choices in order to survive. Seasoned professionals and new graduates who once commanded high salaries and choice assignments found themselves facing a tough job market. The bubble had burst. If nothing else, we learned that things can change quickly and without warning.

As you read this, think about what is going on in the field of IT right now. Is the demand for IT professionals and IT projects strong? Or, are there fewer jobs and projects available? If the demand for IT projects and professionals to work on these projects is strong, many organizations will probably have to choose from among projects that have been sitting on the backburner for some time. On the other hand, if time, money, and resources for many organizations are limited, then only a few, select IT projects can be funded.

In both good times and bad, senior management will make a certain level of funding available for IT projects. The budgeted amount will depend upon such things as the economy, competitor's actions within the industry, and the organization's strategic plan. Regardless whether an organization's budget for IT projects shrinks or grows, the resources available for any given period will be relatively fixed. Quite often the total funding requirements for the proposed projects will be greater than the available budget. As a result, any project that receives funding will do so at the expense of another project. The competition for funding IT projects proposed by the various business units within an organization will be especially keen when the budget is tight. Projects that do not receive any funding will either have to wait or fall by the wayside. Therefore, the decision to fund specific projects will always be an important management decision because it will have a major impact on the organization's performance.

The decision to fund or invest in an IT project should be based on the value that the completed project will provide the organization. Otherwise, what is the point of spending all that time, effort, and money? Although senior management must make the difficult decision as to which IT projects receive funding and which ones do not, others must plan and carry out the project work. Which situation is worse: Successfully building and implementing an information system that provides little or no value to the organization, or implementing an information system that *could have* provided value to the organization, but was developed or managed poorly? It is probably moot. In either situation everyone with a direct or indirect interest in the project's outcome loses.

How This Book Is Organized

The goal of this book is to help you to plan and manage information technology projects. We will focus on a number of different theories, but the main focus will be on applying the methods, tools, techniques, and processes for planning and managing an IT project from start to finish. If you are a project manager (or will be one soon), this book will help you to understand and apply project management principles in order to better manage your IT project. If you are just starting out in the field, this book will help you to understand the big picture of what an IT project is all about. This knowledge will help you to become a better team member and prepare you for the next several progressions in your career.

Many of the principles of project management can be applied to just about any project, but IT projects are unique in several ways. Throughout the text, we will discuss what makes IT projects different from other types of projects and how the principles and methods of system development can be integrated to define the IT project management discipline. Although many of the concepts for developing an information system will be integrated throughout, this is not a systems analysis and design text. More specifically, we will not delve too deeply into the systems analysis and design techniques that are used during systems development. We will leave that for other books and classes.

The remainder of this chapter provides a foundation for project initiation by providing an understanding of the nature of information technology projects. Before getting too involved with definitions and concepts, however, it is important to understand the motivation behind IT project management. In the next section we will focus on the software crisis, which for many people has become a call to arms for more effective management of IT projects. Then, we will introduce and define projects and project management. Subsequently, we will look at the relationship between the project life cycle and the systems development life cycle. At the end of the chapter, you will be introduced to the nine areas that make up the Project Management Body of Knowledge (PMBOK) that will be integrated throughout the remaining chapters of this text.

THE SOFTWARE CRISIS

Although IT is becoming more reliable, faster, and less expensive, the costs, complexities, and risks of IT projects continue to increase. In 1995, a consulting firm called The Standish Group conducted a survey of 365 IT managers. The widely cited report, appropriately called *CHAOS,* was startling.

For example, although the United States spent over $250 billion each year on IT application development projects, 31 percent of these projects were canceled before completion. Almost 53 percent were completed, but they were over-budget and over-schedule and did not meet the original specifications. The average cost overrun for a medium-size company surveyed was 182 percent of the original estimate, while the average schedule overrun was 202 percent. That is, the results of the survey, summarized in Table 1.1, suggest that a medium-sized project originally estimated to cost about $1 million and to take a year to develop, actually cost $1,820,000, took just over two years to complete, and only included 65 percent of the envisioned features and functions! Sadly, 48 percent of the IT managers surveyed believed there were more failures at the time than five and ten years earlier.

Why IT Projects Fail

The *CHAOS* report also provides some interesting insight as to why some projects succeed while others fail. According to the survey, user involvement, executive

Table 1.1 Summary of the CHAOS Study Results

Company Size	Average Cost of Development	Average Cost Overruns	Average Schedule Overrun	Original Features and Functions Included	Successful Projects [a]	Challenged Projects [b]	Impaired Projects [c]
Large	$2,322,000	178%	230%	42%	9%	61.5%	29.5%
Medium	$1,331,000	182%	202%	65%	16.2%	46.7%	37.1%
Small	$ 434,000	214%	239%	74%	28%	50.4%	21.6%

[a] Completed on-time and on-budget

[b] Completed, but over-budget, over schedule, and includes fewer features and functions than originally envisioned

[c] Cancelled before completion

SOURCE: Adapted from The Standish Group, *CHAOS* (West Yarmouth, MA: 1995), http://www.standishgroup.com /visitor/chaos.htm.

management support, and a clear statement of requirements ranked at the top of the list of factors essential for IT project success. On the other hand, lack of user involvement and incomplete requirements appear to be the two main factors for projects being challenged or canceled before completion.

Tables 1.1 and 1.2 summarize some of the key findings of the *CHAOS* report. First, larger projects report a success rate of only 9 percent and appear to be much more risky than medium and smaller projects. Technology, business models, and cycle times are changing too quickly to develop systems that take much more than a year to complete. This data also supports the need to break up large projects into smaller, more manageable ones that can be completed in less than a year. Companies such as Sears, Roebuck and Co., for example, have new, stricter IT project deadlines that require all web-based projects be completed within three months (Hoffman and King 2000).

In addition, one can look at the project factors for successful and not-so-successful projects to see what may be happening on those projects. User involvement leads the list as the most important factor in project success. This should come as no surprise since the client's expertise is needed to identify problems and opportunities and to define requirements. Moreover, active participation by the client keeps them interested in and excited about the project. Individuals will also begin to take ownership of a project if they feel that they have a stake in the project's success or failure. Effective communication between the techies and non-techies allows for a clearer definition of the project's goals and requirements. Working together, developers and users have more realistic expectations because they themselves set those expectations together. Management is then more compelled to support a popular project.

On the other hand, lack of user input or involvement ranks at or near the top in factors affecting challenged and impaired projects. One can almost picture the chain of events. Without close support of the key users, the project team will have a difficult time understanding the goals of the project and defining the requirements. As a result, suspicion and hostility may arise, and there can easily be an "us versus them" situation. Without effective communication and a clear direction, changes to the project's requirements always seem to appear, and both groups may set unrealistic expectations. Chaos sets in. Management begins to find fewer reasons to support an

Table 1.2 Summary of Factor Rankings for Successful, Challenged, and Impaired Projects

Rank	Factors for Successful Projects	Factors for Challenged Projects	Factors for Impaired Projects
1	User involvement	Lack of user input	Incomplete requirements
2	Executive management support	Incomplete requirements	Lack of user involvement
3	Clear statement of requirements	Changing requirements & specifications	Lack of resources
4	Proper planning	Lack of executive support	Unrealistic expectations
5	Realistic expectations	Technology incompetence	Lack of executive support
6	Smaller project milestones	Lack of resources	Changing requirements specifications
7	Competent staff	Unrealistic expectations	Lack of planning
8	Ownership	Unclear objectives	Didn't need it any longer
9	Clear vision & objectives	Unrealistic time frames	Lack of IT management
10	Hard-working, focused team	New technology	Technology illiteracy

SOURCE: Adapted from The Standish Group, *CHAOS* (West Yarmouth, MA: 1995), http://www.standishgroup .com /visitor/chaos.htm.

unpopular project and more and more resources are diverted away from it. The project is barely successful, or a failure.

Improving the Likelihood of Success

How can we improve the chances for IT project success and avoid repeating past mistakes? Here are three approaches that will be focal points throughout this book.

A Socio-Technical Approach   In the past, organizations have attempted to improve the chances of IT project success by focusing on the tools, techniques, and methodologies of IT development. A purely technical approach, however, focuses attention on the technology. We can easily end up developing an application that no one asked for or needs. Applications to support electronic commerce, supply chain management, and integration require that at least equal attention be paid to the organizational side. The days of being good order takers are over. We can no longer be content with defining a set of user requirements, disappearing for several months, and then knocking on the user's door when it is time to deliver the new system. IT professionals must understand the business and be actively creative in applying the technology in ways that bring value to the organization. Similarly, the clients must become stakeholders in the project. This means actively seeking and encouraging their participation, involvement, and vision. The successful application of technology and the achievement of the project's goal must be an equal responsibility of the developers and users.

TAXPAYERS PAY $50 BILLION A YEAR FOR IRS MISTAKES

A *Computerworld* investigation reports that delays in overhauling the federal tax system have cost the U.S. government approximately $50 billion a year in uncollected taxes. Although the Internal Revenue Service (IRS) had spent hundreds of millions of dollars in an attempt to modernize its computer systems, critics claim that much of that money has been wasted because of mismanagement and primitive development practices. Government and private groups believe that there are several reasons for the problems:

- Failure to redesign the business processes before beginning systems development
- No overall systems architecture or development plan
- Primitive and sometimes "chaotic" software development methodologies
- Failure to manage information systems as investments

- Lack of information security

Both Congress and the General Accounting Office have directed the IRS to carry out the following recommendations:

- Put in place a rigorous process for selecting, prioritizing, controlling, and evaluating major information systems investments
- Improve system development practices from ad hoc to ones that can be repeated and improve the likelihood of success
- Develop organization-wide plans that focus on an integrated systems architecture, security, data architecture, and configuration management

SOURCE: Adapted from Gary H. Anthes, "IRS Project Failures Cost Taxpayers $50B Annually," *Computerworld,* October 14, 1996, http://www.computerworld.com/news/1996/story/0,11280,10332,00.html.

A Project-Management Approach   One suggestion of the *CHAOS* study was the need for better project management. But, isn't building an information system a project? Haven't organizations used project management in the past? And aren't they using project management now? While many organizations have applied the principles and tools of project management to IT projects, many more—even today—build systems on an ad hoc basis. Success or failure of an IT project depends largely on who is, or is not, part of the project team. Applying project management principles and tools across the entire organization, however, should be part of a **methodology**—the step-by-step activities, processes, tools, quality standards, controls, and deliverables that are defined for the entire project. As a result, project success does not depend primarily on the team, but more on the set of processes and infrastructure in place. A common set of tools and controls also provides a common language across projects and the ability to compare projects throughout the organization.

In addition, other reasons for project management to support IT projects include:

- *Resources*—When developing or purchasing an information system, all IT projects are capital projects that require cash and other organizational resources. Projects must be estimated accurately, and cost and schedules must be controlled effectively. Without the proper tools, techniques, methods, and controls in place, the project will drain or divert resources away from other projects and areas of the organization. Eventually, these uncontrolled costs could impact the financial stability of the organization.

- *Expectations*—Today, organizational clients expect IT professionals to deliver quality products and services in a professional manner. Timely status updates and communication, as well as sound project management practices, are required.

- *Competition*—Internal and external competition has never been greater. An internal IT department's services can easily be outsourced if the quality or

---

COUNTER THINKING?

Many people find it easier to avoid failure than accept it. Yet, failure can be helpful and, at times, even desirable. Failure can be a valuable experience because one can learn more from failure than from success since the benefits of taking risks often outweigh the consequences of failure. In addition, Harold Kerzner makes three points about failure:

1. A company is not taking enough business risks if its projects are 100 percent successful.
2. Terminating a project early can be viewed as successful if the resources originally dedicated to the project can be reassigned to more profitable activities

or the technology needed for the project does not exist or cannot be invented cost-effectively within a reasonable time period.

3. Excellence in project management requires a continuous stream of successfully managed projects. But you can still have project failures.

SOURCE: Adapted from Alan S. Horowitz, "The Sweet Smell of Failure," *Computerworld,* http://www.computerworld.com/home /online9676.nsf/all/980209; Harold Kerzner, *In Search of Excellence in Project Management: Successful Practices in High Performance Organizations* (New York: John Wiley, 1998).

---

cost of providing IT services can be bettered outside the organization. Today, competition among consultants is increasing as they compete for business and talent.

■ *Efficiency and Effectiveness*—Peter Drucker, the well-known management guru, defined **efficiency** as doing the thing right and **effectiveness** as doing the right thing. Many companies report that project management allows for shorter development time, lower costs, and higher quality. Just using project management tools, however, does not guarantee success. Project management must become accepted and supported by all levels within the organization, and continued commitment in terms of training, compensation, career paths, and organizational infrastructure must be in place. This support will allow the organization to do the right things and do them right.

A Knowledge-Management Approach A socio-technical approach and a commitment to project management principles and practices are important for success. However, excellence in IT project management for an individual or an organization takes time and experience. **Knowledge management** is a relatively new area. It is a systematic process for acquiring, creating, synthesizing, sharing, and using information, insights, and experiences to transform ideas into business value. Although many organizations today have knowledge management initiatives under way, and spending on knowledge management systems is expected to increase, many others believe that knowledge management is just a fad or a buzzword.

What about learning from experience? Experience can be a great teacher. These experiences and the knowledge gained from these experiences, however, are often fragmented throughout the organization. Chances are that if you encounter what appears to be a unique problem or situation, someone else in your organization has already dealt with that problem, or one very similar. Wouldn't it be great to just ask that person what they did? What the outcome was? And, would they do it again the same way? Unfortunately, that person could be on the other side of the world or down the hall—and you may not even know!

Knowledge and experience, in the form of lessons learned, can be documented and made available through the technologies accessible today, technologies such as the World Wide Web or local versions of the web called intranets. **Lessons learned** that document both reasons for success and failure can be valuable assets if maintained and used properly. A person who gains experience is said to be more mature. Similarly, an organization that learns from its experiences can be more mature in its processes by taking those lessons learned and creating **best practices**—simply, doing things in the most efficient and effective manner. In terms of managing IT projects, managing knowledge in the form of lessons learned can help an organization develop best practices that allow all of the project teams within the organization to do the right things and then to do them right. As summarized in the *CHAOS* report:

> There is one aspect to be considered in any degree of project failure. All success is rooted in either luck or failure. If you begin with luck, you learn nothing but arrogance. However, if you begin with failure and learn to evaluate it, you also learn to succeed. Failure begets knowledge. Out of knowledge you gain wisdom, and it is with wisdom that you can become truly successful (Standish Group 1995, 4).

THE CONTEXT OF PROJECT MANAGEMENT

What Is a Project?

Although the need for effectively managing projects has been introduced, we still require a working definition of a project and project management. The Project Management Institute (PMI), an organization that was founded in 1969, has grown to become the leading non-profit professional association in the area of project management. In addition, PMI establishes many project management standards and provides seminars, educational programs, and professional certification. It also maintains the *Guide to the Project Management Body of Knowledge (PMBOK Guide)*. The *PMBOK Guide* (Project Management Institute 2000) provides widely used definitions for **project** and **project management.**

> A *project* is a temporary endeavor undertaken to accomplish a unique purpose (4).

> *Project management* is the application of knowledge, skills, tools, and techniques to project activities in order to meet or exceed stakeholder needs and expectations from a project (6).

Attributes of a Project Projects can also be viewed in terms of their attributes: time frame, purpose, ownership, resources, roles, risks and assumptions, interdependent tasks, organizational change, and operating in an environment larger than the project itself.

Time Frame Because a project is a temporary endeavor, it must have a definite beginning and end. Many projects begin on a specific date and the date of completion is estimated. Some projects, on the other hand, have an immovable date when the project must be completed. In this case, it is necessary to work backwards to determine the date when the project must start. Keep in mind that your career should not consist of a single project, but a number of projects.

Purpose Projects are undertaken to accomplish something. An IT project can produce any number of results—a system, a software package, or a recommendation based on a study. Therefore, a project's goal must be to produce something tangible and of value to the organization. A project must have a goal to drive the project in terms of defining the work to be done, its schedule, and its budget, and to provide the project team with a clear direction.

Because it sets expectations that will directly influence the client's level of satisfaction, the project's goal must be clearly defined and agreed upon. The definition for project management suggests that project activities *must meet or exceed stakeholder needs and expectations.* Expectations and needs, however, cannot be met if the project's goal is not achieved. It is, therefore, important to keep in mind that a project should only be undertaken to provide some kind of value to the organization. Moreover, a specific and measurable project goal can be evaluated after the project is completed.

Ownership   The project must provide something of value to an individual or group who will own the project's product after it is completed. Determining who owns this product is not always easy. For example, different groups may fight over who does or does not own the system, the data, the support, and the final cost of implementing and maintaining the system. Although a project may have many **stakeholders** (i.e., people or groups who have a vested interest in the project's outcome), a project should have a clearly defined sponsor. The **sponsor** may be the end user, customer, or the client who has the ability and desire to provide direction, funding, and other resources to the project.

Resources   IT projects require time, money, people, and technology. Resources provide the means for achieving a project's goal and also act as a constraint. For example, the project's **scope,** or work to be accomplished, is determined directly by the project's goal—that is, if we know what we have to accomplish, we can then figure out how to accomplish it. If the project sponsor asks that an additional feature be added to the system, however, this request will undoubtedly require additional resources in terms of more work on the part of the project team. The use of a project resource has an associated cost that must be included in the overall cost of the project.

In the past, computer technology was relatively more expensive than the labor needed to develop a system. Today, the labor to build a system is relatively more expensive than the technology. As IT salaries increase, the cost of IT projects will become even more expensive. Therefore, if team members must do additional work, their time and the costs associated with time spent doing unscheduled work must be added to the project's schedule and budget. In other words, if scope increases, the schedule and budget of a project must increase accordingly. If the project's schedule and resources are fixed, then the only way to decrease the cost or schedule of the project may be to reduce the project's scope. Scope, schedule, and budget must remain in a sort of equilibrium to support a particular project goal. This relationship, sometimes referred to as the **triple constraint,** is illustrated in Figure 1.1. It should be a consideration whenever making a decision that affects the project's goal, scope, schedule, or budget.

Scope

Schedule

Project goal
&
expectations

Budget

Figure 1.1   The Scope, Schedule, and Budget Relationship—the Triple Constraint

Roles   Today, IT projects require different individuals with different skill sets. Although these skills may be different on different projects, a typical project may include the following:

- *Project Manager*—The project manager is the team leader and is responsible for ensuring that all of the project management and technical development processes are in place and are being carried out within a set of specific requirements, defined processes, and quality standards.

- *Project Sponsor*—The project sponsor may be the client, customer, or organizational manager who will act as a champion for the project and provide organizational resources and direction when needed.

- *Subject Matter Expert(s) (SME)*—The subject matter expert may be a user or client who has specific knowledge, expertise, or insight in a specific functional area needed to support the project. For example, if the organization wishes to develop a system to support tax decisions, having a tax expert on the project team who can share his/her knowledge will be more productive than having the technical people try to learn everything about tax accounting while developing the system.

- *Technical Expert(s) (TE)*—Technical expertise is needed to provide a technical solution to an organizational problem. Technical experts can include systems analysts, network specialists, programmers, graphic artists, trainers, and so forth. Regardless of their job title, these individuals are responsible for defining, creating, and implementing the technical and organizational infrastructure to support the product of the IT project.

Risks and Assumptions   All projects have an element of risk, and some projects entail more risk than others. Risk can arise from many sources, both internal and external to the project team. For example, **internal risks** may arise from the estimation process or from the fact that a key member of the project team could leave in the middle of the project. **External risks,** on the other hand, could arise from dependencies on other contractors or vendors. **Assumptions** are what we use to estimate scope, schedule, and budget and to assess the risks of the project. There are many unknown variables associated with projects, and it is important to identify and make explicit all of the risks and assumptions that can impact the IT project.

Interdependent Tasks   Project work requires many interdependent tasks. For example, a network cannot be installed until the hardware is delivered, or certain requirements cannot be incorporated into the design until a key user is interviewed. Sometimes the delay of one task can affect other subsequent, dependent tasks. The project's schedule may slip, and the project may not meet its planned deadline.

Organizational Change   Projects are planned organizational change. Change must be understood and managed because implementation of the IT project will change the way people work. The potential for resistance, therefore, exists, and a system that is a technical success could end up being an organizational failure.

Operating in an Environment Larger than the Project Itself   Organizations choose projects for a number of reasons, and the projects chosen can impact the organization (Laudon and Laudon 1996). It is important that the project manager and team understand the company's culture, environment, politics, and the like.

These organizational variables will influence the selection of projects, the IT infrastructure, and the role of IT within the organization. For example, a small, family-owned manufacturing company may have a completely different corporate culture, strategy, and structure than a start-up electronic commerce company. As a result, the projects selected, the technical infrastructure, and the role of IT for each organization will be different. The project team must understand both the technical and organizational variables so that the project can be aligned properly with the structure and strategy of the organization. Moreover, understanding the organizational variables can help the project team understand the political climate within the organization and identify potential risks and issues that could impede the project.

■ THE PROJECT LIFE CYCLE AND IT DEVELOPMENT

The **project life cycle** (PLC) is a collection of logical stages or phases that maps the life of a project from its beginning to its end in order to define, build, and deliver the product of a project—that is, the information system. Each phase should provide one or more deliverables. A **deliverable** is a tangible and verifiable product of work (i.e., project plan, design specifications, delivered system, etc.). Deliverables at the end of each phase also provide tangible benefits throughout the project and serve to define the work and resources needed for each phase.

Projects should be broken up into phases to make the project more manageable and to reduce risk. **Phase exits, stage gates,** or **kill points** are the phase-end review of key deliverables that allow the organization to evaluate the project's performance and to take immediate action to correct any errors or problems. Although the deliverables at the end of a stage or phase usually are approved before proceeding to the next stage, **fast tracking** or starting the next phase before approval is obtained can sometimes reduce the project's schedule. Overlapping of phases can be risky and should only be done when the risk is deemed acceptable.

Like all living things, projects have life cycles where they are born, grow, peak, decline, and then terminate (Gido and Clements 1999; Meredith and Mantel 2000). Although project life cycles may differ depending upon the industry or project, all project life cycles will have a beginning, a middle, and an end (Rosenau 1998; Gido and Clements 1999). Figure 1.2 provides a generic life cycle that describes the common phases or stages shared by most projects.

Define Project Goal

Defining the project's overall goal should be the first step of the project. This goal should focus on providing business value to the organization. A well-defined goal gives the project team a clear focus and drives the other phases of the project. In addition, most projects seem to share the following characteristics:

- The effort, in terms of cost and staffing levels, is low at the start of the project, but then increases as the project work is being done, and then decreases at the end as the project is completed.

- Risk and uncertainty are the highest at the start of a project. Once the goal of the project is defined and the project progresses, the probability of success should increase.

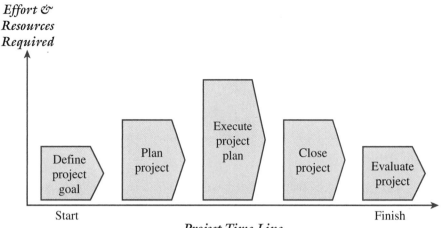

Figure 1.2 A Generic Project Life Cycle

- The ability for stakeholders to influence the scope and cost of the project is highest at the beginning of the project. The cost of changing the scope and correcting errors becomes more expensive as the project progresses.

Plan Project

Once the project's goal has been defined, developing the project plan is a much easier task. A project plan essentially answers the following questions:

- What are we going to do?
- Why are we going to do it?
- How are we going to do it?
- Who is going to be involved?
- How long will it take?
- How much will it cost?
- What can go wrong and what can we do about it?
- How did we estimate the schedule and budget?
- Why did we make certain decisions?
- How will we know if we are successful?

In addition, the deliverables, tasks, resources, and time to complete each task must be defined for each phase of the project. This initial plan, called a **baseline plan**, defines the agreed upon scope, schedule, and budget and is used as a tool to gauge the project's performance throughout the life cycle.

Execute Project Plan

After the project's goal and plan have been defined, it's time to put the plan into action. As work on the project progresses, scope, schedule, budget, and people must be actively managed to ensure that the project achieves its goal. The project's progress must be documented and compared to the project's baseline plan. In addition, project performance must be communicated to all of the project's stakeholders. At the end of this phase, the project team implements or delivers a completed product to the organization.

Close Project

As was mentioned, a project should have a definite beginning and end. The closing phase of a project ensures that all of the work is completed as planned and as agreed to by the project team and the sponsor. Therefore, there should be some kind of formal acknowledgement by the sponsor that they will accept (and pay for!) the product delivered. This closure is often capped with a final project report and presentation to the client that documents that all promised deliverables have been completed as specified.

Evaluate Project

Sometimes the value of an IT project is not readily known when the system is implemented. For example, the goal of a project to develop an electronic commerce site should be to make money—not to build or install hardware, software, and web pages on a particular server platform. The technology and its subsequent implementation are only a means to an end. Therefore, the goal of the electronic commerce site may be to produce $250,000 within six months. As a result, evaluating whether the project met its goal can be made only after the system has been implemented.

However, the project can be evaluated in other ways as well. The project team should document its experiences in terms of lessons learned—those things that it would do the same and those things it would do differently on the next project, based on its current project experiences. This post mortem should be documented, stored electronically, and shared throughout the organization. Subsequently, many of these experiences can be translated into best practices and integrated into future projects.

In addition, both the project team and the project itself should be evaluated at the end of the project. The project manager may evaluate each project team member's performance in order to provide feedback and as part of the organization's established merit and pay raise processes and procedures. Often, however, an outside third party, such as a senior manager or partner, may audit the project to determine whether the project was well-managed, provided the promised deliverables, followed established processes, and met specific quality standards. The project team and project manager may also be evaluated in terms of whether they acted in a professional and ethical manner.

The IT Product Life Cycle

Although projects follow a project life cycle, information systems development follows a product life cycle. The most common product life cycle in IT is the **Systems Development Life Cycle** (SDLC), which represents the sequential phases or stages an information system follows throughout its useful life. The SDLC establishes a logical order or sequence in which the system development activities occur and indicates whether to proceed from one system development activity to the next (McConnell 1996). Although there is no generally accepted version of the SDLC, the life cycle depicted in Figure 1.3 includes the generally accepted activities and phases associated with systems development. Keep in mind that these concepts are generally covered in great detail in system analysis and design books and courses. For some, this may be a quick review, while for others it will provide a general background for understanding how IT project management and information system development activities support one another.

Planning, analysis, design, implementation, and maintenance and support are the five basic phases in the systems development life cycle.

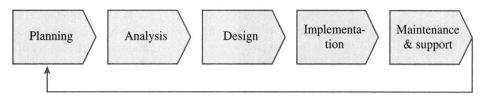

Figure 1.3 Systems Development Life Cycle

Planning   The planning stage involves identifying and responding to a problem or opportunity and incorporates the project management and system development processes and activities. Here a formal planning process ensures that the goal, scope, budget, schedule, technology, and system development processes, methods, and tools are in place.

Analysis   The analysis phase attempts to delve into the problem or opportunity more fully. For example, the project team may document the current system to develop an "as is" model to understand the system currently in place. In general, systems analysts will meet with various stakeholders (users, managers, customers, etc.) to learn more about the problem or opportunity. This work is done to identify and document any problems or bottlenecks associated with the current system. Generally, the "as is" analysis is followed by a requirements analysis. Here the specific needs and requirements for the new system are identified and documented. Requirements can be developed through a number of means—interviewing, joint applications development (JAD), conducting surveys, observing work processes, and reading company reports. Using process-oriented, data-oriented, and/or object-oriented modeling techniques, the current system, user requirements, and logical design of the future system called the "to be" system are represented and documented (Dennis and Haley 2000).

Design   During the design phase, the project team uses the requirements and "to be" logical models as input for designing the architecture to support the new information system. This architecture includes designing the network, hardware configuration, databases, user interface, and application programs.

Implementation   Implementation includes the development or construction of the system, testing, and installation. In addition, training, support, and documentation must be in place.

Maintenance and Support   Although maintenance and support may not be a true phase of the current project, it is still an important consideration. Once the system has been implemented, it is said to be in production. Changes to the system, in the form of maintenance and enhancements, are often requested to fix any discovered errors (i.e., bugs) within the system, to add any features that were not incorporated into the original design, or to adjust to a changing business environment. Support, in terms of a call center or help desk, may also be in place to help users on an as-needed basis.

Eventually, the system becomes part of the organizational infrastructure and becomes known as a legacy system. At this point, the system becomes very similar to a car. Let's say you buy a brand new car. Over time, the car becomes less and less new, and parts have to be replaced as they wear out. Although, a system does not wear out like a car, changes to the system are required as the organization changes. For example, a payroll system may have to be changed to reflect changes in the tax laws, or an electronic commerce site may have to be changed to reflect a new line of products that the company wishes to introduce. As the owner of an older or classic car, you may find yourself replacing part after part until you make the decision to trade in the old junker for something newer and more reliable. Similarly, an organization may find itself spending more and more on maintaining a legacy system. Eventually, the organization will decide that it is time to replace this older system with a newer one that will be more reliable, require less maintenance, and better meets its needs. Subsequently, a new life cycle begins.

Putting the SDLC into Practice

There are basically two ways to implement the SDLC. Today, an IT project will follow either a structured approach or a newer approach called Rapid Applications Development (RAD).

Structured Approach to Systems Development   A structured approach to systems development has been around since the 1960s and 1970s when large mainframe applications were developed. These applications were built when (1) systems were relatively simple and independent from each other, (2) computer hardware was relatively more expensive than the labor, and (3) development and programming tools were primitive compared to today (Satzinger, Jackson, Burd 2002).

The **Waterfall method** in Figure 1.4 follows the SDLC in a very sequential and structured way. Planning overhead is minimized because it is all done up-front and a tangible system is not produced until the end of the life cycle (McConnell 1996). The idea of a waterfall is a metaphor for a cascading of activities from one phase to the next. This approach stresses a sequential and logical flow of development activities. For example, the design activities begin only after the analysis and requirement activities are complete. Subsequently, the actual development, or programming activities, will not start until the design phase is complete. Although one can go back to a previous stage, it is not always easy or desirable.

This approach is suitable when developing structured systems and assumes, or at least hopes, that the requirements defined in the analysis stage do not change very much over the remainder of the project. In addition, because it will provide a solid structure that can minimize wasted effort, this method may work well when the project team is inexperienced or less technically competent (McConnell 1996).

Rapid Applications Development (RAD)   On the other hand, one can take a less-structured approach to developing systems. Today, taking less time to conceive,

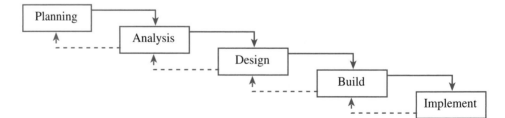

Figure 1.4 Waterfall Model

develop, and implement an information system can provide the organization with a competitive advantage. In addition, as evidenced by the *CHAOS* study, larger projects that take longer to develop are riskier than smaller and shorter projects. Satzinger, Jackson, and Burd (2002, 533) define RAD as "a collection of development approaches, techniques, tools, and technologies, each of which has been proven to shorten development schedules under some conditions." This means that different development approaches, tools, techniques, and so forth can be mixed and matched depending on the project. For some projects, it means that the Waterfall approach is the most appropriate; however, RAD often follows one of the following iterative approaches:

- *Prototyping*—Prototyping is an iterative approach to systems development where the developer and user work together very closely to develop a partially or fully functional system as soon as possible, usually within a few days or weeks. The prototype application will go through a number of iterations as functional requirements are defined or changed. This approach is most useful when the requirements of the new system are difficult to define or when working with a new technology where the capabilities of that technology are unknown or not understood very well. A prototype may be either a throwaway system or a fully usable system. A throwaway prototype may be used to discover or refine system requirement specifications that can be used as a model for developing the real system. On the other hand, the prototype may become the actual system after it has gone through a number of refinements over time.

- *Spiral Development*—Another way to expedite the SDLC is the spiral approach first proposed by Barry Boehm (1988). The spiral model provides a risk-oriented approach where a software project is broken up into a number of miniprojects where each addresses one or more major risks until all major risks have been addressed (McConnell 1996). A risk can be defined as a poorly understood requirement or architecture or as a potential problem with the technology or system performance. The basic idea is to begin development of the system on a small scale where risks can be identified. Once identified, the development team then develops a plan for addressing these risks and evaluates various alternatives. Next, deliverables for the iteration are identified, developed, and verified before planning and committing to the next iteration. Subsequently, completing each iteration brings the project closer to a fully functional system. Reviews after each iteration provide a means of controlling the overall risk of the project. Major problems or challenges will surface early in the project and, therefore, provide the potential to reduce the total cost of the project. The disadvantages to the spiral development approach center on its complexity (Satzinger, Jackson, Burd 2002). These types of projects are more complex to manage because many people may be working on a number of different parallel activities.

- *Extreme Programming (XP)*—Kent Beck introduced the idea of XP in the mid-1990s. Under XP, the system is transferred to the users in a series of versions called releases. A release may be developed using several iterations and should be developed and tested within a few weeks or months. Each release is a working system that only includes one or several functions that are part of the full system specifications. XP includes a number of activities where the user requirements are first documented as a user story. The user stories are then documented using an object-oriented model called the class diagram, and the release is developed over the course of several iterations. A set of acceptance tests for each user story is then developed. Releases that pass the acceptance test are then considered complete. XP provides the continuous testing and integration of different software modules and components while supporting active user involvement. In addition, XP often incorporates team programming where two programmers work together on the same workstation. Small teams of developers often work in a common room where workstations are positioned in the middle and workspace for each team member is provided around the perimeter. Developers often are prohibited from working more than 40 hours a week in order to avoid burnout and the mistakes that often occur because of fatigue (Satzinger, Jackson, Burd 2002).

The PLC versus the SDLC

You may be still wondering about the difference between the project life cycle and the systems development life cycle. Although they may seem to be quite similar, the difference is that the product life cycle focuses on the processes of managing a project, while the SDLC focuses on creating and implementing a product—the information system. In this text we will focus primarily on the PLC, although the SDLC and the particular approach we choose will have a direct bearing on the project's scope (i.e., the deliverables that the project team must provide) and the work activities needed to produce those deliverables. Consequently, the number of activities, their sequence, time-to-complete, and resources required will directly determine the project's schedule and budget.

As illustrated in Figure 1.5, the SDLC is really part of the PLC because many of the activities for developing the information system occur during the execution phase. The last two stages of the PLC, closing and evaluating the project, occur after the implementation of the information system.

The integration of project management and system development activities is one important component that distinguishes IT projects from other types of projects. A

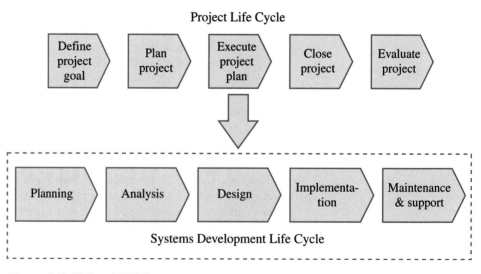

Figure 1.5 PLC and SDLC

methodology will be presented in Chapter 2 and will illustrate how the project life cycle and systems development life cycle can be combined to manage the process and product of IT projects. This methodology will provide a foundation for the concepts, processes, tools, and techniques throughout this text.

THE PROJECT MANAGEMENT BODY OF KNOWLEDGE (PMBOK)

As was mentioned earlier, the *Guide to the Project Management Body of Knowledge* is a document available from the Project Management Institute (PMI)—an international, nonprofit, professional organization with more than 55,000 members worldwide. The original document was published in 1987, and the updated version provides a basis for identifying and describing the generally accepted principles and practices of project management. However, as PMBOK is quick to point out, "generally accepted" does not mean these principles and practices work the same way on each and every project. It does mean that many people over time believe that these principles and practices are useful and have value. Determining what is appropriate is the responsibility of the team and comes from experience. (Perhaps experiences that can be documented and shared?)

This text will use the *PMBOK Guide* as a foundation but will also integrate a number of concepts and ideas that are part of the body of knowledge that makes up the field of information systems. Ideally, you will then understand not only what many IT project managers and organizations throughout the world think are important, but also the language and the processes.

PMI provides a certification in project management through the Project Management Professional (PMP) certification exam. This text can also help you prepare for the PMP certification exam. To pass, you must demonstrate a level of understanding and knowledge about project management, satisfy education and experience requirements, and agree to and adhere to a professional code of ethics.

Project Management Knowledge Areas

The *Guide to the Project Management Body of Knowledge* defines nine knowledge areas for understanding project management. These nine knowledge areas are illustrated in Figure 1.6 and will be covered in more detail in later chapters.

- *Project Integration Management*—Integration focuses on coordinating the project plan's development, execution, and control of changes.
- *Project Scope Management*—A project's scope is the work to be completed by the project team. Scope management provides assurance that the project's work is defined accurately and completely and that it is completed as planned. In addition, scope management includes ways to ensure that proper scope change procedures are in place.
- *Project Time Management*—Time management is important for developing, monitoring, and managing the project's schedule. It includes identifying the project's phases and activities and then estimating, sequencing, and assigning resources for each activity to ensure that the project's scope and objectives are met.
- *Project Cost Management*—Cost management assures that the project's budget is developed and completed as approved.

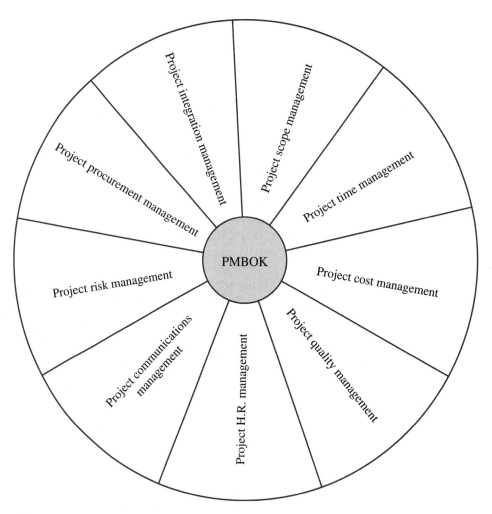

Figure 1.6 Project Management Body of Knowledge (PMBOK)

- *Project Quality Management*—Quality management focuses on planning, developing, and managing a quality environment that allows the project to meet or exceed stakeholder needs or expectations.

- *Project Human Resource Management*—People are the most important resource on a project. Human resource management focuses on creating and developing the project team as well as understanding and responding appropriately to the behavioral side of project management.

- *Project Communications Management*—Communication management entails communicating timely and accurate information about the project to the project's stakeholders.

- *Project Risk Management*—All projects face a certain amount of risk. Project risk management is concerned with identifying and responding appropriately to risks that can impact the project.

- *Project Procurement Management*—Projects often require resources (people, hardware, software, etc.) that are outside the organization. Procurement management makes certain that these resources are acquired properly.

CHAPTER SUMMARY

This chapter provides an introduction to the text and to the area of information technology project management (ITPM). As evidenced by the *CHAOS* report published by The Standish Group, many IT projects are late and over-budget and include only a fraction of the functionality originally envisioned. Although many factors contribute to a project's success or failure, the product and process associated with the development of an information system must be actively managed. This management includes taking a socio-technical approach that focuses not only on the technology, but also on the organizational side. In addition, individuals and organizations can learn and share their experiences. These experiences, in the form of lessons learned, can be used to develop new ideas and best practices that can be implemented in an organization's systems development and project management policies and methods.

The *Guide to the Project Management Body of Knowledge (PMBOK Guide)* defines a project as a temporary endeavor undertaken to accomplish a unique purpose and project management as the application of knowledge, skills, tools, and techniques to project activities in order to meet or exceed stakeholder needs and expectations. Projects can also be viewed in terms of their attributes. These attributes include the project's time frame, purpose, ownership, resources, roles, risks and assumptions, tasks, and the impact the project will have on the organization. Projects also operate in an environment larger than the project itself. The company's culture, environment, politics, strategy, structure, policies, and processes can influence the selection of projects, the IT infrastructure, and the role of IT within the organization. Similarly, the selection of projects, the IT infrastructure, and the role of IT within the organization can influence the organizational variables.

The project life cycle (PLC) is a collection of logical stages or phases that maps the life of a project from its beginning to its end. It also helps in defining, building, and delivering the product of a project. Projects are broken up into phases to make the project more manageable and to reduce risk. In addition, each phase should focus on providing a deliverable—a tangible and verifiable product of work. A generic project life cycle was introduced. Its phases included (1) defining the project goal, (2) planning the project, (3) executing or carrying out the project, (4) closing the project, and (5) evaluating the project. Although projects follow a project life cycle, information systems development follows a product life cycle.

The Systems Development Life Cycle (SDLC) represents the sequential phases or stages an information system follows throughout its useful life. The SDLC described in this chapter includes the following phases: (1) planning, (2) analysis, (3) design, (4) implementation, (5) maintenance and support. In addition, the SDLC can be implemented using a structured approach (the Waterfall model) or by means of more iterative approaches. By following a rapid applications development (RAD) approach, systems developers can combine different approaches, tools, and techniques in order to shorten the time needed to develop an information system. The SDLC is really a component of the PLC, and choice of a particular approach for systems development will influence the activities, their sequence, and the estimated time to complete. In turn, this will directly impact the project's schedule and budget.

The *Guide to the Project Management Body Knowledge* outlines nine knowledge areas for understanding project management. These nine areas include: (1) project integration management, (2) project scope management, (3) project time management, (4) project cost management, (5) project quality management, (6) project human resources management, (7) project communications management, (8) project risk management, and (9) project procurement management. Along with a number of concepts and principles that make up the body of knowledge for information systems, these nine PMBOK areas will be integrated in the chapters throughout this text.

REVIEW QUESTIONS

1. Describe the software crisis in your own words.
2. How is a successful project defined in the *CHAOS* study?
3. How is a challenged project defined in the *CHAOS* study?
4. How is an impaired project defined in the *CHAOS* study?
5. Why are many IT projects late, over budget, and with fewer features and functions than originally envisioned?
6. What is the socio-technical approach to systems development?
7. What are the benefits to using a project management approach to developing information systems?

8. What is a methodology? What are the advantages of following a methodology when developing an information system?

9. How does sharing experiences in the form of lessons learned lead to best practices in managing and developing information systems?

10. What is a project?

11. What is project management?

12. What are the attributes of a project?

13. Describe the relationship among scope, schedule, and budget.

14. Describe the different roles and skill sets needed for a project.

15. Describe three risks that could be associated with an IT project.

16. Why should assumptions associated with a project be documented?

17. Discuss the statement: Projects operate in an environment larger than the project itself.

18. Describe the project life cycle.

19. What are phase exits, stage gates, and kill points? What purpose do they serve?

20. What is fast tracking? When should fast tracking be used? When is fast tracking not appropriate?

21. Describe the Systems Development Life Cycle (SDLC).

22. Describe the Waterfall model for systems development. When should the Waterfall model be used?

23. Describe the prototyping approach to systems development. When is prototyping appropriate?

24. Describe the Spiral approach for iterative development. What advantages does this model have in comparison with the Waterfall model?

25. Describe extreme programming (XP). How does XP accelerate the SDLC?

26. What is knowledge management? Although many people believe knowledge cannot be managed, why do you think many companies are undertaking knowledge management initiatives?

27. Although the *Guide to the Project Management Body of Knowledge* describes the generally accepted principles and practices of project management, why wouldn't these principles and practices work for every project?

▰ EXTEND YOUR KNOWLEDGE

1. Using the web or library, find an article that describes either a successful or an unsuccessful IT project. Discuss whether any of the project factors listed in Table 1.2 had any bearing on the project.

2. Design a template that could be used by a project team to document its experiences and lessons learned. Describe or show how these experiences could be catalogued and shared with other members and other teams.

3. Using the web or library as a resource, write a one-page position paper on knowledge management. You should provide a definition of knowledge management and your opinion as to whether an organization should invest in a knowledge management initiative.

▰ BIBLIOGRAPHY

Boehm, B. W. 1988. A Spiral Model of Software Development and Enhancement. *Computer* (May): 61–72.

Dennis, A. and W. B. Haley. 2000. *Systems Analysis and Design: An Applied Approach.* New York: John Wiley.

Gido, J. and J. P. Clements. 1999. *Successful Project Management.* Cincinnati, OH: South-Western College Publishing.

Hoffman, T. and J. King. 2000. Y2K Freeze Melts In January Thaw. *Computerworld,* January 17. http://www.computerworld.com /home/print.nsf/all/000117E04A.

Laudon, K. C. and J. P. Laudon. 1996. *Management Information Systems: Organization and Technology.* Upper Saddle River, NJ: Prentice Hall.

McConnell, S. 1996. *Rapid Development: Taming Wild Software Schedules.* Redmond, WA: Microsoft Press.

Meredith, J. R. and S. J. Mantel, Jr. 2000. *Project Management: A Managerial Approach.* New York: John Wiley.

Project Management Institute (PMI). 2000. *A Guide to the Project Management Body of Knowledge (PMBOK Guide).* Newtown Square, PA: PMI Publishing.

Rosenau, M. D. J. 1998. *Successful Project Management.* New York: John Wiley.

Satzinger, J. W., R. B. Jackson, and S. D. Burd. 2002. *Systems Analysis and Design in a Changing World.* Boston: Course Technology.

Standish Group. 1995. *CHAOS.* West Yarmouth, MA: The Standish Group.

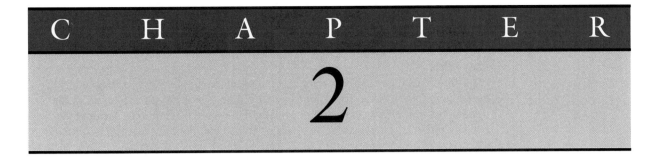

CHAPTER

2

Conceptualizing and Initializing The IT Project

CHAPTER OVERVIEW

Chapter 2 describes how IT projects are conceptualized and initialized. After studying this chapter, you should understand and be able to:

- Define what a methodology is and describe the role it serves in IT projects.
- Identify the phases and infrastructure that make up the IT project methodology introduced in this chapter.
- Develop and apply the concept of a project's measurable organizational value (MOV).
- Describe and be able to prepare a business case.
- Distinguish between financial models and scoring models.
- Describe the project selection process as well as the Balanced Scorecard approach.

GLOBAL TECHNOLOGY SOLUTIONS

Tim Williams sat across from Kellie Matthews as the waiter brought their orders and refilled the water glasses. After the waiter left, Tim handed a folder with GTS embossed on the cover to Kellie. "I've been giving this a great deal of thought," Tim said as he reached for the peppershaker. Kellie began to look over the contents of the folder while Tim waited.

"It's a methodology that I'm working on to help us organize the Husky Air project," Tim explained. "In fact," he added, "I think we can use it as a blueprint for all of our projects. Of course, I'm trying to make it flexible so we can add to it or change it over time as we learn better ways of doing things."

Kellie thought for a moment. "Will it restrict the project team's creativity?" she asked. "Husky Air's management is counting on us to come up with some innovative

23

solutions for them. I know I've always hated the feeling of being constrained by too many rules."

Tim was ready with his answer: "Think of this methodology as a road map. If you were planning a trip, the first thing you would have to do is decide on a destination based upon your interests. For our purposes, that would be similar to defining the project's goal. Once you decide where you're going, you then need to figure out how to get there and how much it will cost."

"Some kind of plan?" Kellie interjected.

"Exactly!" exclaimed Tim. "A travel plan would help you figure out whether to drive, fly, take a train, or use a combination to get to your destination. It really depends on where you're going and how much you want to spend."

Kellie reflected for a moment. "But when I'm on vacation, I like to be spontaneous!" she said. "Planning every minute of a vacation takes the fun out of it."

"Aha!" Tim replied. "You see that's the difference between a methodology and a plan. The methodology would help you to plan your plan."

"What?" said Kellie, "Are you playing a game with words?"

Tim grinned. "No, not really," he answered. "Let's say you went on vacation and had a terrible time. And maybe you even spent more than you budgeted for your vacation."

"I've had a few of those experiences," Kellie reflected.

"So the next time you decide to take a vacation, you might want to do things differently," Tim explained. "What you might do is organize the way you plan your vacation. First, you may try to come up with a better way of choosing a vacation spot. Then, you go about picking a mode of travel and reserve your accommodations. Finally, you figure out what you want to see and do while on your vacation. You may schedule your vacation by the minute, or you can have a list of places to visit or see while you're there—it really depends on what would make your vacation enjoyable."

The waiter returned and refilled their water glasses. Kellie thought for a moment. "I guess we really owe it to our client to have a game plan," she said. "After all, we can't really just wander in any direction and hope we'll somehow end up at our destination. They're paying us by the hour, and time is money. Besides, we owe it to them to meet their needs in the most efficient and effective way possible. So, what's our first step? We're meeting with Husky Air's management tomorrow morning."

"Glad you asked," Tim smiled. "If you take a look at the methodology, you'll see that the first thing we need to do is prepare a business case. That's where we'll figure out our destination—I mean, the overall goal of this project. Once we know where we're headed, we can identify several options for Husky Air. After one is approved, we'll develop a project charter and plan that defines the detailed schedule and budget. That will tell us what needs to be done, when, by whom, and how much it will cost. In addition, the methodology will help make sure that our plan is being followed, or changed when necessary."

"Sounds good," said Kellie, "But there's just one more thing."

"What's that?" asked Tim.

Kellie grinned. "It's your turn to buy lunch."

Things to Think About:

1. What are the advantages of having and following a project methodology?
2. Why should a methodology be flexible?
3. What perceptions might a client have if GTS has a methodology in place? If they don't?

INTRODUCTION

This chapter will introduce a framework for an IT project methodology that will be integrated into this text. A methodology provides a game plan for planning and managing the IT project and recommends the phases, steps, tools, and techniques to be followed and used throughout the project life cycle. All projects, however, are unique. A project methodology must be flexible in order to be useful. Moreover, a methodology should evolve to include the best practices that are derived from an organization's lessons learned. Over time, the methodology will better fit the organization and may even provide some kind of competitive advantage.

After the IT project methodology is introduced, the remainder of this chapter will focus on conceptualizing and initializing the project. Through high-level strategic planning, the overall project goal is defined. Defining this goal (and getting agreement) may be the most difficult part of the methodology and the project itself. The project's goal, if achieved, should provide direct and measurable value to the organization. A project, however, will have specific objectives that support this overall goal. These objectives, in terms of project's scope, schedule, budget, and product quality, are important, but not necessarily sufficient, conditions for defining the project's success or lack of success. A project should have only one goal, but may have several objectives.

Once the project's goal is defined, the IT project methodology introduced in this chapter recommends that the project team develop a **business case.** A business case is a deliverable that documents the project's goal, as well as several alternatives or options. The feasibility, costs, benefits, and risks for each alternative are analyzed and compared, and a recommendation to approve and fund one of the alternatives is made to senior management. The first phase of the IT project methodology, as in all of its phases, ends with a review of the project by the client or sponsor.

Most organizations have limited resources, and a particular project may have to compete with other projects within the organization for those resources. As a result, only one or a few select projects that make up the IT project portfolio can be funded at any given time. Therefore, many organizations have a formal selection process for taking on a project. This chapter will review some of the common techniques and tools for selecting IT projects. If a project has a clear and measurable goal that brings value to the organization, it will have a greater likelihood of being selected. Approval of the business case provides authority to proceed to the next phase of the methodology. This next phase focuses on developing a project charter and plan that details the organization of the project as well as the its schedule and budget.

AN INFORMATION TECHNOLOGY PROJECT METHODOLOGY (ITPM)

A **methodology** provides a strategic-level plan for managing and controlling IT projects. Think of a methodology as a template for initiating, planning, and developing an information system. Although information systems may be different, it is the product, and not necessarily the process, of managing the project that makes them different. As you can see in Figure 2.1, the methodology recommends the phases, deliverables, processes, tools, and knowledge areas for supporting an IT project. The key word is *recommends* because different types of projects, such as electronic commerce (EC), customer relations management (CRM), or data warehousing applications, may require different tools and approaches.

PLC Phases

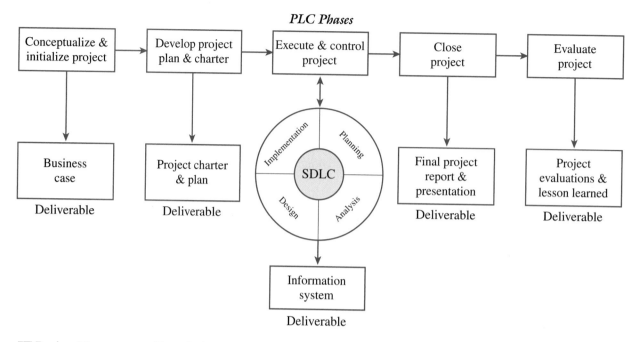

IT Project Management Foundation

PM processes:	Initiating, planning, executing, controlling, closing
PM objectives:	Scope, schedule, budget, quality
Tools:	Project management, information systems development
Infrastructure:	Organizational, project, technical
PMBOK areas:	Integration mgmt, scope mgmt, time mgmt, cost mgmt, quality mgmt, H.R. mgmt, communications mgmt, risk mgmt, procurement mgmt

Figure 2.1 An Information Technology Project Methodology

Methodologies provide the project team with a game plan for implementing the project and product life cycles. The team can then focus on the tasks at hand, instead of always worrying about what they are supposed to do next. In addition, a methodology also provides a common language that allows the project team, project sponsor, and others within the organization to communicate more effectively. By standardizing a methodology throughout the organization, management can compare different projects more objectively because each project's planned and actual progress is reported the same way. Ideally, this will allow management to make better-informed and more objective decisions with respect to which projects get selected and whether funding should continue to support a particular project.

A good methodology should be flexible and adapt to the needs of the project organization over time. For example, whether a structured or rapid applications development (RAD) approach is used depends upon the project and application system. During the analysis and design phases of the systems development life cycle, a team may use one modeling approach or a combination (i.e., process modeling, data modeling, or object-oriented modeling).

The development and modeling approach used, however, depends on a number of factors. These factors may include the organization's experiences, the knowledge

THE PROJECT MANAGEMENT OFFICE

In the past, many companies did not use a project management approach in the development of IT projects, and as a result, most IT projects were late and over budget. Companies these days are trying to establish a project management culture, and establishing a project office is one way of developing that culture while improving results and cutting cost. In fact, Forrester Research, Inc. in Cambridge, Massachusetts, has conducted a study of thirty companies that suggests the mission of project offices is "to bring order out of the chaos of project management." The study also suggests that the biggest challenges focus on managing multiple projects, cross-functional projects, global projects, overlapping projects, interdependent projects, project resource allocation, politics, sponsorship, and culture.

The role of a project office is to provide support and collect data while providing tools and methodologies. Collecting information about projects company-wide gives the project office a means to study the company's portfolio of IT projects. Eventually, this historical information can be used as a basis for estimating and conducting reality checks for projects. Many view these project offices as centers of excellence for project management. Some benefits of a project office include:

- Pointing out minefields in project processes, such as estimating costs.
- Enforcing priorities and/or controls that keep the project on track.
- Coordinating cross-functional projects that may stumble as a result of politics that arise when intra-organizational boundaries are crossed.
- Providing a standardized way for all projects to be planned, managed, and reported.
- Showing the real value of projects by comparing projected costs and benefits with actual results.
- Coordinating more or larger projects than the organization could handle in the past.
- Allowing IT to support its requests for additional staff or resources.

SOURCE: Adapted from Kathleen Melymuka, "Here Comes the Project Office," *Computerworld,* August, 2, 1999, http://www.computerworld.com/news/1999/story/0,11280,36545,00.html.

and skill sets of the project team, the IT and organizational infrastructure to support the development effort and the application, and the nature of the project itself—that is, the project's size, degree of structure, development time frame, and role within the organization. Many IS development methodologies have been proposed, but most focus on the *product* of the development effort. As discussed in Chapter 1, whether or not an organization follows a formal IS development methodology, the development effort should fit within, or be part of, an overall project management methodology.

Although many IT projects fail or experience significant challenges, a methodology can incorporate the experiences of and lessons learned by the project team members. Developing and implementing an IT product then becomes more predictable and the likelihood of success increases. Over time, an organization's methodology incorporates a set of best practices that fits the organization and the projects it undertakes. These best practices should lead to fewer wasted resources and projects that provide true value to the organization. The organization will find more opportunities for competitive advantage as efficiency and effectiveness increase.

Phase 1: Conceptualize and Initialize

The first stage of the IT project methodology focuses on defining the overall goal of the project. A project is undertaken for a specific purpose, and that purpose must be to add tangible value to the organization. Defining the project's goal is the most important step in the IT project methodology. As you will see, the project's goal aids in defining the project's scope and guides decisions throughout the project life cycle. It will also be used at the end of the project to evaluate the project's success.

Alternatives that would allow the organization to meet its goal must be identified. Then, the costs and benefits, as well as feasibility and risk, of each alternative must be analyzed. Based upon these analyses, a specific alternative is recommended for funding. Finally, the project's goal and the analysis of alternatives that support the goal are summarized in a deliverable called the business case. Senior management will use the business case during the selection process to determine whether the proposed project should be funded. The details of developing the project goal and business case will be discussed in more detail later in this chapter.

Phase 2: Develop the Project Charter and Detailed Project Plan

The **project charter** is a key deliverable for the second phase of the IT project methodology. It defines how the project will be organized and how the project alternative that was recommended and approved for funding will be implemented. The project charter provides another opportunity to clarify the project's goal and defines the project's objectives in terms of scope, schedule, budget, and quality standards. In addition, the project charter identifies and gives authority to a project manager to begin carrying out the processes and tasks associated with the systems development life cycle (SDLC). The project plan provides all the tactical details concerning who will carry out the project work and when. The project charter and plan answer the following questions:

- Who is the project manager?
- Who is the project sponsor?
- Who is on the project team?
- What role does everyone associated with the project play?
- What is the scope of the project?
- How much will the project cost?
- How long will it take to complete the project?
- What resources and technology will be required?
- What approach, tools, and techniques will be used to develop the information system?
- What tasks or activities will be required to perform the project work?
- How long will these tasks or activities take?
- Who will be responsible for performing these tasks or activities?
- What will the organization receive for the time, money, and resources invested in this project?

In addition, the project's scope, schedule, budget, and quality objectives are defined in detail. Although some may wish to combine the business case with the project charter and plan, the IT project methodology presented in this text recommends that the business case and project charter/plan remain separate. There are a number of reasons to justify separation.

First, much time and effort must be devoted to understanding the "big picture." This process involves high-level strategic planning. Defining and agreeing to the project's goal and making a recommendation are not easy, nor is getting agreement on which projects should be funded. However, once the project's goal and recommended strategy are defined and agreed to, it will help define the details of the project, that is, who does what and when. The focus of the *conceptualize and initialize phase* is to determine whether a proposed project should and can be done.

The second reason is that the project charter and plan are the products of tactical planning. Here, the details will define how the project's goal will be achieved, by defining the approach and tasks to support the SDLC. Combining strategic planning with tactical planning can confuse the project's goal and objectives with how they should be achieved. It then becomes easy for people to fall into a trap where they worry too much about how they are going to get someplace when they have not even decided where they are going!

The third reason to separate the phases is time. It is better to pull the plug on a project with a high probability of failure or without the expected business value as early as possible. Why spend the time, money, and resources on developing a detailed plan for a project that should not be undertaken? Therefore, a project should be *doable* and *worth doing* before an organization spends resources determining *how* the project should be done. Reviews at the end of each phase provide the decision-making controls to ensure that resources are committed appropriately.

Phase 3: Execute and Control the Project

The third phase of the IT project methodology focuses on execution and control—carrying out the project plan to deliver the IT product and managing the project's processes to achieve the project's goal. It is during this phase that the project team uses a particular approach and set of systems analysis and design tools for implementing the systems development life cycle (SDLC).

In addition, the project manager must ensure that the environment and infrastructure to support the project includes:

- Acquisition of people with the appropriate skills, experience, and knowledge
- The technical infrastructure for development
- IS development methods and tools
- A proper work environment
- Scope, schedule, budget, and quality controls
- A detailed risk plan
- A procurement plan for vendors and suppliers
- A quality management plan
- A change management plan
- A communications plan
- A testing plan
- An implementation plan
- A human resources system for evaluation and rewards

Phase 4: Close Project

After the information system has been developed, tested, and installed, a formal acceptance should transfer control from the project team to the client or project sponsor. The project team should prepare a final project report and presentation to document and verify that all the project deliverables have been completed as defined in the project's scope. This gives the project sponsor confidence that the project has been completed and makes the formal approval and acceptance of the project go more smoothly.

At this time, the final cost of the project can be determined. Subsequently, the consultant may invoice the client for any remaining payments, or the accounting department may make any final internal charges to appropriate accounts. In addition, the project manager and team must follow a set of processes to formally close the project. These processes include such things as closing all project accounts, archiving all project documents and files, and releasing project resources.

Phase 5: Evaluate Project Success

The final phase of the methodology should focus on evaluating four areas. First, a postmortem," or final project review, should be conducted by the project manager and team. This review should focus on the entire project and attempt to assess what went well and what the project team could have done better. Subsequently, the lessons learned from the project team's experience should be documented and shared with others throughout the organization. In addition, the project manager and team should identify best practices that can be institutionalized throughout the organization by incorporating them into the methodology. As a result, the methodology evolves and better suits the organization's processes, culture, and people.

The second type of evaluation should take place between the project manager and the individual project team members. Although this performance review may be structured in terms of the organization's performance and merit review policies and procedures, it is important that each member of the team receive honest and useful feedback concerning his or her performance on the project. Areas of strength and opportunities for improvement should be identified so that plans of action can be developed to help each person develop to his or her potential.

In addition, an outside third party should review the project, the project manager, and project team. The focus of this review should be to answer the following questions:

- What is the likelihood of the project achieving its goal?
- Did the project meet its scope, schedule, budget, and quality objectives?
- Did the project team deliver everything that was promised to the sponsor or client?
- Is the project sponsor or client satisfied with the project work?
- Did the project manager and team follow the processes outlined in the project and system development methodologies?
- What risks or challenges did the project team face? And how well did they handle those risks and challenges?
- How well did the project sponsor, project team, and manager work together? If there were any conflicts, how well were they addressed and managed?
- Did the project manager and team act in a professional and ethical manner?

Lastly, the project must be evaluated in order to determine whether the project provided value to the organization. The goal of the project should be defined in the first phase of the project. In general, the value an IT project brings to the organization may not be clearly discernable immediately after the project is implemented. Therefore, it may be weeks or even months before that value is known. However, time and resources should be allocated for determining whether the project met its intended goal or not.

IT Project Management Foundation

The box under the phases in Figure 2.1 defines the IT project management foundation. This includes the project management processes, objectives, tools, infrastructure, and knowledge areas that are needed to support the IT project.

Project Management Processes   According to the Project Management Body of Knowledge (PMBOK), a **process** is a series of activities that produce a result. **Project management processes** describe and help organize the work to be accomplished by the project, while **product-oriented processes** focus on the creation and delivery of the product of the project. These management and product-oriented processes tend to overlap and are integrated throughout the project's life cycle. Each phase of the methodology should include the following:

- *Initiating processes*—to start or initiate a project or phase once commitment is obtained.
- *Planning processes*—to develop and maintain a workable plan to support the project's overall goal.
- *Executing processes*—to coordinate people and other resources to execute the plan.
- *Controlling processes*—to ensure proper control and reporting mechanisms are in place so that progress can be monitored, problems identified, and appropriate actions taken when necessary.
- *Closing processes*—to provide closure in terms of a formal acceptance that the project or a project's phase has been completed satisfactorily.

Project Objectives   In addition to an overall goal, a project will have several objectives. These objectives support the overall goal and may be defined in terms of the project's scope, schedule, budget, and quality standards. Separately, each of these objectives cannot define success; however, together they must support the project's goal. This relationship is illustrated in Figure 2.2.

Tools   Tools support both the processes and product of the project. These project management tools, include tools and techniques for estimation, as well as tools to develop and manage scope, schedule, budget, and quality. Similarly, tools support the development of the information system. For example, computer aided software engineering (CASE) tools and models support the analysis and design phases of development.

Infrastructure   Three infrastructures are needed to support the IT project. These include:

- *An organizational infrastructure*—The organizational infrastructure determines how projects are supported and managed within the organization. The organizational infrastructure influences how project resources are allocated, the reporting relationships of the project manager and the project team members, and the role of the project within the organization.
- *A project infrastructure*—The project infrastructure supports the project team in terms of the project environment and the project team itself. It includes:
  - *The project environment*—The physical workspace for the team to meet and work.
  - *Roles and responsibilities of the team members*—This determines the reporting relationships, as well as the responsibilities and authorities of the individual team members.

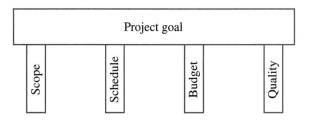

Figure 2.2 Project Objectives

- *Processes and controls*—Processes and controls provide support for managing all aspects of the project. They ensure that the project's goal and objectives are being met.

- *A technical infrastructure*—The technical infrastructure provides the hardware and software tools to support the project team. It may include such things as project management software, e-mail, voice mail, word processing, access to the Internet, and so on. The technical infrastructure allows the project team to do its work.

Project Management Knowledge Areas   The Project Management Body of Knowledge (PMBOK) encompasses nine areas generally accepted as having merit for effectively managing projects. These nine areas support both the project processes and product by providing a foundation of knowledge for supporting projects within a particular organization.

As an organization gains more experience with projects over time, the lessons learned from every project contribute to each of these nine areas. Ideally, these lessons will lead to an IT project management knowledge base that can be used to identify best practices that adapt the IT project methodology to an organization's needs, culture, and IT project environment. This base of knowledge can then be institutionalized throughout the organization and its projects.

THE BUSINESS CASE

What Is a Business Case?

Although organizations have increasingly turned to information technology to improve effectiveness and levels of efficiency, many projects have been undertaken without a thorough understanding of their full costs and risks. As a result, numerous IT projects have failed to return benefits that compensate adequately for the time and resources invested.

A business case provides the first deliverable in the IT project life cycle. It provides an analysis of the organizational value, feasibility, costs, benefits, and risks of several proposed alternatives or options. However, a business case is *not* a budget or the project plan. The purpose of a business case is to provide senior management with all the information needed to make an informed decision as to whether a specific project should be funded (Schmidt 1999).

For larger projects, a business case may be a large, formal document. Even for smaller projects, however, the process of thinking through why a particular project is being taken on and how it might bring value to an organization is still useful.

Because assumptions and new information are sometimes used to make subjective judgments, a business case must also document the methods and rationale used for quantifying the costs and benefits. Different people who work independently to develop a business case can use the same information, tools, and methods, but still come up with different recommendations. Therefore, it is imperative that decision makers who read the business case know and understand how it was developed and how various alternatives were evaluated.

One can also think of a business case as an investment proposal or a legal case. Like an attorney, the business case developer has a large degree of latitude to structure arguments, select or ignore evidence, and deliver the final presentation. The outcome depends largely on the ability to use compelling facts and logic in order to influence an individual or group with decision-making authority. Thus, a good IT business case should be (1) thorough in detailing all possible impacts, costs, and benefits; (2) clear and logical in comparing the cost/benefit impact of each alternative; (3) objective through including all pertinent information; and (4) systematic in terms of summarizing the findings (Schmidt 1999).

Developing the Business Case

The purpose of a business case is to show how an IT solution can create business value. Although IT projects can be undertaken for any number of reasons, organizational value generally focuses on improving effectiveness and/or efficiency. For example, an IT project may be undertaken to:

- Reduce costs
- Create a new product or service
- Improve customer service
- Improve communication
- Improve decision making
- Create or strengthen relationships with suppliers, customers, or partners
- Improve processes
- Improve reporting capabilities
- Support new legal requirements

Although these are just some of the reasons for proposing an IT project, it is up to management to evaluate, select, and fund projects on the basis of the value they bring to the organization. Therefore, the business case must show explicitly how an investment in IT will lead to an increase in business value. Figure 2.3 depicts the process for developing a business case.

Step 1: Select the Core Team   Rather than have one person take sole responsibility for developing the business case, a core team should be recruited. If possible, developing a business case should include many of the stakeholders affected by the project or involved in its delivery. The core team should, therefore, include managers, business specialists, and users who understand the requirements to be met, as well as IT specialists who understand the opportunities, limitations, and risks associated with IT. In general, there are several advantages for having a core team develop the business case (Schmidt 1999):

- *Credibility*—A team made up of individuals from various organizational areas or departments can provide access to critical expertise and information that may not be readily accessible to others outside that particular area. Moreover, a team can provide different points of view and provide a check for important items that an individual may overlook.

- *Alignment with organizational goals*—Higher-level managers can help connect the business case with the organization's long-term strategic plan and mission. This alignment may be beneficial in understanding and presenting how the expected business value of the IT project will support the overall goals and mission of the organization. Moreover, it may facilitate prioritizing, legitimizing, and assigning value of the IT project to the organization's

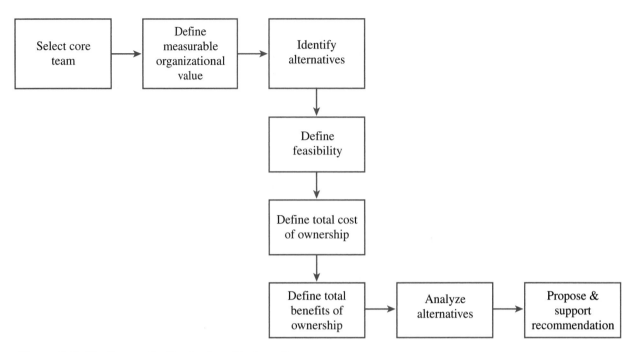

Figure 2.3 The Process for Developing a Business Case

strategic business objectives. In other words, the business case should outline how the successful completion of the proposed project will help the organization achieve its overall mission, goals, and objectives.

- *Access to the real costs*—Core members with certain expertise or access to important information can help build more realistic estimates in areas such as salaries, overhead, accounting and reporting practices, training requirements, union rules and regulations, and hiring practices.

In addition, the core team that develops the business case can play a crucial role when dealing with various areas or departments within the organizational boundary. The advantages include:

- *Ownership*—A cross-functional team can spread a sense of ownership for the business case. A project that includes other areas from the outset has a better chance of reducing the political problems associated with territorial domains.

- *Agreement*—If you develop a business case in isolation, it is very likely that you will have to defend your assumptions and subjective judgments in a competitive or political setting. However, if a core team develops the business case, the critics may be more apt to argue the results rather than the data and methods used.

- *Bridge building*—The core team may serve as an effective tool for handling critics of the business case. One tactic may be to include critics on the core team or to at least allow recognition and consideration for their positions. This may lead to fewer surprises and attacks later on.

Step 2. Define Measurable Organizational Value (MOV)   The core team's objective should be to define the problem or opportunity and then identify several alternatives that will provide direct and measurable value to the organization. To provide real value to an organization, however, IT projects must align with and support the organization's goals, mission, and objectives. Therefore, any recommended alternative by the core team must have a clearly defined purpose and must map to the goals and strategy of the organization. The goal of the project then becomes the project's measure of success (Billows 1996; Smith 1999). In the IT project management methodology, the project's overall goal and measure of success is referred to as the project's **measurable organizational value (MOV).** As the name implies, the MOV must:

- *Be measurable*—Measurement provides focus for the project team in terms of its actions. Instead of implementing an information system, the project team attempts to achieve a specific performance target. Moreover, an MOV provides a basis for making decisions that affect the project through its remaining phases. Why do additional work or make decisions that affect the project if they do not help you achieve the MOV?

- *Provide value to the organization*—Resources and time should not be devoted to a project unless they provide some kind of value to the organization. Keep in mind that information technology in itself cannot provide value. Technology is only an enabler—that is, IT enables organizations to do things.

- *Be agreed upon*—A clear and agreed upon MOV sets expectations for the project stakeholders. It is important that all project stakeholders understand and agree to the project's MOV. It is not easy to get everyone to agree to the project's goal so early; but it will be well worth the time and effort in the later stages of the project (Billows 1996).

- *Verifiable*—At the end of the project, the MOV must be verified to determine if the project was a success.

The MOV guides all the decisions and processes for managing the IT project and serves as a basis for evaluating the project's achievements. In other words, a project cannot be properly planned or evaluated unless the goal of the project is clearly defined and understood. An organization should not undertake projects that are not clearly linked to its overall mission.

The IT value chain depicted in Figure 2.4 suggests that an organizational goal leads to or defines an organizational strategy. In turn, a project's measurable organizational value then supports this organizational strategy. This mapping shows how a project's goal aligns with an organization's strategy and goal. At the end of the project, the project's actual achievements can be compared to its initial MOV to determine whether the project was successful. If the project is a success (i.e., it either met or exceeded its MOV), then one can see explicitly how that project will support the organization.

For example, if we follow Michael Porter's (Porter 1980; Porter 1985) competitive forces model, one organizational goal may be to prevent customers from leaving or switching to a competitor. Therefore, an organizational strategy to support this goal may be to develop tight linkages with customers. To support this organizational

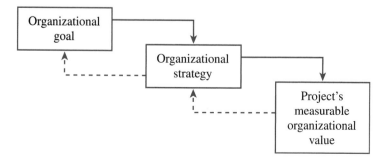

Figure 2.4 The IT Value Chain

strategy and goal, the organization may consider developing a business-to-business (B2B) application that will allow customers to check inventory status, place orders, track shipments, receive an invoice, pay an invoice, and receive various reports online.

Will the installation of hardware and a network mean that the B2B application was a success? Will the development and implementation of the application software? What if the project is completed not only on time, but also within budget? A yes answer here is only partially correct. Although all of these achievements are important, they cannot be true measures of a project's success.

More specifically, installing hardware and a network are activities. Having them in place is a necessary, but not sufficient, condition for success. In other words, hardware and software can be in place, but unless they support the organizational goal and strategy, their mere installation does not bring much value to the organization. One can also view budget and schedule in the same light. You can have a project that is finished on time and within budget, but unless it brings value to the organization in terms of supporting a goal and strategy, it will not be of much use.

But what if a project goes over schedule and over budget? How will that impact the project's value to the organization? The answer is that it depends. A project that is late and over budget certainly can impact the project's value to the organization, but success or failure really depends on the amount of value a project will provide. For example, should a project that is one day late and a dollar over budget be considered unsuccessful? Probably not. What about a project that is one week late and $1,000 over budget? That depends on how these overruns compare to the original schedule and budget. If the original schedule and budget were two years and $1 million, then most people would agree that the schedule and cost variation is no big deal.

What's more important is the value the project brings to the organization. A consultant friend once told a story of a CEO who was ecstatic because an e-commerce project the company was taking on was only one year late and only $12 million over budget. In this case, schedule and cost did not matter all that much because once the e-commerce site was up and running the company would make the deficit up within six months. The moral of the story is that business value is the most important criteria for IT projects.

A project's MOV should be based on the organization's goal and strategy. An excellent example of an MOV is the following statement that John F. Kennedy made back in the 1960s, "Our goal is to land a man on the moon and return him safely by the end of the decade."

This simple yet powerful statement mobilized an entire nation and fueled the space race with the then Soviet Union. What is interesting about this statement is how clear and measurable the goal becomes:

- A human being is to land on the moon—not an unmanned spacecraft or a spacecraft with a chimpanzee.
- We will not just get a human to the moon or get that person just back halfway. This person must make the whole trip and come back safely.
- This will all be done before 1970.

What is equally interesting is that Kennedy never told anyone *how* to do this. That was NASA's job, not his. The goal was to beat the Soviets to the moon, and the project's MOV defined this explicitly.

But how do we go about developing a project's MOV? There are six basic steps. Let's follow that process using as an example a company that would like to develop and implement a business-to-consumer (B2C) electronic commerce application that it hopes will allow it to expand its current bricks and mortar operations.

Identify the Desired Area of Impact   The first step involves identifying the desired impact the IT project will play in supporting the organization. One approach might be to adapt the criteria used by *CIO* magazine's Enterprise Value Awards.[1] The guidelines summarized in Table 2.1 are used by the judges to define IT value and provide a good starting point for developing the MOV and business case. You should feel free to adapt these areas of impact as needed. The important question to answer at this point is why are we thinking of doing this project?

In our B2C example, the project manager would meet with the project sponsor and first determine how the idea for the project came about. Although the reasons could be broad and numerous (i.e., all of our competitors are doing it, it is part of our long-term strategy, we think we can make a lot of money, B2C will make our company look hip), identifying them will provide a background for understanding how and why decisions are made by the sponsor's organization. In this example, we will say that the reasons for considering this project are both strategic and financial because the company wants to expand its current brick and mortar operations. The idea is not to neatly categorize the project, but to understand the nature of the project and how it will impact the organization.

Identify the Desired Value of the IT Project   Once the desired area of impact is identified, the next step involves determining the desired value the IT project will bring to the organization. This area is can be tricky, but having a process helps. In simplest terms, we can identify the value of an IT project by providing answers to the following four questions:

- *Better*—What does the organization want to do better? (For example, improve quality or increase effectiveness?)
- *Faster*—What does the organization want to do faster? (Increase speed, increase efficiency, or reduce cycle times?)
- *Cheaper*—What does the organization want to do cheaper? (Reduce costs?)
- *Do more*—What does the organization want to do more than it is currently? (Growth or expansion?[2])

The key words to identifying the value an IT project will provide an organization are *better, faster, cheaper,* and *do more.* The first three criteria—better, faster, and cheaper—focus on quality, effectiveness, and efficiency, while doing more of something focuses on growth. For example, if an organization has identified increasing profits as its desired area of impact, it makes sense that it would like to make more money than it currently does. Therefore, value to this organization would be in the form of growth. On the other hand, another organization may be faced with high inventory costs as a result of having too much inventory in its warehouse. The value that an IT project would bring to this organization would not be from growth; it does not want to do more of what it is currently doing. The value comes from doing something better (e.g., improved quality to reduce waste or rework), faster (e.g., fewer manufacturing bottlenecks or reduced cycle times), or even cheaper (e.g., lower overhead costs).

---

[1] Since 1993, *CIO* magazine has conducted a competition to identify and honor organizations that create enterprise value through the innovative use of IT. Entrants must submit an entry following contest guidelines. A team made up of *CIO* editors and consultants selects finalists. Entries are judged on the value of the achievement that an IT investment provides and how it serves the organizations mission.

[2] Value to an organization may also result by doing *less* of something. For example, a company may develop a safety program to reduce the number of accidents. Reducing accidents can be viewed as negative growth or as an increase in safety as a result of doing something better (i.e., quality). It just depends on one's viewpoint.

Table 2.1 Potential Areas of Impact for IT Projects

Potential Area	Examples of Desired Impact
Strategic	<ul><li>Penetration of new markets</li><li>Transformation of the terms of competition within the market</li><li>Increased market share</li></ul>
Customer	<ul><li>Customers have more choices of products or services</li><li>Customers receive better products or services</li><li>Transaction processes are more efficient or effective</li></ul>
Financial	<ul><li>Increased profit</li><li>Increased margins</li></ul>
Operational	<ul><li>Lower costs due to streamlined operations</li><li>Increased operational effectiveness</li><li>Improvements to supply chain</li></ul>
Social	<ul><li>Education</li><li>Health</li><li>Safety</li><li>Environment</li></ul>

SOURCE: Adapted from *CIO* magazine's Enterprise Value Awards Application Form and Elaine M. Cummings, "Judgment Call," *CIO*, February 2, 2000, http://www.cio.com/awards/eva/index.html.

While the question in the first step focuses on why an organization wants to take on the project, this second step focuses on the question "how will this project help us achieve what we want to achieve?" At this point, the project manager and client should identify one or two value areas to emphasize. If all four of the value areas appear important, it is a good idea to rank them in order of importance. Keep in mind, however, that not having a clear idea of the desired impact or value of the project may well mean that the problem or opportunity is not clearly understood. The project team may end up treating the symptoms rather than the real problem.

Following our example of the B2C project, the value critical to the organization may be doing more through the project's ability to enable to organization to expand its current operations. Value from improved customer service and improved operations could also support the organization in doing things better, faster, and cheaper as well. This step provides an excellent vehicle for all project stakeholders to discuss and identify the expected value of the project.

Develop an Appropriate Metric   Once there is agreement as to the value the IT project will bring to the organization, the next step is to develop a metric or set of metrics that (1) provides the project team with a target or directive, (2) sets expectations among all stakeholders, and (3) provides a means for evaluating whether the project is a success later on. In general, tangible benefits to the organization are easier to define than intangible ones; however, this can be done with some creativity. For example, knowing whether profits increased should be fairly straightforward, but customer satisfaction may require surveys or interviews. Often evaluation requires benchmarking so that a before and after comparison can be made.

To develop a metric, the project manager and sponsor should agree on a specific number or range of numbers. When not obvious, the target metric should indicate whether an increase or decrease from the organization's current state is desired. The metrics may be expressed as dollars, percentages, or numbers. For example, an organization that wishes to increase profits may state this as a 20 percent increase or an increase of $1 million from the last month, quarter, or fiscal year. On the other hand, an organization that would like to grow its customer base may set a goal of one hundred new customers. Therefore, the metrics to support an MOV may be one or a combination of the following:

- Money (in dollars, euros, etc.)   (increase or decrease)
- Percentage (%)   (increase or decrease)
- Numeric Value   (increase or decrease)

The company in our example would like to grow strategically, that is, expand its current base of operations. There are a number of relevant metrics that could be used. The question is how will this company determine whether this project is a success. Keep in mind that the organization will make a significant investment by the time the project is completed. Will the B2C application be successful when the Web site is finished and anyone with an Internet connection can view the site? It is important to have a working Web site, but that alone will not make up for the investment and subsequent maintenance and support for keeping the site up and running. What about using a hit counter so that the organization can tell how many times the B2C site was visited? Having traffic to the Web site is also important, but people who just visit will not keep the company in business nor will visitors justify the investment and cost of keeping the B2C Web site up and running.

It should now be obvious that the company must make money from its B2C Web site. Only a profit can justify the time, effort, and resources needed to develop and support the application. The questions then become how much profit and are there any other metrics that should be considered. Assume that management has determined that a 20 percent return will be adequate for covering all expenses and for providing the desired return. Also assume that management is interested in developing new customers. Therefore, the company has set a target of five hundred new customers. Why a 20 percent return and five hundred new customers? Those numbers are not developed by the project manager or project team on their own. The 20 percent return and five hundred new customers' metrics can only be determined by the project sponsor. The project manager and project team only guide the process.

Set a Time Frame for Achieving the MOV Once you have agreement on the target metrics that will provide the desired impact to the organization, the next step is to agree on a specific time frame. For example, a company may focus on increasing profits or reducing costs, but the question is when will these results be achieved. Keep in mind that the scheduled completion of the project is not the same thing as the agreed upon time frame for achieving the MOV. Scope, schedule, budget, and quality are project objectives. The MOV is the project goal. Rarely will the installation of an information system provide the desired or expected value right away. A project with an immovable deadline may, however, have a specific date as part of the MOV. For example, there may be cause for putting a deadline date in the MOV in 01/01/10000, when all the dates in computers, or whatever they are using then, have to be changed once more.

The project manager and sponsor should also agree upon how and when the project's MOV will be evaluated. Continuing with the example, let's say that management would like to see a 20 percent return and five hundred new customers within one year after the system goes online. But what happens after the first year? Perhaps the company would like to maintain this growth annually over the useful life of the system. There is, however, no reason why different targets cannot be set for different time periods. For example, a 20 percent return and five hundred new customers may be sufficient for the first year, but these targets may change as word spreads and more and more people know about the B2C Web site. Therefore, the company may establish a target of a 25 percent return and one thousand new customers in the second year, while a 30 percent return with 1,500 new customers is set for the third year. The MOV should be flexible to accommodate the expectations and needs of the project sponsor.

Verify and Get Agreement from the Project Stakeholders The next step in developing the MOV is to ensure that it is accurate and realistic. In short, will the successful completion of this project provide the intended value to the organization? And is the MOV realistic? The development of the MOV requires a close working relationship between the project manager and the sponsor. The project manager's responsibility is to guide the process, while the sponsor must identify the value and target metrics. This joint responsibility may not always be easy, especially when several sponsors or individuals need to agree upon what will make an IT project successful or what exactly will bring value to the organization. Still, it is better to spend the time arguing and getting consensus now rather than during later phases of the project. While the project manager is responsible for guiding the process, he or she needs to be confident that the MOV can be achieved. Being challenged is one thing; agreeing to an unrealistic MOV is another. The latter can be detrimental to your career, the project team, and everyone's morale.

Summarize the MOV in a Clear, Concise Statement or Table   Once the impact and value to the organization are verified and agreed upon by all the project stakeholders, the MOV should be summarized in a single statement or table. Summarizing the MOV (1) provides an important chance to get final agreement and verification, (2) provides a simple and clear directive for the project team, and (3) sets explicit expectations for all project stakeholders. The easiest way to summarize the MOV in a statement form is to complete the following statement:

This project will be successful if _____.

For example, using a single statement format, the MOV would be:

MOV: The B2C project will provide a 20 percent return on investment and five hundred new customers within the first year of its operation.

However, if the MOV includes a growth component, a table format may be clearer. For example, the project's MOV over three years could be summarized as shown in Table 2.2.

Notice that the MOV does not include any explicit statements about technology. More specifically, it does not mention that a particular relational database vendor's product will be used or that the system will be programmed in a particular language. It is up to the project team to figure out how to build the system and determine what technology will be employed to achieve the project goal. At this point in the project, we are concerned with the organization—not with the technology!

The project team's directive will be to achieve the MOV, not just develop and implement a B2C Web site. Although information technology will play an important role, the designers and developers of the information system cannot be expected to know everything or be solely responsible for achieving the project goal.

In the past, purely technical approaches were often applied to organizational problems. A system would be built, but did it really support or have a significant, positive impact on the organization? Judging from the *Chaos* study, most IT projects have not lived up to management's expectations. In short, the technical people may understand and be very good at working with the technology, but achieving this MOV will also require an organizational approach and commitment. A cross-functional project team that includes a number of non-technical experts will be required so that the burden of achieving this MOV does not rest squarely on the shoulders of the technical experts. Therefore, the selection of the project team becomes a crucial project management decision.

Table 2.2 Sample MOV Using Table Format

Year	MOV
1	20% return on investment 500 new customers
2	25% return on investment 1,000 new customers
3	30% return on investment 1,500 new customers

Step 3: Identify Alternatives   Since no single solution generally exists for most organizational problems, it is imperative to identify several alternatives before dealing directly with a given business opportunity. The alternatives, or options, identified in the business case should be strategies for achieving the MOV.

It is also important that the alternatives listed include a wide range of potential solutions as well as a **base case alternative** that describes how the organization would perform if it maintained the status quo—i.e., if it did not pursue any of the options described in the business case. In some situations, maintaining the status quo may be the best alternative. It is important to be open to and objective on all viable options.

The base case should also delve into the realistic costs of maintaining the current system over time. Include such things as increased maintenance costs of hardware and software, as well as the possibility for more frequent system failures and downtime. However, if the demand for service decreases, maintaining a legacy system may be a more viable alternative than a proposed new system.

On the other hand, other options may provide the best solution. These options should consider a spectrum of choices that include:

- Changing the existing business processes without investing in IT
- Adopting or adapting an application developed by a different area or department within the organization
- Reengineering the existing system
- Purchasing an off-the-shelf application package from a software vendor
- Custom building a new application using internal resources or outsourcing the development to another company

Step 4: Define Feasibility and Assess Risk   Each option or alternative must be analyzed in terms of its feasibility and potential risk. **Feasibility** should focus on whether a particular alternative is *doable* and *worth doing.* **Risk,** on the other hand, focuses on *what can go wrong* and *what must go right.* Analyzing the feasibility and risk of each alternative at this point may act as a screening process for ruling out any alternatives that are not worth pursuing. Feasibility may be viewed in terms of:

- *Economic feasibility*—Although a cost/benefit analysis will be conducted to look at the alternatives in greater depth, some alternatives may be too costly or simply not provide the benefits envisioned in the problem statement. At this point, an organization may evaluate an alternative in terms of whether funds and resources exist to support the project. For example, although you may be in a market for a new car, the reality of your limited income rules out the fancy sports car. Conducting an economic feasibility should serve as a reality check for each option or alternative.

- *Technical feasibility*—Technical feasibility focuses on the existing technical infrastructure needed to support the IT solution. Will the current infrastructure support the alternative? Will new technology be needed? Will it be available? Does the current IT staff have the skills and experience to support the proposed solution? If outsourcing, does the vendor or company have the skills and experience to develop and implement the application?

- *Organizational feasibility*—Organizational feasibility considers the impact on the organization. It focuses mainly on how people within the organization will adapt to this planned organizational change. How will people and the way they do their jobs be impacted? Will they accept this change willingly? Will business be disrupted while the proposed solution is implemented?

- *Other feasibilities*—Depending on the situation and the organization, a business case may include other issues, such as legal and ethical feasibility.

Risk should focus on:

- *Identification*—What can go wrong? What must go right?
- *Assessment*—What is the impact of each risk?
- *Response*—How can the organization avoid or minimize the risk?

Step 5: Define Total Cost of Ownership The decision to invest in an IT project must take into account all of the costs associated with the application system. **Total Cost of Ownership (TCO)** is a concept that has gained widespread attention in recent years and generally refers to the total cost of acquiring, developing, maintaining, and supporting the application system over its useful life. TCO includes such costs as:

- *Direct or up-front costs*—Initial purchase price of all hardware, software, and telecommunications equipment, all development or installation costs, outside consultant fees, etc.
- *Ongoing costs*—Salaries, training, upgrades, supplies, maintenance, etc.
- *Indirect costs*—Initial loss of productivity, time lost by users when the system is down, the cost of auditing equipment (i.e., finding out who has what and where), quality assurance, and post implementation reviews.

It is important to note that TCO goes beyond the original purchase or development costs. In fact, the TCO is really an organized list of all possible cost impacts. When preparing the business case, it is also important to document all data sources, assumptions, and methods for determining the various costs.

Step 6: Define Total Benefits of Ownership Similarly, the **Total Benefits of Ownership (TBO)** must include all of the direct, on-going, and indirect benefits associated with each proposed alternative. The TBO should address the benefits of an alternative over the course of its useful life. Benefits can arise from:

- *Increasing high-value work*—For example, a salesperson may spend less time on paperwork and more time calling on customers.
- *Improving accuracy and efficiency*—For example, reducing errors, duplication, or the number of steps in a process.
- *Improving decision-making*—For example, providing timely and accurate information.
- *Improving customer service*—For example, new products or services, faster or more reliable service, convenience, etc.

Tangible benefits associated with an IT project are relatively easy to identify and quantify. They will usually arise from direct cost savings or avoided costs. On the other hand, intangible benefits may be easy to identify, but they are certainly more difficult to quantify. It is important to try and quantify all of the benefits identified. One way to quantify intangible benefits is to link them directly to tangible benefits that can be linked to efficiency gains. For example, a corporate telephone directory on an intranet not only improves communication, but also can cut paper, printing, and labor costs associated with creating and distributing a paper-based telephone book.

Another way to quantify intangible benefits is to estimate the level of service. For example, one could determine how much someone is willing to pay for a particular service or compare prices of products or services that have or do not have a particular feature. Moreover, if an electronic data interchange (EDI) application allows a company to collect its accounts receivable more quickly, it can estimate the value of this benefit by determining the return it could earn by investing that money.

Step 7: Analyze Alternatives Once costs and benefits have been identified, it is important that all alternatives be compared with each other consistently. Understanding the financial and numeric tools and techniques required by financial people and senior management is critical, even for the technically savvy. Being able to communicate effectively using their terms and tools increases one's credibility and the chances of getting projects approved and funded. There are several ways to analyze the proposed alternatives. The most common are financial models and scoring models.

Financial models focus on either profitability and/or cash flows. Cash flow models focus on the net cash, may be positive or negative, and are calculated by subtracting the cash outflows from the cash inflows. In general, one could view the benefits associated with a particular alternative as a source of cash inflow and the costs as the source of outflows. Using a tool such as an electronic spreadsheet application, one could conduct a sensitivity analysis to view how changes in the initial investment or net cash flows would impact the risk of a particular project alternative.

The most commonly used cash flow models include payback, breakeven, return on investment, net present value, and scoring.

Payback The payback method determines how long it will take to recover the initial investment. For example, if a company spends $100,000 developing and implementing an application system and then receives a net cash return of $20,000 a year, the payback period for that investment would be:

$$\text{Payback Period} = \frac{\text{Initial Investment}}{\text{Net Cash Flow}}$$
$$= \frac{\$100,000}{\$20,000}$$
$$= 5 \text{ years}$$

Although the payback period is fairly straightforward to calculate and understand, it does not consider the time value of money or cash flows beyond the payback period. Still, the payback period is useful for highlighting the risk of a particular investment because a riskier investment will have a longer payback period than a less risky investment. Depending on the situation and the organization's policy, net cash flow may be either before tax or after tax.

Breakeven Similar to the payback method, the breakeven method attempts to determine the point at which a project would begin to recoup its original investment. This method is useful if a certain number of transactions allow the original investment to be recovered. For example, let's say that you would like to create a Web site to sell golf putters that you manufacture. If you spent $100,000 to create the site, how many golf putters would you have to sell to break even if you sell each putter for $30? To determine this point, you have to look at the cost of selling a putter. These costs may include the following:

Materials (putter head, shaft, grip, etc.)	$12.00
Labor (0.5 hours at $9.00/hr)	$ 4.50
Overhead (rent, insurance, utilities, taxes, etc.)	$ 8.50
Total	$25.00

If you sell a golf putter for $30 and it costs $25 to make it, you have a profit margin of $5. The breakeven point is computed as follows:

$$\text{Breakeven Point} = \frac{\text{Initial Investment}}{\text{Net Profit Margin}}$$
$$= \frac{\$100,000}{\$5}$$
$$= 20,000$$

Therefore, you would have to sell 20,000 putters over your Web site to break even.

Like the payback period method, the breakeven method is generally easy to compute and can provide a measure of risk. In general, riskier project alternatives will have a higher breakeven point than less risky project alternatives.

Return on Investment In a strict financial sense, **return on investment (ROI)** is an indicator of a company's financial performance. From a project management point of view, ROI provides a measure of the value expected or received from a particular alternative or project. It is calculated by dividing the net income, or return, of a project alternative by its total cost. So, if a project alternative, for example, is expected to cost $100,000 but provide $115,000 in expected benefits, its ROI would be:

$$\text{Project ROI} = \frac{\text{total expected benefits} - \text{total expected costs}}{\text{total expected costs}}$$
$$= \frac{\$115,000 - \$100,000}{\$100,000}$$
$$= 15\%$$

The above formula shows the expected ROI for a project alternative; a completed project's ROI would use the actual costs and benefits derived and can be compared to its expected ROI to provide a comparison at the end of the project. The usefulness of a project's ROI depends on two important assumptions. First, there must be the ability to define accurately the total costs and benefits expected or realized. Second, the returns must arise as a direct result of the initial investment. For example, if you purchased a lottery ticket for $1 and won $1 million, you can determine the ROI directly because the $1 million return can be related to the $1 lottery ticket you purchased. Even though the chances of winning a lottery are pretty slim, the ROI calculated as ($1,000,000 − $1) ÷ $1 = 99,999,900 percent would be quite acceptable for most people. In complex business situations, however, ROI analysis may be difficult because intervening variables and conditions may have an indirect influence.

Regardless, with ROI one can see the relationship between a project's costs and benefits. A project's ROI will increase as the benefits increase and/or the expected costs decrease. When comparing two or more projects or alternatives, those with the higher ROI would be the most desirable (all other things being equal). Many organizations even have a required ROI, whereby no project or alternative may be considered unless a certain ROI value can be achieved. The idea is that it is not worth investing time and resources in a project that does not provide a certain level of value to the organization and its shareholders.

Net Present Value **Net Present Value (NPV)** focuses on the time value of money. For example, if you borrow $20 today, you may have to agree to pay back the original $20 plus another $2 at the end of the month. Someone may also be willing to give you either $18 today or $20 at the end of the month. If you could take the $18 and invest it, ending up with $20 at the end of the month, you might feel indifferent as to whether you collected $18 today or $20 at the end of the month. The point here is that there is a cost associated with time when it comes to money.

It is going to take time and resources (i.e., costs) before any particular project or alternative is completed and provides the returns we originally envisioned. NPV takes this into account by discounting streams of cash flows a particular alternative or project returns in the future so that we can determine if investing the time, money, and resources is worth the wait. Very simply put, only a project or alternative with a positive NPV should be considered. Let's say that one alternative is an application system that is expected to cost $200,000 and will be completed in the current year (Year 0). In addition, over the following four years the project's benefits will provide inflows of cash, while the costs to build, maintain and support this application will require outflows of cash. The expected cash flows for the next five years may look something like:

	Year 0	Year 1	Year 2	Year 3	Year 4
Total Cash Inflows	$0	$150,000	$200,000	$250,000	$300,000
Total Cash Outflows	$200,000	$85,000	$125,000	$150,000	$200,000
Net Cash Flow	($200,000)	$65,000	$75,000	$100,000	$100,000

To discount the net cash flows, a **discount rate** is required. This rate is sometimes called a **cutoff rate** or **hurdle rate** because it basically defines the organization's required rate of return. In short, the discount rate is the minimum return a company would expect from a project if the company were to make an equivalent investment in an opportunity of similar risk. This discount rate is usually set by management. The NPV is calculated using the formula:

$$NPV = -I_O + \sum \left(\frac{\text{Net Cash Flow}}{(1+r)^t} \right)$$

Where:
I = total cost (or investment) in the project
r = discount rate
t = time period

Therefore, if we use a discount rate of 8 percent, we can discount the net cash flow for each period and add them up to determine the NPV.

Time Period	Calculation	Discounted Cash Flow
Year 0	($200,000)	($200,000)
Year 1	$65,000 \div (1 + .08)^1$	$60,185
Year 2	$75,000 \div (1 + .08)^2$	$64,300
Year 3	$100,000 \div (1 + .08)^3$	$79,383
Year 4	$100,000 \div (1 + .08)^4$	$73,503
Net Present Value (NPV)		$77,371

This alternative would be acceptable because a NPV of $77,371 is positive. One can compare the NPV for different alternatives and projects. In general, the project or alternative with a higher NPV would be more desirable. Remember, increasing the discount rate will decrease the NPV.[1]

Scoring models provide a method for comparing alternatives or projects based on a weighted score. Scoring models also allow for quantifying intangible benefits or for different alternatives using multiple criteria. Using percentage weights, one can assign values of importance to the different criteria. The weights must sum to 100 percent, and when multiplied by a score assigned to each criterion they allow a composite score that is the weighted average. For example, one could compare several alternatives using the following formula:

$$\text{Total Score} = \sum_{i=1}^{n} w_i c_i$$

Where:
w_i = criterion weight
c_i = criterion score
$0 \le w_i \le 1$

Table 2.3 compares three project alternatives using this system. The scoring model in Table 2.3 highlights several important ideas:

- *The scoring model can combine both qualitative and non-qualitative items.* Whether one assigns more weight to intangible or intangible criteria depends on the philosophy of management or the client.

- *Weights and scores can be largely subjective.* This scoring is a two-edged sword. People use their judgment, or gut feelings, in assigning weights and scores, but may not necessarily have the same judgments. Thus, getting agreement among individuals may be difficult. One suggestion is to have different individuals assign weights and scores to the different criteria and then average these individual responses to create a composite score. Even if people don't agree, at least they have an opportunity to express their opinions. Another suggestion would be to use a relative score whenever possible. For example, let's say that the NPVs for the three alternatives were as follows:

	Alternative		
	A	**B**	**C**
NPV	$200	$400	$1,000

Since Alternative C has the highest NPV, we can determine a relative score (on a basis of 0 to 10) for each alternative as follows:

Alternative	NPV	Calculation	Relative Score
A	$1,000	($1,000 ÷ $1,000) × 10	10
B	$400	($400 ÷ $1,000) × 10	4
C	$200	($20 ÷ $1,000) × 10	2

---

[1] Closely related to the concept of Net Present Value is the popular concept called Internal Rate of Return (IRR). The IRR focuses on streams of cash flows and is the discount rate where the total present value of future cash flows equals the cost of the investment. In short, it is the rate where the NPV is equal to zero. Therefore, alternatives or projects with higher IRR are more desirable. Management may set a minimum desired IRR that an alternative or project must meet in order to be considered. IRR can be readily computed with a financial calculator or by using specific spreadsheet or program functions; otherwise, the exact IRR must be interpolated.

Table 2.3 Comparison of Project Alternatives

Criterion		Weight	Alternative A	Alternative B	Alternative C
Financial	ROI	15%	2	4	10
	Payback	10%	3	5	10
	NPV	15%	2	4	10
Organizational	Alignment with strategic objectives	10%	3	5	8
	Likelihood of achieving project's MOV	10%	2	6	9
Project	Availability of skilled team members	5%	5	5	4
	Maintainability	5%	4	6	7
	Time to develop	5%	5	7	6
	Risk	5%	3	5	5
External	Customer satisfaction	10%	2	4	9
	Increased market share	10%	2	5	8
Total Score		**100%**	**2.65**	**4.85**	**8.50**

Note: Risk scores have a reverse scale—i.e., higher scores for risk imply lower levels of risk.

The scores used in this example range from 0 to 10; but there is nothing sacred about this range. One could use a scale of 0 to 100. Consistency rather than any particular scale is the key.

- *Financial models can be biased towards the short run.* Although financial models are important and should be considered, they focus solely on the periods used in discounting cash flows. Scoring models go beyond this limitation because they allow for multi-criteria (Meredith and Mantel 2000).

- *Some criteria can be reversed-scored.* In our example, higher scores for certain criteria make sense. For instance, higher financial performance measures inherently have higher scores. However, a criterion such as risk can be reversed-scored with lower risk alternatives having higher scores. If you reverse-score any criterion, it is beneficial to note these assumptions conspicuously for the reader.

- *Past experience may help create a more realistic business case.* As mentioned before, many of the weights and scores are subjective. Instead of relying on guesswork, past experience with past projects can provide guidelines and a reference for ensuring that the selection models are relevant and realistic. Although the business situation, technology, and data will change over time, the process or method of preparing a business case and analyzing alternatives will remain much the same. Learning from past experience can improve the process and product associated with business cases and thus improves the likelihood of a project being approved and funded.

Step 8: Propose and Support the Recommendation   Once the alternatives have been identified and analyzed, the last step is to recommend one of the options. It is important to remember that a proposed recommendation must be supported. If the analysis was done diligently, this recommendation should be a relatively easy task.

The business case should be formalized in a professional-looking report. Remember that the quality and accuracy of your work will be a reflection on you and your organization. A potential client or project sponsor may not give you a second chance. Figure 2.5 provides a template for developing a business case.

PROJECT SELECTION AND APPROVAL

The objective of the business case is to obtain approval and funding for a proposed alternative. However, a proposed project may have to compete against several others.

The criteria for selecting a **project portfolio,** a set of projects that an organization may fund, are very similar to the analysis and subsequent selection of the proposed project alternatives. Similar to portfolio theory in finance, an organization may wish to select a portfolio of IT projects that have varying levels of risk, technological complexity, size, and strategic intent (McFarlan 1981; Marchewka and Keil 1995). An IT project portfolio mainly comprised of projects with low risk or those that do not attempt to take advantage of new technology may lead to stagnation. The organization may not move ahead strategically and the IT employees may fail to grow professionally due to lack of challenge. On the other hand, an organization that focuses too heavily on risky projects employing cutting-edge technology may end up in a precarious position if the IT projects experience serious problems and failures. Learning from mistakes can be useful, unless the same mistakes are repeated over and over. Thus, an organization should attempt to balance its IT project portfolio with projects that have varying degrees of risk, cutting-edge technologies, and structure.

Unfortunately, as Harold Kerzner (Kerzner 2000, 120) points out, "What a company wants to do is not always what it can do." He contends that companies generally have a number of projects that they would like to undertake, but because of

---

The following provides a suggested outline for developing and writing a business case:

Cover Page
- Title and subtitle
- Author and address
- Date

Executive Summary
- Brief description of the problem or opportunity
- Brief description of organization's goal and strategy
- Brief description of project's MOV and how it ties to the organizational goal and strategy
- Brief description of each option or alternative analyzed
- Brief explanation of which alternative is being recommended and why

Introduction
- Background
- Current situation
- Description of the problem or opportunity

- Project's measurable organizational value
- How achieving the project's MOV will support the organization's goal and strategy
- Objectives of writing this business case

Alternatives
- Description of alternative 1 (Base Case)
- Description of alternative 2 …
- Description of alternative N

Analysis of Alternatives
- Methodology of how alternatives will be analyzed
  - Data collection methods
  - Metrics used and explanation why they are relevant
- Presentation of results that compares each alternative
  - Metrics
  - Sensitivity analysis
  - Risks
  - Assumptions
- Proposed recommendation
- Required funding and support

Figure 2.5 Business Case Template

limited resources, they must prioritize and fund projects selectively. Depending on the demand for IT professionals or the state of the economy, it is not always feasible to hire new employees or to have them trained in time.

The IT Project Selection Process

Although each organization's selection process is different, this section describes the general process for selecting and funding a given project. The selection process determines which IT projects will be funded in a given period. This period can be for a quarter, year, or a time frame used by the organization. In order to weed out projects that have little chance of being approved, many organizations use an initial screening process in which business cases submitted for review are compared with a set of organizational standards that outline minimum requirements.

Projects that meet the minimum requirements are then forwarded to a decision-making committee of senior managers who have the authority to approve and provide the resources needed to support the project. On rare occasions an individual might make such decisions, but most organizations of any size prefer to use committees. The committee may compare several competing projects based on the costs, benefits, and risks to projects currently under development and to those already implemented. Projects selected should then be assigned to a project manager who selects the project team and then develops a project charter and detailed plan.

The Project Selection Decision

Even though each project proposal should be evaluated in terms of its value to the organization, it is important to reiterate that IT projects should not be undertaken for technology's sake. The decision to approve an IT project requires a number of conditions be met:

- The IT project must map directly to the organization's strategies and goals.
- The IT project must provide measurable organizational value that can be verified at the completion of the project.
- The selection of an IT project should be based upon diversity of measures that include:
    - Tangible costs and benefits
    - Intangible costs and benefits
    - Various levels throughout the organization (e.g., individual, process, department, and enterprise)

One way to select an IT project portfolio is to use the same methods that were used and discussed when analyzing the project alternatives in the business case. Today, however, there are several ways to measure the expected and realized value of IT to an organization. One method that is becoming increasingly popular is the **Balanced Scorecard** approach that was introduced by Robert S. Kaplan and David Norton in a 1992 *Harvard Business Review* article. Instead of focusing solely on the financial impact of a decision, the Balanced Scorecard approach helps balance traditional financial measures with operational metrics across four different perspectives: finance, customer satisfaction, internal business processes, and the organization's ability to innovate and learn (Kaplan and Norton 1992; Kaplan and Norton 1993).

An organization that utilizes the Balanced Scorecard approach must create a set of measurements, or key performance indicators, for each of the perspectives illustrated in Figure 2.6. In turn, these measures are used to create a report or scorecard for the organization that allows management to track, or keep score, of the organization's performance. The four perspectives provide a balanced approach in terms of tangible and intangible benefits and long and short term objectives, as well as how each perspective's desired outcomes and drivers impact the other perspectives.

■ *Financial perspective*—The Balanced Scorecard approach encourages managers to consider measures other than traditional financial measures for strategic success. Most financial measures are useful for understanding how an organization performed in the past, and some have likened this to steering the ship by watching the wake. Traditional financial measures, however, are still important and can be a cornerstone for ensuring that an organization's strategies are being implemented properly. More importantly, the Balanced Scorecard approach provides a means for linking financial performance with customer focused-initiatives, internal operations, and investments in employees and the infrastructure to support their performance. Although traditional financial measures that include operating income—ROI, NPV, IRR, and so forth—are still useful, many organizations are now using new financial measures as well. One financial measure that has been receiving a great deal of attention and scrutiny recently is **Economic Value Added (EVA).** EVA is a measurement tool to determine if an organization is earning

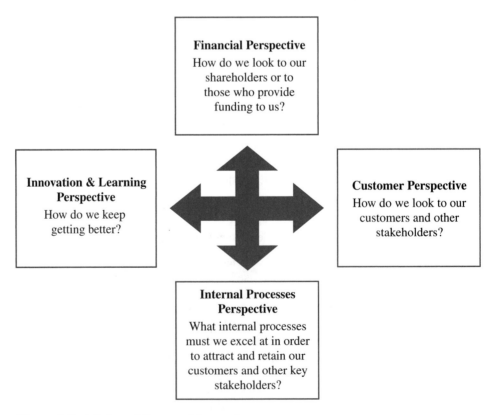

Figure 2.6 A Balanced Scorecard Approach

more than its true cost of capital. Supporters of EVA believe it provides a clearer picture on whether management is creating or destroying shareholder wealth. EVA is calculated by considering the cost of debt (e.g., the interest rate a bank would charge) and the cost of equity (e.g., what shareholders could earn elsewhere). Subsequently, a positive EVA indicates that positive wealth has been created.

- *Customer perspective*—How an organization performs in its customers' eyes largely determines customer satisfaction. In turn, satisfied customers can mean repeat business and referrals for new business. As a result, measures or targets for customer satisfaction can be linked to financial rewards. They create a value chain for establishing customer-focused initiatives that can be linked to financial performance. Customer-based measurements may focus on areas that determine the level of satisfaction with the products and services of the company and how well those product and services are delivered.

- *Internal process perspective*—The internal process perspective focuses on the processes—both long term and short term—that an organization must excel at in order to achieve its customer and financial objectives. Customer satisfaction can be achieved through improved operational activities by the organization, which in turn leads to improved financial performance. Therefore, internal-based measurements should focus on the efficiency and effectiveness of the organization's processes.

- *Innovation and learning perspective*—The abilities, capabilities, and motivations of the people within an organization determine the outcomes of the operational activities, financial performance, and levels of customer satisfaction within the organization. Thus, an organization relies heavily on its people not only to support the other three perspectives, but also to provide continuous improvements in these areas. An organization's ability to innovate and learn at the individual level is critical for supporting the organization as a whole. Therefore, the Balanced Scorecard approach gives considerable support to the importance of investing in the future by investing in people and makes investing in human infrastructure at least as important as investing in technical and physical infrastructures. Measures for the innovation and learning perspective may include training, certifications, and employee satisfaction and retention.

By measuring the value of an IT project across these four areas, the scorecard approach compels an organization's management to consider the impact and context of a project from an organization-wide view. It also limits the potential for overemphasizing traditional financial measurement at the expense of perspectives that include both tangible and intangible benefits. Still, the Balanced Scorecard can fail for a number of reasons (Schneiderman 1999):

- The nonfinancial measurement variables are incorrectly identified as the primary drivers for stakeholder satisfaction.

- Metrics are not properly defined.

- Goals for improvements are negotiated and not based on stakeholder requirements, fundamental process limits, or capabilities.

- No systematic way to map high-level goals with subprocess levels where the actual improvement activities reside.

- Reliance on trial and error as a methodology for improvement.

- There is no quantitative linkage between the nonfinancial and expected financial results.

The Balanced Scorecard approach is an overall performance management system that is useful for selecting all projects in an organization, monitoring their progress, and then evaluating their overall contribution. As illustrated in Figure 2.7, the MOV concept introduced earlier supports the Balanced Scorecard approach.

The MOV can be developed and reviewed in terms of how it supports the four Balanced Scorecard perspectives. However, the MOV concept can also support organizations that use other means of identifying a project's value to the organization.

CHAPTER SUMMARY

A methodology provides a blueprint or template for planning, managing, and controlling a project throughout its life cycle. Although the products of information systems projects are different, many of the processes are the same. In this chapter, a framework for an IT project methodology was introduced. This framework will be used throughout the remainder of this text and provides a basic foundation that will allow organizations to adapt it to their particular needs and from their lessons learned.

In addition, the concept of a project's measurable organizational value or MOV was introduced because it is an important tool for defining a project's goal and value to the organization. The MOV becomes the project's measure of success and must be measurable, agreed upon, and verifiable at the end of the project. A project's MOV must align with the organization's goals and strategies in order to provide value to the organization.

A business case defines the problem or opportunity, MOV, feasibility, costs, and benefits of several alternatives that an organization may choose in order to achieve its goals and strategies. Based on the analysis of the alternatives identified, a recommendation is made to approve and fund a specific project.

The business case is formalized in a report to senior management who may review several proposed projects. The decision to fund a particular project and add it to the organization's project portfolio depends largely on the resources available and the value of the project to the organization. One increasingly popular method for defining value to an organization is the Balanced Scorecard approach. This approach focuses on four perspectives—financial, customer, internal processes, and innovation and learning. Regardless of the selection approach, an organization should make the project selection decision based on a diverse set of measures and in terms of how well the project supports the goals and strategies of the organization.

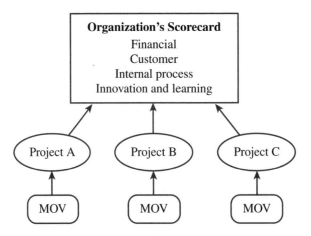

Figure 2.7 MOV and the Organization's Scorecard

REVIEW QUESTIONS

1. What are the advantages of having and following a project methodology?

2. Describe the five phases of the IT project methodology.

3. Why is it important to have deliverables for each phase of the IT project methodology?

4. How can the experiences of and lessons learned by past project team members be incorporated into a project methodology?

5. Describe the conceptualize and initialize phase of the IT project methodology

6. What is a project charter?

7. What are the advantages of developing a detailed project plan after a project has been approved for funding?

8. Describe the execute and control phase of the IT project methodology.

9. Describe the close project phase of the IT project methodology.

10. Describe the evaluate project success phase of the IT project methodology.

11. Describe the five project management processes

12. Why can a project that is developed under budget and before its deadline still not be considered successful?

13. What kinds of tools would be needed to support an IT project?

14. How does an organizational infrastructure support a project?

15. What is a project infrastructure?

16. Describe a technical infrastructure that would be needed to support a consulting team working at a client site.

17. Discuss how the project management knowledge areas support the IT project methodology.

18. What is a business case?

19. Why should an organization develop a business case?

20. What is the purpose of selecting a core team to develop a business case?

21. What is a project's measurable organizational value (MOV)?

22. Develop a MOV for an organization that is contemplating developing a corporate intranet.

23. Why must a project's MOV be agreed upon?

24. Describe how a project's MOV can support an organization's goals and strategies.

25. Describe how an IT project can bring value to an organization.

26. What is a base case alternative? Why should a business case even consider a base case alternative?

27. Describe Economic Feasibility.

28. Describe Technical Feasibility.

29. Describe Organizational Feasibility.

30. What other types of feasibility issues should an organization consider?

31. How should the risk of each business case alternative be analyzed?

32. What is Total Cost of Ownership?

33. What is Total Benefits of Ownership?

34. What is the difference between tangible and intangible benefits? Give an example of each.

35. What are some ways of quantifying intangible benefits?

36. Describe the payback method. What are some advantages and disadvantages of this method?

37. Describe the breakeven method. What are some advantages and disadvantages of this method?

38. Describe the ROI method. What are some advantages and disadvantages of this method?

39. Describe the NPV method. What are some advantages and disadvantages of this method?

40. What effect does increasing the discount rate have on a project's NPV?

41. What are the advantages of using a scoring model when comparing several project alternatives? Any disadvantages?

42. What is an IT project portfolio?

43. Why shouldn't an organization always take on less challenging projects?

44. Describe the criteria that should be used to make a project selection decision?

45. Describe the Balanced Scorecard approach.

46. Describe the financial perspective of the Balanced Scorecard approach.

47. Describe the customer perspective of the Balanced Scorecard approach.

48. Describe the internal process perspective of the Balanced Scorecard approach.

49. Describe the innovation and learning perspective of the Balanced Scorecard approach.

50. How does the concept of MOV support the Balanced Scorecard approach?

EXTEND YOUR KNOWLEDGE

1. Using the Web or the library as a resource, write a one-page position paper on the Balanced Scorecard approach. Why does this approach seem to be gaining popularity?

2. Determine the Total Cost of Ownership (TCO) and Total Benefits of Ownership (TBO) for purchasing, maintaining, and supporting a personal computer of your choice over the next three years. You may want to use a spreadsheet package to conduct your analysis.

3. Analyze the TCO and TBO that you conducted in Question 2 using the payback, ROI, and NPV methods.

4. Create a scoring model to analyze whether to purchase a new car. Your alternatives are: keep your current mode of transportation, purchase a used car, or purchase a new car. Be sure to include both tangible and intangible costs and benefits.

5. Develop a Balanced Scorecard for an organization contemplating an Internet-based application that would allow its customers to look up their order status online.

6. Suppose a bank's goal is to gain competitive advantage by developing tighter relationships with its customers. Its strategy is to create focused differentiation through a customer relationship management (CRM) system. Develop project MOV and discuss how this MOV supports the goal and strategy of this organization.

BIBLIOGRAPHY

Billows, D. 1996. *Project and Program Management: People, Budgets, and Software.* Denver: The Hampton Group, Inc.

Kaplan, R. S. and D. Norton. 1992. The Balanced Scorecard: Measures that Drive Performance. *Harvard Business Review* (January–February): 71–79.

Kaplan, R. S. and D. Norton. 1993. Putting the Balanced Scorecard to Work. *Harvard Business Review* (September–October): 134–147.

Kerzner, H. 2000. *Applied Project Management: Best Practices on Implementation.* New York: John Wiley.

Marchewka, J. T. and M. Keil 1995. A Portfolio Theory Approach for Selecting and Managing IT Projects. *Information Resources Management Journal* 8: 5–14.

McFarlan, F. W. 1981. Portfolio Approach to Information Systems. *Harvard Business Review* (September–October).

Meredith, J. R. and S. J. Mantel, Jr. 2000. *Project Management: A Managerial Approach.* New York: John Wiley.

Porter, M. 1980. *Competitive Strategy.* New York: Free Press.

Porter, M. 1985. *Competitive Advantage.* New York: Free Press.

Schmidt, M. J. 1999. *The IT Business Case: Keys to Accuracy and Credibility.* Solution Matrix, Ltd.: www.solutionmatrix.com.

Schmidt, M. J. 1999. *What's a Business Case? And Other Frequently Asked Questions.* Solution Matrix, Ltd.: www.solutionmatrix.com.

Schneiderman, A. M. 1999. Why Balanced Scorecards Fail. *Journal of Strategic Performance Management* (January): 6–12.

Smith, D. K. 1999. *Make Success Measurable.* New York: John Wiley.

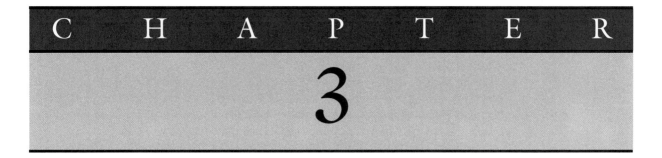

Developing the Project Charter and Baseline Project Plan

CHAPTER OVERVIEW

Chapter 3 focuses on developing the project charter and project plan. After studying this chapter, you should understand and be able to:

- Describe the five project management processes and how they support each phase of the project life cycle.
- Define the project management knowledge area called project integration management and describe its role in project plan development, project plan execution, and overall change control.
- Develop a project charter and describe its relationship to the project plan.
- Identify the steps in the project planning framework introduced in this chapter and describe how this framework links the project's measurable organizational value (MOV) to the project's scope, schedule, and budget.

GLOBAL TECHNOLOGY SOLUTIONS

The quiet drive back to the office was a welcome respite for Tim Williams, even though he was catching the tail end of rush hour traffic. Traffic was moving well below the speed limit, so the time alone gave him a chance to reflect on the activities of the last few weeks. The business case for Husky Air was complete, and Tim had presented it to the company's senior management not more than thirty minutes ago.

Just as Tim was about to turn on the car's radio, his cell phone rang and he was immediately brought back to reality. Tim answered, and heard his business partner Kellie Matthews ask, "So, how did it go?"

"Not bad!" Tim replied. "In fact, senior management approved our recommendation and is willing make funds available for us to go on to the next step."

Kellie laughed and teased, "I guess that means we can pay the office rent next month. So what's our next step?"

The traffic had now come to a complete stop, so Tim didn't feel that talking on his cell phone was a distraction. "Now that we've completed the business case and Husky Air gave us the approval and funds, I would say that the first phase of our project methodology is complete," he said. "The next thing we need to do is develop a project charter and baseline plan that will outline what we're going to do, how we're going to do it, when we're going to do it, and how much it will cost."

"Wow," exclaimed Kelly, "I thought that was all outlined in the business case."

"The business case was a strategic plan, the project charter and baseline project plan are going to be our tactical plan," Tim explained. "This will also be a reality check to make sure that we can deliver the application to our client within the guidelines that were specified in the business case."

"Will this require another approval by Husky Air's management?" asked Kelly.

"Actually, there will be several more," answered Tim. "In fact, the CEO was pleased that our methodology has approval or review points throughout the project life cycle. He said that Husky Air hired a consulting firm a few years ago to develop an inventory system. The consultants never kept senior management informed after the project was approved. So the CEO was surprised to find out that the project was only half complete when the agreed upon project deadline arrived. Husky Air's management had only two choices: Cancel the project and take the loss, or bite the bullet and continue funding a project that would cost twice as much as originally planned. Needless to say, they never intend on hiring that consulting firm again."

"Well if the client is happy then we should be happy as well," Kelly said.

The traffic started moving again, and Tim said "I'll see you in the office tomorrow morning. We have a lot of work ahead of us."

Kellie agreed, and they both said good-bye before hanging up. Tim relaxed as the traffic started to move again. Even though there was still much work to be done before the actual work on the system would begin, he felt good that they had cleared the first hurdle. "What the heck," he thought. He turned off at the next exit and headed for his favorite Italian restaurant. "It's important to celebrate the small but important successes along the way," he told himself. "Pizza is perfect."

Things to Think About

1. Why is it important to have several status review and decision points throughout the project's life cycle?

2. Aside from *reality checks* what other purposes do status reviews and decision points throughout the project's life cycle provide?

3. How does a business case differ from the project charter/project plan?

4. Why is it important to celebrate the small but important successes?

INTRODUCTION

Up to this point, we have looked at IT project management from a very high or strategic level. The first phase of the IT project management methodology focuses on conceptualizing and initializing the project. The primary deliverable or work effort of this phase is the development of a business case. The business case defines the project's goal and value to the organization and includes an analysis and feasibility of several alternatives. Moreover, the business case plays an important role in the project selection process by providing sufficient, reliable information to senior management so that a decision whether the organization should support and fund the project can be made.

The basic question when conceptualizing and initializing the project is, What is the value of this project to the organization? Making the right decision is critical. Abandoning a project that will provide little real value to an organization at this early stage will save a great deal of time, money, and frustration. On the other hand, failure to fund a project that has a great deal of potential value is an opportunity lost.

The development of the business case and its subsequent approval represents an important milestone in the project's life cycle. Approval also represents closure for the first phase of the IT project methodology and the beginning of the next. This second phase, developing the project charter and plan, requires the review and approval of another project deliverable before even more time, resources, and energy are committed. At this point the question becomes, How should we do it? This requires a subtle yet important transition from a strategic mindset to a more tactical one.

Unfortunately, the knowledge, tools, and techniques required to develop a tactical project plan cannot be presented in a single chapter. Therefore, the next several chapters will focus on the human side of project management, defining and managing the project's scope, and on learning how to use or apply a number of estimation methods and project management tools.

Before we get to the details, this chapter provides an overview of the project planning process. This overview will include a more detailed discussion of the five project processes that were briefly introduced in Chapter 2 as part of the IT project methodology. More specifically, it explains how these processes are integrated with the various project management knowledge areas in order to support the development of the project's tactical plan. In fact, it will concentrate on one of the nine knowledge areas called project integration management. This particular area supports and coordinates: (1) project plan development, (2) project plan execution, and (3) overall change control.

The project charter and detailed project plan make up the project's tactical plan. The project charter defines the project infrastructure and identifies the project manager, the project team, the stakeholders, and the roles each will play within the project. In addition, the project charter formalizes the project's MOV, scope, supporting processes and controls, required resources, risks, and assumptions. This project infrastructure provides the foundation for developing a detailed project plan that answers four major questions: How much will the project cost? When will the project be finished? Who will be responsible for doing the work? And, what will we ultimately get at the end of the project?

In addition, a project planning framework will be introduced in this chapter that links the project's MOV to the project's scope, schedule, and budget. This framework outlines the steps necessary to create a detailed project plan so that management can determine whether the project's budget aligns with the cost analysis conducted in the business case. If the budget exceeds the overall cost envisioned in the business case, iterations to change the plan may be necessary to bring the project's scope, schedule, and budget in line. Cost cutting measures may require using less expensive resources or trade-offs in terms of reducing the scope and schedule. If the total cost of the project exceeds the expected organizational value, then the decision to cancel the project may be appropriate before more time, money, energy, and resources are committed to the next phase. However, once the project plan is approved, it then becomes the project's baseline plan that will be executed and used to benchmark actual progress.

PROJECT MANAGEMENT PROCESSES

Processes are an integral component of project management. They support all of the activities necessary to create and implement the product of the project. As described in Chapter 2, project management processes are concerned with defining and coordinating

D'OH!

The Center for Project Management in San Ramon, California examined twenty-four IT projects and compiled a list of ten dumb mistakes. The center then presented this list to fifty conference attendees and asked them to grade their organizations on each mistake. The average grade was between a C+ and D.

1. Mistaking every half-baked idea for a viable project.
2. Overlooking stakeholders, forgetting the champions, and ignoring the nemesis.
3. Not assessing the project's complexity.
4. Not developing a comprehensive project charter.
5. Not developing a comprehensive project plan.
6. Not designing a functional project organization.
7. Accepting or developing unrealistic or unachievable estimates.
8. Accepting status reports that contain mostly noise and not enough signal.
9. Looking back and not ahead.
10. Not following a robust project process architecture.

SOURCE: Adapted from "F.Y.I.", *Computerworld,* February 26, 1996, http://www.computerworld.com/news/1996/story/0,11280,14953,00.

the activities and controls needed to manage the project. On the other hand, **product-oriented processes** focus on the tangible results of the project, such as the application system itself. The product-oriented processes require specific domain knowledge, tools, and techniques in order to complete the work. For example, you would need completely different subject matter experts (SME), tools, and methods to build a house than you would to build a spacecraft to land on Mars. As Figure 3.1 suggests, there must be a balance between project management processes and product-oriented processes. An emphasis or sole focus on the project management processes does not provide the expertise or ability to define the project's scope or develop a quality system. However, a more product-oriented focus does not provide the management or controls to ensure that the work is completed as required. Therefore, a balance is needed to complete an IT project successfully.

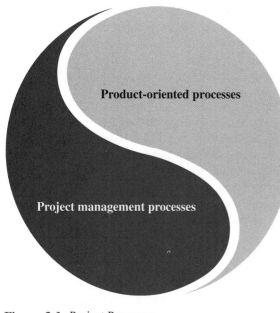

Figure 3.1 Project Processes

Project Management Process Groups

The five process groups were introduced briefly in Chapter 2. As illustrated in Figure 3.2, these process groups overlap within and between the different phases of the project life cycle since the outcome of one process group within a phase becomes the input or catalyst for a process group of the next phase.

Initiating The initiating process signals the beginning of the project or phase. It requires an organization to make a commitment in terms of time and resources. For example, the first phase of the IT project methodology recommends the development of a business case to identify several viable alternatives that can support a particular organization's strategy and goals. In short, the time and effort needed to develop the business case does not come without a cost. One can measure this cost directly in terms of the labor cost and time spent, and indirectly by the time and effort that could have been devoted to some other endeavor.

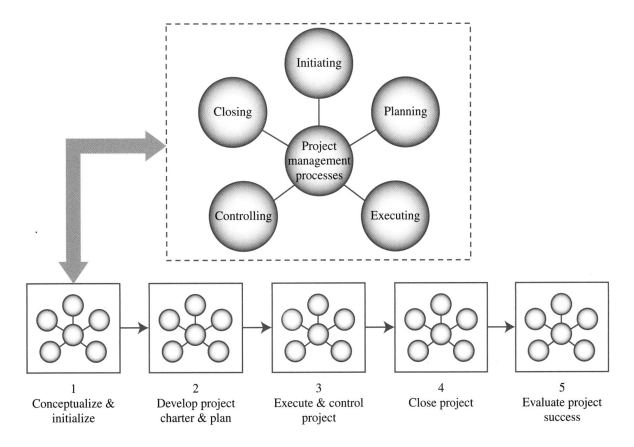

Figure 3.2 Project Management Processes and ITPM Phases

Therefore, some type of organizational commitment is needed even during the earliest stages of a project.

Similarly, a business case recommendation, once approved, becomes a project. This decision requires an even greater commitment in terms of time and resources; however, the next phase, when the actual work on the project commences, requires a commitment of even more time and resources. Although all phases of the project should have some type of initiating process, the first phase of the IT project methodology, conceptualize and initialize, requires the most detail and attention.

Planning Since projects are undertaken to create something of value that generally has not been done before, the planning process is of critical importance. The planning process should be in line with the size and complexity of the project—that is, larger, complex projects may require a greater planning effort than smaller, less complex projects. Although planning is important for each phase of the project, the second phase of the IT project methodology, developing the project charter and project plan, requires the most planning activities. In addition, planning is usually an iterative process. A project manager may develop a project plan, but senior management or the client may not approve the scope, budget, or schedule. In addition, planning is still more of an art than a science. Experience and good judgment are just as important as, and perhaps even more important to quality planning than, using the latest project management software tool. It is important that the project manager and project team develop a realistic and useful project plan. Supporting processes include scope planning, activity planning, resource planning, cost estimating, schedule estimating, organizational planning, and procurement planning.

Executing Once the project plan has been developed and approved, it is time to execute the activities of the project plan or phase. The product-oriented processes play an important role when completing the project plan activities. For example, the tools and methods for developing and/or implementing a system become critical for achieving the project's end result. Supporting processes include quality assurance, risk management, team development, and an implementation plan. Although executing processes are part of every project phase, the majority of the executing processes will occur during the execute and control phase of the IT project methodology.

Controlling The controlling process group allows for managing and measuring the progress towards the project's MOV and the scope, schedule, budget, and quality objectives. Controls not only tell the project team when deviations from the plan occur, but also measure progress towards the project's goal. Supporting processes include scope control, change control, schedule control, budget control, quality control, and a communications plan. The emphasis on controlling processes will occur during the execution and control phase of the IT project methodology.

Closing The closing process group focuses on bringing a project or project phase to a systematic and orderly completion. The project team must verify that all deliverables have been satisfactorily completed before the project sponsor accepts the project's product. In addition, the final product—the information system—must be integrated successfully into the day-to-day operations of the organization. Closure of a project should include **contract closure** and **administrative closure.** Contract closure ensures that all of the deliverables and agreed upon terms of the project have been completed and delivered so that the project can end. It allows resources to be reassigned and settlement or payment of any account, if applicable. Administrative closure, on the other hand, involves documenting and archiving all project documents. It also includes evaluating the project in terms of whether it achieved its MOV. Lessons learned should be documented and stored in a way that allows them to be made available to other project teams, present and future. Although each phase must include closing processes, the major emphasis on closing processes will occur during the close project phase of the IT project methodology.

PROJECT INTEGRATION MANAGEMENT

The Project Management Body of Knowledge (PMBOK) views project integration management as one of the most important knowledge areas because it coordinates the other eight knowledge areas and all of the project management processes throughout the project's life cycle. It is up to the project manager to ensure that all of the activities and processes are coordinated in order for the project to meet or exceed its MOV. All of these knowledge areas and processes must come together to support the development of the project plan, its execution, and overall change control. As Figure 3.3 illustrates, project integration management includes: (1) project plan development, (2) project plan execution, and (3) overall change control. This section describes how these processes and various knowledge areas interact with each other.

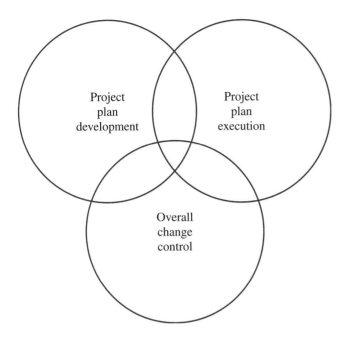

Figure 3.3 Project Integration Management

Project Plan Development

The purpose of project plan development is to create a useable, flexible, consistent, and logical document that will guide the work or activities of the project. In addition, the project plan provides a control mechanism for coordinating changes across the entire project.

As you will soon find out for yourself, project planning is an iterative process. A first cut or draft of the project plan is developed based on the business case and any other information as it becomes available. Historical information from past projects can be a useful resource for understanding how these project plans fared in terms of the accuracy and completeness of their estimates. They can also serve as a source for drawing upon new ideas and lessons learned.

In addition, the policies and procedures of the organization must be taken into account when developing the project plan. For example, formal accounting procedures may have to be followed for the disbursement of funds for such things as travel, training, or payments to vendors. On the other hand, an organization may have either formal or informal policies for such things as hiring and firing employees or conducting performance and merit reviews. Internal project teams may be familiar with these organizational policies, while outside consultants may have to learn them as they go along. Regardless of whether the project team is internal or external to the organization, it is important that the project manager and team learn, understand, and follow these policies, because they can impact the project plan estimates.

Various constraints and assumptions must also be taken into consideration and documented when developing the project plan. **Constraints** are things that can limit the project and usually can have an impact on scope, schedule, budget, or quality. For example, the project may have to be completed by a specific date or within a predefined budget. On the other hand, **assumptions** can be thought of as things that must go right in order for the project plan to be completed as planned. Assumptions can be, for example, a skilled and experienced programmer being available by a specific date or a vendor delivering hardware and/or software in time for a development activity to begin. Constraints and assumptions are closely related to risk. The development of a risk management plan should be part of the project plan.

A method for project planning is a critical element for developing a project plan, all projects should follow a structured process. Various software tools, such as Microsoft Project, can be useful for developing the project plan.

A software tool, however, cannot create the perfect project plan by itself. The project manager should engage various stakeholders throughout the planning process. These stakeholders can be managers or subject matter experts (SME) who can contribute valuable knowledge or expertise to refine the project plan. In short, the project plan should also consider who will be needed, when they will be needed, and how they will be needed to help create the product of the project.

Project Plan Execution

The purpose of the project planning process is to create a document that can be carried out in order to achieve the project's MOV. It is important to have a realistic and usable project plan because the project will expend the majority of its assigned resources executing it. It is, therefore, necessary that the plan be used not only to coordinate the resources that will perform certain scheduled activities, but also to gauge the project's progress towards its goal.

Today, most organizations use some type of project management software tool such as Microsoft Project to manage and control the project. Project management software tools not only help to create and track a project's progress, but also act as an information system for reporting project performance and making decisions.

The project's product will directly determine the skills and knowledge areas needed by the project team members. The project manager must ensure that specific team members either have specific skills or knowledge coming into the project or that they will acquire them in due time through training.

The execution of the project plan must also have some type of **work authorization system** in place. A work authorization system is just a way of sanctioning or authorizing project team members to perform a specific activity or group of related activities to ensure that the right things are done in the proper sequence.

Depending on the size and complexity of the project, the work authorization system can be either formal or informal. For smaller projects, a work authorization system may be nothing more than the project manager giving a project team member verbal approval to begin working on a specific activity outlined in the project plan. On the other hand, activities on larger, more complex projects may require a more formal approval because each team member may be working on a piece of the application system. In turn, their activities may depend upon the activities of someone else or some other group. The project manager must have the larger picture in mind, and specific activities must be verified as being complete before other activities can begin. For example, one set of activities for an IT application system may be the gathering and documenting of requirements during the systems analysis phase. Several individuals or groups may work on this activity together. Design and programming activities should not begin until the information requirements are complete and verified; otherwise, time and resources will be wasted if changes must be made later. Experience has shown that the cost of making changes or correcting errors in the later stages of a project is more expensive.

Status review meetings are a useful tool for coordinating the project processes and activities. Status review meetings are regularly scheduled meetings that the project manager and project team members have with key stakeholders. The purpose of these meetings is to keep everyone informed as to the status of the project. Project status meetings can be formal or informal and can include different levels of stakeholders. Regularly scheduled status meetings not only keep everyone informed, but help focus the project team's attention on meeting key deadlines for deliverables. Meetings with project stakeholders tend to go more smoothly when the project is progressing as planned.

Overall Change Control

Status review meetings provide a catalyst or at least an opportunity for change. For instance, a project stakeholder may introduce an idea that would change or expand the scope of the project. Regardless whether this change increases or decreases the project's value to the organization, the project must have controls in place to manage change. Overall change controls must: (1) ensure that a process is in place to evaluate the value of a proposed change, (2) determine whether an accepted change has been implemented, (3) include procedures for handling emergencies—that is, automatic approval for defined situations, and (4) help the project manager manage change so that change does not disrupt the focus or work of the project team.

Many organizations have a Change Control Board (CCB) made up of various managers responsible for evaluating and approving change requests. If an organization does not have an overall change control process in place, the project manager should develop one as part of the project charter.

THE PROJECT CHARTER

The **project charter** and baseline project plan provide a tactical plan for carrying out or executing the IT project. More specifically, the project charter serves as an agreement or contract between the project sponsor and project team—documenting the project's MOV, defining its infrastructure, summarizing the project plan details, defining roles and responsibilities, showing project commitments, and explaining project control mechanisms.

- *Documenting the Project's MOV*—Although the project's MOV was included in the business case, it is important that the MOV be clearly defined and agreed upon before developing or executing the project plan. At this point, the MOV must be cast in stone. Once agreed upon, the MOV for a project should not change. As you will see, the MOV drives the project planning process and is fundamental for all project-related decisions.

- *Defining the Project Infrastructure*—The project charter defines all of the people, resources, technology, methods, project management processes, and knowledge areas that are required to support the project. In short, the project charter will detail everything needed to carry out the project. Moreover, this infrastructure must not only be in place, but must also be taken into account when developing the project plan. For example, knowing who will be on the project team and what resources will be available to them can help the project manager estimate the amount of time a particular task or set of activities will require. It makes sense that a highly skilled and experienced team member with adequate resources should require less time to complete a certain task than an inexperienced person with inadequate resources. Keep in mind, however, that you can introduce risk to your project plan if you develop your estimates based upon the abilities of your best people. If one of these individuals should leave sometime during the project, you may have to replace them with someone less skilled or experienced. As a result, you will either have to revise your estimates or face the possibility of the project exceeding its deadline.

- *Summarizing the Details of the Project Plan*—The project charter should summarize the scope, schedule, budget, quality objectives, deliverables, and milestones of the project. It should serve as an important communication tool that provides a consolidated source of information about the project that can be referenced throughout the project life cycle.

- *Defining Roles and Responsibilities*—The project charter should not only identify the project sponsor, project manager, and project team, but also when and how they will be involved throughout the project life cycle. In addition, the project charter should specify the lines of reporting and who will be responsible for specific decisions.

ARE IT PROJECTS DIFFERENT?

Many organizations view project management as an investment to improve the likelihood of success of IT projects. However, Gopal K. Kapur believes that the principles and practices of project management have been developed by the engineering profession. Based upon his experience, first as a civil engineer and then as an IT project manager, Kapur strongly believes that IT projects are more difficult to manage than engineering projects. For IT project management to work, the IT profession must adapt and expand the engineering Project Management Body of Knowledge. Kapur lists seven key differences:

1. The engineer uses artists' renderings, architectural models, and drawings that describe clearly the final product or end state *before* construction begins. However, the final product or end state of an IT project is not always clearly defined or known until the later stages of the project.

2. The phases of a construction project are more linear, and the boundaries for each phase are well defined. On the other hand, the phases of an IT project are more complex because they tend to overlap or spiral.

3. The construction process for engineering projects is based on fabricating the end product from pretested and predesigned components, while the code for most IT projects must be developed or written from scratch.

4. The deliverables for most engineering projects are defined precisely in terms of specifications. Deliverables for IT projects, however, are seldom defined as precisely and may be open to interpretation by various stakeholders.

5. Engineering projects often have extensive databases that contain accurate cost information that are available to estimators. IT estimation generally is based on best guess estimates because there are few sources that can provide historical information.

6. In engineering projects, the roles and responsibilities of team members are generally well defined (e.g., carpenters, plumbers, electricians, painters, and so forth), while a single person on an IT project may have to take on several roles or responsibilities.

7. Engineering drawings and specifications make use of standardized symbols, terms, and text. Little confusion arises from blueprints that depict electrical wiring or a map of the landscape. IT vendors, on the other hand, tend to try to create new terms, symbols, or text in order to distinguish themselves from their competition.

SOURCE: Adapted from Gopal K. Kapur, Why IT Project Management is So Hard to Grasp, *Computerworld,* May 3, 1999, http://www.computerworld.com/managementtopics/management/project/story/0,1080 1,35529,00.html.

- *Showing Explicit Commitment to the Project*—In addition to defining the roles and responsibilities of the various stakeholders, the project charter should detail the resources to be provided by the project sponsor and specify clearly who will take ownership of the project's product once the project is completed. Approval of the project charter gives the project team the formal authority to begin work on the project.

- *Setting Out Project Control Mechanisms*—Changes to the project's scope, schedule, and budget will undoubtedly be required over the course of the project. But, the project manager can lose control and the project team can lose its focus if these changes are not managed properly. Therefore, the project charter should outline a process for requesting and responding to proposed changes.

In general, the project charter and project plan should be developed together—the details of the project plan need to be summarized in the project charter, and the infrastructure outlined in the project charter will influence the estimates used in developing the project plan. It is the responsibility of the project manager to ensure that the project charter and plan are developed, agreed upon, and approved. Like the business case, the project charter and plan should be developed with both the project team and the project sponsor to ensure that the project will support the organization and that the goal and objective of the project are realistic and achievable.

What Should Be in a Project Charter?

The framework for a project charter should be based on the nine project management knowledge areas and processes. Although the formality and depth of developing a project charter will most likely depend on the size and complexity of the project, the fundamental project management processes and areas should be addressed and included for all projects. This section presents an overview of the typical areas that may go into a project charter; however, organizations and project managers should adapt the project charter based on best practices, experience, and the project itself.

Project Identification   It is common for all projects to have a unique name or a way to identify them. It is especially necessary if an organization has several projects underway at once. Naming a project can also give the project team and stakeholders a sense of identity and ownership. Often organizations will use some type of acronym for the project's name. For example, instead of naming a project something as mundane as the Flight Reservation System in 1965, American Airlines named its system SABRE. Today, SABRE has become a well-recognized product that connects travel agents and online customers with all of the major airlines, car rental companies, hotels, railways, and cruise lines.

Project Stakeholders   It is important that the project charter specifically name the project sponsor and the project manager. This reduces the likelihood of confusion when determining who will take ownership of the project's product and who will be the leader of the project. In addition, the project team should be named along with their titles or roles in the project, their phone numbers, and e-mail addresses. This section should describe who will be involved in the project, how they will be involved, and when they will be involved. Formal reporting relationships can be specified and may be useful on larger projects. In addition, including telephone numbers and e-mail addresses can provide a handy directory for getting in touch with the various participants.

Project Description   The project charter should be a single source of information. Therefore, it may be useful to include a description of the project to help someone unfamiliar with the project understand not only the details, but the larger picture as well. This may include a brief overview or background of the project as to the problem or opportunity that became a catalyst for the project and the reason or purpose for taking on the project. It may also be useful to include the vision of the organization or project and how it aligns with the organization's goal and strategy. Much of this section could summarize the total benefits expected from the project that were described in the business case. It is important that the project description focus on the business and not the technology.

Measurable Organizational Value (MOV)   The MOV should be clear, concise, agreed upon, and made explicit to all of the project stakeholders. Therefore, the project's MOV should be highlighted and easily identifiable in the project charter.

Project Scope   The project's scope is the work to be completed. A specific section of the project charter should clarify not only what will be produced or delivered by the project team, but also what will *not* be part of the project's scope. This distinction is important for two reasons. First, it provides the foundation for developing the project plan's schedule and cost estimates. Changes to the project's scope will impact the project's schedule and budget—that is, if resources are fixed, expanding the amount work you have to complete will take more time and money. Therefore, the creation of additional work for the project team will extend the project's schedule and invariably increase the cost of the project. Formal procedures must be in place to control and manage the project's scope. Secondly, it is important for the project manager to manage the expectations of the project sponsor and the project team. By making the project's scope explicit as to what is and what is not to be delivered, the likelihood of confusion and misunderstanding is reduced.

For example, the project team and several users may have several discussions regarding the scope of a project. One user may suggest that the system should allow for the download of reports to a wireless personal digital assistant (PDA). After discussing this idea in depth, management may decide that the cost and time to add this wireless PDA capability would not be in the organization's best interest. In this case, it would be a good idea to explicitly state in the project charter that wireless PDA capability will not be part of the project's scope. Although *you* may be clear on this issue, others may still have different expectations. The project's scope should, therefore, define key deliverables and/or high-level descriptions of the information system's functionality. The details of the system's features and functionality will, however, be determined later in the systems development life cycle when the project team conducts an information requirements analysis.

Project Schedule Although the details of the project's schedule will be in the project plan, it is important to summarize the detail of the plan with respect to the expected start and completion dates. In addition, expected dates for major deliverables, milestones, and phases should be highlighted and summarized at a very high level.

Project Budget A section of the project charter should highlight the total cost of the project. The total cost of the project should be summarized directly from the project plan.

Quality Issues Although a quality management plan should be in place to support the project, a section that identifies any known or required quality standards should be made explicit in the project charter. For example, an application system's reports may have to meet a government agency's requirements.

Resources Because the project charter acts as an agreement or contract, it may be useful to specify the resources required and who is responsible for providing those resources. Resources may include people, technology, or facilities to support the project team. It would be somewhat awkward for a team of consultants to arrive at the client's organization and find that the only space available for them to work is a corner table in the company cafeteria! Therefore, explicitly outlining the resources needed and who is responsible for what can reduce the likelihood for confusion or misunderstanding.

Assumptions and Risks Any risks or assumptions should be documented in the project charter. Assumptions may include things that must go right, such as a particular team member being available for the project, or specific criteria used in developing the project plan estimates. Risks, on the other hand, may be thought of as anything that can go wrong or things that may impact the success of the project. Although a risk management plan should be in place to support the project team, the project charter should summarize the following potential impacts:

- *Key situations or events that could significantly impact the project's scope, schedule, or budget.* These risks, their likelihood, and the strategy to overcome or minimize their impact should be detailed in the project's risk plan.

- *Any known constraints that may be imposed by the organization or project environment should be documented.* Known constraints may include such things as imposed deadlines, budgets, or required technology tools or platforms.

■ *Dependencies on other projects internal or external to the organization.* In most cases, an IT project is one of several being undertaken by an organization. Subsequently, dependencies between projects may exist, especially if different application systems or technology platforms must be integrated. It may also be important to describe the project's role in relation to other projects.

■ *Impacts on different areas of the organization.* As described in Chapter 1, IT projects operate in a broader environment than the project itself. As a result, the development and implementation of an IT solution will have an impact on the organization. It is important to describe how the project will impact the organization in terms of disruption, downtime, or loss of productivity.

■ *Any outstanding issues.* It is important to highlight any outstanding issues that need further resolution. These may be issues identified by the project sponsor, the project manager, or the project team that must be addressed and agreed upon at some point during the project. They may include such things as resources to be provided or decisions regarding the features or functionality of the system.

Project Administration   Project administration focuses on the controls that will support the project. It may include:

■ A *communications plan* that outlines how the project's status or progress will be reported to various stakeholders. This plan also includes a process for reporting and resolving significant issues or problems as they arise.

■ A *scope management plan* that describes how changes to the project's scope will be submitted, logged, and reviewed.

■ A *quality management plan* that details how quality planning, assurance, and control will be supported throughout the project life cycle. In addition, a plan for testing the information system will be included.

■ A *change management* and *implementation plan* that will specify how the project's product will be integrated into the organizational environment.

■ A *human resources plan* for staff acquisition and team development.

Acceptance and Approval   Since the project charter serves as an agreement or contract between the project sponsor and project team, it may be necessary to have key stakeholders sign off on the project charter. By signing the document, the project stakeholder shows his/her formal acceptance of the project and, therefore, gives the project manager and team the authority to carry out the project plan.

References   In developing the project charter and plan, the project manager may use a number of references. It is important to document these references in order to add credibility to the project charter and plan, as well as to provide a basis for supporting certain processes, practices, or estimates.

Terminology   Many IT projects use certain terms or acronyms that may be unfamiliar to many people. Therefore, to reduce complexity and confusion, it may be useful to include a glossary giving the meaning of terms and acronyms, allowing all the project's stakeholders to use a common language. Figure 3.4 provides a template for a project charter. Feel free to adapt this template as needed.

PROJECT PLANNING FRAMEWORK

In this section, a project planning framework will be introduced. This framework is part of the IT project methodology and provides the steps and processes necessary to develop the detailed project plan that will support the project's MOV.

A project plan attempts to answer the following questions:

- *What* needs to be done?
- *Who* will do the work?
- *When* will they do the work?
- *How long* will it take?
- *How much* will it cost?

The project planning framework illustrated in Figure 3.5 consists of several steps and processes. We will now focus on each of these steps to show how the project's schedule and budget are derived.

Project Name or Identification

Project Stakeholders
- Names
- Titles or roles
- Phone numbers
- E-mail addresses

Project Description
- Background
- Description of the challenge or opportunity
- Overview of the desired impact

Measurable Organizational Value (MOV)
- Statement or table format

Project Scope
- What will be included in the scope of this project
- What will be considered outside the scope of this project

Project Schedule Summary
- Project start date
- Project end date
- Timeline of project phases and milestones
- Project reviews and review dates

Project Budget Summary
- Total project budget
- Budget broken down by phase

Quality Issues
- Specific quality requirements

Resources Required
- People

- Technology
- Facilities
- Other
- Resources to be provided
  - Resource
  - Name of resource provider
  - Date to be provided

Assumptions and Risks
- Assumptions used to develop estimates
- Key risks, probability of occurrence, and impact
- Constraints
- Dependencies on other projects or areas within or outside the organization
- Assessment project's impact on the organization
- Outstanding issues

Project Administration
- Communications plan
- Scope management plan
- Quality management plan
- Change management plan
- Human resources plan
- Implementation and project closure plan

Acceptance and Approval
- Names, signatures, and dates for approval

References

Terminology or Glossary

Appendices (as required)

Figure 3.4 Project Charter Template

The MOV

The first step of the project planning framework entails finalizing the definition of and agreement on the project's measurable organizational value or MOV. Although an in-depth discussion of a project's MOV was provided in Chapter 2, it is important here to focus on a few salient points. First, it is important that the project's MOV be defined and agreed upon before proceeding to the other steps of the project planning framework. The project's MOV provides a direct link to the organization's strategic mission; however, as Figure 3.5 illustrates, a project's MOV links directly to the project plan. Therefore, a project's MOV acts as a bridge between the strategic mission and objectives of the organization and the project plans of individual projects it undertakes. The MOV guides many of the decisions related to scope, schedule, budget, and resources throughout the project's life cycle.

Define the Project's Scope

Once the project's MOV has been defined and agreed upon by the project's stakeholders, the next step of the project planning framework is to define the project's scope.

The Project Management Body of Knowledge defines scope as the product or services to be provided by the project and includes all of the project deliverables. One can think of scope as the work that needs to be completed in order to achieve the project's MOV. Project scope management is one of the nine project management knowledge areas and entails the following processes:

- *Initiation*—Once the project's MOV has been defined and agreed upon, the organization must make a commitment, in terms of time and resources, to define the project's scope in order to create the project plan.

- *Planning*—The project team must develop a written statement that defines the work to be included, as well as the work not to be included in the project plan. The scope statement will be used to guide future project-related decisions and to set stakeholder expectations.

- *Definition*—The project's scope must be organized into smaller and more manageable packages of work. These work packages will require resources and time to complete.

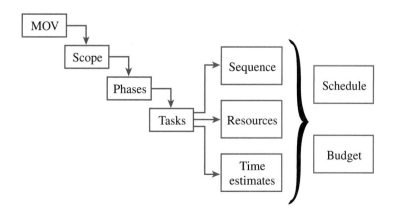

Figure 3.5 The Project Planning Framework—Defining the MOV

- *Verification*—Once the project's scope has been defined, the project team and stakeholders must verify it to ensure that the work completed will in fact support the project in achieving its MOV.

- *Change Control*—Controls must be in place to manage proposed changes to the project's scope. Scope changes can either move the project closer to its MOV or result in increased work that drains the project's budget and causes the project to exceed it scheduled deadline. Proper scope control procedures can ensure that the project stays on track.

Subdivide the Project into Phases

Once the project's scope has been defined and verified, the work of the project can be organized into phases in order to deliver the project's product. **Phases** are logical stages. Although the IT project methodology defines five high-level phases, IT projects should be further divided into subphases that follow the phases of the systems development life cycle (SDLC).

Breaking a project down into phases and subphases reduces complexity and risk. In many cases it is easier to focus on the pieces instead of the whole; however, it is important to never lose sight of the big picture. More specifically, each phase should focus on providing at least one specific deliverable—that is, a tangible and verifiable piece of work. In addition, a **milestone** is a significant event or achievement that provides evidence that that deliverable has been completed and that the phase or subphase is complete.

Tasks—Sequence, Resources, and Time Estimates

Once the project is divided into phases, tasks are then identified. A **task** may be thought of as a specific activity or unit of work to be completed. Examples of some tasks in an IT project may be to interview a particular user, write a program, or test links in a Web page. When considering tasks, it is important to consider sequences, resources, and time.

Sequence Some tasks may be linear—i.e., have to be completed in a particular sequence—while others can be completed in parallel—i.e., at the same time. Performing parallel tasks often provides an opportunity to shorten the overall length of the project. For example, assume that a project has two tasks—A and B. Task A will require only one day to complete; task B requires two days. If these tasks are completed one after the other, the project will finish in three days. On the other hand, if these tasks are performed in parallel, the length of the project will be two days. In this case, the length of the project is determined by the time it takes to complete the longest task (i.e., task B). This simple example illustrates two important points: (1) A project is constrained by the longest tasks, and (2) any opportunity to perform tasks in parallel can shorten the project schedule.

Resources Resources on an IT project may include such things as technology, facilities (e.g., meeting rooms), and people. Tasks require resources, and there is a cost associated with using a resource. The use of a resource may be accounted for by using a per-use charge or on a prorated basis—that is, a charge for the time you use that resource. For example, a developer earns $50,000 a year and is assigned to work on a task that takes one day to complete. The cost of completing that particular task would be prorated as $191 (assuming an eight-hour, five-day work week).

Time   It will take a resource a specific amount of time to complete a task. The longer it takes a resource to complete a specific task, however, the longer the project will take to finish and the more it will cost. For example, if we plan on assigning our developer who earns $50,000 a year to a task that takes two days, then we would estimate the cost of completing that task to be approximately $400. If the developer completes the task in one half the time, then the cost of doing that task will be about $200. Moreover, if the developer were then free to start the next task, our schedule would then be ahead by one day. Unfortunately, the reverse is true. If we thought the task would take two days to complete (at a cost of $400) and it took the developer three days to complete, the project would be one day behind schedule and $200 over budget. However, if two tasks could be performed in parallel, with our developer working on Task A (one day) and another $50,000/year-developer working on Task B (two days), then even if Task A takes two days, our project schedule would not be impacted—as long as the developer working on Task B completes the task within the estimated two days. While this parallel work may save our schedule, our budget will still be $200 over budget because task A took twice as long to complete. Understanding this relationship among tasks, resources, and time will be important when developing the project plan and even more important later if it is necessary to adjust the project plan in order to meet schedule or budget constraints.

Schedule and Budget—The Baseline Plan

The detailed project plan is an output of the project planning framework. Once the tasks are identified and their sequence, resources required, and time-to-complete estimated, it is a relatively simple step to determine the project's schedule and budget. All of this information can be entered into a project management software package that can determine the start and end dates for the project, as well as the final cost.

Once the project plan is complete, it should be reviewed by the project manager, the project sponsor, and the project team to make sure it is complete, accurate, and, most importantly, able to achieve the project's MOV. Generally, the project plan will go through several iterations as new information becomes known or if there are compromises with respect to scope, schedule, and budget. In addition, many of the details of the project plan are summarized in the project charter in order to provide a clearer picture as to how the plan will be carried out. Once the project plan is approved, it becomes the baseline plan that will serve as a benchmark to measure and gauge the project's progress. The project manager will use this baseline plan to compare the actual schedule to the estimated schedule and the actual costs to budgeted costs.

THE KICK-OFF MEETING

Once the project charter and project plan are approved, many organizations have a **kick-off meeting** to officially start work on the project. The kick-off meeting is useful for several reasons. First, it brings closure to the planning phase of the project and signals the initiation of the next phase of the IT project methodology. Second, it is a way of communicating to everyone what the project is all about. Many kick-off meetings take on a festive atmosphere in order to energize the stakeholders and get them enthusiastic about working on the project. It is important that everyone starts working on the project with a positive attitude. How the project is managed from here on will determine largely whether that positive attitude carries through.

CHAPTER SUMMARY

Processes are important to project management because they support all of the activities needed to develop and manage the development of an IT solution. Product-oriented processes focus on the development of the application system itself and require specific domain knowledge, tools, and techniques. On the other hand, project management processes are needed to manage and coordinate all of the activities of the project. A balance of both product-oriented processes and project management processes is needed; otherwise, the result may be a solution that is a technical success but an organizational failure. In addition, five project management process groups were introduced that support both the project and each phase of the project. These include: (1) initiating, (2) planning, (3) executing, (4) controlling, and (5) closing.

Project integration management is one of the most important Project Management Body of Knowledge areas. It coordinates and integrates the other knowledge areas and all of the project processes. Project integration management is concerned with three areas: (1) project plan development so that a useable, flexible, and consistent project plan is developed, (2) project plan execution so that the project plan is carried out in order achieve the project's MOV, and (3) overall change control to help manage change so that change does not disrupt the focus of the project team.

The project charter serves as an agreement and as a communication tool for all of the project stakeholders.

The project charter documents the project's MOV and describes the infrastructure needed to support the project. In addition, the project charter summarizes many of the details found in the project plan. A well-written project charter should provide a consolidated source of information about the project and reduce the likelihood of confusion and misunderstanding. In general, the project charter and project plan should be developed together—the details of the project plan need to be summarized in the project charter, and the infrastructure outlined in the project charter will influence the estimates used to develop the project plan.

The project plan provides the details of the tactical plan that answers these questions: What needs to be done? Who will do the work? When will they do the work? How long will it take? How much will it cost?

A project planning framework was introduced and recommended a series of steps to follow in order to develop a detailed project plan. The details with respect to carrying out these steps will be the focus of subsequent chapters. Once the project charter and plan are approved, the project plan serves as a baseline plan that will allow the project manager to track and access the project's actual progress to the original plan. A kick-off meeting usually brings closure to the second phase of the IT project methodology and allows the project team to begin the work defined in the plan.

REVIEW QUESTIONS

1. What are project management processes? Give one example.
2. What are product-oriented processes? Give one example.
3. Why must a balance exist between project management processes and product-oriented processes?
4. Describe the initiating processes. Give one example of an initiating process to support a particular phase of the IT project methodology.
5. Describe the planning process. Give one example of a planning process to support a particular phase of the IT project methodology.
6. Describe the executing process. Give one example of an executing process to support a particular phase of the IT project methodology.
7. Describe the controlling process. Give one example of a controlling process to support a particular phase of the IT project methodology.
8. Describe the closing process. Give one example of a closing process to support a particular phase of the IT project methodology.
9. Describe how the output of project management process groups in one phase becomes the input or catalyst for the process group in the next phase. Provide an example.
10. What is the difference between contract closure and administrative closure?
11. Describe project integration management and its relationship to the other eight Project Management Body of Knowledge areas.
12. Describe project plan development and its importance to the second phase of the IT project methodology.
13. Describe project plan execution and its importance to project plan development.

14. Describe overall change control and its importance to the project team.
15. What is the purpose of a project charter?
16. Why can a project charter serve as an agreement or a contract?
17. Why is a project charter a useful communication tool?
18. Why should the project charter and project plan be developed together?
19. How does the project charter support the project plan?
20. How does the project plan support the project charter?
21. Describe the project planning framework.
22. Why is it important that the project's MOV be cast in stone.
23. Describe how the project's MOV supports the development of the project's scope, schedule, and budget.

24. What is a project's scope?
25. Why should a project be divided into phases?
26. What is a deliverable? What is the relationship between phases and deliverables?
27. What is a milestone? Why are milestones useful?
28. What is a task? Provide three examples of some typical tasks in an IT project.
29. What impact can the sequence of tasks have on a project's schedule?
30. How can resources impact the schedule of a project?
31. What is a baseline plan? What purpose does it serve once the project team begins to execute the project plan?
32. What is a kick-off meeting? What purpose does it serve?

■ EXTEND YOUR KNOWLEDGE

1. You have just been hired by a local swim team to develop a Web site. This Web site will be used to provide information to boys and girls between the ages of six and eighteen who are interested in joining the team. In addition, the Web site will provide information about practices and the swim meet schedule for the season. The team would also like to be able to post the meet results. The head coach of the swim team is the project sponsor. He would also like the Web site to include pictures of the three assistant coaches and of the different swimmers at swim meets and practice. The swim team is supported largely by an association of parents who help run the swim meets and work the concession stand. Several of the parents have asked that a volunteer schedule be part of the Web site so that the parent volunteers can see when they are scheduled to work at a particular meet. The head coach, however, has told you that he believes this project can wait and should not be part of the Web site now. Two people will be helping you on the project. One is a graphic artist; the other is person who is very familiar with HTML, Java, Active Server Pages (ASP), and several Web development tools. Based upon the information provided, develop the basics of a project charter. Although you will not be able to develop a complete project charter at this point, you can get started on the following:

   a. Come up with a name for the project.
   b. Identify the project stakeholders, their roles, and their titles.
   c. Provide a brief description of the project.
   d. Develop a MOV for this project.
   e. Specify the project's scope in terms of the high-level features or functionality that should be included in the Web site.
   f. Specify what should not be included in the project's scope.
   g. Specify the resources that will be required and provide an estimated cost for each resource. (Be sure to include a reference or sound basis to justify the cost for each resource).
   h. Identify some of the risks associated with this project.
   i. You are free to make assumptions as needed, but be sure to document them!

2. Suppose a company is interested in purchasing a call center software package to improve its customer service. Describe the project management processes that would be needed to support the first two phases of the IT project methodology.

3. Plan a kick-off meeting for a project team.

C H A P T E R

4

The Human Side of Project Management

CHAPTER OVERVIEW

Chapter 4 focuses on the human side of project management. After studying this chapter, you should understand and be able to:

- Describe the three major types of formal organizational structures: functional, pure project, and matrix.
- Discuss the advantages and disadvantages of the functional, pure project, and matrix organizational structures.
- Describe the informal organization.
- Develop a stakeholder analysis.
- Describe the difference between a work group and a team.
- Describe and apply the concept of learning cycles and lessons learned as a basis for knowledge management.

GLOBAL TECHNOLOGY SOLUTIONS

Tim Williams thought he was going to be the first one to arrive at the office, but as he turned into the parking lot, he could see Kellie Matthews' car in its usual spot. Tim parked his car next to Kellie's and strode into the GTS office. This was going to be an exciting and busy day because several new employees were going to report for their first day of work at GTS. He wanted to get to the office early so he could greet them and prepare for their day of orientation.

As Tim walked through the office door, he made a beeline for the small kitchen area where a fresh pot of coffee was waiting. The smell brought a smile to his face as he poured the dark liquid into his favorite coffee mug. Tim turned around as Kellie entered the kitchen area. "Good morning!" Kellie exclaimed. Tim never had been a morning person, and he wondered to himself how anyone could be so cheerful this early. He tried to be as cheerful as possible given that he hadn't had his first cup of coffee. "Good morning to you, too." Tim could see that Kellie was at least one cup of coffee ahead of him, which gave him some consolation. "Care for another cup?" Tim asked as he offered to pour a cup for Kellie. "Sure, thanks," said Kellie as she held the cup out.

As Tim poured the coffee for Kellie, she smiled and said, "After you left yesterday, I received a phone call from Sitaramin. He said that he would accept our offer and join us at GTS next week." That news seemed to wake Tim up. "That's great!" Tim exclaimed.

Both Tim and Kellie have been busy during the last two weeks interviewing and negotiating with a number of candidates to join GTS. With the addition of Sitaramin, the team for the Husky Air project would be complete.

Kellie sipped her coffee and said, "Well, our budget for salaries is going to be slightly higher than we had planned, but I guess that can be expected given the job market for information systems professionals and the fact that we had to pay a premium because we're a start-up company. But if all goes well, I'm pretty sure that the Husky Air project will still be profitable for us. We can develop a detailed project plan and use the latest software metrics for planning the project schedule and budget, but the success of this project rests largely on how well this team performs."

Tim agreed, looked at his watch and said, "We have about an hour before our new employees arrive. I suggest we go over the details of the day's agenda one more time." Tim refilled his coffee mug and Kellie's before they made their way to the conference room where the orientation would be held. As they walked down the hall, Tim thought about what Kellie had said. He knew that it was going to be a challenge to form a cohesive and high-performance team from people who would meet for the first time in less than an hour.

Things to Think About

1. What feelings might a new employee have when starting a new job?
2. What could GTS do to help new employees transition successfully to their new jobs?
3. Why does the success of a project rest largely on the performance of the team?
4. How can a group of individuals become a cohesive and high-performing team?

INTRODUCTION

The key ingredients to IT Project management are people, processes, and technology. Technology is a tool, while processes provide a structure and path for managing and carrying out the project. The success of a project, however, is often determined by the various project stakeholders, as well as who is (or who is not) on the project team.

In this chapter, we will discuss the human side of project management. According to the Project Management Body of Knowledge, the area of project human resource management entails: (1) organizational planning, (2) staff acquisition, and (3) team development.

Organizational planning focuses on the roles, responsibilities, and relationships among the project stakeholders. These individuals or groups can be internal or external to the project. Moreover, organizational planning involves creating a project structure that will support the project processes and stakeholders so that the project is carried out efficiently and effectively.

Staff acquisition includes staffing the project with the best available human resources. Effective staffing involves having policies, procedures, and practices to guide the recruitment of appropriately skilled and experienced staff. Moreover, it may include negotiating for staff from other functional areas within the organization. Team development involves creating an environment to develop and support the individual team members and the team itself.

This chapter will expand upon these three PMBOK concepts and integrate several relatively recent concepts for understanding the human side of IT project management. In the next section, we will focus on project and organizational planning. Three primary organizational structures—the **functional, project, and matrix**—will be described. In addition, the various opportunities and challenges for projects conducted under each structure will be discussed. As a project manager or project team member, it is important to understand an organization's structure since this will determine authorities, roles, responsibilities, communication channels, and availability of resources.

While the formal organizational structure defines official roles, responsibilities, and reporting relationships, informal relationships will exist as well. It is important to understand why these informal structures and relationships exist and how they can influence the relationships among the different project stakeholders. In addition, understanding both the formal and informal organizations will help you to understand not only who makes certain decisions, but also why certain decisions are made.

We will also focus on the various roles of the project manager. In general, one of the greatest responsibilities of the project manager is the selection and recruitment of the project team. Once the project team is in place, the project manager must also ensure that the project team members work together to achieve the project's MOV. Therefore, the language and discipline of *real teams* versus *work groups* will be introduced. These concepts will provide the basis for understanding the dynamics of the project team.

Once the project team is in place, it is important that the project team learn from each other and from past project experiences. Thus, the idea of learning cycles will be introduced as a tool for team learning and for capturing lessons learned that can be documented, stored, and retrieved using a knowledge management system.

In the last section of this chapter, we will focus on the project environment. In addition to staffing the project, the project manager must create an environment to support the project team. If necessary, this includes appropriating a suitable place for the team to work and ensuring that the team has the proper tools and supplies needed to accomplish their work.

ORGANIZATION AND PROJECT PLANNING

The performance of an organization or a project is influenced largely by how well its resources are organized. In general, structures are created within an organization to manage the input, processing, and output of resources. For example, departments or areas based on the specialized skills needed to manage a particular resource are created—i.e., accounting and finance manages the money resources, personnel manages the human resources, and information systems manages the information resource. As a result, many organizations adopt a structure based upon function. Other organizations may adopt a structure based on the products it sells or its customers. These structures may use brand management or geographical divisions.

However, the structure of an organization must fit its strategy, and since organizations may follow different strategies, it makes sense that no single structure can work well for every organization. Therefore, there are different organizational structures and ways to efficiently and effectively manage not only the organizational resources but also the work and processes involved. As long as the firm performs well, a particular structure and strategy will exist. On the other hand, when a firm performs poorly, a change in structure and/or strategy may be required.

Projects are part of an organization and can be thought of as micro organizations that require resources, processes, and structure. Moreover, these resources, processes, and structures are determined largely by the organizational structure of the supporting or parent organization, which may determine or influence the availability of resources, reporting relationships, and project roles and responsibilities. Therefore, it is important to understand how the project interfaces with the host or parent organization and how the project itself will be organized. In this section, we will focus on three formal structures that tie projects explicitly to the organization. Each structure provides distinct opportunities and challenges, and choosing and implementing the correct structure can have a major impact on both the project and the organization.

The Formal Organization

An organization's structure reveals the formal groupings and specializations of activities. Generally, these groupings and activities are documented in an organizational chart to clarify and portray the lines of authority, communication, reporting relationships, and responsibilities of individuals and groups within the organization. Although an organization's formal structure does not tell us anything about the informal lines of communication among its subunits, it does provide us with an indication of how a project will interface with the parent or supporting organization. In other words, the formal organizational structure will determine how resources are allocated, who has authority over those resources, and who is really in charge of the project.

Figure 4.1 illustrates the three most common structures—the functional, matrix, and project-based organization. Keep in mind that these organizations are not exhaustive—they represent a continuum of approaches that may evolve over time or as the result of a unique situation. An organization may choose to combine these forms any number of ways to create a hybrid organization such as a **functional matrix** or **project matrix.**

The Functional Organization   The functional organizational structure may be thought of as the more traditional organizational form. This particular structure is based upon organizing resources to perform specialized tasks or activities in order to attain the goals of the organization. As Figure 4.2 illustrates, individuals and subunits (i.e., groups of individuals) perform similar functions and have similar areas of expertise. Subsequently, projects are managed within the existing functional hierarchy.

Projects in a functional organization are typically coordinated through customary channels and housed within a particular function. For example, a project to install a new machine would be a self-contained project within the manufacturing function because the expertise required for the project would reside within the manufacturing subunit. The project manager would most likely be a senior manufacturing manager, and the project team would be made up of individuals from the engineering and production areas. As a result, the manufacturing subunit would be responsible for managing the project and for supplying and coordinating all of the resources dedicated to the project.

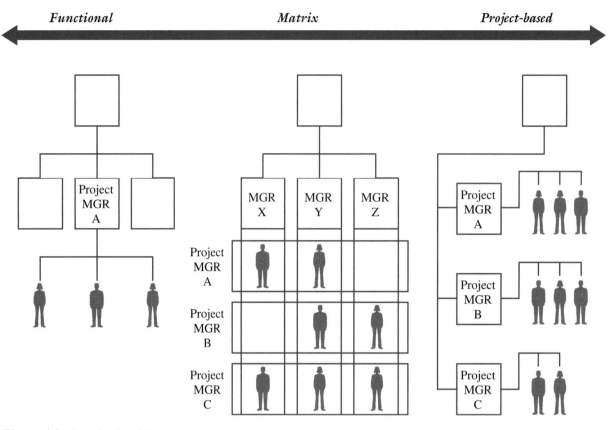

Figure 4.1 Organizational Structures

However, a project may cross functional boundaries. In the case of an information technology project, the knowledge and expertise to design and develop an application may reside in the information systems subunit, while the domain or functional knowledge resides in one of the functional subunits. As a result, the project team may consist of individuals from two or more functional areas. There are two main issues that must be resolved at the outset of a project: Who will be responsible for the project? What resources will each subunit provide?

There are a number of advantages for projects sponsored by organizations with functional structures. These include:

- *Increased flexibility*—Subject matter experts and other resources can be assigned to the project as needed. In addition, an individual can be part of the project team on a full-time or part-time basis. Once the project is completed, the project team members can return to their respective functional units.

- *Breadth and depth of knowledge and experience*—Individuals from a particular subunit can bring a wealth of knowledge, expertise, and experience to the project. This knowledge can be expanded even further as a result of their experiences with the project. As a result, the project experience may lead to greater opportunities for career advancement within the subunit. If the project crosses functional areas, an opportunity exists for these individuals to learn from each so that a less parochial solution can be developed.

- *Less duplication*—Coordination of resources and activities can lead to less duplication of resources across projects since specialization of skills and

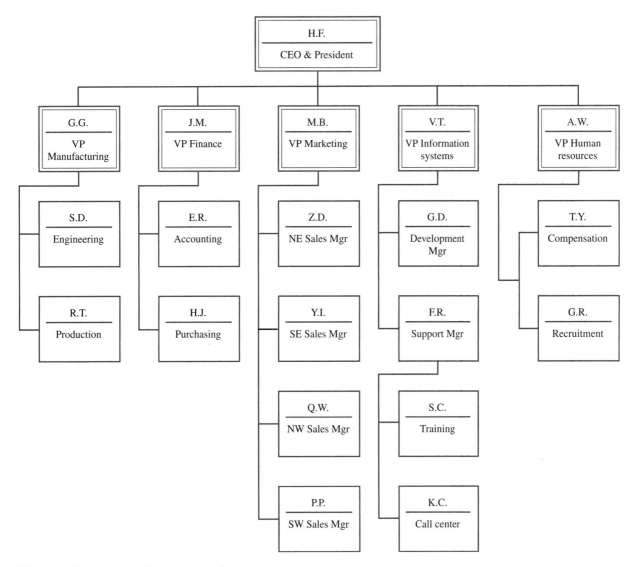

Figure 4.2 Functional Organizational Structure

resources are housed within a functional area. The project also tends to be more focused because a primary functional area is responsible for and ultimately takes ownership of the project.

There are, however, several disadvantages associated with projects sponsored by organizations with functional structures. These include:

- *Determining authority and responsibility*—As was mentioned previously, determining who has authority and responsibility for a project must be resolved at the outset, especially when the project involves more than one functional area. For example, in an IT project, will the project manager be from the IS department or from the functional area? A project manager from the IS area may have knowledge and expertise with respect to the technology, but lack critical knowledge about the business. On the other hand, a project manager from the functional area may understand the business, but lack an understanding of the technology. Furthermore, there is a

WARRING TRIBES

According to Allen Alter, the reason the IS function sometimes has a poor reputation in an organization may be due to strong in-group loyalty he calls tribalism. Alter contends that the typical IS department, made up of support centers, data centers, programmers, and network administration, is really several clans that tend to stick together with others of "similar backgrounds or status." As a result, some tribes "regularly knock heads" because of conflicting interests or because they do not communicate well with each other. Often when a project is in trouble, one tribe will not go out of its way to help another. Then, the business suffers because this indifference results in delays and wasted time. Ideas and suggestions for IT initiatives are also held back or fail globally because no one is able to see and understand the big picture. Alter suggests that tribes should not

be abolished because highly skilled and specialized individuals are comfortable working this way. It is, however, important that communication form a bridge between groups. Communication can be helped by bringing the whole function together in meetings and social events. But, it is imperative to pick a manager who can encourage people from different groups to communicate. Alter also suggests that unless IS tribes communicate effectively with each other, they will have even more difficulty working with another important tribe—the users.

SOURCE: Adapted from Allen E. Alter, Think Tribally, Fail Globally, *Computerworld,* November 17, 1997, http://www.computerworld .com/news/1997/story/0,11280,11174,00.html.

chance that the project manager will have an insular view of the project—that is, the project manager's allegiance and loyalty to a particular functional area may lead her or him to focus primarily on the interests of that area. The likelihood of this happening increases when the project expands across several functional boundaries. Other functional areas may begin to ask if there is anything in it for them and withhold resources unless their needs and expectations are met. The project manager may not have the authority for acquiring and providing the resources, but she or he will certainly be accountable for the failure of the project.

■ *Poor response time*—The normal lines of authority and communication delineated by the functional structure determine who makes specific decisions. Projects may take longer if important decisions have to pass through several layers of management and across several functional areas. Unfortunately, what's important to you may not be important to me if a particular functional unit has a dominant role or interest in a project. Due to the potential for parochial interests, problem resolution may break down because of finger pointing, trying to place blame for the problem rather than focusing on problem resolution.

■ *Poor integration*—The culture of the organization may encourage functional areas to insulate themselves from the rest of the organization as a way to avoid many of these parochial issues. However, this can result in two problems: First, the individuals in a functional area may act in their own best interests instead of taking a holistic or organizational view of the project. Second, the functional area may attempt to become self-sufficient by acquiring knowledge, expertise, and technology outside of its normal area of specialization. While specialization of skills and resources can *reduce* duplication of activities and resources, the functional structure can also *increase* this duplication. It may lead to an organization of warring tribes as functional areas compete for resources and blur lines of responsibility.

The Project Organization   At the other end of the spectrum from the functional organization is the project organization (see Figure 4.3). Sometimes referred to as the *pure project organization,* this organizational structure supports projects as the dominant form of business. Typically, a project organization will support multiple projects at one time and integrate project management tools and techniques throughout the organization. Each project is treated as a separate and relatively independent unit within the organization. The project manager has sole authority over and responsibility for the project and its resources, while the parent or supporting organization provides financial and administrative controls. Both the project manager and the project team are typically assigned to a particular project on a full-time basis.

There are advantages and disadvantages associated with projects supported by the project organization. Advantages include:

- *Clear authority and responsibility—* Unlike the projects in a functional organization, the project manager here is fully in charge. Although he or she must provide progress reports and is ultimately responsible to someone who has authority over all the projects (e.g., a program manager), the project manager has full authority over and responsibility for the assigned project. Moreover, the project team reports directly to the project manager, thus providing clear unity of command. This structure may allow the project team to better concentrate on the project.

- *Improved communication—*A clear line of authority results in more effective and efficient communication. In addition, lines of communication are shortened because the project manager is able to bypass the normal channels of distribution associated with the functional organizational structure. This structure thus results in more efficient communication and fewer communication problems.

- *High level of integration—*Since communication across the organization is increased, the potential for a higher level of cross integration across the organization exists. For example, the project team may include experts with technical skills or knowledge of the business. Fewer conflicts over resources arise since each project has resources dedicated solely to it.

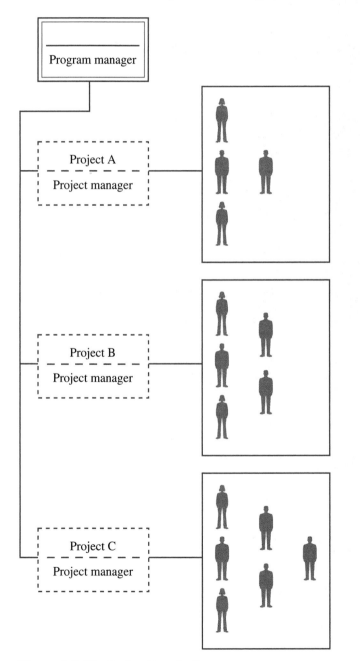

Figure 4.3 The Project Organization

Projects supported by project organization structures face several disadvantages. These disadvantages include:

- *Project isolation*—Since each project may be thought of as a self-contained unit, there is the potential for each project to become isolated from other projects in the organization. Unless a project management office or program manager oversees each project, inconsistencies in policies and project management approaches may occur across projects. In addition, project managers and project teams may have little opportunity to share ideas and experiences with other project managers and project teams, thus hindering learning throughout the organization.

- *Duplication of effort*—While the potential for conflicts over resources is reduced, various projects may require resources that are duplicated on other projects. Project managers may try to stockpile the best people and other resources that could be shared with other projects. Each project must then support the salaries of people who are part of the dedicated project team but whose services are not needed at all times. There is then the problem of what to do with these people when the project is completed and they have not been assigned to another project. Many consulting firms, for example, refer to people who are between projects as being on *the beach* or *on the bench*. While awaiting the next assignment, consultants are often sent to training in order to make the most of their idle time.

- *Projectitis*—Projectitis sometimes occurs when the project manager and project team develop a strong attachment to the project and to each other. As a result, these individuals may have a difficult time letting go, and the project begins to take on a life of its own with no real end in sight (Meredith and Mantel 2000). The program manager or project office must ensure that proper controls are in place to reduce the likelihood of this happening.

The Matrix Organization   The third type of organizational form is the matrix structure. The matrix organization is a combination of the vertical functional structure and the horizontal project structure (see Figure 4.4). As a result, the matrix organization provides many of the opportunities and challenges associated with the functional and project organizations.

The main feature of the matrix organization is the ability to integrate areas and resources throughout an organization. Moreover, people with specialized skills can be assigned to the project either on a part-time or on a more permanent basis. Unfortunately, **unity of command** is violated since each project team member will have more than one boss, leading to the possibility of confusion, frustration, conflict, and mixed loyalties. The functional manager will be responsible for providing many of the people and other resources to the project, while the project manager is responsible for coordinating these resources. In short, the project manager coordinates all the project activities for the functional areas, while the functional areas provide the wherewithal to carry out those activities.

The matrix organization can take on various forms that can create **hybrid organizations.** The most common forms include:

- *Balanced matrix*—In the balanced matrix form, the project manager focuses on defining all of the activities of the project, while the functional managers determine how those activities will be carried out.

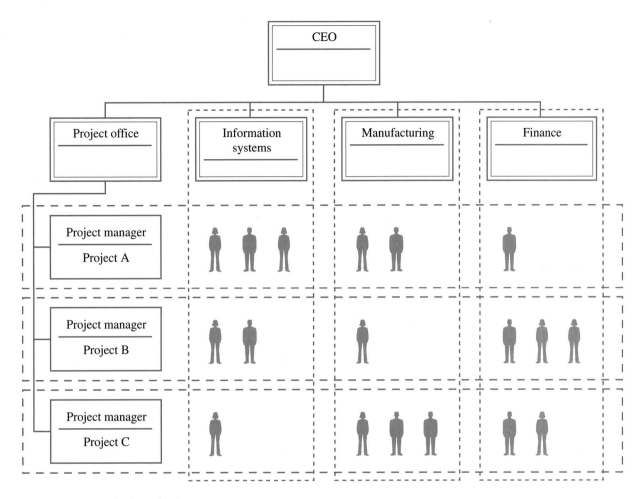

Figure 4.4 Matrix Organization

- *Functional matrix*—The functional matrix organization tends to take on more of the qualities of a functional organization. Here the project manager focuses on coordinating the project activities, while the functional managers are responsible for completing those activities that are related to their particular area.

- *Project matrix*—It follows, then, that a project matrix structure would take on more of the qualities of a project organization. In this case, the project manager has most of the authority and responsibility for defining and completing the project activities, while the functional managers provide guidance and resources, as needed.

There are several advantages and disadvantages for projects supported by a matrix organization. The advantages include:

- *High level of integration*—The cross-functional nature of the matrix structure allows for the access and sharing of skilled people and resources from across the organization, and people within the organization can be assigned to more than one project. This ability to share can result in less duplication of resources and activities.

- *Improved communication*—Due to the high level of integration, communication channels are more efficient and effective. As a result, problems and issues can be addressed by the project manager and functional managers, and decisions can be made more quickly than in a functional organization.

- *Increased project focus*—Because a project under the matrix organization has improved communication channels and access to a repository of resources and skilled expertise, the project team can focus on the activities of the project. This ability to focus should increase the likelihood of projects being completed on time and meeting the needs of the organization better.

On the other hand, there are several disadvantages for projects supported by the matrix organization. These include:

- *Higher potential for conflict*—Since power is distributed, project team members may wonder who really is their boss. They may receive conflicting orders, especially if the project and functional area managers have different goals or are fighting over scarce resources. In general, power may depend on which manager has the fewest direct reports to the chief executive office. The project manager may be required to be a skillful mediator and negotiator in order to keep the project on track.

- *Poorer response time*—Because the concept of unity of command is violated in a matrix structure, there can be confusion, mixed loyalties, and various distributions of power. Communication can become bogged down, and decisions may require agreement from individuals who are in conflict with each other. As a result, the project may stall and the project team may begin to experience low moral, little motivation, and the pressure to pick sides.

Which Organizational Structure Is Best? Unfortunately, there are no simple answers. It really depends on factors such as the nature of the organization's products and services it provides, the business environment, and its culture—that is, the personality of the organization. Projects supported under a functional organizational structure may work best when the organization focuses on a few internal projects. On the other hand, a project organizational structure may work better if an organization takes on a large number of external projects. Subsequently, most consulting firms follow the project organization structure. On the other hand, the matrix organizational structure may work best when an organization takes on projects that require a cross-functional approach.

There has been some research in this area. For example, Larson and Gobeli (1988) surveyed more than 1,600 project management professionals. The results of their study suggest that both project and functional managers have a strong preference for the project or project matrix organization. The functional and functional matrix organizational structures were viewed as the least effective, and the balanced matrix structure was seen as only marginally effective. Larson and Gobeli suggest that the success of a project is linked directly to the project manager's degree of autonomy and authority.

The success of large, complex projects may require a concentrated project focus that can be best supported by the project or project-matrix organization. On the other hand, the matrix organizational structure may work well when an organization cannot dedicate scarce staff and resources to a project or when a cross-functional focus is needed. If a project is undertaken within one specific area of the organization, then a functional-matrix structure would be effective. Although there is little evidence to support the effectiveness of projects supported under a functional organization, it would make sense that the best organizational structure would balance the needs of the project with those of the organization (Gray and Larson 2000).

The Informal Organization

The formal organization is the published structure that defines the official lines of authority, responsibilities, and reporting relationships. While the formal structure tells us how individuals or groups within an organization *should* relate to one another, it does not tell us how they *actually* relate (Nicholas 1990). In many cases the informal organization bypasses the formal lines of communication and authority because of the inevitable positive and negative relationships that occur over time in any organization. While communication in the formal organization is supposed to flow through published channels, it can flow in any direction and at a much faster pace through the network of informal relationships—the famous grapevine. Power in an organization, therefore, is not only determined by one's place in the hierarchy, but also how well one is connected in the informal network. A person's degree of connectedness in the informal organization largely determines what information is received or not received.

Stakeholders   Stakeholders are individuals, groups, or even organizations that have a stake, or claim, in the project's outcome. Often we think of stakeholders as only those individuals or groups having an interest in the successful outcome of a project, but the sad truth is that there are many who can gain from a project's failure. While the formal organization tells us a little about the stakeholders and what their interests may be, the informal organization paints a much more interesting picture.

Stakeholder Analysis   A published organizational chart is usually fairly easy to acquire or create. The informal organization may be more difficult to understand or explain, even for those well-connected individuals. To help the project manager and project team understand the informal organization better, one can develop a stakeholder analysis as a means of determining who should be involved with the project and understanding the role that they must play. To develop a stakeholder analysis, one may start with the published organizational chart and then add to it as the complexities of the informal organization become known. Since the purpose of the stakeholder analysis is to understand the informal organization, it may be best to view this as an exercise rather than a formal document to be made public. The following steps provide a guide for developing a stakeholder analysis:

1. Develop a list of stakeholders. Include individuals, groups, and organizations that must provide resources to the project or who have an interest in the successful or unsuccessful outcome of the project.

2. Next to each stakeholder, identify the stakeholder's interest in the project by giving the stakeholder a "1" if they have an positive interest in the project's outcome or a "–1" if they have a negative interest. Neutral individuals or groups can be given a "0". If you are not sure, then give a stakeholder a "?".

3. Next, it may be useful to gauge the amount of influence each stakeholder has over the project. One can use a scale from 0 to 5, with zero meaning no influence and five meaning extremely high influence—that is, this person or group could terminate the project.

4. The fourth step involves defining a role for each of the stakeholders. For example, every project should have a champion or someone prominent within the organization who will be a public supporter of the project. In addition, it is important to identify the owner of the project. This list may include an individual, group, or organization that will accept the transfer of the project's product. Other roles may include consultant, decision maker, advocate, ally, rival, foe, and so forth. Use adjectives or metaphors that provide a clear meaning and picture of the stakeholder.

5. Once you determine who has an interest in the project, what that interest is, and what influence they may have, it may be useful to identify an objective for each stakeholder. This may include such things as providing specific resources, expertise, or guidance navigating through the political waters of the organization. In the case of potential adversarial stakeholders, this may require getting their acceptance or approval concerning certain aspects of the project.

6. Lastly, it is important to identify various strategies for each stakeholder. These strategies may require building, maintaining, improving, or re-establishing relationships. In short, this list should include a short description of how the objective could be attained.

The exercise for developing a stakeholder analysis can be conducted and summarized in a table such as the template illustrated in Figure 4.5.

THE PROJECT TEAM

The word *team* has different meanings for each of us. As a result of past experiences with teams, those meanings probably have both positive and negative connotations. Information technology projects require various resources; but people are the most valuable resource and have the greatest influence on the project's outcome. Indeed, the human resource of a systems development project will consume up to 80 percent of its budget (McLeod and Smith 1996). It is important, then, that the project manager and project team members be chosen wisely. In addition, people must be sure to support the project team so that project success is not a random event.

The Roles of the Project Manager

One of the most critical decisions in project management is selecting a project manager or team leader. The project manager is usually assigned to the project at the earliest stages of the project life cycle, but a new one may be brought in as replacement in the later stages of a project.

Stakeholder	Interest	Influence	Role	Objective	Strategy

Figure 4.5 Stakeholder Analysis Chart

The project manager must play many roles. First, the project manager must play a managerial role that focuses on planning, organizing, and controlling. The project manager, for example, is responsible for developing the project plan, organizing the project resources, and then overseeing execution of the plan. The project manager must also perform many administrative functions, including performance reviews, project tracking and reporting, and other general day-to-day responsibilities.

Although this work sounds fairly simple and straightforward, even the best thought-out plans do not always go the way we expect. Thus, the project manager must know when to stay the course and when to adapt or change the project plan by expediting certain activities or acting as a problem solver.

The success of the project, of course, depends not only on the project team, but also on the contributions and support of all project stakeholders as well. Therefore, the project manager must build and nurture the relationships among the various stakeholders. To do this effectively, the project manager must play a strong leadership role. While the managerial role focuses on planning, organizing, and controlling, leadership centers on getting people motivated and then headed down the right path towards a common goal.

Choosing a project manager for a project is analogous to hiring an employee. It is important to look at his or her background, knowledge, skill sets, and overall strengths and weaknesses. Some attributes of a successful project manager include:

- *The ability to communicate with people*—A project manager must have strong communication skills. A project manager need not to be a great motivational speaker, but should have the ability to connect with people, share a common vision, and get everyone to respond or head in the right direction.

- *The ability to deal with people*—Aside from being a good communicator, a project manager must have the soft skills for dealing with people, their egos, and their agendas. The project manager must be a good listener, hearing what people say and understanding what they mean. This skill allows the project manager to get below the surface of issues when people are not being completely honest or open without being annoying or alienating them. A project manager must also have a sense of humor. Often, project managers and project teams are expected to perform during stressful situations, and a sense of humor can make these situations more manageable. Although a project manager does not have to be everyone's best friend, people should feel that they are at least approachable and should be comfortable talking with him or her. In addition, the project manager must also be willing to share knowledge and skills with others and be willing to help each individual develop to her or his fullest potential.

- *The ability to create and sustain relationships*—A good project manager must be able to build bridges instead of walls. Acting as a peacemaker or negotiator among the project client or sponsor, top management, the project team, customers, suppliers, vendors, subcontractors, and so forth may be necessary. In addition, the project manager should be a good salesperson. An effective project manager must continually sell the value of the project to all of the stakeholders and influence others over whom he or she has no direct authority.

- *The ability to organize*—A project manager must be good at organizing—developing the project plan, acquiring resources, and creating an effective project environment. The project manager must also know and understand both the details and the big picture, which requires a familiarity with the details of the project plan and also an understanding of how contingencies may impact the plan.

Team Selection and Acquisition

Another critical task of a project manager is selecting and staffing the project. Staffing involves recruiting and assigning people to the project team. Selecting the right mix of people, with both technical and non-technical skills, is a decision that can influence the outcome of the project. Although a project manager should strive to acquire the brightest and the best, project team members should be chosen based on the following skills:

- *Technology skills*—Depending upon the nature of the project, members with specific technology skill sets— programmers, systems analysts, network specialist, and so forth—will be required.

- *Business/organization skills*—Although technology skills are important in IT projects, it is also important to have people or access to people with domain knowledge. These skills include knowledge or expertise within a specific domain (e.g., compensation planning) as well as knowledge of a particular organization or industry (e.g., healthcare) to augment the technical skill requirements.

- *Interpersonal skills*—The ability to communicate with other team members and other stakeholders is an important skill for team members. It is important not only for the team members to understand one another, but also for the project team to understand the project sponsor's needs. Due to the nature of many projects, other desirable characteristics should include creativity, a tolerance for ambiguity, acceptance of diversity, flexibility in adapting to different roles, and the capacity to take calculated risks.

The size or scope of the project will determine the size of the project team. Although smaller teams have the potential to work faster and develop a product in a shorter time, larger teams can provide a larger knowledge base and different perspectives. Unfortunately, there is also a tendency for larger teams to function more slowly. One solution to this latter problem may be creating subgroups to make the project more manageable and to facilitate communication and action.

The project manager may recruit project team members internally or externally. For example, in the functional or matrix organization, people may be acquired from the functional areas. In a project organization, a project manager may recruit people who are currently in-between projects or who will be soon *rolling off* an existing project. The project manager may have to negotiate with other managers for specific individuals with specific skills or areas of expertise. On the other hand, a project manager may have to hire individuals from outside the organization. In either case, for a particular project, training may be required. Therefore, the timing of when a particular individual can begin work on the project is a significant factor that can impact the project's schedule.

Team Performance

The project team has a direct influence on the outcome of the project. Therefore, it is important the team's performance be of the utmost concern to the project manager. In *The Wisdom of Teams,* Jon R. Katzenbach and Douglas K. Smith (1999) provide an insightful and highly usable approach for understanding the language and discipline

IS SWAT TEAMS

SWAT (Special Weapons And Tactics) teams are law enforcement teams that are highly trained to respond to special situations. The term *SWAT* has also been applied to expert teams in the IS world. Drawing upon the analogy of police SWAT teams, these IS teams came about to respond effectively to client/server projects; but this same idea could be applied to many other types of projects. The basic idea of an IS SWAT team is to assemble a small team of highly skilled developers who are experts in the latest technology. By pooling the knowledge, expertise, and talents of a select few individuals, the team can harness the creative power of the group and develop a solution that is much more effective than an individual could. Because everyone is a highly skilled technologist, IS SWAT teams give individual team members the opportunity to learn more from each other than they would on their own. In addition, working in groups allows the team members to hone their people skills because working in a group requires greater communication and the art of compromise. On the downside, people working on IS SWAT teams must be comfortable working in a very unstructured environment. Often, the beginning of the project is chaotic and the teams reflect the individual personalities of the individuals involved. In addition, IS SWAT teams involve high profile projects. While success can lead to career advancement for the team members, project failure can reflect badly on them.

SOURCE: Adapted from Linda Wilson, SWAT Teams, *Computerworld,* October 23, 1995, http://www.computerworld.com/news/1995/story /0,11280,1946,00.html.

of teams. In refining the language of teams, they provide a distinction between work groups and several types of teams.

Work Groups The work group is based on the traditional approach where a single leader is in control, makes most of the decisions, delegates to subordinates, and monitors the progress of the assigned tasks. Therefore, the performance of a work group depends greatly on the leader.

A work group can also include members who interact to share information, best practices, or ideas. Although the members may be interested in each other's success, work groups do not necessarily share the same performance goals, do not necessarily provide joint work-products, and are not necessarily held mutually accountable. A study group is an example of a work group. You and several members of a class may find it mutually beneficial to study together for an exam, but each of you (hopefully!) will work on the exam individually. The grade you receive on the exam is not a direct result of the work produced by the study group, but rather of your individual performance on the exam. In an organizational context, managers may form work groups to share information and help decide direction or policy, but performance will ultimately be a reflection of each manager and not the group. Work groups or single leader groups are viable and useful in many situations.

Real Teams In cases where several individuals must produce a joint work product, teams are a better idea. More specifically, Katzenbach and Smith (1999) define a team as:

> a small number of people with complimentary skills who are committed to a common purpose, performance goals, and approach for which they hold themselves mutually accountable. (45)

Moreover, calling a group of people a team does not make it one nor does working together make a group a team. Teamwork focuses on performance, not on becoming a team. Subsequently, there are several *team basics* that define a real team:

- *A small number of people*—Ideally, a project team must be between two and twelve people. Although a large number of people can become a team, a large team can become a problem in terms of logistics and communication. As a result, a large team should break into subteams rather than try to function as one large unit.

- *Complementary skills*—For achieving the team's goal, a team must have or develop the right mix of skills that are complementary. These skills include:
  - Technical or functional expertise
  - Problem-solving or decision-making skills
  - Interpersonal skills—that is, people skills

- *Commitment to a common purpose and performance goals*—Katzenbach and Smith distinguish between activity goals (e.g., install a local area network) and performance goals (e.g., ship all orders within twenty-four hours of when they are received). The concept of a performance goal is similar to the concept of the MOV and sets the tone and aspirations of the team while providing a foundation for creating a common team purpose. As a result, the team develops direction, momentum, and commitment to its work. Moreover, a common performance goal and purpose inspires pride because people understand how their joint work product will impact the organization. A common goal also gives the team an identity that goes beyond the individuals involved.

- *Commitment to a common approach*—Although teams must have a common purpose and goal, they must also develop a common approach to how they will work together. Teams should spend as much time developing their approach as they do defining their goal and purpose. A common work approach should focus not only on economic and administrative issues and challenges, but also on the social issues and challenges that will shape how the team works together.

- *Mutual accountability*—A group can never become a team unless members hold themselves mutually accountable. The notion that "we hold ourselves accountable" is much more powerful than "the boss holds me accountable." Subsequently, no team can exist if everyone focuses on his or her individual accountability. Mutual accountability requires a sincere promise that each team member makes to herself or himself and to the other members of the team. This accountability requires both commitment and trust because it counters many cultures' emphasis on individualism. In short, it can be difficult for many people to put their careers and reputations in the hands of others. Unless a common approach and purpose has been forged as a team, individuals may have a difficult time holding themselves accountable as a team.

Based upon their in-depth study of several teams, Katzenbach and Smith provide several common sense findings:

- *Teams tend to flourish on a demanding performance challenge.* A clear performance goal is more important to team success than team-building exercises, special initiatives, or seeking team members with ideal profiles.

- *The team basics are often overlooked.* The weakest of all groups is the pseudo team, which is not focused on a common performance goal. If a team cannot shape a common purpose, it is doomed to achieving mediocre results. We cannot just tell a group of individuals to be a team.

- *Most organizations prefer individual accountability to team accountability.* Most job descriptions, compensation plans, and career paths emphasize individual accomplishments and, therefore, tend to make people uncomfortable trusting their careers to outcomes dependent on the performance of others.

Katzenbach and Smith provide some *uncommon sense* findings as well:

- *Strong performance goals tend to spawn more real teams.* A project team cannot become a real team just because we call them a team or require them to participate in team-building activities or exercises. However, their findings suggest that real teams tend to thrive as a result of clearly defined performance-based goals.

- *High performance teams are rare.* In their study of teams, Katzenbach and Smith identified high performance teams. These are real teams that outperform all other teams and even the expectations given. This special type of team requires an extremely high level of commitment to other team members and cannot be managed.

- *Real teams provide the basis of performance.* Real teams combine the skills, experiences, and judgments of the team members to create a synergy that cannot be achieved through the summation of individual performance. Teams are also the best way to create a shared vision and sense of direction throughout the organization.

- *Teams naturally integrate performance and learning.* Performance goals and common purposes translate into team members developing the skills needed to achieve those goals. As a result of open communication and trust, the members of a team are more apt to share their ideas and skills so that they may learn from one another. Moreover, successful teams have more fun, and their experiences are more memorable for both what the team accomplished and in terms of what each member learned as a result of the team process.

Project Teams and Knowledge Management

The primary challenge of real teams is to develop shared performance goals and a common purpose. For project teams following the IT project methodology, this challenge requires defining and getting agreement on the project's MOV. It also requires that the team members learn from each other and from other project teams' experiences.

In *The Radical Team Handbook,* John Redding (2000) describes a fundamentally new and different form of teamwork based on learning. Based on a study of twenty teams, Redding suggests that traditional teams tend to:

- *Accept background information at face value.* In short, most teams accept the project challenge as it is first defined and do not challenge preconceived notions about the problem or opportunity and what they must do.

- *Approach projects in a linear fashion.* Projects have a beginning and end, and the project plan outlines all of the steps needed to complete the project on time and within budget. Traditional teams tend to focus on the project's schedule and, therefore, base project success on completing the project on time and within budget.

- *Provide run-of-the-mill solutions.* Since the team focuses on the challenge as it was handed to them (i.e., the way the challenge was originally framed), they never really understand the challenge and subsequently provide a solution that has minimal impact on the organization. In other words, the team may focus on a symptom and, therefore, never focus on the real problem or opportunity since the solutions remain within the original *frame* or how the challenge was originally presented to them.

In contrast, Redding describes a radical team as a team that is able to get to the root or fundamental issue or challenge. In general, radical teams do not accept the original performance challenge at its face value. The core objective of a radical team is to question and challenge the original framing of the problem or challenge at hand.

The way the problem or challenge is defined may very well be the problem. Too often a team is handed a performance challenge that is framed by a senior manager. For example, the team may be told by a senior manager that the company is losing money and, therefore, the team should focus on cutting costs. If the team accepts this framing of the challenge, they will develop a solution aimed at saving money. If, however, a team challenges this original frame, they may find out that the real reason why the organization is losing money is because customers are leaving due to poor service. Unless the project team understands the real problem in this case, its solution to cut costs will have little impact on the organization and the organization will continue to lose money.

Learning Cycles and Lessons Learned

Learning cycle theory was originally proposed by John Dewey in 1938 and used to describe how people learn (Kolb 1984). More recently, the concept of **learning cycles** has been applied to project teams and knowledge management. More specifically, learning cycles provide a way to resolve ambiguous situations through the repeated pattern of thinking through a problem (Dewey 1938). Figure 4.6 illustrates a team learning cycle.

Redding (2000) suggests that a team learning cycle has four phases:

1. *Understand and frame the problem*—It is important that a project team not accept the issues and challenges presented to them at face value. Assumptions must be surfaced and tested because the problem or issue as it is originally framed may not be the real problem after all. Thus, the project team must get to the root of the problem. At the beginning of a project, the team member's understanding may be quite general, or they may feel that they really do not understand the challenge assigned to them. Unfortunately, few people are willing to admit that they do not have all the answers or that their understanding of the team's challenge is

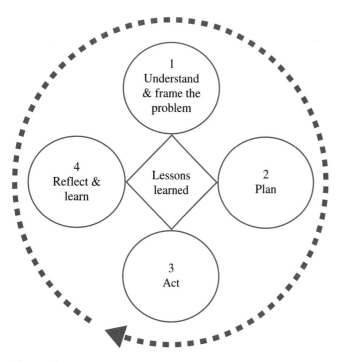

Figure 4.6 A Learning Cycle

Source: *The Radical Team Handbook*, John Redding, Jossey-Bass 2000. Reprinted by permission of John Wiley & Sons, Inc.

limited. On the other hand, other members of the team may approach the project with a high degree of certainty—that is, they may act as though they know what the solution is and, therefore, the team just needs to work out the details of how to go about implementing the solution. Opinions are often accepted without question and can result in erroneous assumptions that lead the project team in the wrong direction or keep the team from getting at the real problem. Moreover, there is often pressure for the team to take immediate action so that the project can be completed on time and within budget. In either case, the team runs the risk of not getting to the root of the problem and may propose solutions that have minimal impact on the organization.

Therefore, the project team must come to understand two things: Preconceived solutions are likely to produce run-of-the-mill results, and teams should encourage open humility. In other words, it is all right for team members to recognize and admit that they do not have all the answers, especially at the beginning of a project. As a result, team members may feel more comfortable admitting they have more questions than answers and the potential for preconceived ideas leading to mediocre solutions is reduced.

2. *Plan*—To help teams understand and reframe the problem, teams should create a shared understanding of the problem or opportunity. This understanding includes defining what the team is trying to accomplish and how they are going to go about it. Figure 4.7 provides a template to guide a team through the exercise of separating facts from assumptions.

Using the team learning record as shown in Figure 4.7, the team can brainstorm "what they know" (the facts), "what they think they know" (assumptions), and "what they don't know" (questions to be answered). Early in the project, a team may have more questions and assumptions than facts. That is to be expected because the team may not understand the problem or challenge fully. Assumptions are ideas, issues, or concepts that must be tested (e.g., "the users will never agree to this" or "senior management will never spend the money"). Often, a person can make an assumption sound like a fact, especially if she or he says it with enough authority. Therefore, it is every team member's job to separate the facts (proof, evidence, or reality) from assumptions (theories, opinions, or guesses). On the other hand, if the team identifies things it does not know, these can be classified as questions to be answered. Once the project team identifies what it knows, what it thinks it knows, and what it doesn't know, it can create a plan of action. Each team member can volunteer or be assigned to specific tasks that require him or her to test assumptions or to learn answers to questions that were identified in the team learning record (Figure 4.7). As a

What We Know *(Facts)*	*What We Think We Know* *(Assumptions)*	*What We Don't Know* *(Questions to be Answered)*

Figure 4.7   Team Learning Record

SOURCE: *The Radical Team Handbook*, John Redding, Jossey-Bass 2000. Reprinted by permission of John Wiley & Sons, Inc.

result, the team creates a plan of action and can document the actions to be learned in a format similar to Figure 4.8

3. *Act*—The key to team learning is carrying out the actions defined in the team's action plan. Team members can work on their own or together to test out assumptions, try out hunches, experiment, or gather and analyze data. The purpose of these actions should be to generate knowledge and test assumptions, not to complete a series of tasks like a to-do list. Thus, the purpose of these actions is to confirm or disconfirm assumptions and learn answers to questions the team does not know. Redding suggests that what teams do outside of meetings is just as important as the meeting itself because only by acting do teams have the opportunity to learn.

4. *Reflect and learn*—After the team has had a chance to carry out the action items in the action-learning plan, the team should meet to share its findings and reflect upon what everyone has learned. To be effective, this reflection must take place in an environment of openness, honesty, and trust. Once the team has a chance to meet and reflect on the information it has acquired, the team can document what it has learned. One format Redding suggests is for the team to answer the following questions:

   - What do we know now that we didn't know before?
   - Have we encountered any surprises? Have we gained any new insights? If so, what were they?
   - What previous assumptions have been supported or refuted by what we have learned so far?
   - How does the team feel the project is progressing at this point in time?
   - How effective has the team been so far?

   Another approach for documenting **lessons learned** is the United States Army's After Action Review (AAR). The format for an AAR is:

   - *What was the intent?* Begin by going back and defining the original purpose and goal of the action.
   - *What happened?* Describe as specifically and objectively as possible what actually occurred.
   - *What have we learned?* Identify key information, knowledge, and insights that were gained as a result.
   - *What do we do now?* Determine what will be done as a result of what has been learned, dividing actions into three categories: Short-term, mid-term, and long-term.
   - *Take action.*
   - *Tell someone else.* Share what has been learned with anyone in the organization who might benefit.

What Needs To Be Done?	*By Whom?*	*By When?*

Figure 4.8 Action Plan for Team Learning

The team learning cycles and lessons learned can be documented and shared with other project teams. However, the completion of a team's lessons learned marks the ending of one learning cycle and the beginning of another. Based on the learning that has transpired, the team can focus once again on understanding and reframing the problem and then repeat the plan, act, reflect and learn phases again. Figure 4.9 illustrates this concept.

As illustrated in Figure 4.9, an entire project can be viewed as a series of learning cycles. An initial team meeting can examine the initial problem or challenge assigned to the team. During that meeting, the team can develop an initial action plan. Between meetings, the members of the team can then carry out their assigned tasks for testing assumptions or gathering information. At the next meeting, the team can reflect on what it has learned, document the lessons learned, and then start the beginning of a new cycle. Each cycle should be used to challenge the framing of the problem and create new opportunities for learning.

Teams do not always begin and end learning cycles at each meeting. Some learning cycles may take longer, and some can be accomplished in a shorter time if face-to-face meetings are not needed. Redding suggests, however, that three dimensions can be used to assess team learning: speed, depth, and breadth.

- *Speed*—First, a team should follow a learning cycle approach rather than a traditional, linear approach. Second, speed refers to the number of learning cycles completed. Therefore, the opportunity to learn can be increased if a team can complete more cycles in a given amount of time.

- *Depth*—Just increasing the number of learning cycles does not guarantee that teams will increase their learning. Subsequently, depth of learning refers to the degree to which a team can deepen its understanding of the project from cycle to cycle. This learning includes challenging the framing of the problem and various assumptions. In short, depth focuses on how well the team is able to dig below the surface in order to get to the root of the problem. Redding suggests that a team can measure depth by asking the following question: Was the team's conception of the project at the end any different from what it was in the beginning? (47)

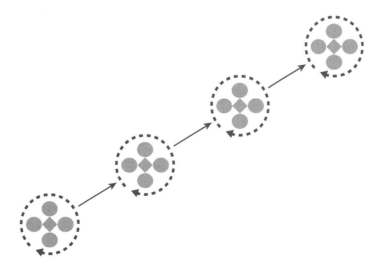

Figure 4.9 Team Learning Cycles Over the Project Life Cycle

SOURCE: *The Radical Team Handbook,* John Redding, Jossey-Bass 2000. Reprinted by permission of John Wiley & Sons, Inc.

■ *Breadth*—The breadth of learning refers to the impact the project has on the organization. It also focuses on whether the learning that has taken place within the team stays within the team or is shared and used throughout the organization. If a team can uncover complex relationships, it can develop a solution that impacts the whole organization. For example, what originally was thought to be a marketing problem could very well cross several functional or departmental boundaries.

THE PROJECT ENVIRONMENT

The project manager is responsible for many things. In addition to acquiring human resources, the project manager must also focus on the project environment. The project environment includes not only the physical space where the team will work, but also the project culture as well. More specifically, the project environment includes:

■ *A place to call home*—It may seem obvious, but a project team must have adequate space to work and meet. If the project team is internal to the organization, a work area may already be available to the team. However, consultants often are found camped out in a conference room or even the organization's cafeteria because no other space in the organization is available. Therefore, the project manager should make sure that the team has a place to call home and a place to meet as a team for the duration of the project.

■ *Technology*—In addition to having an adequate work area, the team will also need adequate technology support. Support may include a personal computer and appropriate software, Internet access, electronic mail, and a telephone. In addition, many teams today are geographically dispersed. Technology provides a means for teams to collaborate when they cannot meet at the same time in the same place. Collaboration tools not only can improve communication, but also can increase the speed of the team's learning cycles by allowing the team to store and share minutes of team meetings, action plans, and lessons learned.

■ *Office supplies*—Aside from technology resources, the team will need various office supplies, such as paper, pens, pencils, staplers, and so forth.

COLLABORATION AND CULTURE

Groupware can be an important business tool that allows people to work together without the limitation of having to meet at the same time or in the same place. However, implementing groupware technology and expecting people from different cultures to embrace it can lead to many problems. For example, a U.S. manager may expect workers in different departments and locations to use a groupware system to electronically kick around ideas informally. Unfortunately, that may violate cultural protocols in countries that adhere to a more hierarchical business structure. To talk to another co-worker, an individual may have to first let her or his manager know, who, in turn, would have to check with the co-worker's manager. Moreover, some cultures encourage people to be selective about what client data they make available to others. For example, Margaret Matthews, a knowledge director at Andersen Consulting (now Accenture), found that the company's Japanese users were more likely to call a client "a worldwide electronics distributor" than to name the company, because of a strong bias toward protecting client confidentiality.

SOURCE: Adapted from Rebecca Sykes, Collaboration Kinks, *Computerworld,* December 8, 1997, http://www.computerworld .com/news/1997/ story/0,11280,14715,00.html.

■ *Culture*—Each organization has its own culture, but a project team should have its own culture as well. Culture reflects the values and norms of the team. One way of establishing a culture for the project team is to have the project team develop a team charter early on in the project. The team charter allows the team to agree on a set of values and expectations that will help define the project team culture. This charter includes:

▧ What is expected from each member?

▧ What role will each team member play?

▧ How will conflicts be resolved?

Figure 4.10 provides an example of an actual team charter. Because many organizations operate globally today, many projects teams are made up of people from different backgrounds and cultures. The project manager and the project team members must be sensitive to these cultural differences.

CHAPTER SUMMARY

Organizations create a specific structure to support a particular strategy. If the organization performs poorly, then the firm will often develop a new strategy and/or formal organizational structure. Three different formal organizational structures were discussed in this chapter: the functional organization, the project organization, and the matrix organization. These organizational structures represent a continuum of possible structures, and an organization can create structures that are between functional and matrix organizations or matrix and project organizations.

Each organizational structure presents opportunities and challenges for projects in terms of flexibility, knowledge and expertise available, and authority and responsibilities. While the formal organization, in terms of an organizational or hierarchical chart, defines the official line of authority and communication, the informal organization includes the informal relationships and internetworking of people within the organization that develops over time. Understanding the formal and informal sides of an organization is important because it will help the project manager and project team better understand the politics and culture of the organization and provide greater insight into the decision-making process.

The project manager is a key position that should be filled at the earliest stages of the project. The project manager plays many important roles that include not only the traditional roles of a manager, but also roles specific to the nature of projects. Therefore, the project manager must be a skillful communicator, negotiator, organizer,

Expectations and Team Values

■ Everybody's ideas and opinions count

■ Everyone must learn something new technically and with the business

■ Work hard, but have fun

■ Produce necessary, quality periodic deliverables throughout the course of the product

■ Add values to clients' organization

■ Heavy team commitment

■ Show up for team meetings

■ Team coordination

■ Accountability

■ Assistance

■ Communication with clients and team

■ No such thing as a stupid question

■ *RESPECT for everyone*

■ Research: expanding knowledge base as well as comfort zone

■ Extend ourselves (Leave our comfort zones)

■ Punctuality and group attendance

■ Equal contributions from members

■ Be prepared for meetings: check e-mail and team web site before every meeting

■ Trust one another

Grievance Resolution

■ Try to resolve issue with each team member first

Figure 4.10 Project Team Charter

and relationship builder. In addition, the project manager must perform several critical tasks, including selecting and acquiring members of the project team and creating the project environment.

Two relatively new approaches to managing project teams were introduced in this chapter. First, *The Wisdom of Teams* by Jon R. Katzenbach and Douglas K. Smith (1999) provides a new language and discipline for project teams. For example, a work group can follow a traditional approach where a single leader or boss is in control, makes most of the decisions, and delegates to subordinates who work independently from each other. Or a work group can include several individuals who come together to share information or set policy, but work independently from one another and do not necessarily share the same performance goals or work products. On the other hand, real teams are a special type of team, with a few individuals with complimentary skills who focus on a performance-based goal and share a common purpose and approach. Based on their study of teams, Katzenbach and Smith found that real teams consistently outperform work groups.

Project team members must learn from each other and from other project team experiences if they are to provide a solution that gets to the root of the problem and not just a symptom. Learning cycle theory has been around since 1938, but has recently been applied to team learning and knowledge management. In *The Radical Team Handbook,* John Redding (2000) provides an interesting approach for teams based on learning cycles. Here, it is important that a team not accept the problem

or challenge as it is originally presented to them. Following a learning cycle, the team follows four phases: (1) understand and frame the problem, (2) plan, (3) act, and (4) reflect and learn. The conclusion of a learning cycle and the beginning of the next is marked by the documentation of lessons learned.

Instead of developing a solution prematurely, the project team is to encourage open humility by acknowledging that it does not have all the answers, especially at the beginning of a project. Therefore, the project team is encouraged to discuss and separate facts from assumptions or opinions. The team then creates an action plan to research questions and test assumptions. When the team meets, the members reflect on and learn from the information collected. Surprises, insights, and confirmed (or disconfirmed) assumptions are then documented as lessons learned. A team's learning can be assessed using three dimensions: (1) speed or the number of learning cycles, (2) depth or the degree to which the team deepened its understanding of the project, and (3) breadth or the impact of the team's proposed solution on the organization.

Although the project manager is responsible for overseeing many project activities, it is his or her responsibility to ensure that the project team has an adequate work environment. A suitable workspace and the technology to support the team are necessary. In addition, each project should define its own culture. It is helpful to have the team develop a team charter that outlines the roles, values, expectations, and methods for resolving conflict in order to set proper expectations.

▮ REVIEW QUESTIONS

1. What is the relationship between an organization's strategy and organizational structure?

2. What is meant by the formal organization?

3. Why is it important for a project manager to understand the formal organization?

4. Describe the functional organizational structure.

5. What are some challenges for IT projects under the functional organizational structure?

6. What are some opportunities for IT projects under the functional organizational structure?

7. Describe the project organizational structure.

8. What are some challenges for IT projects under the project organizational structure?

9. What are some opportunities for IT projects under the project organizational structure?

10. Describe the matrix organizational structure.

11. What are some challenges for IT projects under the matrix organization structure?

12. What are some opportunities for IT projects under the matrix organizational structure?

13. What is projectitis? When might you expect to encounter projectititis? How could an organization minimize the likelihood of projectitis?

14. Describe the balanced matrix, functional matrix, and project matrix organizational structures.

15. Describe what is meant by the informal organization. Why should the project manager or project team be concerned with understanding the informal organization?

16. What is a stakeholder?

17. How does conducting a stakeholder analysis help the project manager and project team understand the informal organization?

18. Why would the project manager and project team not want to make a stakeholder analysis public to the entire organization?

19. In conducting a stakeholder analysis, why is it important not only to identify those who will gain from the project's success, but also those who may gain from its failure?

20. What is the purpose of defining a role and objective for each stakeholder identified in the stakeholder analysis?

21. Describe the roles of a project manager.

22. What qualities are required for a good project manager? Can you come up with any on your own?

23. What skills or qualities are important in selecting a project team?

24. What is the difference between a work group and a real team?

25. What is the difference between a performance-based goal and an activity-based goal? Give an example of each.

26. Why is focusing on a performance-based goal, such as a project's MOV, more important than having the team go through a series of team-building exercises?

27. Why do you think many teams accept the project opportunity at face value and never question the way the project was originally framed?

28. Describe the concept of a learning cycle?

29. What purpose does creating a lesson learned at the end of a learning cycle provide?

30. What advantage does a team have when it encourages open humility instead of trying to solve the problem or provide a solution as soon as possible?

31. What is meant by the speed of learning cycles? How is speed associated with team learning?

32. What is meant by depth of learning cycles? How is depth associated with team learning?

33. What is meant by breadth of learning cycles? How is breadth associated with team learning?

34. What is the project environment? Why must a project manager ensure that a proper project environment is in place?

▨ EXTEND YOUR KNOWLEDGE

1. Develop and write a job description for hiring a project manager to manage an Enterprise Resource Planning (ERP) project. Once the job description is complete, describe how you might go about finding this person externally. What sources would you use?

2. If you are working on a semester assignment with other individuals in your class, complete a stakeholder analysis using the Stakeholder Analysis Chart in Figure 4.5.

3. What kind of projects are you best suited for? Using the World Wide Web, point your browser to the following Web sites and take an online assessment.
   - Quiz 1: http://www.project-manager.com/pmpage19.html
   - Quiz 2: http://www.project-manager.com/pmpage20.html

4. If you are working with other students on a semester project assignment, do you consider yourselves more of a work group or a team? Why? How effectively has this worked for you? What would you like to change? What would you like to leave the same?

5. If you are working with a team on a class project, go through a learning cycle as a team.

   - Write down the problem or challenge assigned to your team as you originally understood it. What is MOV (i.e., performance-based goal) that your team is trying to achieve?
   - Using the following table as a guide, write down what you know (facts), what you think you know (assumptions), and what you don't know (questions to be answered). Be sure to challenge any opinions or assumptions before concluding they are facts.

What We Know (Facts)	What We Think We Know (Assumptions)	What We Don't Know (Questions to be Answered)

   - Once you and your team members finish brainstorming facts, assumptions, and questions, develop an action plan and assign responsibilities for each member of the team using the following table as a guide. Agree on a meeting day and time so that each member has a chance to complete his or her assignment and so that the team can meet to discuss these findings.

Actions to Learn	Who's Responsible

- After everyone has had a chance to complete his or her action-learning assignments, the team should meet to share this information. Each member should take a turn presenting what he or she found. While a team member is presenting what they found, the other members must listen carefully and not challenge any of the information presented. Clarification questions are fine. After each member has had a chance to present her or his findings, the team should focus on the following questions:

a. Is there anything we know now that we didn't know before?

b. Were there any surprises? Have we gained any new insights? If so, what are they?

c. What assumptions have been supported and not supported?

d. How well is the team progressing?

e. The answers to these questions should be documented. Once documented, the team has completed one full learning cycle. The next step is to start over and reframe the project challenge as you did in Part a.

BIBLIOGRAPHY

Dewey, J. 1938. *Logic: The Theory of Inquiry.* New York: Holt, Rinehart, and Winston.

Gray, C. F. and E. W. Larson 2000. *Project Management: The Managerial Process.* Boston: Irwin McGraw-Hill.

Katzenbach, J. R. and D. K. Smith 1999. *The Wisdom of Teams.* New York: HarperCollins Publishers.

Kolb, D. 1984. *Experiential Learning.* Upper Saddle River, N.J.: Prentice Hall.

Larson, E. W. and D. H. Gobeli 1988. Organizing for Product Development Projects. *Journal of Product Innovation Management* 5: 180–190.

McLeod, G. and D. Smith 1996. *Managing Information Technology Projects.* Danvers, Mass: Boyd & Fraser Publishing Company.

Meredith, J. R. and S. J. Mantel, Jr. 2000. *Project Management: A Managerial Approach.* New York: John Wiley.

Nicholas, J. M. 1990. *Managing Business and Engineering Projects: Concepts and Implementation.* Upper Saddle River, N.J.: Prentice Hall.

Redding, J. C. 2000. *The Radical Team Handbook.* San Francisco: Jossey-Bass.

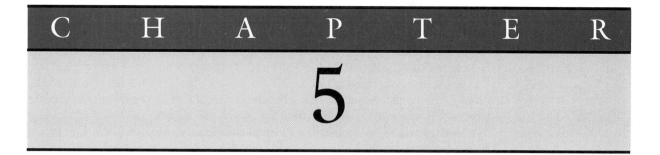

5

Defining and Managing Project Scope

CHAPTER OVERVIEW

Chapter 5 focuses on developing a scope management plan to define and manage the project and product deliverables of the project. After studying this chapter, you should understand and be able to:

- Identify the five processes that support project scope management. These processes, defined by the Project Management Body of Knowledge (PMBOK), include initiation, planning, scope definition, scope verification, and scope change control.

- Describe the difference between product scope (i.e., the features and functions that must support the IT solution) and project scope (i.e., the deliverables and activities that support IT project methodology).

- Apply several tools and techniques for defining and managing the project's scope.

GLOBAL TECHNOLOGY SOLUTIONS

On Friday evening Matt and Kellie were still at the GTS office, working on the project charter and project plan for Husky Air. Rubbing her eyes, Kellie asked, "I know we defined the goal of the project by developing the MOV, but what about the work that has to be done to get us there?"

"Glad you asked," Matt said as he put down his personal digital assistant on the desk in front of him. "I think we're ready to start defining the scope of the project, which will help us define all of the deliverables and activities that support the MOV."

"I remember working on a project that never seemed to end," she replied. "The users always wanted to add more bells and whistles to the system, and the project ended up missing its deadline and costing a lot more than we had planned."

Matt thought for a moment, then asked. "So, what can we learn from that experience?"

Kellie smiled. "First of all," she said. "I think we need to have a plan in place to make sure that the scope of the project is well-defined. I think part of our problem was that we never really got a clear idea of the project's goal; so we never defined the scope of the project properly. And secondly, we should've had some kind of process in place to control scope changes once we started the project."

Matt agreed. "That sounds like an excellent idea. But why not just say no to any scope change requests?"

Kellie sat back in her chair. "The way I see it, if we say yes to each and every scope change request, we run the risk of escalating the project's schedule and, in turn, the project's budget. On the other hand, if we say no to all scope change requests, we run the risk of missing some opportunities or appearing non-responsive to our client's needs."

"Good point, but how do you know when to say yes to a scope change and when to say no?" asked Matt.

"I guess we could let the project's MOV be our guide," she answered. "If a scope change supports the MOV, then it's worth doing. Otherwise, if it doesn't support the MOV, then the scope change isn't worth the time or money. Besides, the client has to make the decision whether the change in scope is worth the increase in schedule and cost. All we can do is keep the schedule and budget under control and then point out to them how any requested scope change will impact the project."

Matt stood up, saying "I think what we need is a scope management plan that can be part of the project charter. It's also important that we let everyone involved with the project know about it. Let's call it a day and get started on it first thing Monday morning."

Kellie agreed. "That's the best idea I've heard all day. Why don't you go ahead? I'll lock up after I make a few phone calls."

Things to Think About

1. What is the importance of ensuring that the scope of a project has been defined completely and accurately?
2. What is the relationship between the project's MOV and its scope?
3. What is the importance of having scope control procedures in place?
4. Why should a scope control process be communicated to all of the stakeholders of a project?

▌ INTRODUCTION

This chapter focuses on defining and managing the work that must be accomplished by the project team over the course of the project. The term **scope** is used to define the work boundaries and deliverables of the project so what needs to get done, gets done—and only what needs to get done, gets done. Therefore, it is important to define not only what is part of the project work, but also what is not part of the project work. Any work not part of the project is considered to be outside of the project's scope.

Project Scope Management Processes

The Project Management Body of Knowledge (PMBOK) defines five processes to support the knowledge area of project scope management, as shown in Table 5.1. This process group begins with a **scope initiation** process whereby the project sponsor gives

Table **5.1** Scope Management Processes

Scope Management Process	*Description*
Project scope initiation	Ensuring that authority and resources are committed to developing a scope management plan.
Scope planning	Setting the scope boundary to determine what is and what is not included in the project work.
Scope definition	Identifying the product and project deliverables that support the project's MOV.
Scope verification	Confirming that the project's scope is accurate, complete, and supports the project's MOV.
Scope change control	Ensuring that controls are in place to manage scope changes once the project's scope is set. These procedures must be communicated to all project stakeholders.

the project manager the authority and resources to define the scope of the project. In the context of the IT project methodology, the authority to commit time and resources to define the project's scope is included in the second phase when the project charter and project plan are developed.

Once the commitment and resources to develop the project charter and plan are in place, the next process focuses on **scope planning.** This planning process entails setting the boundary of the project in order to determine what is and what is not to be included in the project work.

The third process centers on **scope definition.** While scope planning defines the project boundary, scope definition identifies the project deliverables (as identified in the IT project methodology) and the product deliverables (the high-level functionality or features of the IT product to be delivered by the project team). As a result, the boundary and deliverables defined by the scope planning and definition processes provide a key component for developing the project charter and plan. Moreover, the boundary and deliverables become critical inputs for estimating the project's schedule and budget.

Once the scope is defined, the process of **scope verification** confirms that the scope is complete and accurate. The project team and sponsor must agree to all of the project deliverables. This not only sets expectations, but also focuses the project team on what needs to get done and what is outside the scope of the project.

Time and resources will be wasted needlessly if the scope of the project is never defined accurately or agreed upon. However, changes to the scope may be inevitable as new information becomes available or if the needs of the organization change. Therefore, a process called **scope change control** is needed to handle these changes so that if a scope change is appropriate, the change can be approved in order to amend the project's schedule and budget accordingly. In addition, scope change control procedures also protect the scope boundary from expanding as a result of *increasing featurism,* requests by project stakeholders to keep adding additional features and functions (i.e., bells and whistles) to the project once the scope has been set. Remember that the scope, schedule, and budget relationships suggest that increasing the project's scope (i.e., expanding the scope boundary) will generally require an increase in schedule and budget. Therefore, adding additional work to the project's scope will ultimately lead to a project that misses its deadline and costs more than originally estimated. Subsequently, once the project's scope has been set, approved changes to the project's scope must be reflected in the project's baseline plan.

Together, the processes and techniques for defining and managing scope make up the **scope management plan.** Depending on the size and nature of the project, this plan can be separate and/or summarized in the project charter. Regardless, the procedures for defining and managing the scope of a project must be communicated and understood by all of the project's stakeholders to minimize the likelihood of misunderstandings. Moreover, the project's scope must align and support the project's MOV. Why spend time and resources to perform work that will not add any value to the organization or help the project achieve its MOV? Again, work that does not add value consumes valuable time and resources needlessly. Figure 5.1 summarizes the components and processes of a scope management plan.

PROJECT SCOPE INITIATION

Scope initiation provides a beginning process that formally authorizes the project manager and team to develop the scope management plan. In terms of the IT project methodology, this authorization is given after the project is formally accepted and funds are committed to developing the project charter and plan by the project sponsor or client. The business case provides important information about the project's description, MOV, risks, assumptions, and feasibility. In addition, the business case provides information about the background of the project in terms of why it was proposed and how it aligns with the organization's overall strategic plan.

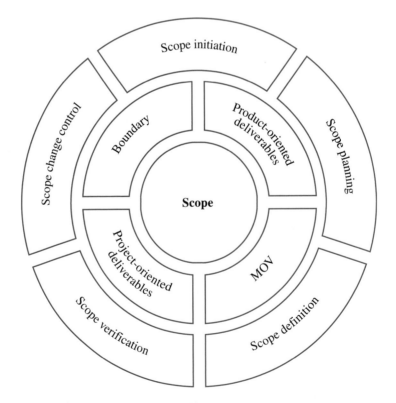

Figure 5.1 Scope Management Plan

Project Scope Planning

> Failure to define what is part of the project, as well as what is not, may result in work being performed that was unnecessary to create the product of the project and thus lead to both schedule and budget overruns.
>
> Olde Curmudgeon, *PM Network Magazine,* 1994.

Scope planning is a process for defining and documenting the project work. More specifically, a project's scope defines all the work, activities, and deliverables that the project team must provide in order for the project to achieve its MOV. It is an important step in developing the project plan since one must know what work must be done before an estimate can be made on how long it will take and how much it will cost.

Scope Boundary

Defining the scope boundary is the first step to establishing what is, and what is not, part of the project work to be completed by the project team. Think of the scope boundary as a fence designed to keep certain things in and other things out. As Figure 5.2 illustrates, any work within the scope boundary should include only the work or activities that support the project's MOV. This work is what we want to capture and keep within our fence. On the other hand, a project team can spend a great deal of time doing work and activities that will not help the project achieve its MOV. As a result, the project will consume time and resources with very little return. Therefore, the scope boundary must protect the scope from these activities once it is set and agreed upon by the project stakeholders. Having a clear and agreed upon definition of the project MOV is critical for defining and managing the scope boundary.

The Scope Statement

One way to define the scope boundary is to create a **scope statement** that documents the project sponsor's needs and expectations. For example, let's say we are outside consultants hired to develop an electronic commerce application for a bank. After developing and presenting a business case to our client, we have been given the authority to develop the project charter and plan. Although the business case provides a great deal of relevant information, we will still set up several meetings and interviews with key stakeholders in the bank. Based upon these meetings and interviews, we create a scope statement.

Scope Statement

1. Develop a proactive electronic commerce strategy that identifies the processes, products, and services to be delivered through the World Wide Web.

2. Develop an application system that supports all of the processes, products, and services identified in the electronic commerce strategy.

3. Integrate the application system with the bank's existing enterprise resource planning system.

It is just as important to clarify what work is not to be included, that is, what work is outside the scope of the project. Often the

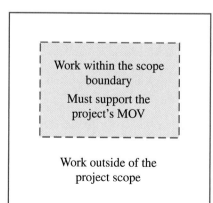

Figure 5.2 Scope Boundary

scope of a project is defined through interviews, meetings, or brainstorming sessions. Stakeholders often suggest ideas that are interesting, but not feasible or appropriate for the current project.

Let's say that in our example a certain bank vice president pushed for a customer relationship management (CRM) and a data mining component to be included in the application system. The bank's president, however, has decided that the time and effort to add these components cannot be justified because launching the Web site in eight months is vital to bank's competitive strategy. Let's also assume that conducting technology and organizational assessments of our client's current environment is an important piece of our project methodology. But because the bank would like to control some of the costs of this project, we agree that its IT department will conduct that study. The results of this study will then be documented and provided to us.

In this case, it is critical that we define explicitly both what is and what is not part of the project scope. Individuals from both organizations may believe that specific project work (i.e., the assessment study), system features, or functionality (i.e., CRM and data mining) will be part of this project. These beliefs may result in misunderstandings that lead to false expectations or needless work. To manage these expectations, it is useful to list explicitly what is *not* part of the project's scope.

Out of Scope for this Project

1. Technology and organizational assessment of the current environment
2. Customer resource management and data mining components

Setting the scope boundary for the project not only sets expectations, but also can define the constraints of the project and how the product of the organization fits within the organization, that is, the system must integrate with the organization's existing systems.

The scope statement provides a very general and high-level view of the project work and provides only a starting point for defining the scope of our project. At the beginning of a project understanding of the project's scope may be limited. However, as we work more closely with our client more information is uncovered and our understanding of the project increases. Subsequently, the project scope will evolve from being very general and high level to more detailed and defined.

THE OREGON DEPARTMENT OF MOTOR VEHICLES

In 1993, the Oregon Department of Motor Vehicles (DMV) began a project to automate its manual system. The project was originally scheduled to be completed in five years and cost $50 million; but state officials envisioned saving $7.5 million a year by reducing its DMV staff by 20 percent. By 1995, the project's deadline had been extended to 2001 with expected costs escalating to $123 million. A prototype was implemented in a test office in 1996, but soon lines of people backed up around the block. The system was considered a total failure, and the project was cancelled. The project failed because the project team did not accurately define the project's scope. The state's procurement and development rules were followed, and the project's vendor delivered everything promised on time But no one thought to have the vendor integrate the new system. Subsequently, there was a strict process, but no tangible result from the project.

SOURCE: Adapted from When Bad Things Happen to Good Projects, *CIO*, October 15, 1997, http://www.cio.com/archive/101597/bad.html.

PROJECT SCOPE DEFINITION

Developing a scope statement is a useful first step for defining the scope of the project and setting a boundary. A project's scope, however, should also be defined in terms of the deliverables that the team must provide. These deliverables can be divided into project-oriented deliverables and product-oriented deliverables. This separation gives the team a clearer definition of the work to be accomplished and improves the likelihood of accurately assigning resources and estimating the time and cost of completing the work. Moreover, a clear definition of the project's deliverables sets unambiguous expectations and agreement among all of the project stakeholders.

Project-Oriented Scope

Project-oriented deliverables, or scope, support the project management and IT development processes that are defined in the information technology project methodology (ITPM). Project scope includes such things as the business case, project charter, and project plan and defines the work products of the various ITPM phases. Project-oriented deliverables also include specific deliverables such as a current systems study, requirements definition, and the documented design of the information system. These are deliverables supported by the systems development life cycle (SDLC) component of the overall ITPM.

Project-oriented deliverables require time and resources and, therefore, must be part of the overall project schedule and budget. Their role is to ensure that the project processes are being competed so that the project's product (i.e., the information system) achieves the project's MOV and objectives. Project-oriented deliverables also provide tangible evidence of the project's progress (or lack of progress). Finally, they allow the project manager to set a baseline for performance and quality control because they usually require some form of approval before work on the next project phase or deliverable begins.

Project-Oriented Scope Definition Tools   All of the project deliverables must have a clear and concise definition. One way to communicate the project's deliverables is to create a **deliverable definition table (DDT).** An example of a DDT for our bank's electronic commerce system is illustrated in Table 5.2.

The purpose of the DDT is to define all of the project-oriented deliverables to be provided by the project team. Each deliverable should have a clear purpose. In addition, it is important to define the structure of the deliverable. For example, a deliverable could be a document (paper or electronic), prototype, presentation, or the application system itself. This sets the expectation of what will be *delivered* by the project team. Moreover, the standards provide a means to verify whether the deliverable was produced correctly. These standards could be defined within the IT Project methodology, controlling agency (e.g., International Organization for Standardization), or through various quality standards established by the organization. Each deliverable must be verified and approved generally by the project sponsor and/or the project manager. It is important that the responsibility for approving a deliverable be clearly defined as well. Once a deliverable is approved, the project team is authorized to begin work on the next deliverable. This provides authorization control as well as a basis for logically sequencing the work. Finally, it is important that the resources required to complete the deliverable be defined. This will provide the foundation for determining not only what resources will be needed for the project, but also for estimating the time and cost in completing each deliverable.

Table 5.2 Deliverable Definition Table

Deliverable	Structure	Standards	Approval Needed By	Resources Required
Business case	Document	As defined in the project methodology	Project sponsor	Business case team & office automation (OA) tools
Project charter & project plan	Document	As defined in the project methodology	Project sponsor	Project manager, project sponsor, & OA tools
Technology & organizational assessment	Document	As defined in the project methodology	Project manager & project sponsor	Bank's systems analysts users, case tool, and OA tools
Requirements definition	Document	As defined in the project methodology	Project manager	System analyst, users, case tool, & OA tools
User interface	Prototype	As defined in the user interface guidelines	Project sponsor	System analyst, programmer, users, & integrated development environment (IDE)
Physical & technical design	Document	As defined in the project methodology	Project manager & project sponsor	System analyst, programmer, & case tool
Application system	Files & database	As defined in the project methodology	Project sponsor	Programmers, system analysts, network specialists, program development tools, and relational database management system
Testing plan	Document	As defined in the project methodology	Project manager	System analysts & OA tools
Testing results	Document	As defined in the test plan	Project manager	Programmers, system analysts, & OA tools
Change management and implementation plan	Document	As defined in the project methodology	Project manager	Systems analysts & OA tools
Training program	User documentation & training class	As defined in the implementation plan	Project manager & project sponsor	Trainers, documentation writers, & OA tools
Final report & presentation	Document	As defined in the project methodology	Project sponsor	Project Sponsor, project manager, & OA tools
Project evaluations & lessons learned	Document	As defined in the project methodology	Project manager & senior	Project team, knowledge management system

SOURCE: Inspired by Graham McLeod and Derek Smith, *Managing Information Technology Projects* (San Francisco: Boyd & Fraser, 1996), 51–52.

Once the deliverables have been defined in the DDT, a **deliverable structure chart (DSC)** can be developed as an interim step to define detailed work packages that will be used to estimate the project schedule and budget. Later on, these work packages will be used to create a **work breakdown structure (WBS)**—a tool used to help create the project plan. For example, Figure 5.3 provides an example of a

PROJECT SCOPE: KEEP IT SIMPLE

Since 1994, the Standish Group has studied over twenty-three thousand projects. It found that the number of IT projects delivered on time and within budget for *Fortune* 500 companies increased from 9 percent in 1994 to 24 percent by 1998. The average cost of IT projects has decreased from $2.3 million to $1.2 million as a result of a reduction in project scope. It appears that the likelihood of a project being developed on time and within budget is negatively correlated with project size. In other words, projects that take less than six months, have fewer than six people, and cost less than $750,000 have the highest probability of meeting the schedule and budget objectives. According to

Jim Johnson, president of Standish Group International, the best way to design and manage projects is to follow an iterative process that focuses on the most key features. Although more features can be added later on, they will probably be deemed unnecessary. The study also found that user involvement, executive support, experienced project management, clear business objectives, and good communication were important to project success.

SOURCE: Adapted from Kathleen Melymuka, With IT Projects, Small is Beautiful, *Computerworld,* June 18, 1998. http://www.computerworld.com/news/1998/story/0,11280,25731,00.html

Deliverable Structure Chart that maps the project life cycle and systems development life cycle phases to the deliverables defined in the DDT.

Product-Oriented Scope

Although the electronic commerce application system is listed as a project-oriented deliverable, we really do not have any idea what exactly will be delivered to the client. In general, the application system will be the largest project deliverable and will, therefore, require the most time and resources to complete. Identifying the features and functionality of the application system (and their complexity) will be pivotal for estimating the time and cost of producing this deliverable.

Product-Oriented Scope Definition Tools   Product scope therefore focuses on identifying the features and functionality of the information system to be implemented.

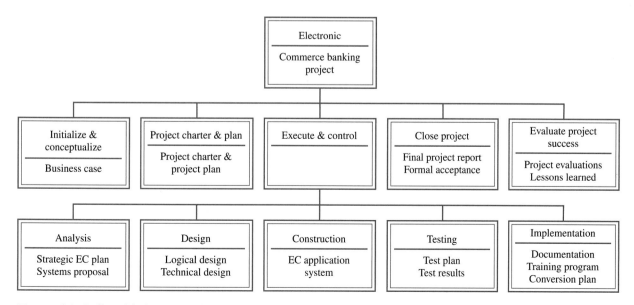

Figure 5.3 Deliverable Structure Chart (DSC)

A useful tool for refining the scope boundary and defining what the system must do is a modeling tool called a context level **data flow diagram (DFD).** A DFD is a process model that has been available for quite some time and is often taught in systems analysis and design courses. A context level DFD, however, presents a high-level representation of the system that has one process (i.e., a circle or rounded rectangle that represents the system as a whole) and depicts all the inflows and outflows of data and information between the system and its external entities. The external entities are usually represented by a square and can be people, departments, or other systems that provide or receive flows of data. Arrows represent the directional flow of data between external entities and the system. Each arrow and entity should be labeled appropriately. Lower level DFDs can be developed later to model the processes and flows of data in greater detail. An example of a context level DFD for our banking electronic commerce system is provided in Figure 5.4. As you can see, the high level features and functionality of the system focus on what the system must do.

Another useful tool for defining the product scope is the **use case diagram,** which has been used in the object-oriented world as part of the Unified Modeling Language (UML). While Jacobson (Jacobson, Cristerson et al. 1992) introduced the use case as a tool for software development, a use case diagram can provide a high level model for defining, verifying, and reaching agreement upon the product scope.

The use case diagram is a relatively simple diagram in terms of symbols and syntax, but it is a powerful tool for identifying the main functions or features of the system and the different users or external systems that interact with the system. At this early stage of the project, the use case can provide a high level diagram that can be further refined and detailed during requirements analysis later in the project.

Actors are people (i.e., users, customers, managers, etc.) or external systems (i.e., the bank's ERP system) that interact, or *use,* the system. Think of actors in terms of roles (e.g., customer) instead of as specific individuals (e.g., Tom Smith). A **use case,**

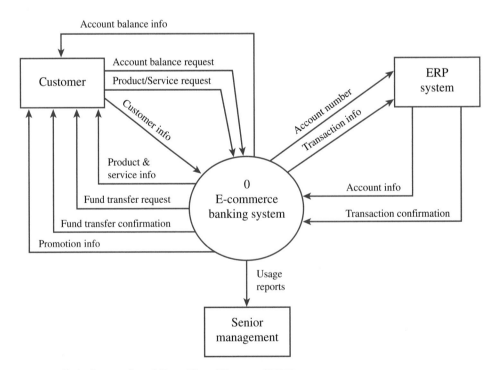

Figure 5.4 Context Level Data Flow Diagram (DFD)

on the other hand, depicts the major functions the system must perform for an actor or actors. When developing a use case diagram, actors are identified using stick figures, while use cases are defined and represented using ovals. Figure 5.5 provides an example of a use case diagram for the bank example.

As you can see in Figure 5.5, the use case diagram provides a simple yet effective overview of the functions and interactions between the use cases and the actors. The box separating the use cases from the actors also provides a system boundary that defines the scope boundary. Use cases inside the boundary are considered within the scope of the project, while anything outside of the boundary is considered outside the scope of the project. Listing the actors provides an opportunity to identify various stakeholders and can be useful for understanding the needs of the organization as a whole. It can be useful not only for addressing competing needs among various stakeholders, but also for identifying security issues as well (Fowler and Scott 1997). The development of a use case diagram is an iterative process that can be developed during a **joint application development (JAD)** session. JAD is a group-based method where the users and systems analysts jointly define the system requirements or design the system (Turban, Rainer and Potter 2001).

The use case diagram used to define the product scope can be used to refine the level of detail and functionality later on in our project. Following our example, the use case diagram in Figure 5.5 identifies the customer actor as using the system to transfer payments. However, a scenario or set of scenarios could be developed during the analysis and design phases of our project to determine how a customer would transfer funds successfully, while another scenario might focus on what happens when a customer has insufficient funds in their account. This level of detail is more suited to the requirements definition rather than the scope definition. At this point, it is more important to identify that the system must allow a customer to transfer funds than to identify how the funds may be transferred. Later on, the product scope can be compared or measured against the detailed requirements. These detailed requirements will be defined during the SDLC component of the ITPM.

But what is the appropriate level of detail for defining the product scope? Knowing the right level of detail is more an art than a science. The right level allows the project manager to estimate the time it will take to produce the application system accurately. As the next chapter shows, estimating the time and effort to produce the application system deliverable depends on the size of the application, the number of features incorporated, and their level of complexity. Therefore, the quality of the estimates will be greatly influenced by our understanding of the information system to be delivered.

The time and resources committed to developing the project charter and plan may limit the amount of time and energy we can devote to defining the details of the information system. Thus, the objective during this planning stage of the project should be to secure enough detail about the information system to allow us to estimate the time and effort needed to produce this deliverable. During the analysis and design phases, we can commit more time and resources to increasing our understanding and to documenting the level of detail needed to built and deliver the system.

PROJECT SCOPE VERIFICATION

Once the project's scope has been defined, it must be verified. **Project scope verification** is the scope management process that provides a mechanism for ensuring that the project deliverables are completed according to the standards described in the

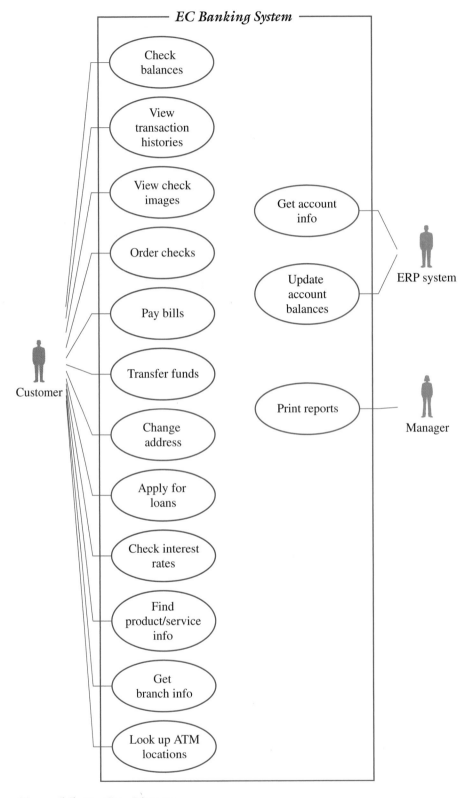

Figure 5.5 Use Case Diagram

DDT. Gray and Larson (2000) provide a project scope checklist for ensuring that the deliverables are completed—and completed correctly. This checklist has been adapted to include the MOV concept.

- *MOV*—Are the project's MOV clearly defined and agreed upon? Failure to define and agree upon the MOV could result in scope changes later in the project, which can lead to added work impacting the project's schedule and budget.

- *Deliverables*—Are the deliverables tangible and verifiable? Do they support the project's MOV?

- *Quality standards*—Are controls in place to ensure that the work was not only completed, but also completed to meet specific standards?

- *Milestones*—Are milestones defined for each deliverable? Milestones are significant events that mark the acceptance of a deliverable and give the project manager and team the approval to begin working on the next deliverable. In short, milestones tell us that a deliverable was not only completed, but also reviewed and accepted.

- *Review and acceptance*—Are both sides clear in their expectations? The project's scope must be reviewed and accepted by the project stakeholders. The project sponsor must formally accept the boundary, product to be produced, and the project-related deliverables. The project team must be clear on what it must deliver. In both cases, expectations must be realistic and agreed upon.

SCOPE CHANGE CONTROL

According to the PMBOK, **scope change control** is concerned with ensuring that any changes to the project scope will be beneficial, with determining that an actual scope change has occurred, and with managing the actual changes when and as they occur. Scope control is also concerned with:

- *Scope grope*—Scope grope is a metaphor that describes a project team's inability to define the project's scope. This situation is common early in a project when the project team and sponsor have trouble understanding what the project is supposed to accomplish. Scope grope can be minimized by having a clearly defined MOV and by following or applying the processes, concepts, and tools described in this chapter.

- *Scope creep*—Scope creep refers to *increasing featurism,* adding small yet time- and resource-consuming features to the system once the scope of the project has been approved. For example, a project sponsor may try to add various bells and whistles to the project scope. Yet, scope creep does not always come from the project sponsor side. The project team itself may come across interesting or novel ideas as the project work progresses. Its enthusiasm for adding these ideas can divert its attention or add features and functions to the system that the project sponsor did not ask for and does not need. Scope creep must be identified and controlled throughout the project because it will lengthen the project schedule and, in turn, lead to cost overruns.

- *Scope leap*—If scope creep is caused by increasing featurism, scope leap suggests a fundamental and significant change in the project scope. For example, the original scope for the bank's electronic commerce project was

SIX MYTHS OF SCOPE MANAGEMENT

Myth 1: User involvement will result in an IS project grounded in the realities of business needs.

Reality: Often user involvement is really a vaguely stated idea from senior management handed off to someone in the user community. Involvement by proxy can create problems if the original *concept person* is too busy or unavailable to discuss the details.

Myth 2: A scope statement will clearly define what a project will do.

Reality: A good scope statement will also make it clear as to what the project will not attempt to do, which is especially important when specifying roles and responsibilities. Setting scope is much like putting a fence around the project. It not only keeps things in, it also keeps things out.

Myth 3: Once the scope of the project is defined, hold firm because any deviation from the original plan is a sign that the project is out of control.

Reality: Scope change is inevitable. Often schedules and budgets are set before enough details of the project are known. Early estimates should be revised as new information is acquired. Good scope management, however, involves a change management committee of senior management who review proposed changes and decide whether an additional feature or requirement should be added to the project's scope.

Myth 4: A function of a scope change committee is to arbitrate user requests for additional features or functionality beyond the original project charter.

Reality: Scope problems go beyond additional user demands. Scope changes will affect schedule, budget, or both. Slippage of the schedule will require additional resources or reduced functionality. It is also important that the project not get off track while the scope change committee reviews a particular change.

Myth 5: Regular and frequent meetings with senior management will ensure they are kept up to date and will result in goodwill and support.

Reality: They may not be listening. It is important to keep their attention and involvement by focusing on the benefits of the system.

Myth 6: You can always make up schedules and budgets later on if they slip a little bit.

Reality: Catching up is a rare occurrence. Projects rarely fail overnight, and project managers must be vigilant for early warning signs. If there are minor setbacks, it is important that the project manager be candid with senior management.

SOURCE: Adapted from Alice LaPlante, Scope Grope, *Computerworld*, March 20, 1995, http://www.computerworld.com/news/1995/story /0,11280,1340,00.html.

to provide new products and services to its customers. Scope creep may be adding a new feature, such as a new product or service, not originally defined in the project's scope. Scope leap, on the other hand, is an impetus to change the project so that the electronic commerce system would allow the bank to obtain additional funding in the open market. Adding this activity would dramatically change the entire scope and focus of the project. Scope leap can occur as a result of changes in the environment, the business, and the competitive makeup of the industry. Scope leap entails changing the MOV and, therefore, requires that the organization rethink the value of the current project. If this change is critical, the organization may be better off pulling the plug on the current project and starting over by conceptualizing and initiating a new project.

Scope Change Control Procedures

A scope change procedure should be in place before the actual work on the project commences. It can be part of, or at least referenced in, the project charter so that it is communicated to all project stakeholders. This procedure should allow for the identification and handling of all requested changes to the project's scope. Scope change requests can be made, and each request's impact on the project can be assessed. Then, a decision whether to accept or reject the scope change can be made.

JUST ONE MORE BELL—ONE MORE WHISTLE

Scope creep is a widespread problem. A *Computerworld* survey of 160 IS professionals revealed that 80 percent of the respondents said scope creep "always" or "frequently" occurs. Moreover, 44 percent responded that "poor initial requirements definition" was the leading cause for scope creep. In addition, only 16 percent of the respondents said "no" when users demanded significant changes once the project was well under way. To reduce scope creep, 63 percent of the respondents use JAD and 25 percent use prototyping. A classic case of scope creep is provided in a research study by Mark Keil of Georgia State University, which focused on an artificial intelligence application designed to help sales people of a large computer vendor configure computer systems. Although scope creep may arise as a result of not getting the scope of a project defined

properly, Keil found that sales staff did not care for the system because they, the system's would-be users, were rewarded on sales volume and not the accuracy or completeness of the order. Thus, they began to make excuses for not using the system. These excuses became scope changes, and the project began to take on a life of its own that led to project escalation. The company eventually canceled the project after the company spent tens of millions of dollars over eleven years.

SOURCE: Adapted from Mark Keil, Pulling the Plug: Software Project Management and the Problem of Project Escalation, *MIS Quarterly*, December 1995, 421–447; and Gary H. Anthes, No More Creeps: Are You a Victim of Creeping User Requirements? *Computerworld*, May 2, 1994, http://www.computerworld.com/news/1994/story/0,11280 ,15919,00.html.

A scope change procedure may include a scope change request form. An example of a scope change request form is illustrated in Figure 5.6. The individual or group making the scope change request should complete the form.

Regardless of the format for a scope change request form, it should contain some basic information. First, the description of the change request should be clearly defined so that the project manager and project team understand fully the nature and reason for the scope change. Second, the scope change should be justified, which separates the *would likes* from the *must haves*. In addition, several alternatives may be listed in order to assess the impact on scope, schedule, resources, and cost. Often a trade-off or compromise will be suitable if the impact of the scope change is too great. The project sponsor must understand and approve these impacts because the baseline project plan will have to be adjusted accordingly. Alternatives may include reducing functionality in other areas of the project, extending the project deadline, or adding more resources in terms of staff, overtime, or technology. Finally, all scope changes must be approved so that additional resources can be committed to the project.

However, nothing can be more frustrating than making a request and then not hearing anything. Too often requests fall through the cracks, leading to credibility concerns and accusations that the project manager or project team is not being responsive to the client's needs. Therefore, a scope change control procedure should be logged with the intention that each request will be reviewed and acted upon. As seen in Figure 5.7, an example of a Change Request Log includes information as to who has the authority to make the scope change decision and when a response can be expected.

Although this may seem like the beginning of a bureaucracy, it is really designed to protect all project stakeholders. Too often the project manager and project team feel the pressure to say yes to each and every scope change request because their refusal may be interpreted as being uncooperative. Unfortunately, introducing scope creep will impact the schedule and budget. As the deadline passes or as costs begin to overrun the budget, the project manager and team then may come under fire for not controlling the project objectives.

Scope change request form

Requestor name: _____   Request date: _____

Request title: _____   Request number: _____

Request description:

Justification:

Possible alternatives:

Impacts	Alternative 1	Alternative 2	Alternative 3
Scope			
Schedule			
Resources required			
Cost			

Recommendation:

Authorized by   *Date*

_____   _____

Figure 5.6 Scope Change Request Form

Request Number	Request Title	Date of Request	Requested By	Priority (L, M, H)	Authority to Approve Request	Expected Response Date	Scope Change Approved? (Y/N)

Figure 5.7 Scope Change Request Log

Still, a project manager and team should not say no to every scope change request. Some changes will be beneficial and warranted as the project proceeds. The question then becomes, What should be the basis for making a scope change decision?

As you have seen, the project's MOV guides the project planning process. Similarly, the project's MOV can also guide scope change decisions. A scope change request should be approved if—and only if—the scope change can bring the project closer to achieving its MOV; otherwise, why bother adding additional work, resources, time, and money to activities that will not bring any value to the organization?

Benefits of Scope Control

The most important benefit of scope change control procedures is that they keep the project manager in control of the project. More specifically, they allow the project manager to manage and control the project's schedule and budget. Scope control procedures also allow the project team to stay focused and on track in terms of meeting its milestones because it does not have to perform unnecessary work.

CHAPTER SUMMARY

Although scope is the work to be performed on the project, a project's scope can be defined as the boundary and deliverables that the project team will provide to the project sponsor. A scope boundary acts as a fence to ensure that what needs to get done, gets done—and only what needs to get done, gets done. Performing work that does not help the project achieve its MOV needlessly consumes valuable time and resources. Therefore, the project's boundary helps the project team define the limits of the project and how it will interact with its environment. In addition, deliverables are tangible units of work that ensure that the project is on track. Deliverables may be product-oriented or project-oriented. Product-oriented deliverables focus on the high level features and functionality of the application system—the project's product. On the other hand, project-oriented deliverables focus on the project's processes as defined in the IT project methodology.

The Project Management Body of Knowledge identifies five processes that make up the scope management process group. These processes include: (1) Scope Initiation, (2) Scope Planning, (3) Scope Definition, (4) Scope Verification, and (5) Scope Change Control. Figure 5.8 summarizes these processes and the tools used to support them.

Scope grope is a common occurrence in the early stages of the project. Often the project team struggles to define what the project is all about and what work must be done. By applying the concept of an MOV and the tools introduced in this chapter, the time a project team spends searching for these answers should be reduced. Scope creep, on the other hand, is a common occurrence in many projects. It entails adding additional features or functions to the scope once the scope has been set and approved. This phenomenon can increase the schedule and budget, causing the project to miss its deadline and budget targets. Scope creep can be managed by (1) verifying that the scope is accurate and complete by using a scope verification checklist, and (2) ensuring that appropriate scope changes are approved and reflected in the baseline plan by having scope change procedures. The MOV concept can guide this decision process. For example, scope changes that move the project closer to achieving its MOV should be approved, while those that do not merely waste time and resources. Lastly, scope leap entails a major and fundamental change to the project scope. It may be the result of a changing business environment or the competitive makeup of the industry. Such a radical departure from the original business case may require the project stakeholders to rethink the viability of the current project.

REVIEW QUESTIONS

1. What is meant by project scope?
2. Briefly describe the five scope management processes.
3. What is the project's scope initiation process? When does it occur? Why is it important?
4. How is a project's scope initiation process supported by the IT project methodology?
5. Briefly describe the scope planning process.
6. Briefly describe the scope definition process.
7. Briefly describe the scope verification process.

Scope Management Processes

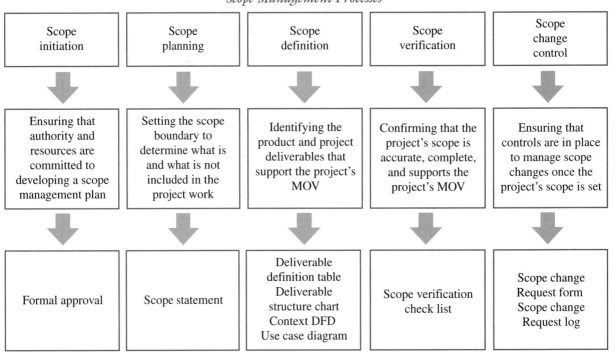

Figure 5.8 Scope Management Processes and Tools

8. Briefly describe the scope change control process.

9. Describe the scope management plan in Figure 5.1.

10. Why is it important to define the project's scope accurately and completely?

11. What is a scope boundary? What purpose does it serve?

12. What is the difference between product-oriented deliverables and project-oriented deliverables?

13. How does a project's scope support the MOV concept?

14. What is a scope statement? What purpose does it serve?

15. What is a context dataflow diagram (DFD)? What purpose does it serve?

16. How does a use case diagram help to define the project's scope?

17. What is a deliverable definition table (DDT)? What purpose does it serve?

18. What is a deliverable structure chart (DSC)? How does it map to a deliverable definition table (DDT)?

19. What is a work breakdown structure (WBS)? How does it map to the DDT and DSC?

20. Briefly describe what must be included in a scope verification checklist?

21. What is the purpose of verifying a project's scope?

22. What is the purpose of scope change control procedures?

23. Briefly describe scope grope.

24. Briefly describe scope creep.

25. Briefly describe scope leap.

26. What are the benefits of having scope control procedures?

27. Briefly describe what should be included on a scope change request form.

28. What is the purpose of a scope change request log?

EXTEND YOUR KNOWLEDGE

1. Using the Web or library, find an article about an unsuccessful IT project. Discuss whether poor scope management had any bearing on the project being unsuccessful.

2. Discuss the statement: Failing to define what is not part of the project is just as important as failing to define what is part of the project.

3. Choose a company that sells a product or service on the Web. Using this Web site as a guide, develop the following (even though the application is already in existence). You may make assumptions where necessary, but be sure to document them.

   a. Scope statement

   b. Context level DFD

   c. Use case diagram

BIBLIOGRAPHY

Fowler, M. and K. Scott 1997. UML Distilled: Applying the Standard Object Modeling Language. Reading, Mass.: Addison-Wesley.

Gray, C. F. and E. W. Larson 2000. Project Management: The Managerial Process. Boston: Irwin McGraw-Hill.

Jacobson, I., M. Cristerson, P. Jonsson, and G. Overgaard 1992. Object-Oriented Software Engineering: A Use-Case Driven Approach. Reading, Mass.: Addison-Wesley.

Turban, E., R. K. Rainer, Jr., and R.E. Potter 2001. Introduction to Information Technology. New York: John Wiley.

6

The Work Breakdown Structure and Project Estimation

CHAPTER OVERVIEW

Chapter 6 focuses on developing the work breakdown structure, as well as on introducing a number of project estimation approaches, tools, and techniques. After studying this chapter, you should understand and be able to:

- Develop a work breakdown structure.
- Describe the difference between a deliverable and a milestone.
- Describe and apply several project estimation methods. These include the Delphi technique, time boxing, top-down estimation, and bottom-up estimation.
- Describe and apply several software engineering estimation approaches. These include lines of code (LOC), function point analysis, COCOMO, and heuristics.

GLOBAL TECHNOLOGY SOLUTIONS

The white board in the GTS conference room was filled with multicolor markings reflecting the ideas and suggestions from the Husky Air team. Several empty pizza boxes were piled neatly in the corner. It had been an all-day working session for the Husky Air project team. Although it was late in the day, the energy in the room was still high. Everyone felt they were drawing closer to a first draft of the project plan.

Tim Williams stood up and walked over to the electronic white board. Addressing the group, he said, "It looks like we have just about everything we need, but I would like to make sure all of the activities or tasks in the systems testing phase are defined more clearly. Let's start out by identifying what deliverables we need to produce as a result of the testing phase."

Sitaramin paged through his notes and said that the team had identified a test plan and a test results report as part of the project scope. Yan, the project's database administrator, suggested that the test report summarize not only the results of the system tests, but also what was tested and how the tests were conducted. The rest of the team agreed, and Tim wrote *TESTING PHASE* in capital letters on the board and then *Deliverable: Test Results Report* underneath it. Yan then suggested that the phase needed a milestone. Sitaramin said that the testing phase would not be completed when the report was finished, but only when the test results were acceptable to the client. The rest of the team agreed and Tim wrote *Milestone: Client signs off on test results.*

Tim then asked what specific activities or tasks the team would have to do to create the test results report. For the next ten minutes, the entire team brainstormed ideas. Tim dutifully wrote each idea on the board without judgment and only asked for clarification or help spelling a particular word. After working together for only a short time, the team had already adopted an unwritten rule that no one was to evaluate an idea until after they finished the brainstorming activity. They had found that this encouraged participation from everyone and allowed for more creative ideas.

After a few minutes, the frequency of new ideas suggested by the team started to slow. Tim then asked if any of these ideas or suggestions were similar—i.e., did they have the same meaning or could they be grouped. Again, everyone had ideas and suggestions, and Tim rewrote the original list until the team agreed on a list of activities that would allow them to develop the test results plan.

"This looks pretty good!" exclaimed Tim. Then he added, "But do all of these activities have to be followed one after the other? Or can some of these activities be completed in parallel by different team members?"

Once again, the team began making suggestions and discussing ideas of how to best sequence these activities. This only took a few minutes, but everyone could to see how the testing phase of the project was taking shape. Tim paused, took a few steps back, and announced, "Ok, it looks like we're headed in the right direction. Now who will be responsible for completing these tasks and what resources will they need?"

Since everyone on the team had a specific role, the assigning of team members to the tasks was pretty straightforward. Some of the tasks required only one person, while others needed two or more. The team also identified a few activities where the same person was assigned to tasks scheduled at the same time. The team's discussion also identified an important activity that was overlooked and needed to be added.

Tim joked that he was glad they were using a white board that could easily be erased as he carefully updated the activities and assignments. Then he smiled and said, "Our work breakdown structure is almost complete. All we need to do now is estimate how long each of these testing activities will take. Once we have these estimates, we can enter the work breakdown structure into the project management software package we're using to get the schedule and budget. I think we'll need to review our project plan as a team at least one more time before we present it to our client. I'm sure we'll have to make some changes along the way, but I would say the bulk of our planning work is almost complete."

It was getting late in the day, and the team was starting to get tired. Ted, a telecommunications specialist, suggested that they all meet the next day to finalize the time estimates for the testing phase activities. He also asked that before they adjourned, the team should once again develop an action plan based upon facts the team knew to be true, any assumptions to be tested, and what they would need to find out in order to estimate each of the testing phase activities.

The rest of the team agreed, and they began another learning cycle.

Things to Think About

1. What are some advantages of a project team working together to develop the project plan? What are some disadvantages?

2. Why should the project team members not be too quick to judge the ideas and suggestions provided during a brainstorming session?

3. How can the concept of learning cycles support the project planning process?

INTRODUCTION

In the last chapter, you learned about defining and managing the project's scope, i.e., the work to be done in order to achieve the project's MOV or goal. Defining and understanding what you have to do is an important first step to determining how you're going to do the work that has to be done. In this chapter, we will focus on defining the tasks or activities that need to be carried out in order to complete all of the scope-related deliverables as promised. Moreover, we also need to estimate or forecast the amount of time each activity will take so that we can determine the overall project schedule.

The Project Management Body of Knowledge (PMBOK) area called **project time management** focuses on the processes necessary to develop the project schedule and to ensure that the project is completed on time. As defined in the PMBOK, project time management includes:

- *Activity definition*—identifying what activities must be completed in order to produce the project scope deliverables.

- *Activity sequencing*—determining whether activities can be completed sequentially or in parallel and any dependencies that may exist among them.

- *Activity duration estimation*—estimating the time to complete each activity.

- *Schedule development*—based upon the availability of resources, the activities, their sequence, and time estimates, a schedule for the entire budget can be developed.

- *Schedule control*—ensuring that proper processes and procedures are in place in order to control changes to the project schedule.

In this chapter, we will concentrate on two of these processes: activity definition and activity estimation. These are key processes that deserve special attention because they are required inputs for developing the project network model that will determine the project's schedule and budget. In the next chapter, you will see how we put this all together to develop the detailed project plan.

The remainder of this chapter will introduce several important tools, techniques, and concepts. A **work breakdown structure (WBS)** is discussed first. It provides a hierarchical structure that outlines the activities or work that needs to be done in order to complete the project scope. The WBS also provides a bridge or link between the project's scope and the detailed project plan that will be entered into a project management software package.

Today, most project management software packages are relatively inexpensive and rich in features. It is almost unthinkable that anyone would plan and manage a project without such a tool. Project success, however, will not be determined by one's familiarity with a project management software package or the ability to produce nice looking reports and graphs. It is the thought process that must be followed before using the tool that counts! Thinking carefully through the activities and their estimated durations first will make the use of a project management software package much more effective. You can still create nice looking reports and graphs, but you'll have more confidence in what those reports and graphs say.

Once the project activities are defined, the next step is to forecast, or estimate, how long each activity will take. Although a number of estimation methods and techniques are introduced here. Estimation is not an exact science. It is dependent upon a number of variables—the complexity of activity, the resources (i.e., people) assigned to complete the activity, and the tools and environment to support those individuals working on the activity (i.e., technology, facilities, etc.). Moreover, confidence in estimates will be lower early in the project because a full understanding of the problem or opportunity at hand is probably lacking. However, as we learn and uncover new information from our involvement in the project, our understanding of the project will increase as well. Although estimates may have to be revised periodically, we should gain more confidence in the updated schedule and budget. Even though no single estimation method will provide 100 percent accuracy all of the time, using one or a combination of methods is preferable to guessing.

THE WORK BREAKDOWN STRUCTURE (WBS)

In the last chapter, you learned how to define and manage the project's scope. As part of the scope definition process, several tools and techniques were introduced. For example, the deliverable definition table (DDT) and deliverable structure chart (DSC) identify the deliverables that must be provided by the project team.

Once the project's scope is defined, the next step is to define the activities or tasks the project team must do to fulfill the scope deliverable requirements. The work breakdown structure (WBS) is a useful tool for developing the project plan and links the project's scope to the schedule and budget. According to Gregory T. Haugan (2002),

> The WBS represents a logical decomposition of the work to be performed and focuses on how the product, service, or result is naturally subdivided. It is an outline of what work is to be performed. (17)

The WBS provides a framework for developing a tactical plan to structure the project work. PMBOK originally defined the WBS as a "deliverable-oriented hierarchy," but much debate and confusion has existed as to what a WBS should look like and how one should be built. Recently, the Project Management Institute formed a committee to recommend standards for the WBS. That committee recommends that no arbitrary limits should be imposed because the WBS should be flexible. Subsequently, the WBS can be used in different ways depending on the needs of the project manager and team.

Work Packages

The WBS decomposes, or subdivides, the project into smaller components and more manageable units of work called **work packages.** Work packages provide a logical basis for defining the project activities and assigning resources to those activities so that all the project work is identified (Haugan 2002). A work package makes it possible to develop a project plan, schedule, and budget and then later monitor the project's progress.

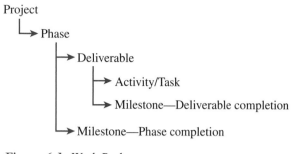

Figure 6.1 Work Package

As illustrated in Figure 6.1, a work package may be viewed as a hierarchy that starts with the project itself. The project is then decomposed into phases, with each phase having one or more deliverables as defined in the deliverable definition table and deliverable structure chart. More specifically, each phase should provide at least one specific deliverable—that is, a tangible and verifiable piece of work. Subsequently, activities or tasks are identified in order to produce the project's deliverables.

Deliverables and Milestones

One departure from most traditional views of a WBS is the inclusion of milestones. A **milestone** is a significant event or achievement that provides evidence that that deliverable has been completed or that a phase is formally over.

Deliverables and milestones are closely related, but they are not the same thing. Deliverables can include such things as presentations or reports, plans, prototypes, and the final application system. A milestone, on the other hand, must focus on an achievement. For example, a deliverable may be a prototype of the user interface, but the milestone would be a stakeholder's formal acceptance of the user interface. Only the formal acceptance or approval of the user interface by the project sponsor would allow the project team to move on to the next phase of the project.

In theory, if a project team succeeds in meeting all of its scheduled milestones, then the project should finish as planned. Milestones also provide several other advantages. First, milestones can keep the project team focused. It is much easier to concentrate your attention and efforts on a series of smaller, short-term deliverables than on a single, much larger deliverable scheduled for completion well into the future. On the other hand, if milestones are realistic, they can motivate a project team if their attainment is viewed as a success. If meeting a milestone signifies an important event, then the team should take pleasure in these successes before gearing up for the next milestone.

Milestones also reduce the risk of a project. The passing of a milestone, especially a phase milestone, should provide an opportunity to review the progress of the project. Additional resources should be committed at the successful completion of each milestone, while appropriate plans and steps should be taken if the project cannot meet its milestones.

Milestones can also be used to reduce risk by acting as **cruxes** or proof of concepts. Many times a significant risk associated with IT projects is the dependency on new technology or unique applications of the technology. A crux can be the testing of an idea, concept, or technology that is critical to the project's success. For example, suppose that an organization is building a data warehouse using a particular vendor's relational database product for the first time. A crux for this project may be the collection of data from several different legacy systems, cleansing this data, and then making it available in the relational database management system. The team may ensure that this can be accomplished using only a small amount of test data. Once the project team solves this problem on a smaller scale, they have proof that the concept or technique for importing the data from several legacy systems into the data warehouse can be done successfully. This breakthrough can allow them to incorporate what they have learned on a much larger scale. Subsequently, solving this crux is a milestone that would encourage the organization to invest more time and resources to complete the project.

Milestones can also provide a mechanism for quality control. Continuing with our example, just providing the users with an interface does not guarantee that it will be acceptable to them. Therefore, the completion of user interface deliverable should end only with their acceptance; otherwise, the team will be forced to make revisions. In short, the deliverable must not only be done, but must be done right.

Developing the WBS

Developing the WBS may require several versions until everyone is comfortable and confident that all of the work activities have been included. It is also a good idea to involve those who will be doing the work—after all, they probably know what has to be done better than anyone else.

The WBS can be quite involved, depending upon the nature and size of the project. To illustrate the steps involved, let's continue with our electronic commerce project example from the last chapter. As you may recall, we created a DDT and DSC to define the scope of the project. To make things easier to follow, let's focus on only one portion of the project—creating a document called the test results report. Figure 6.2 provides the DSC that we developed in Chapter 5. As you can see, two deliverables—the test plan and test results report—are to be completed and delivered during the testing phase of the project.

The DSC defines the phases and deliverables for our project. The next step is to develop sets of work packages for each of the phases and deliverables. After a team meeting, let's say that we have identified and discussed several activities that we need to do in order to produce the test results document:

- Review the test plan with the client so that key stakeholders are clear as to what we will be testing, how we will conduct the tests, and when the tests

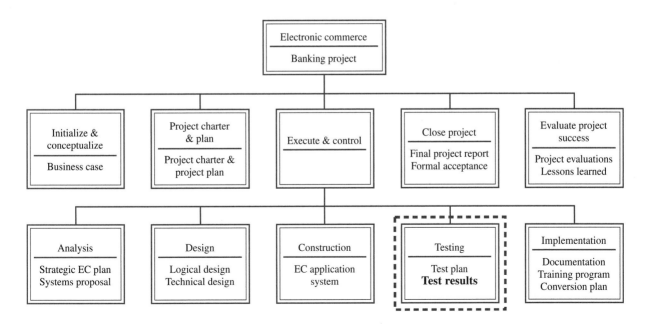

Figure 6.2 Deliverable Structure Chart (DSC) for EC Example

will be carried out. This review may be done as a courtesy or because we need specific support from the client's organization and, therefore, must inform them when that support will be required.

- After we have informed the client that we will test the system, we basically carry out the tests outlined in the test plan.
- Once we have collected the test results, we need to analyze them.
- After we analyze the results, we will need to summarize them in the form of a report and presentation to the client.
- If all goes well, then the client will approve or signoff on the test results. Then, we can move on to the implementation phase of our project. If all does not go well, we need to address and fix any problems. Keep in mind, that the test phase is not complete just because we have developed a test plan and created a test report. The client will sign off on the test results only if the system meets certain predetermined quality standards.

Figure 6.3 provides an example of a WBS with the details shown for only the testing phase of the project. As you can see, the WBS implements the concept of a work package for the project, phase, deliverable, task/activity, and milestone components that were illustrated in Figure 6.1. This particular WBS follows an outline format with a commonly used decimal numbering system that allows for continuing levels of detail.[1] If a software package is used to create the WBS, signs in front of each item can either hide or show the details. For example, clicking on "–6.2 Test Results Report" would roll up the details of this work package into "+6.2 Test Results Report". Similarly, clicking on any item with a "+" in front of it would expand that item to show the details associated with it.

The skills to develop a useful WBS generally evolve over time with practice and experience. Everyone, experienced or not, should keep in mind the following points when developing a WBS.

The WBS Should Be Deliverable-Oriented   Remember, the focus of a project should be to produce something, not merely on completing a specified number of activities. Although the WBS does not provide for any explicit looping, some activities may have to be repeated until the milestone is achieved. For example, software testing may uncover a number of problems or bugs that make the software system unacceptable to the client. As a result, these problems will have to be addressed and fixed and the same tests may have to be conducted again. This process may be repeated a number of times (while consuming the project schedule and budget) until the quality standards are met.

The WBS Should Support the Project's MOV   The WBS should include only tasks or activities that allow for the delivery of the project's deliverables. Before continuing with the development of the project plan, the project team should ensure that the WBS allows for the delivery of all the project's deliverables as defined in the project's scope. In turn, this will ensure that the project is more likely to achieve its MOV.

---

[1] Many people prefer to develop a WBS using a chart format, and the DSC in Figure 6.3 could be easily adapted by adding the work package levels. Although a graphic WBS can be visually appealing, it can also become extremely complex and confusing as more detail is added. Feel free to experiment with the WBS. The correct form will depend on the situation or your preference.

```
–0.0  EC Bank Project
        +1.0  Conceptualize & initialize project
        +2.0  Develop charter & plan
        +3.0  Analysis
        +4.0  Design
        +5.0  Construction
   ┌ ─ ─ ─ ─ ─ ─ ─ ─ ─ ─ ─ ─ ─ ─ ─ ─ ─ ─ ─ ─ ─ ─ ─ ─ ─ ─ ─ ─ ─ ┐
   │  –6.0  Testing                                              │
   │        +6.1  Test plan                                      │
   │    ┌──────────────────────────────────────────────────┐    │
   │    │ –6.2  Test results report                         │    │
   │    │        6.2.1   Review test plan with client       │    │
   │    │        6.2.2   Carry out test plan                │    │
   │    │        6.2.3   Analyze results                    │    │
   │    │        6.2.4   Prepare test results report and presentation │ │
   │    │        6.2.5   Present test results to client     │    │
   │    │        6.2.6   Address any software issues or problems │ │
   │    │        6.2.7   **Milestone:** client signs off on test results │ │
   │    └──────────────────────────────────────────────────┘    │
   │        +6.3  **Milestone:** testing completed               │
   └ ─ ─ ─ ─ ─ ─ ─ ─ ─ ─ ─ ─ ─ ─ ─ ─ ─ ─ ─ ─ ─ ─ ─ ─ ─ ─ ─ ─ ─ ┘
        +7.0  Implementation
        +8.0  Close project
        +9.0  Evaluate project success
```

Figure 6.3 Work Breakdown Structure

Haugen (2002) also suggests that the **100 percent rule** is the most important criterion in the developing and evaluating the WBS. The rule states: "The next level decomposition of a WBS element (child level) must represent 100 percent of the work applicable to the next higher (parent) element." (17) In other words, if each level of the WBS follows the 100 percent rule down to the activities, then we are confident that 100 percent of the activities will have been identified when we develop the project schedule. Moreover, 100 percent of the costs or resources required will be identified when we create the budget for our project.

The Level of Detail Should Support Planning and Control   The WBS provides a bridge between the project's scope and project plan—that is, the schedule and budget. Therefore, the level of detail should support not only the development of the project plan but also allow the project manager and project team to monitor and compare the project's actual progress to the original plan's schedule and budget. The two most common errors when developing a WBS are too little or too much detail. Too little detail may result in a project plan that overlooks and omits important activities and tasks. This will lead to an overly optimistic schedule and budget. On the other hand, the WBS should not be a to-do list of one-hour tasks. This excessive detail results in micromanagement that can have several adverse effects on the project. First, this may impact the project team's morale because most people on projects are professionals who do not want someone constantly looking over their shoulders. Second, the progress of each and every task must be tracked. As a result, the project plan will either not be updated frequently or clerical staff will have to be hired (at a cost to the project) just to keep everything current.

Developing the WBS Should Involve the People Who Will Be Doing the Work
One way to ensure that the WBS has the appropriate level of detail is to ensure that
the people who do the work are involved in its development. A person who has experience and expertise in a particular area probably has a better feel for what activities
need to be performed in order to produce a particular project deliverable. Although
the project manager is responsible for ensuring that a realistic WBS is developed, the
people who must carry out the activities and tasks may be more committed to the plan
if they are involved in its development.

Learning Cycles and Lessons Learned Can Support the Development of a WBS
By using the concept of learning cycles, the project team can focus on what they know
(the facts), what they think they know (assumptions), and what they need to find out
(research) in order to develop a more useful WBS. Lessons learned from previous
projects can be helpful in ensuring that the WBS and subsequent project plan are realistic and complete.

PROJECT ESTIMATION

Once the project deliverables and activities have been defined, the next step in developing the project schedule and budget is to estimate each activity's duration. One of
the most crucial—and difficult—activities in project management is estimating the
time it will take to complete a particular task. Since a resource generally performs a
particular task, a cost associated with that particular resource must be allocated as part
of the time it takes to complete that task. The time estimated to complete a particular
task will have a direct bearing on the project's budget as well. As T. Capers Jones
(Jones 1998) points out:

> The seeds of major software disasters are usually sown in the first
> three months of commencing the software project. Hasty schedul-
> ing, irrational commitments, unprofessional estimating techniques,
> and carelessness of the project management function are the factors
> that tend to introduce terminal problems. Once a project blindly
> lurches forward toward an impossible delivery date, the rest of the
> disaster will occur almost inevitably. (120)

In this section, we will review several estimation techniques—guesstimating,
Delphi, top-down and bottom-up estimating.

Guesstimating

Estimation by guessing or just picking numbers out of the air is not the best way to
derive a project's schedule and budget. Unfortunately, many inexperienced project
managers tend to **guesstimate,** or guess at the estimates, because it is quick and easy.
For example, we might guesstimate that testing will take two weeks. Why two weeks?
Why not three weeks? Or ten weeks? Because we are picking numbers out of thin air,
the confidence in these estimates will be quite low. You might as well pick numbers
out of a hat. The problem is that guessing at the estimates is based on feelings rather
than hard evidence.

However, many times a project manager is put on the spot and asked to provide
a ballpark figure. Be careful when quoting a time frame or cost off the record, because
whatever estimates you come up with often become on the record.

People are often overly optimistic and, therefore, their guesstimates are overly optimistic. Underestimating can result in long hours, reduced quality, and unmet client expectations. If you ever find yourself being pressured to guesstimate, your first impulse should be to stall until you have enough information to make a confident estimate. You may not, however, have that luxury so the best approach is to provide some kind of confidence interval. For example, if you think something will probably take three months and cost $30,000, provide a confidence interval of three to six months with a cost of $30,000 to $60,000. Then quickly offer to do a little more research to develop a more confident estimate. Notice that even though three months and $30,000 may be the most likely estimate, an estimate of two to six months was not made. Why? Because people tend to be optimists and the most likely case of finishing in three months is probably an optimistic case.

Delphi Technique

The **Delphi technique** involves multiple experts who arrive at a consensus on a particular subject or issue. Although the Delphi technique is generally used for group decision-making, it can be a useful tool for estimating when the time and money warrant the extra effort (Roetzheim and Beasley 1998).

To estimate using the Delphi technique, several experts need to be recruited to estimate the same item. Based upon information supplied, each expert makes an estimate and then all the results are compared. If the estimates are reasonably close, they can be averaged and used as an estimate. Otherwise, the estimates are distributed back to the experts who discuss the differences and then make another estimate.

In general, these rounds are anonymous and several rounds may take place until a consensus is reached. Not surprisingly, using the Delphi technique can take longer and cost more than most estimation methods, but it can be very effective and provide reasonable assurance when the stakes are high and the margin for error is low.

Time Boxing

Time boxing is a technique whereby a *box* of time is allocated for a specific activity or task. This allocation is based more on a requirement rather than on just guesswork. For example, a project team may have two (and only two) weeks to build a prototype. At the end of the two weeks, work on the prototype stops, regardless of whether the prototype is 100 percent complete.

Used effectively, time boxing can help focus the project team's effort on an important and critical task. The schedule pressure to meet a particular deadline, however, may result in long hours and pressure to succeed. Used inappropriately or too often, the project team members become burned out and frustrated.

Top-Down Estimating

Top-down estimating involves estimating the schedule and/or cost of the entire project in terms of how long it *should* take or how much it *should* cost. Top-down estimating is a very common occurrence that often results from a mandate made by upper management (e.g., Thou shalt complete the project within six months and spend no more than $500,000!).

Often the schedule and/or cost estimate is a product of some strategic plan or because someone *thinks* it should take a certain amount of time or cost a particular amount. On the other hand, top-down estimating could be a reaction to the business environment. For example, the project may have to be completed within six months as a result of a competitor's actions or to win the business of a customer (i.e., the customer needs this in six months).

Once the target objectives in terms of schedule or budget are identified, it is up to the project manager to allocate percentages to the various project life cycle phases and associated tasks or activities. Data from past projects can be very useful in applying percentages and ensuring that the estimates are reasonable. It is important to keep in mind that top-down estimating works well when the target objectives are reasonable, realistic, and achievable.

When made by people independent from the project team, however, these targets are often overly optimistic or overly aggressive. These unrealistic targets often lead to what Ed Yourdon (1999) calls a *death march* project:

> I define a death march project as one whose "project parameters" exceed the norm by at least 50 percent. This doesn't correspond to the "military" definition, and it would be a travesty to compare even the worst software project with the Bataan death march during the Second World War, or the "trail of tears" death march imposed upon Native Americans in the late 1700s. Instead, I use the term as a metaphor, to suggest a "forced march" imposed upon relatively innocent victims, the outcome of which is usually a high casualty rate." (2)

Project parameters include schedule, staff, budget or other resources, and the functionality, features, performance requirements, or other aspects of the project. A death march software project means one or more of the following constraints has been imposed (Yourdon 1999):

- The project schedule has been compressed to less than 50 percent of its original estimate.

- The staff originally assigned or required to complete the project has been reduced to less than 50 percent.

- The budget and resources needed have been reduced by 50 percent or more.

- The functionality, features, or other performance or technical requirements are twice what they should be under typical circumstances.

On the other hand, top-down estimating can be a very effective approach to cost and schedule analysis (Royce 1998). More specifically, a top-down approach may force the project manager to examine the project's risks more closely so that a specific budget or schedule target can be achieved. By understanding the risks, trade-offs, and sensitivities objectively, the various project stakeholders can develop a mutual understanding that leads to better estimation. This outcome, however, requires that all stakeholders be willing to communicate and make trade-offs.

Bottom-Up Estimating

Most real-world estimating is made using **bottom-up estimating** (Royce 1998). Bottom-up estimating involves dividing the project into smaller modules and then directly estimating the time and effort in terms of person-hours, person-weeks, or person-months for each module. The work breakdown structure provides the basis for bottom-up estimating because all of the project phases and activities are defined.

The project manager, or better yet the project team, can provide reasonable time estimates for each activity. In short, bottom-up estimating starts with a list of all required tasks or activities and then an estimate for the amount of effort is made. The total time and associated cost for each activity provides the basis for the project's target schedule and budget. Although bottom-up estimated is straightforward, confusing effort with progress can be problematic (Brooks 1995).

Continuing with our earlier example, let's assume that after meeting with our software testers, the following durations were estimated for each of the following activities:

6.2   Test results report

6.2.1 Review test plan with client	1 day
6.2.2 Carry out test plan	5 days
6.2.3 Analyze results	2 days
6.2.4 Prepare test results report and presentation	3 days
6.2.5 Present test results to client	1 day
6.2.6 Address any software issues or problems	5 days

If we add all of the estimated durations together, we find that creating the test results report will take seventeen days. How did we come up with these estimates? Did we guesstimate them? Hopefully not! These estimates could be based on experience—the software testers may have done these activities many times in the past so they know what activities have to be done and how long each activity will take. Or, these estimates could be based on similar or analogous projects. **Analogous estimation** refers to developing estimates based upon one's opinion that there is a significant similarity between the current project and others (Rad 2002).

Keep in mind that estimates are a function of the activity itself, the resources, and the support provided. More specifically, the estimated duration of an activity will first depend upon the nature of the activity in terms of its complexity and degree of structure. In general, highly complex and unstructured activities will take longer to complete than simple, well-structured activities.

The resources assigned to a particular activity will also influence an estimate. For example, assigning an experienced and well-trained individual to a particular task should mean less time is required to complete it than if a novice were assigned. However, experience and expertise are only part of the equation. We also have to consider such things as a person's level of motivation and enthusiasm.

Finally, the support we provide also influences our estimates. Support may include technology, tools, training, and the physical work environment.

These are just some of the variables that we must consider when estimating. You can probably come up with a number of others. Subsequently, estimates will always be a forecast; however, by looking at and understanding the big picture, we can increase our confidence in them.

SOFTWARE ENGINEERING METRICS AND APPROACHES

The discipline of **software engineering** focuses on the processes, tools, and methods for developing a quality approach to developing software (Pressman 2001). **Metrics** on the other hand, provide the basis for software engineering and refers to a broad range of measurements for objectively evaluating computer software.

The greatest challenge for estimating an IT project is estimating the time and effort for the largest deliverable of the project—the application system.

THE MYTHICAL MAN-MONTH

The classic book, *The Mythical Man-Month* by Fredrick P. Brooks, was first published in 1975. Brooks worked at IBM as the manager of a large project that developed the OS/360 operating system. Although the OS/360 was eventually a successful product for IBM, the project was late, took more memory than planned, and cost several times more than originally estimated. In fact, the product did not perform well until after several releases. Based upon his experience, Brooks wrote a number of essays that were embodied in his book. As a result of his timeless advice (and probably due to the fact that some things have not changed, although the term *person-month* may be more appropriate today), a twentieth anniversary edition was issued. The following are some of Brooks' insights:

- "First, our techniques of estimation are poorly developed. More seriously, they reflect an unvoiced assumption which is quite untrue—i.e., that all will go well." (14)
- "Second, our estimating techniques fallaciously confuse effort with progress, hiding the assumption that men and months are interchangeable." (14)

- "Third, because we are uncertain of our estimates, software managers often lack the courteous stubbornness of Antoine's chef (14): Good cooking takes time. If you are made to wait, it is to serve you better, and to please you." (From the menu of Antoine's, a restaurant in New Orleans)
- "Fourth, schedule progress is poorly monitored. Techniques proven and routine in other engineering disciplines are considered radical innovations in software engineering." (14)
- "Fifth, when schedule slippage is recognized, the natural tendency (and traditional) response it to add more manpower. Like dousing a fire with gasoline, this makes matters worse, much worse. More fire requires more gasoline, and thus begins a regenerative cycle which ends in disaster." (14)
- **Brooks Law,** "Adding manpower to a late software project makes it later." (25)

Maintenance projects and the installation of packaged software can experience similar difficulties.

The challenge lies in trying to estimate something that is logical, rather than physical, and that is not well defined until the later stages of the project life cycle. Scope definition can only provide a high-level view of what is and what is not within the scope boundary of the project. Specific requirements, in terms of features and functionality, are generally not defined until later, during the design phase. In addition, the complexity and technical challenges of implementing those features are either unknown or optimistically glossed over in the early stages of the project. As a result, estimating an IT project can be like trying to hit a moving target—hitting either one accurately requires continuous adjustments.

As illustrated in Figure 6.4, the first step to accurately estimating an IT application is determining its size (Jones 1998). In other words, how big is the application? Without getting into too much detail at this point, it should be intuitive that it takes more effort (i.e., in terms of schedule, resources, and budget) to build a larger system than a smaller system. However, the size of the application is only one piece of the estimation puzzle. A good portion of time and effort will be spent on features and functionality that are more complex. As a result, the greater the complexity, the more time and effort that will be spent. Constraints and various influencers will also affect the time and effort needed to develop a particular application. These constraints could be attributes of the application (Jones 1998) or include the processes, people, technology, environment, and required quality of the product as well (Royce 1998). Once the resources and time estimates are known, the specific activities or tasks can be sequenced in order to create the project's schedule and budget.

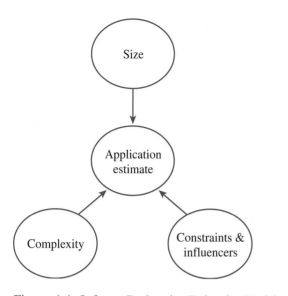

Figure 6.4 Software Engineering Estimation Model
SOURCE: Adapted from Garmus and Herron 1996; Jones 1998, Royce 1998.

Lines of Code (LOC)

Counting the number of lines of code in computer programs is the most traditional and widely used software metric for sizing the application product. It is also the most controversial.

Although counting lines of code seems intuitively obvious—a 1,000 LOC Java program will be ten times larger than a 100 LOC Java program—counting LOC is not all that straightforward. First, what counts as LOC? Do we include comments? Maybe we should not because a programmer could artificially boost his or her productivity by writing one hundred comment lines for every line of code that actually did something. On the other hand, comments are important because they tell us what the code should be doing. This makes it easier to debug and for others to understand what sections of code in the program are doing.

What about declaring variables? Do they count as LOC? In addition, experienced programmers tend to write *less* code than novice programmers. After all, an experienced programmer can write more efficient code, code that does the same thing in fewer lines of code than a novice programmer would use. The same can be said for different programming languages. Writing a program in Assembler requires a great deal more code than writing a similar program in Visual Basic. In fact, one could argue that counting LOC could encourage programmers to write inefficient code, especially when LOC are used as a productivity metric. Finally, it is much easier to count the lines of code after a program is written than it is to estimate how many lines of code will be required to write the program.

Function Points[1]

The inherent problems of LOC as a metric for estimation and productivity necessitated the need for a better software metric. In 1979, Allan Albrecht of IBM proposed the idea of function points at a conference hosted by IBM in Monterey, California (Albrecht 1979). **Function points** are a synthetic metric, similar to ones used every day, such as hours, kilos, tons, nautical miles, degrees Celsius, and so on. However, function points focus on the *functionality* and *complexity* of an application system or a particular module. For example, just as 20 degree Celsius day is warmer than a 10 degree Celsius day, a 1,000 function point application is larger and more complex than a 500 function point application.

The good thing about function points is that they are independent of the technology. More specifically, functionality and the technology are kept separate so we can compare different applications that may or may not use different programming languages or technology platforms. That is, we can compare one application written in COBOL with another application developed in Java. Moreover, function point analysis is reliable—i.e., two people who are skilled and experienced in function point

---

[1] A more thorough discussion of function point analysis is provided in Appendix A.

analysis will obtain function point counts that are the same, that is, within an acceptable margin of error.

Counting function points is fairly straightforward; however, the rules can be complex for the novice. It is recommended that anyone serious about learning function point analysis become certified. Although several function point organizations exist, the two main ones are the International Function Point Users Group (IFPUG) and the United Kingdom Function Point Users Group (UFPUG). Both of these nonprofit organizations oversee the rules, guidelines, standards, and certifications for function point analysis. In addition, there are resources at the end of the chapter if you are interested in learning more about function points.

The key to counting function points is having a good understanding of the user's requirements. Early on in the project, a function point analysis can be conducted based on the project's scope. Then a more detailed analysis of the user's requirements can be made during the analysis and design phases. Then, function point analysis can and should be conducted at various stages of the project life cycle. For example, a function point analysis conducted based on the project's scope definition can be used for estimation and developing the project's plan. During the analysis and design phases, function points can be used to manage and report progress and for monitoring scope creep. In addition, a function point analysis conducted during or after the project's implementation can be useful for determining whether all of the functionality was delivered. By capturing this information in a repository or database, it can be combined with other metrics useful for benchmarking, estimating future projects, and understanding the impact of new methods, tools, technologies, and best practices that were introduced.

Function point analysis is based on an evaluation of five data and transactional types that define the application boundary as illustrated in Figure 6.5.

- *Internal Logical File (ILF)*—An ILF is a logical file that stores data within the application boundary. For example, each entity in an Entity-Relationship Diagram (ERD) would be considered as an ILF. The complexity of an ILF can be classified as low, average, or high based on the number of data elements and subgroups of data elements maintained by the ILF. An example of a subgroup would be new customers for an entity called customer. Examples of data elements would be customer number, name, address, phone number, and so forth. In short, ILFs with fewer data elements and subgroups will be less complex than ILFs with more data elements and subgroups.

- *External Interface File (EIF)*—An EIF is similar to an ILF; however, an EIF is a file maintained by another application system. The complexity of an EIF is determined using the same criteria used for an ILF.

- *External Input (EI)*—An EI refers to processes or transactional data that originate outside the application and cross the application boundary from outside to inside. The data generally are added, deleted, or updated in one or more files internal to the application (i.e., internal logical files). A common example of an EI would be a screen that allows the user to input information using a keyboard and a mouse. Data can, however, pass through the application boundary from other applications. For example, a sales system may need a customer's current balance from an accounts receivable system. Based on its complexity, in terms of the number of internal files referenced, number of data elements (i.e., fields) included, and any other human factors, each EI is classified as low, average, or high.

- *External Output (EO)*—Similarly, an EO is a process or transaction that allows data to exit the application boundary. Examples of EOs include reports, confirmation messages, derived or calculated totals, and graphs or charts. This data could go to screens, printers, or other applications. After the number of EOs are counted, they are rated based on their complexity, like the external inputs (EI).

- *External Inquiry (EQ)*—An EQ is a process or transaction that includes a combination of inputs and outputs for retrieving data from either the internal files or from files external to the application. EQs do not update or change any data stored in a file. They only read this information. Queries with different processing logic or a different input or output format are counted as a single EQ. Once the EQs are identified, they are classified based on their complexity as low, average, or high, according to the number of files referenced and number of data elements included in the query.

Once all of the ILFs, EIFs, EIs, EOs, and EQs, are counted and their relative complexities rated, an Unadjusted Function Point (UAF) count is determined. For example, let's say that after reviewing an application system, the following was determined:

- *ILF:* 3 Low, 2 Average, 1 Complex
- *EIF:* 2 Average
- *EI:* 3 Low, 5 Average, 4 Complex
- *EO:* 4 Low, 2 Average, 1 Complex
- *EQ:* 2 Low, 5 Average, 3 Complex

Using Table 6.1, the (UAF) value is calculated.

The next step in function point analysis is to compute a Value Adjustment Factor (VAF). The VAF is based on the Degrees of Influence (DI), often called the Processing Complexity Adjustment (PCA), and is derived from the fourteen General

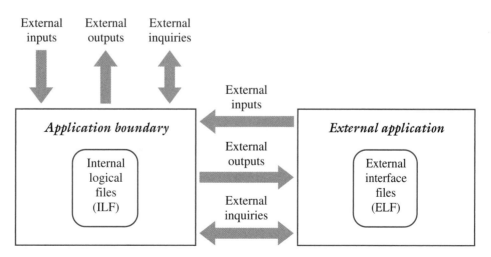

Figure 6.5 The Application Boundary for Function Point Analysis

Table 6.1 Computing UAF

	Complexity			Total
	Low	Average	High	
Internal Logical Files (ILF)	$3 \times 7 = 21$	$2 \times 10 = 20$	$1 \times 15 = 15$	56
External Interface (EIF)	__ $\times 5 =$ __	$2 \times 7 = 14$	__ $\times 10 =$ __	14
External Input (EI)	$3 \times 3 = 9$	$5 \times 4 = 20$	$4 \times 6 = 24$	53
External Output (EO)	$4 \times 4 = 16$	$2 \times 5 = 10$	$1 \times 7 = 7$	33
External Inquiry (EQ)	$2 \times 3 = 6$	$5 \times 4 = 20$	$3 \times 6 = 18$	44
Total Unadjusted Function Points (UAF)				200

Systems Characteristics (GSC) shown in Table 6.2. To determine the total DI, each GSC is rated based on the following scale from 0 to 5:

- 0 = not present or no influence
- 1 = incidental influence
- 2 = moderate influence
- 3 = average influence
- 4 = significant influence
- 5 = strong influence

Continuing with our example, let's say that after reviewing the application, the degrees of influence shown in Table 6.2 were determined to produce 210 total adjusted function points (TAFP). So what do we do with the total adjusted function point number? Once a total adjusted function point count is calculated, the function point count can be transformed into development estimates. The first approach focuses on productivity—i.e., a person, such as a programmer, can produce a certain number of function points in a given amount of time, such as in a day, a week, or a month. Once again, creating a repository of function point information and other metrics allows an organization to compare various projects and support more realistic estimates.

The second approach focuses on converting the function point count into an equivalent number of lines of code. Continuing with our example, we can determine how many lines of code will be required for several different programming languages. Table 6.3 provides an example that approximates the number of lines of code per function point for some of the more popular programming languages. As you can see, the number of lines of code depends on the programming language. An application or module that has 210 total unadjusted function points would require, for example, 134,440 lines of code if programmed in machine language, but only 6,090 lines of code using Visual Basic 5. Again, these estimates not only provide an estimate for the size of the application, but also for the complexity of the application.

In addition, T. Capers Jones has conducted extensive research and has come up with a technique called **backfiring,** which allows direct conversion from an application's source code to an equivalent function point count. Individual programming styles can create variation in the number of LOC so the accuracy of backfiring is not very high. It can, however, provide an easy way to create a function point inventory of an organization's project portfolio if LOC are readily available.

Table 6.2 GSC and Total Adjusted Function Point

General System Characteristic	Degree of Influence
Data communications	3
Distributed data processing	2
Performance	4
Heavily used configuration	3
Transaction rate	3
On-line data entry	4
End user efficiency	4
Online update	3
Complex processing	3
Reusability	2
Installation ease	3
Operational ease	3
Multiple sites	1
Facilitate change	2
Total degrees of influence (TDI)	40
VALUE ADJUSTMENT FACTOR VAF = (TDI * 0.01) + .65	VAF = (40 * .01) + .65 = 1.05
Total adjusted function points = FP = UAF * VAF	FP = 200 * 1.05 = 210

COCOMO

COCOMO is an acronym for COnstructive COst MOdel, which was first introduced in 1981 by Barry Boehm in his book *Software Engineering Economics*. Based on LOC estimates, it is used to estimate cost, effort, and schedule (Boehm 1981). The original COCOMO model received widespread interest and is an open model, meaning that all of the underlying equations, assumptions, definitions, and so on are available to the public. The original COCOMO model was based on a study of 63 projects and is a hierarchy of estimation models.

COCOMO is an example of a **parametric model** because it uses dependent variables, such as cost or duration, based upon one or more independent variables that are quantitative indices of performance and/or physical attributes of the system. Often, parametric models can be refined and fine-tuned for specific projects or projects within specific industries (Rad 2002).

Estimating with COCOMO begins with determining the type of project to be estimated. Project types can be classified as:

- *Organic*—These are routine projects where the technology, processes, and people are expected to all work together smoothly. One may view these types of projects as the easy projects where few problems are expected.

Table 6.3 Function Point Conversion to LOC

Language	Average Source LOC per Function Point	Average Source LOC for a 210 FP Application
Access	38	7,980
Basic	107	22,470
C	128	26,880
C++	53	11,130
COBOL	107	22,470
Delphi	29	6,090
Java	53	11,130
Machine Language	640	134,440
Visual Basic 5	29	6,090

Source: http://www.spr.com

- *Embedded*—An embedded project is viewed as a challenging project. For example, it may be a system to support a new business process or an area that is new ground for the organization. The people may be less experienced, and the processes and technology may be less mature.

- *Semi-Detached*—If organic projects are viewed as easy and embedded as difficult or challenging, then semi-detached fall somewhere in the middle. These projects may not be simple and straightforward, but the organization feels confident that its processes, people, and technology in place are adequate to meet the challenge.

The basic COCOMO model uses an equation for estimating the number of person-months needed for each of these projects types. A person-month can be thought of as a one-month effort by one person. In COCOMO, a person-month is defined as 152 hours. Once the project type is defined, the level of effort, in terms of person-months, can be determined using the appropriate equation:

- Organic: Person-Months = $2.4 \times KDSI^{1.05}$
- Semi-Detached: Person-Months = $3.0 \times KDSI^{1.12}$
- Embedded: Person-Months = $3.6 \times KDSI^{1.20}$
  KDSI = thousands of delivered source instructions, i.e., LOC

Let's suppose that we are developing an application that we estimated to have 200 total adjusted function points. Using Table 6.3, we can convert function points into lines of code. If our application is going to be developed in Java, this would require approximately 10,600 lines of code. If we assume that our project will be of medium difficulty, then the semi-detached equation would be appropriate.

$$
\begin{aligned}
\text{Person-Months} &= 3.0 \times KDSI^{1.12} \\
&= 3.0 \times (10.6)^{1.12} \\
&= 42.21
\end{aligned}
$$

In summary, our 200 function point project will require about 10,600 lines of code and take just over 42.21 person months to complete. Once we have estimated the effort for our project, we can determine how many people will be required. Subsequently, this will determine the time estimate and associated cost for developing our application system.

As Frederick Brooks (1995) points out, people and months are not interchangeable. More people complicate communication and slow things down. Therefore, duration is determined using one of the following formulas:

- Organic: Duration = $2.5 \times Effort^{0.38}$
- Semi-Detached: Duration = $2.5 \times Effort^{0.35}$
- Embedded: Duration = $2.5 \times Effort^{0.32}$

Since our semi-detached project requires 42.21 person-months, the duration of development will be:

$$
\begin{aligned}
\text{Duration} &= 2.5 \times Effort^{0.35} \\
&= 2.5 \times (42.21)^{0.35} \\
&= 9.26 \text{ months}
\end{aligned}
$$

Subsequently, we can determine how many people should be assigned to the development effort:

People Required = Effort ÷ Duration
$$= 42.21 \div 9.26$$
$$= 4.55$$

Therefore, we need 4.55 people working on the project. Okay, so it is pretty tough getting .55 of a person, so we probably will need either four or five people. One could even make an argument that four full-time people and 1 part-time person will be needed for this project.

The above example shows how the basic COCOMO model can be used. There are, however, two other COCOMO models: Intermediate COCOMO and Advanced COCOMO. Intermediate COCOMO estimates the software development effort as a function of size and a set of fifteen subjective cost drivers that include attributes of the end product, the computer used, the personnel staffing, and the project environment. In addition, Advanced COCOMO includes all of the characteristics of Intermediate COCOMO but with an assessment of the cost driver's impact over four phases of development: Product Design, Detailed Design, Coding/Testing, and Integration/Testing.

Today, COCOMO II is available and is more suited for the types of projects being developed using 4GLs or other tools like Visual Basic, Delphi, or Power Builder. However, for more traditional projects using a 3GL, the original COCOMO model can still provide good estimates and is often referred to as COCOMO 81.

Another estimating model that you should be aware of is SLIM, which was developed in the late 1970s by Larry Putnam of Quantitative Software Management (Putnam 1978; Putnam and Fitzsimmons 1979). Like COCOMO, SLIM uses LOC to estimate the project's size and a series of twenty-two questions to calibrate the model.

Heuristics

Heuristics are rules of thumb. Heuristic approaches rely on the fact that the same basic activities will be required for a typical software development project and these activities will require a predictable percentage of the overall effort (Roetzheim and Beasley 1998). For example, when estimating the schedule for a software development task one may, based on previous projects, assign a percentage of the total effort as follows:

- 30 percent Planning
- 20 percent Coding
- 25 percent Component Testing
- 25 percent System Testing

In his book, *Estimating Software Costs,* T. Capers Jones provides a number of heuristics or rules of thumb for estimating software projects based on function points. Some of these rules include:

- Function points raised to the 1.15 power predict approximate page counts for paper documents associated with software projects.
- Creeping user requirements will grow at an average rate of 2 percent per month from the design through coding phases.
- Function points raised to the 1.2 power predict the approximate number of test cases created.

- Function points raised to the 1.25 power predict the approximate defect potential for new software projects.
- Each software test step will find and remove 30 percent of the bugs that are present.
- Each formal design inspection will find and remove 65 percent of the bugs present.
- Each formal code inspection will find and remove 60 percent of the bugs present.
- Maintenance programmers can repair eight bugs per staff month.
- Function points raised to the 0.4 power predict the approximate development schedule in calendar months.
- Function points divided by 150 predict the approximate number of personnel required for the application.
- Function points divided by 750 predict the approximate number of maintenance personnel required to keep the application updated.
- Multiply software development schedules by the number of personnel to predict the approximate number of staff months of effort.

Jones makes an important observation: Rules of thumb are easy, but they are not accurate. As Garmus and Herron point out (Garmus and Herron 1996):

> Accurate estimating is a function of applying a process and recognizing that effort must be expended in creating a baseline of experience that will allow for increased accuracy of that process. Estimating does not require a crystal ball; it simply requires commitment. (142)

Automated Estimating Tools

A number of automated tools can be used for cost, schedule, and resource estimation. These tools include spreadsheets, project management tools, database management systems, software cost estimating, and process or methodology tools. Many of these tools not only help estimate, but also allow the organization to create a database or repository of past projects. In fact, it was found that estimates usually have an accuracy of between 5 and 10 percent when historical data was accurate. Moreover, automated estimating tools are generally more conservative when they are not accurate, as opposed to manual methods that are generally optimistic (Jones 1998).

As the complexity of software development projects increases, the market for software estimation tools will increase as well. Some of the automated tools available include COCOMO II, SLIM, CHECKPOINT, Knowledge Plan, and Cost*Xpert. Research suggests that projects that use a formal estimating tool have a better chance of delivering a system that is on time and within budget.

WHAT IS THE BEST WAY TO ESTIMATE IT PROJECTS?

Unfortunately, no single method or tool is best for accurately estimating IT projects. It may be a good idea to use more than one technique for estimating. You will, however, very likely have two different estimates.

If the estimates from different estimating techniques are fairly close, then you can average them with a fairly high degree of confidence. If the estimates vary widely, then you should probably be skeptical of one or both estimates and review the data that was collected (Roetzheim and Beasley 1998).

Your initial estimates probably will have to be adjusted up or down based on past experience or data from past projects. Many times, however, the initial estimates are negotiated by upper management or the client. For example, you may come up with an estimate that the project will take twelve months and cost $1.2 million. Unless you can substantiate your estimates, upper management may counter and mandate that the project be completed in eight months and cost no more than $750,000. This counter may be a result of a real business need (i.e., they really do need it in eight months and can not spend more than $750,000) or their belief that you inflated the schedule and budget and some of the fat can be trimmed from your estimates. As a result, you may end up working on a death march project.

It basically comes down to whether the project can or cannot be delivered earlier. It is up to the project manager not only to arrive at an estimate, but also to support the estimates. Otherwise, the project's schedule and budget can be very unrealistic. Working long hours and under intense pressure will surely have a negative impact on the project team. A project manager's team must always come first, and protecting them by having a realistic deadline and adequate resources as defined by the project's schedule and budget is the first step.

CHAPTER SUMMARY

Although defining a project's scope in terms of project-oriented and product-oriented deliverables provides an idea of what must be done, the project manager and team must still develop a tactical approach that determines what needs to be done, when it will be done, who will do the work, and how long will it take. The work breakdown structure (WBS) is an important and useful tool for bridging the project's scope with the detailed project plan. More specifically, the WBS provides a logical hierarchy that decomposes the project scope into work packages. Work packages focus on a particular deliverable and include the activities required to produce the deliverable. In addition, milestones provide a mechanism for ensuring that project work is not only done, but also done right.

Once the work packages have been identified, projected durations must be made. Instead of guesstimating, or guessing at the estimates, a number of project estimation methods and techniques were introduced. Traditional approaches to estimating include:

- *The Delphi Technique*—This approach involves multiple experts who arrive at a consensus after a series of round-robin sessions in which information and opinions are anonymously provided to each expert.
- *Time-Boxing*—A technique where a *box* of time is allocated to a specific task. For example, a team may be given two weeks (and only two weeks) to develop a prototype of a user interface.

- *Top-Down Estimating*—This system involves estimating a schedule or budget based upon how long the project or an activity should take or how much it should cost. For example, the project manager may be told that the project must be completed in six months. The project manager then schedules or estimates the project and activities backwards so that the total duration of the activities adds up to six months or less. Although this approach may be used when competitive necessity is an issue, unrealistic expectations can lead to projects with very little chance of meeting their objectives.
- *Bottom-Up Estimating*—Most real-world estimating uses this approach. The WBS outlines the activities that must be completed, and an estimate is made for each of the activities. The various durations are then added together to determine the total duration of the project. Estimates may be analogous to other projects or based on previous experience. These estimates are also a function of the activity itself (e.g., degree of complexity, structuredness, etc.), the resources assigned (e.g., a person's knowledge, expertise, enthusiasm, etc.) and support (e.g., technology, tools, work environment, etc.).

In addition, several software engineering approaches were introduced for estimating the software development effort. These included:

- *Lines of Code (LOC)*—Although counting or trying to estimate the amount of code that must be written may appear intuitively pleasing, there are a number of deficiencies with this approach. The number of LOC may provide an idea of the size of a project, but it does not consider the complexity, constraints, or influencers that must be taken into account.

- *Function Points*—Function points were introduced by Allen Albrecht of IBM in 1979. They are synthetic measures that take into account the functionality and complexity of software. Because function points are independent of the technology or programming language used, one application system can be compared with another.

- *COCOMO*—The COnstructive COst MOdel was introduced by Barry Boehm in 1981. Estimates for a software systems effort are determined by an equation based upon the project's complexity. More specifically, a software project may be classified as organic (relatively simple and straightforward), embedded (difficult), or semi-detached (somewhere in the middle). Once the effort, in terms of person-months, is calculated, a similar procedure using another model can estimate the project's duration.

- *Heuristics*—Heuristics are rules of thumb that are applied to estimating a software project. The basic premise is that the same activities will be repeated on most projects. This approach may include assigning a specific percentage of the project schedule to specific activities or using other metrics such as function points.

Estimating the effort and duration of an IT project is not an exact science. No single method or technique will provide 100 percent accuracy. Using a combination of approaches may help triangulate an estimate, which provides a confidence greater than when merely guessing or using a single estimation technique. To be realistic, estimates should be revised as understanding of the project increases and new information acquired.

WEB SITES TO VISIT

- www.softwaremetrics.com: Articles and examples for learning more about function point analysis
- www.spr.com: The site for Software Productivity Research. Capers Jones articles and information about software estimation and planning tools for IT projects
- www.ifpug.org: International Function Point Users Group
- sunset.usc.edu/research/COCOMOII/index.html: The latest version and information about COCOMO

REVIEW QUESTIONS

1. Describe the PMBOK area of project time management.

2. What is a WBS? What purpose does it serve?

3. Discuss why a project's scope must be tied to the WBS.

4. What is a work package?

5. What is the difference between a deliverable and a milestone?

6. What purpose do milestones serve?

7. What are some advantages of including milestones in the WBS?

8. What is a crux? Why should the project manager and project team identify the cruxes of a project?

9. What is the proper level of detail for a WBS?

10. Why should the WBS be deliverable-oriented?

11. Explain why people who do the work on a project should be involved in developing the project plan?

12. How does the concept of knowledge management support the development of the project plan?

13. How is estimating an IT project different from estimating a construction project?

14. What makes estimating an IT project challenging?

15. What is guesstimating? Why should a project manager not rely on this technique for estimating a project?

16. Describe the potential problems associated with providing an off-the-record estimate?

17. What is the Delphi technique? When would it be an appropriate estimating technique for an IT project?

18. What is time boxing? What are some advantages and disadvantages of time boxing project activities?

19. Describe top-down estimating. What are some advantages and disadvantages of top-down estimating?

20. Describe bottom-up estimating. What are some advantages and disadvantages of bottom-up estimating?

21. What is a death march project? What situations in project planning can lead to a death march project?

22. Discuss why adding people to a project that is already behind schedule can make it later?

23. What is software engineering?

24. Why is counting lines of code (LOC) a popular method for estimating and tracking programmer productivity? What are some problems associated with this method?

25. What is a function point? What advantages do function points have over counting lines of code?

26. How can function point analysis be used to help manage scope creep?

27. What is backfiring? How could an organization use backfiring to improve the accuracy of estimating IT projects?

28. What is COCOMO?

29. Under the COCOMO model, describe the organic, semi-detached, and embedded models.

30. What are heuristics? Discuss some of the advantages and disadvantages of using heuristics for estimating IT projects.

31. What can lead to inaccurate estimates? How can an organization improve the accuracy of estimating IT projects?

32. What is the impact of consistently estimating too low? Too high?

EXTEND YOUR KNOWLEDGE

1. Develop a deliverable-oriented WBS for a surprise birthday party for a friend or relative (perhaps even your instructor?). Be sure to define a measure of success for this party and include milestones.

2. Using the following phases as a guide, develop a WBS for an IT project that will allow Husky Air to keep track of all scheduled maintenance for its chartered aircraft. For each phase, define a deliverable, several activities or tasks, and a milestone.

    1.0 Conceptualize and Initialize Project
    2.0 Develop Project Charter and Plan
    3.0 Analysis
    4.0 Design
    5.0 Construction
    6.0 Testing
    7.0 Implementation
    8.0 Close Project
    9.0 Evaluate Project Success

3. Using the information below, complete a function point analysis in order to use the basic COCOMO model to estimate the duration and number of people needed to develop an application using C++. Assume that the project is relatively simple and straightforward and that the project team is familiar with both the problem and technology. You can perform the calculations by hand, but feel free to use an appropriate software tool.

	Complexity			
	Low	*Average*	*High*	*Total*
Internal logical files (ILF)	__ × 7 = __	__ × 10 = __	__ × 15 = __	
External interface (EIF)	__ × 5 = __	__ × 7 = __	__ × 10 = __	
External input (EI)	__ × 3 = __	__ × 4 = __	__ × 6 = __	
External output (EO)	__ × 4 = __	__ × 5 = __	__ × 7 = __	
External inquiry (EQ)	__ × 3 = __	__ × 4 = __	__ × 6 = __	

	Complexity		
	Low	*Average*	*High*
Internal logical files (ILF)	4	2	0
External interface (EIF)	0	1	0
External input (EI)	3	2	0
External output (EO)	5	7	3
External inquiry (EQ)	2	5	2

Language	*Average Source LOC per Function Point*
Basic	107
C	128
C++	53
COBOL	107
Delphi	29
Java	53
Visual Basic 5	29

General System Characteristic	*Degree of Influence*
Data communications	2
Distributed data processing	3
Performance	3
Heavily used configuration	4
Transaction rate	4
On-line data entry	2
End user efficiency	2
Online update	2
Complex processing	2
Reusability	3
Installation ease	2
Operational ease	2
Multiple sites	1
Facilitate change	1

■ BIBLIOGRAPHY

Albrecht, Allan J. 1979. *Measuring Application Development Productivity.* Proceedings SHARE/GUIDE IBM Applications Development Symposium, Monterey, Calif., October 14–17, 1979.

Brooks, F. P. 1995. *The Mythical Man-Month.* Reading, Mass.: Addison Wesley.

Boehm, B. W. 1981. *Software Engineering Economics.* Englewood Cliffs, N.J.: Prentice Hall.

Brooks, F. P. 1995. *The Mythical Man-Month.* Reading, Mass.: Addison Wesley.

Garmus, D. and D. Herron. 1996. *Measuring the Software Process.* Upper Saddle River, N.J.: Prentice Hall PTR.

Haugan, G. T. 2002. *Efffective Work Breakdown Structures.* Vienna, Va.: Management Concepts, Inc.

Jones, T. C. 1998. *Estimating Software Costs.* New York: McGraw-Hill.

Pressman, R. S. 2001. *Software Engineering: A Practitioner's Approach.* Boston: McGraw-Hill.

Putnam, L. H. 1978. General Empirical Solution to the Macro Software Sizing and Estimating Problem. *IEEE Transactions Software Engineering* SE 4(4): 345–361.

Putnam, L. H. and A. Fitzsimmons. 1979. Estimating Software Costs. *Datamation* 25(Sept–Nov): 10–12.

Rad, P. F. 2002. *Project Estimating and Cost Management.* Vienna, Va.: Management Concepts, Inc.

Roetzheim, W. H. and R. A. Beasley. 1998. *Software Project Cost and Schedule Estimating: Best Practices.* Upper Saddle River, N.J.: Prentice Hall.

Royce, W. 1998. *Software Project Management: A Unified Framework.* Reading, Mass.: Addison Wesley.

Yourdon, E. 1999. *Death March.* Upper Saddle River, N.J.: Prentice Hall.

7

The Project Schedule and Budget

CHAPTER OVERVIEW

Chapter 7 focuses on developing the project schedule and budget and on a number of project management tools for developing the project plan. After studying this chapter, you should understand and be able to:

- Describe the Project Management Body of Knowledge (PMBOK) area called project cost management.
- Develop a Gantt chart.
- Develop a project network diagram using the activity on the node (AON) technique.
- Identify a project's critical path and explain why it must be controlled and managed.
- Develop a PERT diagram.
- Describe the concept of precedence diagramming and identify finish-to-start, start-to-start, finish-to-finish, and start-to-finish activity relationships
- Describe the Project Management Body of Knowledge area called project cost management
- Describe the various costs for determining the project's budget.
- Define what is meant by the baseline project plan.

GLOBAL TECHNOLOGY SOLUTIONS

Kellie Matthews stopped in the doorway of Tim Williams' office. Tim was just finishing a conversation on his cell phone, and he motioned for her to come in and sit down. After pressing the end button, he asked "How did your meeting go this morning?"

Kellie sat back in her chair. "I think it went well," she said. "It was with a local textbook distributor interested in purchasing and implementing a call center software package. There are a number of software packages available from different vendors, but the company is not really sure which one best suits its needs. Its information systems department is stretched pretty thin working on several projects already, so it is considering outsourcing this project. I have another meeting with management later this week, so keep your fingers crossed because we may have another client."

"I will," Tim said. "That might stretch things around here a little bit, but we'll worry about that bridge when we come to it."

Kellie agreed. "So how are thing going with the Husky Air? Have you finished the schedule and budget?"

Tim chuckled and said, "I knew that you were going to ask that. Actually, we are making good progress. The phone call that I just finished was with Husky Air's CEO. He's pretty anxious to find out how much the project will cost and how long it will take to complete. We have a meeting next week to present the project charter and plan to him and several other senior managers."

"Will you be ready?" Kellie asked.

Tim picked up his coffee mug from his desk, took a sip, and then said, "We completed the work breakdown structure yesterday. That helped us to identify all of the tasks or activities, the resources that will be required, and each activity's estimated duration. Right now, we're trying to determine which activities need to be completed sequentially and which can be completed in parallel. That will help us develop a project network of activities that will allow us to develop a schedule and budget once we enter everything into the project management software package. To finally answer your question, I'm pretty confident that we'll have a draft of the project plan ready by next week."

Kellie leaned forward in her chair and asked, "That sounds reasonable. So what do you hope happens at next week's meeting?"

"If this were a perfect world, I'd hope that our client would approve everything and we could get started right away," he said, laughing. "But I know that's not likely to happen. I'm sure that once we present the schedule and budget to them next week, we'll have to make some changes. But, I'm confident that we're close to the original estimates outlined in the business case, so we should only have to make some minor modifications. Once approved, we then have our baseline project plan and we can get started on the real project work."

Kellie stood up to leave. "I have to return a few phone calls before lunch, but please keep me informed and let me know if I can help out," she said.

Tim was grateful and knew that he could count on Kellie's help. As Kellie was walking through the doorway and back to her office, Tim was turning to his computer to answer the six e-mails that had arrived in his inbox since he had last checked them thirty minutes ago.

Things to Think About:

1. How does the work breakdown structure (WBS) link the project's scope to the schedule and budget?

2. Why might a project manager expect a project plan to go through a number of iterations before being accepted by the project sponsor or client?

3. What role does project management software play in developing the project schedule and budget?

INTRODUCTION

The last several chapters have been leading up to the development of the project schedule and budget. Chapter 3 introduced the project-planning framework (see Figure 7.1). To support this framework, subsequent chapters introduced several Project Management Body of Knowledge (PMBOK) areas, including project integration management, human resources management, project scope management, and project time management. In this chapter, you will be introduced to another knowledge area called project cost management, which will bring all of the concepts, tools, and techniques covered in the last several chapters together so that the project plan can be developed.

The project plan contains all of the details of the project's schedule and budget. It will be used to guide the project team and monitor the project's progress throughout the project life cycle. Project time management was introduced in the last chapter; however, our focus was on two important processes: Activity definition and activity duration estimation. These two processes are key ingredients for developing the work breakdown structure (WBS) that links the project's scope to the project plan. The development of a project plan, however, requires a schedule and budget. The project schedule builds upon the WBS by identifying the sequence of activities as well as the interdependencies and relationships. Once the activities, their expected durations, and sequence are identified, various project management tools can be used to map a network of activities to yield the project schedule. This information, in turn, can be entered into a project management software package to make developing the project plan more efficient and to provide a means to monitor and control the project schedule and budget as the plan is executed.

The project budget is determined by the project schedule, the cost of the resources assigned to each of the tasks, and by any other direct or indirect costs and reserves. In addition, a PMBOK area called **project cost management** focuses on the processes, procedures, and techniques to develop and manage the project budget. According to PMBOK, project cost management includes:

- *Resource planning*—Identifying the type of resources (people, technology, facilities, and so forth) and number of resources needed to carry out the project activities.

- *Cost estimating*—Based upon the activities, their time estimates, and resource requirements, an estimate can be developed.

- *Cost budgeting*—Once the time and cost of each activity is estimated, an overall cost estimate for the entire project can be made. Once approved, this estimate becomes the project budget.

- *Cost control*—Ensuring that proper processes and procedures are in place to control changes to the project budget.

Once the project schedule and budget are determined, the total time and cost of each activity can be summed using a bottom-up approach to determine a target deadline and budget. The schedule and budget must, however, be reviewed and accepted by the project sponsor or client. This may require several revisions and possible trade-offs before the scope, schedule, and budget

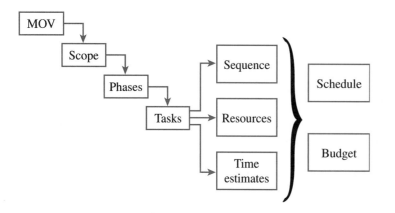

Figure 7.1 The Project Planning Framework

relationship is reasonable and acceptable to *all* of the project stakeholders. Once the schedule and budget are approved by the sponsor or client, the plan becomes the base-line project plan. This milestone is an important achievement that marks the completion of the second phase of the IT project methodology and gives the project manager and team the authority to begin carrying out the activities outlined in the plan.

DEVELOPING THE PROJECT SCHEDULE

> Overeager new manager promises his boss a thirty-day schedule for a project to automate passwords on company's mainframe, midrange, and desktop systems. "We can't do that," desktop support pilot fish tells manager when he sees the project plan. "Have you confirmed that the mainframe and midrange support groups can do the product evaluation in the three days you've allotted?" fish asks. "No," says manager, "but if they don't meet the plan, then it'll be their fault it fails, not mine."
>
> From Shark Tank: That's One Way to Look at It, May 20, 2002. http://www.computerworld.com/careertopics/careers/training /story/0,10801,71293,00.html.

The WBS identifies the activities and tasks that must be completed in order to provide the project scope deliverables. Estimates provide a forecasted duration for each of these activities and are based upon the characteristics of the activity, the resources assigned, and the support provided to carry out the activity. Project networks, on the other hand, support the development of the project schedule by identifying dependencies and the sequencing of the activities defined in the WBS. The project network also serves as a key tool for monitoring and controlling the project activities once the project work begins.

In this section, several project management tools and techniques will be introduced to create a project network plan that defines the sequence of activities throughout the

CRUNCH TIME

The original meaning of the word *deadline* referred to a line drawn around a military prison, beyond which prisoners were shot. A project deadline can be almost as threatening, and as a project manager, you may find yourself dodging political bullets forged by unreasonable expectations and demands with respect the project's schedule and budget. Although tight schedules may be dictated by legal, regulatory, or competitive situations, some deadlines appear to be arbitrary. Arbitrary deadlines result in a *crunch schedule* that will give you less time than you would like to have to do things right. They can be harmful to your career. The trick is to know what and how to negotiate with the senior managers who sometimes make these demands. According to Doug DeCarlo, a project management consultant at ICS Group in Norwalk, Connecticut, crunch schedules normally happen when management dictates a final date for the project rather then asks when it can be done. These crunch schedules can and must be negotiated. Doing so requires political savvy and alternatives. If a project deadline cannot be moved, then perhaps adding temporary help at an additional cost could help make the deadline. Another option may be to break the project into chucks, delivering only those chunks that can be produced on schedule. The political skill comes into play when you break a project into four chunks and have to explain to the fourth-chunk person why his or her part of the project is last. And, how should a project manager handle delays caused by political fighting, turf wars, and team members over whom you have no direct control? The answer is having documented project management processes that are agreed upon by upper management. Without this, a project manager may not have any legitimate authority.

SOURCE: Adapted from Rochelle Garner, Captain of Crunch, *Computerworld,* October 6, 1997. http://www.computerworld.com /news/1997/story/0,11280,9205,00.html.

project and their dependencies. These tools include Gantt charts, activity on the node (AON), critical path analysis, PERT, and the precedence diagramming method (PDM). Many of these tools are integrated into most project management software packages; however, it is important to have a fundamental understanding of how these various project management tools work in order to make the most of an automated tool.

Gantt Charts

Working with the U.S. Army during World War I, Henry L. Gantt developed a visual representation that compares a project's planned activities with actual progress over time. Although **Gantt charts** have been around for a long time, they are still one of the most useful and widely used project management tools.

Figure 7.2 shows how a basic Gantt chart can be used for planning. Estimates for the tasks or activities defined in the WBS are represented using a bar across a horizontal time axis. Other symbols, for example, diamonds, can represent milestones to make the Gantt chart more useful.

The Gantt Chart in Figure 7.2 shows the general sequence of activities or work tasks. In this project example, there are five tasks of varying durations and the project should be completed in fifteen time periods (e.g., days). In addition, the two shaded diamonds following tasks C and E indicate milestone events.

Gantt charts can also be useful for tracking and monitoring the progress of a project. As shown in Figure 7.3, completed tasks can be shaded or filled in, and one can get an accurate picture of where the project stands for a given status or reporting date. In Figure 7.3, tasks A and B have been completed, but it looks like Task C is somewhat behind schedule.

Although Gantt charts are simple, straightforward, and useful for communicating the project's status, they do not show the explicit relationships among tasks or activities. For example, we can see from Figure 7.3 that task C is somewhat behind schedule; however, the Gantt chart does not tell us whether there will be an impact on tasks D or E and whether this impact will push back the project's original deadline. The Gantt chart introduced in this section follows a more traditional form. As you will see, the Gantt chart used in most project management software packages today has been modified to overcome these limitations.

Project Network Diagrams

Project network diagrams include several useful tools for planning, scheduling, and monitoring the project's progress. Similar to Gantt charts, project network diagrams

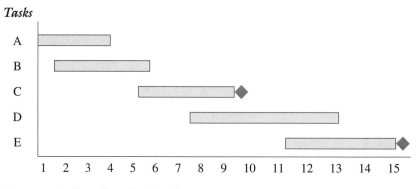

Figure 7.2 Gantt Chart for Planning

Tasks

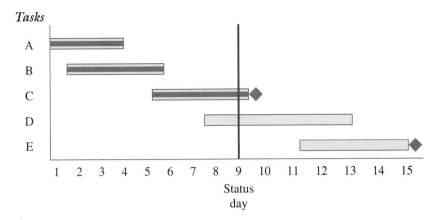

Figure 7.3 Gantt Chart Reporting Project's Progress

use the WBS as a basis to provide a visual representation of the workflow of activities and tasks. However, project network diagrams also provide valuable information about the logical sequence and dependencies among the various activities or tasks. Subsequently, a completion date or project deadline should be developed based on a sound estimating process rather than guesstimating a target date or a date set arbitrarily by upper management or the client.

In addition, project network diagrams provide information concerning when specific tasks must start and finish, and what activities may be delayed without affecting the deadline target date. In addition, the project manager can make decisions regarding scheduling and resource assignments to shorten the time required for those critical activities that will impact the project deadline.

Activity on the Node (AON)[1]   An activity or task focuses on producing a specific project deliverable, generally takes a specific amount of time to complete, and requires resources. **Activity on the Node (AON)** is a project network diagramming tool that graphically represents all of the project activities and tasks, as well as their logical sequence and dependencies. Using AON, activities are represented as boxes (i.e. nodes) and arrows indicate precedence and flow.

To construct an AON network diagram, one begins with the activities and tasks that were defined in the WBS. Estimates for each activity or task defined in the WBS should have an associated time estimate. The next step is to determine which activities are **predecessors, successors, or parallel.** Predecessor activities are those activities that must be completed *before* another activity can be started—e.g., a computer's operating system must be installed before loading an application package. On the other hand, successor activities are activities that must follow a particular activity in some type of sequence. For example, a program must be tested and then documented after it is compiled. A parallel activity is an activity or task that can be worked on at the same time as another activity. Parallel activities may be thought of as an opportunity to shorten the project schedule; however, they also can be a trade-off since doing more than one thing at the same time can have a critical impact on project resources.

---

[1] A project network diagramming technique very similar to Activity on the Node (AON) is Activity on the Arrow (AOA). The AOA approach uses arrows and nodes similar to AON; however, arrows represent the activity and nodes represent an event. Although AON and AOA provide the same answers, AOA sometimes requires the use of *dummy activities* to make things work out properly. The choice of using either AON or AOA is largely a personal one.

The activities, time estimates, and relationships for developing a simple corporate intranet can be summarized in a table similar to Table 7.1.

Once the relationships and time estimates for each activity or task in the WBS have been developed, an AON project network diagram can be created, as in Figure 7.4.

The work in an AON flows from left to right. An activity cannot begin until all of its predecessor activities have been completed. For example, activity F cannot begin until activities C and D are done.

Critical Path Analysis   At this point we have a visual road map of our project. Moreover, the time estimates for each of the activities determines the project schedule and tells us how long our project will take to complete. This is determined by looking at each of the possible paths and computing the total duration for each path, as shown in Table 7.2.

As can be seen in Table 7.2, the longest path in the AON network diagram is nineteen days. This number is significant for two reasons. First, this tells us that our project is estimated to take nineteen days (i.e., the project deadline will be nineteen days after the project starts). Second, and perhaps more importantly, Path 4 is also our **critical path.**

Table 7.1 Activity Analysis for AON

Activity	Description	Estimated Duration (Days)	Predecessor
A	Evaluate current technology platform	2	None
B	Define user requirements	5	A
C	Design Web page layouts	4	B
D	Set-up server	3	B
E	Estimate Web traffic	1	B
F	Test Web pages and links	4	C, D
G	Move Web pages to production environment	3	D, E
H	Write announcement of intranet for corporate newsletter	2	F, G
I	Train users	5	G
J	Write report to management	1	H, I

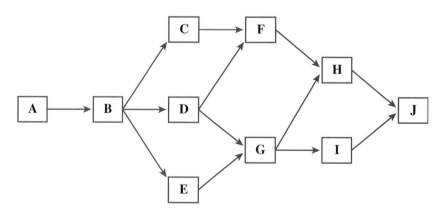

Figure 7.4 Activity on the Node (AON) Network Diagram

Table 7.2 Possible Activity Paths

Possible Paths	Path	Total
Path 1	A + B + C + F + H + J 2 + 5 + 4 + 4 + 2 + 1	18
Path 2	A + B + D + F + H + J 2 + 5 + 3 + 4 + 2 + 1	17
Path 3	A + B + D + G + H + J 2 + 5 + 3 + 3 + 2 + 1	16
Path 4	A + B + D + G + I + J 2 + 5 + 3 + 3 + 5 + 1	19*
Path 5	A + B + E + G + I + J 2 + 5 + 1 + 3 + 5 + 1	17

The critical path is the longest path in the project network and is also the shortest time in which the project can be completed.

Identifying the critical path is a major concern to the project manager because any change in the duration of the activities or tasks on the critical path will affect the project's schedule. In other words, the critical path has zero **slack (or float).** Slack, which is sometimes called float, is the amount of time an activity can be delayed, that is, take longer than expected, before it delays the project. For example, Activity E is not on the critical path. In fact, the only path that includes Activity E is Path 5. Subsequently, the start of Activity E could be delayed for two days or take up to three days to complete before the project schedule is affected. On the other hand, Activities A, B, D, G, I, and J have no float because delaying their start or taking longer to complete that we estimated will increase the total duration of the project by the same amount.

As a result, knowing the critical path can influence a project manager's decisions. For example, a project manager can **expedite,** or **crash,** the project by adding resources to an activity on the critical path to shorten its duration. The project manager may even be able to divert resources from certain activities, for example, Activity E because this activity has some slack or float. Diverting resources will reduce the overall project schedule, but keep in mind that there may be a trade-off—shortening the schedule by adding more resources may inflate the project's budget.

Another way to shorten the project schedule is to look for parallel activity opportunities. Doing two, or several, activities that were originally planned to be completed in sequence at the same time can shorten the critical path. It is known as **fast tracking** the project.

Can the critical path change? The answer is absolutely! As a result, it is imperative that the project manager not only identify the critical path, but also monitor and manage it appropriately. In fact, it is very possible for a project to have more than one critical path.

PERT **Program Evaluation and Review Technique (PERT)** was developed in the late 1950s to help manage the Polaris submarine project. At about the same time, the Critical Path Method (CPM) was developed. The two methods are often combined and called PERT/CPM.

PERT uses the project network diagramming technique to create a visual representation of the scheduled activities that expresses both their logical sequence and interrelationships. PERT also uses a statistical distribution that provides probability for estimating when the project and its associated activities will be completed. This probabilistic estimate is derived by using three estimates for each activity: optimistic, most likely, and pessimistic.

An optimistic estimate is the minimum time in which an activity or task can be completed. This is a best-case scenario where everything goes well and there is little or no chance of finishing earlier. A most likely estimate, as the name implies, is the normally expected time required to complete the task or activity. A pessimistic estimate is a worst-case scenario and is viewed as the maximum time in which an activity can or should be completed.

One can use the following equation to compute a mean or weighted average for each individual activity that will become the PERT estimate:

$$\text{Activity Estimate} = \frac{\text{Optimistic Time} + (4 \times \text{Most Likely Time}) + \text{Pessimistic Time}}{6}$$

The total expected time to complete the project can be easily found by summing each of the individual activity estimates or:

$$\text{Total Expected Time of Project} = \sum_{i=1}^{n} \text{Activity Estimates}$$

For example, on our project used earlier, a project manager and team came up with the estimates presented in Table 7.3.

Analyzing the various paths using PERT provides the critical paths presented in Table 7.4. As can be seen in Table 7.4, the critical path is still Path 4 and the expected completion date of the project is 20.5 or 21 days if we round up. In this case, the deadline increased from nineteen days using the AON method to twenty-one days using the statistical technique associated with PERT. In the first case, the most likely estimates were used, while PERT took into account not only the most likely estimates, but also optimistic and pessimistic estimates as well. PERT is well suited for developing simulations whereby the project manager can conduct a sensitivity analysis for schedule planning and risk analysis. But, like any planning and scheduling tool, its usefulness is highly correlated to the quality of the estimates used.

Precedence Diagramming Method (PDM)   Another tool that is useful for understanding the relationships among project activities is the **Precedence Diagramming Method (PDM).** This tool is also based on the AON project diagram technique and is based on four fundamental relationships shown in Figure 7.5.

- *Finish-To-Start (FS)*—A finish-to-start relationship is the most common relationship between activities and implies a logical sequence. Here, activity or task B cannot begin until task A is completed. For example, a program is

Table 7.3 Activity Analysis for PERT

Activity	Predecessor	Optimistic Estimates (Days) a	Most Likely Estimates (Days) b	Pessimistic Estimates (Days) c	Expected Duration $(a + 4b + c)$ 6
A	None	1	2	4	2.2
B	A	3	5	8	5.2
C	B	2	4	5	3.8
D	B	2	3	6	3.3
E	B	1	1	1	1.0
F	C, D	2	4	6	4.0
G	D, E	2	3	4	3.0
H	F, G	1	2	5	2.3
I	G	4	5	9	5.5
J	H, I	.5	1	3	1.3

Table 7.4 Possible PERT Activity Paths

Possible Paths	Path	Total
Path 1	A + B + C + F + H + J 2.2 + 5.2 + 3.8 + 4.0 + 2.3 + 1.3	18.8
Path 2	A + B + D + F + H + J 2.2 + 5.2 + 3.3 + 4.0 + 2.3 + 1.3	18.3
Path 3	A + B + D + G + H + J 2.2 + 5.2 + 3.3 + 4.0 + 2.3 + 1.3	18.6
Path 4	A + B + D + G + I + J 2.2 + 5.2 + 3.3 + 3.0 + 5.5 + 1.3	20.5*
Path 5	A + B + E + G + I + J 2.2 + 5.2 + 1.0 + 3.0 + 5.5 + 1.3	18.2

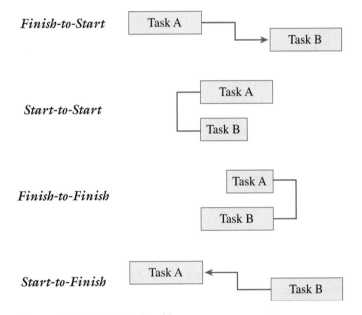

Figure 7.5 PDM Relationships

tested after it is written. Or, in other words, the code is written and then tested. This relationship is similar to the successor and predecessor relationships used in the AON method.

- *Start-To-Start (SS)*—A start-to-start relationship between tasks or activities occurs when two tasks can or must start at the same time. Although the tasks start at the same time, they do not have to finish together—i.e., the tasks can have different durations. A start-to-start relationship would be one type of parallel activity that can shorten a project schedule.

- *Finish-To-Finish (FF)*—Another type of parallel activity is the finish-to-finish relationship. Here, two activities can start at different times, have different durations, but are planned to be competed at the same time. Once both of the FF activities are completed, the next activity or set of activities can be started, or if no more activities follow, the project is complete.

■ *Start-To-Finish (SF)*—The start-to-finish relationship is probably the least common and can be easily confused with the finish-to-start relationship. A SF relationship, as illustrated in Figure 7.5, is exactly the opposite of a FS relationship. In addition, a SF relationship means that task A cannot end until task B starts. An example of a SF relationship in real life might be a nurse working at a hospital. This person may have to work until they are relieved by another nurse who arrives to start the next shift.

An advantage of using PDM is that the project manager can specify **lead** and **lag** times for various activities. More specifically, lead time allows for the overlapping of activities. For example, a project plan may have two activities or tasks that have been identified as a finish-to-start relationship. These two activities may be the setup of computers in a lab followed by the installation of an operating system on those computers. If we had two people, one to set up the computers and one to install the operating systems on each computer, the project plan might specify a finish-to-start relationship where the installation of the operating systems cannot begin until all of the computers have been set up in the lab. Based upon this project plan, the person who installs the operating system must wait and watch while the other person works.

Let's assume, however, that it takes about half the time to install an operating system as it does to set up a computer. Furthermore, there is no reason why the software person cannot begin installing the operating system when the hardware person has about half of the computers set up. In this case, both tasks will finish about the same time, and we have created an opportunity to shorten the project schedule. By scheduling the task of installing the operating systems when the task of setting up the computers is fifty percent complete, we have used the concept of lead time to our advantage.

On the other hand, let's suppose further that before our hardware person starts setting up the computers in the lab, we want the lab walls to be painted. This would be another finish-to-start relationship because we would like to schedule the painting of the lab before we start installing the computers. Using lead time in this case, however, would not make sense because we do not want the hardware person and painters getting in each other's way. In this case, we may even want to give the freshly painted walls a chance to dry before we allow any work to be done in the lab. Therefore, we would like to schedule a lag of one day before our hardware person starts setting up the computers. Another way of looking at this is to say we are going to schedule a negative lead day in our project schedule.

PROJECT MANAGEMENT SOFTWARE TOOLS

A number of software tools are available to make project planning and tracking much easier. In fact, it would be almost unthinkable to plan and manage even a small project without the aid of such a tool. In this section, you will see some examples of how these software tools incorporate and integrate the project management tools and concepts described in the previous section. The overview is intended to show you what these tools do, rather than tell you how to use them.

As you can see in Figure 7.6, the Gantt chart view integrates not only the Gantt chart, but also the project network diagram and PDM techniques. Tasks A and B show a finish-to-start relationship, while tasks B and C show a start-to-start relationship.

GETTING BACK TO THE BASICS OF IT PROJECT MANAGEMENT

The passing of the dot-com boom, along with a downturn in the economy, has led many U.S. companies back to the basics of IT project management. As a result, you probably will not find very many projects with sleepless and caffeine-pumped developers (supported by an open checkbook) working around the clock to be the first to market a snazzy Web site. Many experts agree that economic pressures have required IT projects to return to the fundamentals of project management that emphasize strict schedule and budget control, status reporting, continual user feedback, and documented processes and methodologies. According to Bob Wourms, a director of the consulting firm PM Solutions in Havertown, Pennsylvania, time-to-market and market share were critical a few years ago.

Today, however, the focus is on profitability, which requires the project manager keep the project on time and on budget. It also involves sticking to a goal and knowing when you're done. For example, an electric utility company called PacificCorp in Portland, Oregon, recently embarked on a $10-million customer service and call center project to support its 1.5 million customers. The goal of the eighteen-month project was for PacificCorp's 325 call center agents to handle 80 percent of all incoming calls in less than twenty seconds.

SOURCE: Adapted from Julia King, "Back to Basics," *Computerworld*, April 22, 2002. http://www.computerworld.com/managementtopics/roi/story/0,10801,70253,00.html.

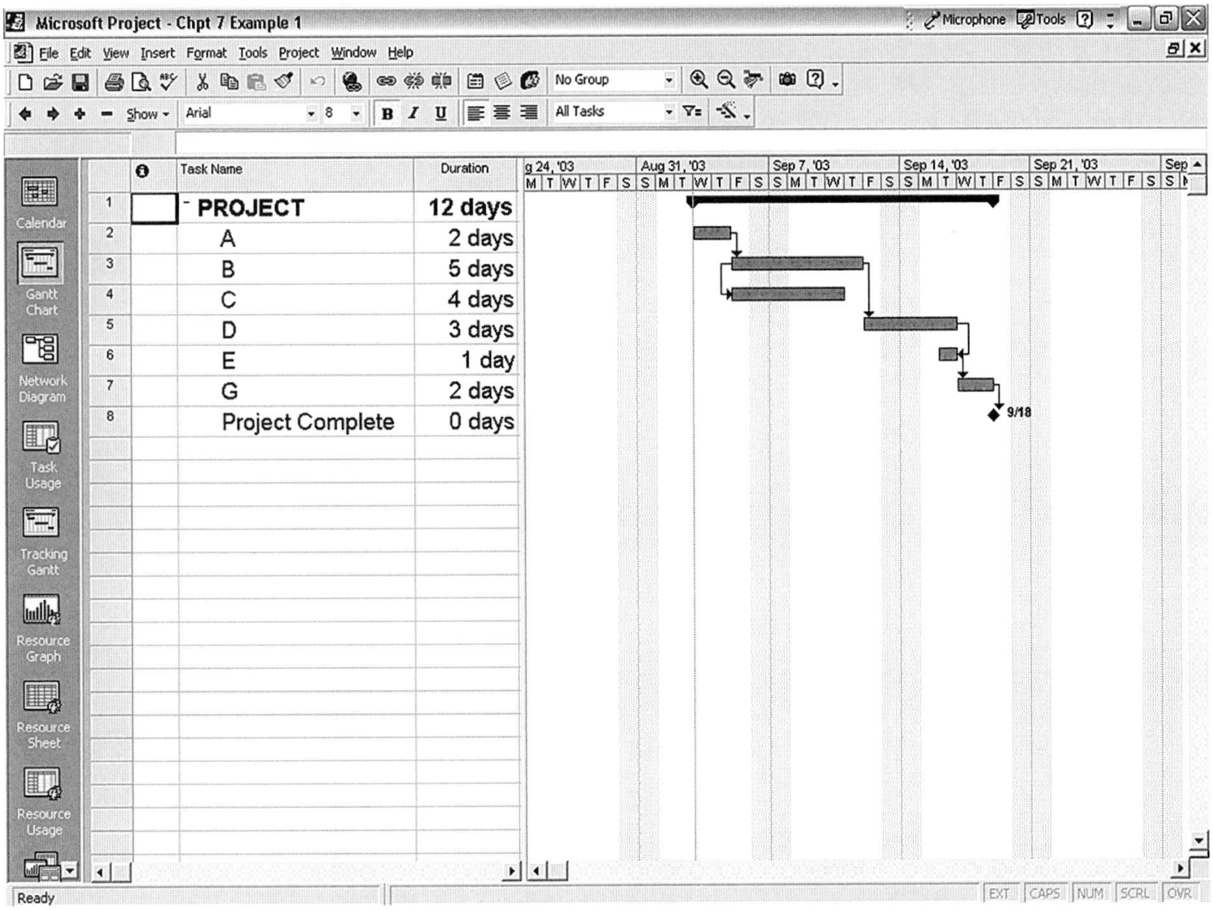

Figure 7.6 Microsoft Project 2000 Gantt Chart View

Tasks D and E show a finish-to-finish relationship. The task Project Complete has a duration of zero days and, therefore, represents a milestone. The Network Diagram View in Figure 7.7 then highlights the project's critical path. One of the most useful tools for scheduling and planning a project is a simple calendar. Figure 7.8 illustrates a Calendar View of the project.

Developing the project schedule and budget is an important planning process that requires that we sometimes define and estimate a large number of activities several months into the future. But, of course, predicting the future is difficult, and detailed project plans will have to be changed frequently to be useful. A technique called **rolling wave** planning is becoming common to help deal efficiently with project planning. Instead of developing a large, detailed project plan requiring frequent updates, the project manager can prepare an overall summary plan, or master schedule, and then develop detailed schedules for only a few weeks or a few months at a time (Haugan 2002). A list of helpful software that is available is listed in Table 7.5.

DEVELOPING THE PROJECT BUDGET

The project's budget is a function of the project's tasks or activities, the duration of those tasks and activities, their sequence, and the resources required. In general, resources used on a project will have a cost, and the cost of using a particular task or activity must be

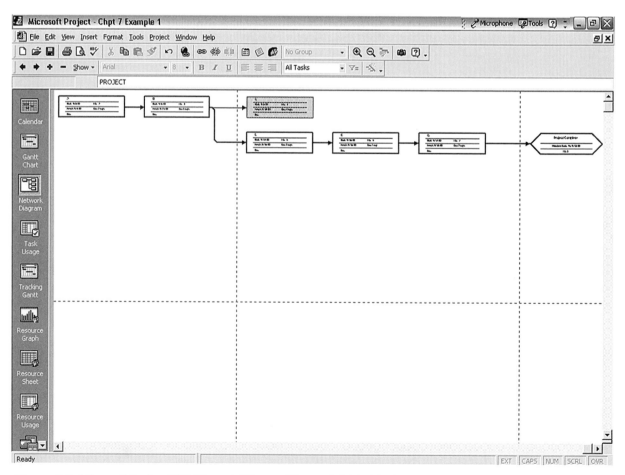

Figure 7.7 Microsoft Project 2000 Network Diagram View and Critical Path

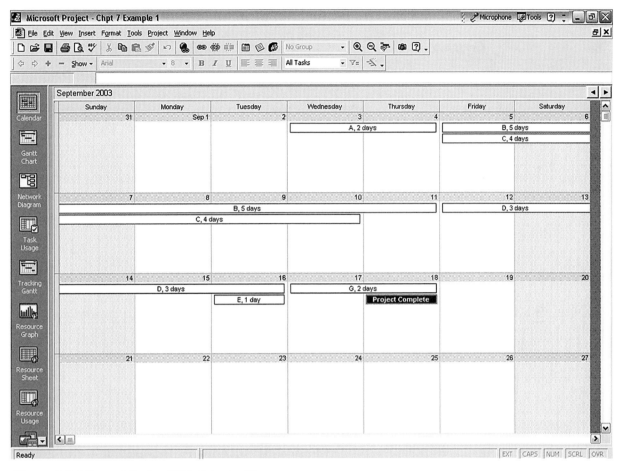

Figure 7.8 Microsoft Project 2000 Calendar View

included in the overall project budget. Unless these costs are accounted for, the project manager and the organization will not know the true cost of the project.

Cost Estimation

Estimating the cost of a particular activity or task with an estimated duration involves five steps:

1. Defining what resources will be needed to perform the work
2. Determining the quantity of resources that are needed
3. Defining the cost of using each resource
4. Calculating the cost of the task or activity
5. Ensuring that the resources are leveled, that is, resources have not been over allocated

For example, let's suppose that we have identified a particular task and estimated that it will take one day to complete and requires one project team member. Let's also assume, for simplicity, that no other resources are needed.

This estimate may require that we define a cost for using this particular resource. For example, if our team member earns $20 an hour, that sum is what our employee sees on his or her paycheck (before taxes and other deductions). The organization,

Table 7.5 Project Management Software

Type	*Company*	*Products*	*Web Site*
High-end enterprise	Artemis International Solutions Corp.	• Viewpoint • Portfolio Director	www.artimispm.com
	Niku Corp.	• Portfolio Manager • Director • Revenue Man	www.niku.com
	PlanView, Inc.	• PlanView	www.planview.com
	Primavera, Inc.	• TeamPlay • Enterprise • Expedition	www.primavera.com
	WST Corp.	• Open Plan • WelcomHome • Cobra	www.welcom.com
Midtier	Microsoft Corp.	• Project 2000 (standard, profession, & server)	www.microsoft.com
	Business Engine Software Corp.	• Business Engine Network	www.businessengine.com
	Pacific Edge Software, Inc.	• Project Office	www.pacificedge.com
	Advanced Management Solutions, Inc.	• RealTime Projects • RealTime Resources	www.amsrealtime.com
Specialty or niche products	Rational Software Corp.	Various products support: • Project management • Requirements analysis • Programming • Modeling • Testing • Documentation	www.rational.com
	QSM, Inc.	Products support: • Schedule & cost estimation • Project tracking • Benchmarking • Process improvement • Forecasting	www.qsm.com
	Software Productivity Research, Inc.	Products support: • Estimation • Benchmarking • Function Point Analysis	www.spr.com

SOURCE: G. H. Anthes, "Competitors," *Computerworld,* March 18, 2002.
http://www.computerworld.com/hardwaretopics/storage/story/0,10801,69118,00.html.

however, may also provide certain benefits to the employee (i.e., health care, life insurance, and so forth) that should be included in the cost for using this particular resource. Since these costs are going to vary from organization to organization, let's assume that our friends in the accounting department have conducted a cost accounting analysis for us and that the true cost of using this particular employee (i.e. hourly wage plus benefits) is $25 an hour. Subsequently, if we pay our employee for one day's work (i.e., an eight-hour day), the cost of completing this particular task is:

$$\textbf{Cost of task} = \text{Estimated duration} \times \text{True cost of the resource}$$
$$= 8 \text{ hours} \times \$25/\text{hour}$$
$$= \$200$$

We can even estimate the cost of a salaried employee by prorating her or his salary. This just means that we assign a portion of that salary to the task at hand. For example, let's say that the fully loaded, or true annual, cost to the organization is $65,000. If this employee works a five-day work week, the associated true cost to the organization would be for $5 \times 52 = 260$ days a year. Therefore, the prorated cost per day would be $65,000 ÷ 260 workdays = $250 a day.

However, this whole process can be greatly simplified if we use a project management software tool. We still have to identify the tasks and accurately estimate their durations, but determining the costs of a particular task and for the whole project becomes painless. Figure 7.9 shows how resources can be assigned to specific tasks on a project.

The project's total budget is computed using a bottom-up approach by summing the individual costs for each task or activity. As shown in Figure 7.10, the basic budget for this project is $5,203.85.

Other Costs

It is important to keep in mind that our example has only considered **direct costs,** or the cost of labor for using this resource directly. In addition to direct labor, resource

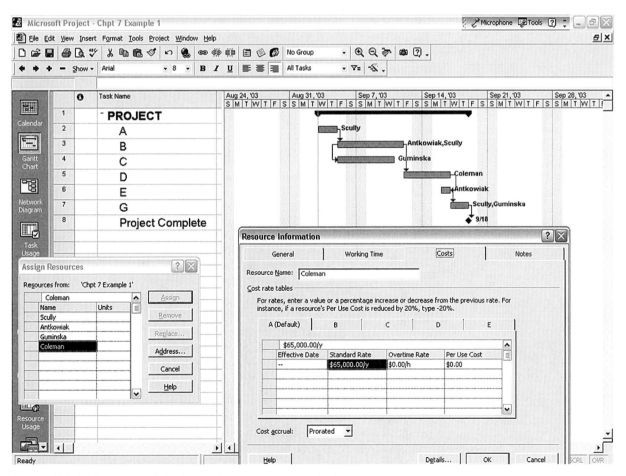

Figure 7.9 Using Microsoft Project to Assign Resources to Tasks

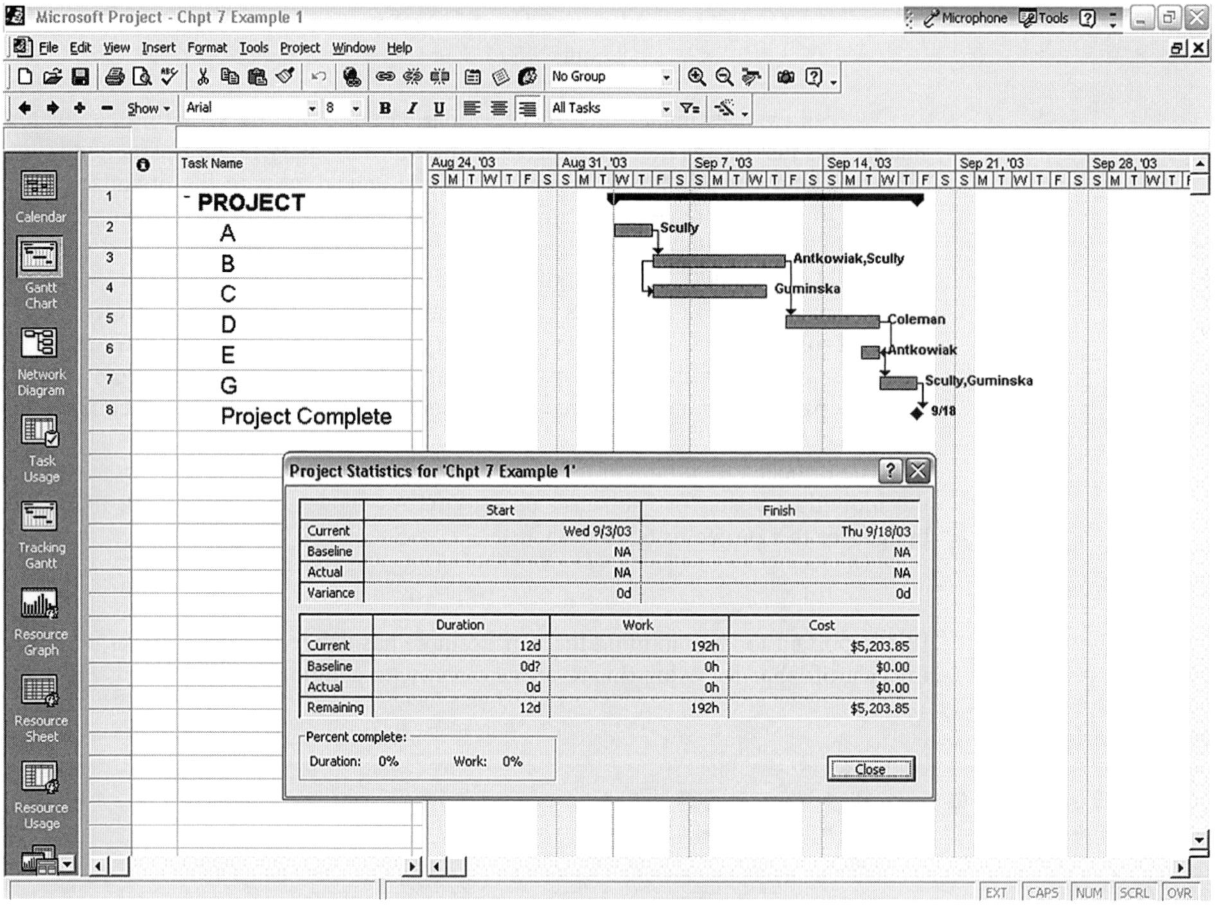

Figure 7.10 Using Microsoft Project 2000 to Compute the Basic Budget

costs include indirect labor, materials, supplies, and reserves (Kinsella 2002). To determine the total project's budget, we also need to include other costs as well. These costs include:

- *Indirect Costs*—These costs include such things as rent, utilities, insurance, and other administrative costs. For example, a consulting firm may charge a client $150 an hour per consultant. Included in that hourly fee would be the salary and benefits of the consultant and enough margin to help cover the administrative and operation costs needed to support the consulting office.

- *Sunk Costs*—Sunk costs are costs that have been incurred prior to the current project. For example, a previous attempt to build an application system may have ended in failure after three months and $250,000. This $250,000 would be considered a sunk cost, regardless of whether any work from the previous project is salvageable or of use to the current project.

- *Learning Curve*—Often we have to "build one and throw it away" in order to understand a problem or use a new technology effectively. In addition, inexperienced people will make mistakes and new technology will usually require a steep learning curve in the beginning. As a result, time and effort can be wasted. This time to learn should be considered in either the project schedule or budget.

■ *Reserves*—Reserves provide a cushion when unexpected situations arise. **Contingency reserves** are based on risk and provide the project manager with a degree of flexibility. On the other hand, a project budget should have some management contingencies built in as well. Of course, reserves are a trade-off. Upper management or the client will view these as fat that can be trimmed from the project budget; however, the wise project manager will ensure that a comfortable reserve is included in the project's budget. For example, it would be sad to think that the project's budget would not allow the project manager to buy pizza or dinner for the team once in a while as a reward for working late to meet an important milestone.

Resource Allocation

Once the resources have been assigned to the project, it is important that the project manager review the project plan to ensure that the resources are level. In other words, resources cannot be over allocated—i.e., a resource cannot be assigned to more than one task at the same time. Although the project manager may catch these mistakes early on, it is important that the level of resources be reviewed once the project schedule and resource assignments have been made. Not catching these mistakes early can have a demoralizing effect on the team and lead to unplanned (i.e., unbudgeted) costs.

A project management tool such as Microsoft Project provides the means for identifying overallocated resources. Figure 7.11 provides an example of the Resource Allocation View where a project team member has been assigned to two tasks at the same time. A project manager has the choice of creating a new relationship for these tasks (e.g., FS) or reassigning another resource to one of the tasks. In addition, many software management tools can level resources automatically for the project manager.

FINALIZING THE PROJECT SCHEDULE AND BUDGET

The project schedule and budget may require several iterations before it is acceptable to the sponsor, the project manager, and the project team. In addition, it is important that the project manager document any and all assumptions used to come up with duration and cost estimates. For example, this documentation may include estimating the salary of a database administrator (DBA) who will be hired at a future date. Instead of allocating a cost of what the project manager *thinks* a DBA will cost (or worse yet, what upper management would like to pay), he or she could use salary surveys or salary information advertised in classified advertisements as a base cost estimate. So, the project manager should document the source of this cost in order to give the cost estimates greater credibility. In addition, the project plan may include several working drafts. Having assumptions documented can help keep things organized as well.

Once the project schedule and project plan are accepted, the project plan becomes the baseline plan that will be used as a yardstick, or benchmark, to track the project's actual progress with the original plan. Once accepted, the project manager and project team have the authority to execute or carry out the plan. As tasks and activities are completed, the project plan must be updated in order to communicate the project's progress in relation to the baseline plan. Any changes or revisions to the project's estimates should be approved and then reflected in the plan to keep it updated and realistic.

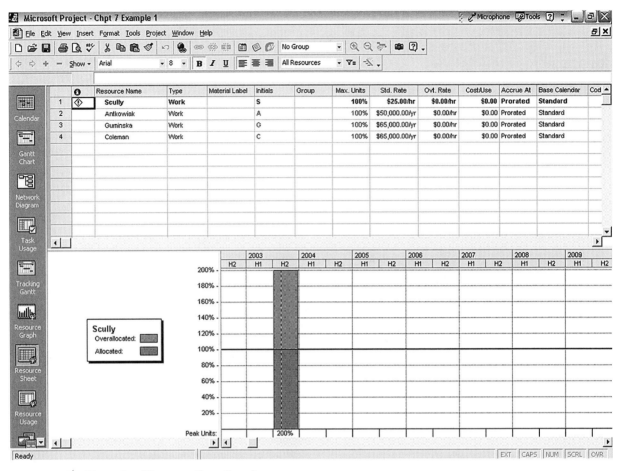

Figure 7.11 Example of Resource Overallocation

CHAPTER SUMMARY

Once project activities or tasks are identified and activity durations are estimated, the sequencing of these activities will help determine the project schedule and estimated completion date. Several techniques were introduced in this chapter. The use of project management software tools can help simplify the development of the project schedule. In addition, these tools can help the project manager identify and monitor activities that are on the critical path. They can help the project manager make decisions with respect to allocation of resources or the rescheduling of activities. In addition, these tools provide a useful information system capable of communicating the actual progress of the project to the original baseline plan.

In general, if a project uses a resource, the cost associated with that resource must be included in the project's budget and must be accounted for as a cost to the project. Project costs are both directly and indirectly related to the resources needed to complete a particular task or activity or support other resources that do. It is important that the right resources and the right quantity of resources be assigned to the project activities.

Together, the approved project schedule and project budget make up the baseline project plan. Approval of this plan by the project client or upper management gives the project manager and team the authority to carry out this plan. Actual progress is then compared to this plan to determine whether the project is on track, ahead of plan, or behind the plan. In order to keep the plan realistic, revisions or changes to the plan should be approved and made.

REVIEW QUESTIONS

1. Describe the PMBOK area of project cost management.
2. Discuss why no project ever failed because of someone's inability to draw a nice looking project network diagram.
3. What are some advantages project network diagrams have over traditional Gantt charts?
4. Define predecessor, successor, and parallel activities. Give a real world example of each.
5. How can parallel activities help shorten the project schedule? Are there any trade-offs?
6. What is meant by slack (or float)?
7. What is the difference between *crashing* and *fast tracking* a project's schedule?
8. What is the difference between AON and PERT?
9. Define the following and give a real world example of each (other than the ones described in this book):

Finish-to-Start; Start-to-Start; Finish-to-Finish; Start-to-Finish

10. What is the difference between lead and lag? Give real world examples (other than the ones used in this book) of how a project manager may use lead and lag in a project schedule.
11. Describe the steps necessary for estimating the cost of a particular activity or task that has an estimated duration.
12. What does prorating the cost of a resource mean?
13. Why should the project manager ensure that the project resources are leveled?
14. Why should assumptions used in estimating be documented?
15. What is a baseline plan?
16. When does the project manager or team have the authority to begin executing the project plan?

EXTEND YOUR KNOWLEDGE

1. Develop a network diagram using the AON technique and calculate the critical path using the information in the table to the right.
2. Enter the information from the above table into a project management software package. What is the critical path?

Task/ Activity	Estimated Duration	Predecessor
A	1 day	None
B	3 days	A
C	4 days	B
D	2 days	B
E	1 day	C
F	3 days	C, D
G	3 days	E
H	1 day	F
I	2 days	G, H
J	5 days	I

BIBLIOGRAPHY

Haugan, G. T. 2002. *Project Planning and Scheduling.* Vienna, Va.: Management Concepts.

Kinsella, S. M. 2002. Activity-Based Costing: Does It Warrant Inclusion in A Guide to the Project Management Body of Knowledge (PMBOK Guide)? *Project Management Journal* 33(2): 49–55.

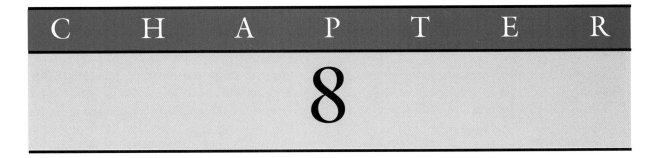

8

Managing Project Risk

CHAPTER OVERVIEW

Chapter 8 focuses on project risk management. After studying this chapter, you should understand and be able to:

- Describe the project risk management planning framework introduced in this chapter.
- Define risk identification and the causes, effects, and integrative nature of project risks.
- Apply several qualitative and quantitative analysis techniques that can be used to prioritize and analyze various project risks.
- Describe the various risk strategies, such as insurance, avoidance, or mitigation.
- Describe risk monitoring and control.
- Describe risk evaluation in terms of how the entire risk management process should be evaluated in order to learn from experience and to identify best practices.

■ GLOBAL TECHNOLOGY SOLUTIONS

The Husky Air project team filed into the GTS conference room, and everyone took a seat at the conference table. No one seemed to know why this urgent meeting had been called, but they knew from Tim Williams' e-mail that they were about to hear some interesting news.

Tim walked into the room and shut the door behind him. Everyone could tell by the expression on his face that the news was not going to be good. Tim took a seat at the head of the table. "Thank you all for being here on such short notice," he said. "As you all know, I had a meeting with our client this morning to go over the project plan we prepared." The look on Tim's face grew more serious, and the tension began to thicken. He paused, then continued, "Husky Air's management has informed me that they are feeling the effects of the downturn in the economy. The company is getting hit from two sides. First, there has been an increase in fuel costs. Second, with the continuing demand for airline pilots, several of its more experienced charter pilots have left to take jobs with the scheduled airlines. With costs up and revenues down, cash flow is a concern."

The project team members looked at each other with puzzled expressions. Sitaramin spoke up, "Tim, how will this affect *our* project?"

Tim looked down at faces of the team members gathered around the table. "When I met with them this morning, a few of the managers were inclined to cancel the project," he said. "However, because we focused on the value that this project is expected to bring to the organization, they decided that the project was too valuable to just cancel outright. But because cash flow is a problem, they need to reduce the cost of the project. After much discussion, it was agreed that we would trim the project's scope in order to decrease the project's budget. The good news is that Husky Air's management believes that the increase in fuel costs will be temporary and they are in the process of recruiting new pilots. However, it may be a few months before they are back on solid financial ground. If that happens, they want us complete the rest of the scope as we had originally planned. In the meantime, we'll have to get back to work and come up with a revised schedule and budget."

Ted, the project's telecommunication specialist, asked, "What about our contract with Husky Air? Can't we hold them to the contract they signed?"

"I just got off the phone with our company's lawyer," Tim answered. "She said that our contract allows either party to cancel the project if they can not fulfill the terms of the agreement. There's a significant financial penalty, of course, but Kellie and I decided that it was in everyone's best interest to renegotiate the contract based on a newly defined scope. We feel legal action is not the best way to build and maintain a good, long-term relationship with our client. Kellie did a quick financial analysis and believes we can still make a profit without having to downsize our project team. Besides, we have leads for several other projects with new clients so all of our eggs are not in one basket."

"Well at least I can still make the payments on my new car!" joked Pat. Everyone in the room laughed.

Sitaramin asked, "Tim, maybe we should think seriously about what else could affect our project?"

Tim looked around the table at the other team members. They seemed to be in agreement with the suggestion. Pat spoke up, "Sitaramin's right. What we need to do is come up with a risk management plan."

Tim laughed, "Okay, it looks like we're in for another brainstorming session. I just hope we have enough color markers. Any suggestions as to how we should get started?"

Even though the team had received bad news just a few minutes earlier, they were energized by thought of tackling another problem together. Yan suggested they focus on identifying different risks and the potential impact they might have on the project. This process would help them come up with strategies for handling risks and reduce the likelihood of surprises. Then, the team could develop a learning cycle to identify the facts, assumptions to be tested, and things to find out. The lessons learned could be documented and made part of the GTS knowledge base. Pat thought that was a good idea, and he suggested that they also identify triggers or flags that warn them when a particular risk might be imminent. This system would allow them to monitor the project's risk throughout the project life cycle and reduce the likelihood of being surprised again.

Tim rolled up his sleeves and walked over to the whiteboard. "Okay, everyone, slow down so I can write these ideas down," he said. "Now, how do you propose we get started?" Tim grinned and thought to himself how much he enjoyed working with this group of people.

Things to Think About:

1. Was the financial downturn of Husky Air a problem that the GTS team could have foreseen and avoided?
2. Can all risks to a project be identified and managed?
3. In addition to identifying threats, why should project stakeholders also look for opportunities?

INTRODUCTION

In the last chapter you learned how to develop a baseline project plan. This project plan is based on a number of estimates that reflect our understanding of the current situation, the information available, and the assumptions we must make. The fact that we must estimate implies a degree of uncertainty in predicting the outcome of future events. Although no one can predict the future with 100 percent accuracy, having a solid foundation, in terms of processes, tools, and techniques, can increase our confidence in these estimates.

Unfortunately, things seldom go according to plan because the project must adapt to a dynamic environment. Project risk management is becoming an important sub-discipline of software engineering. It focuses on identifying, analyzing, and developing strategies for responding to project risk efficiently and effectively (Jones 1994). It is important, however, to keep in mind that the goal of risk management is not to avoid risks at all costs, but to make well-informed decisions as to what risks are worth taking and to respond to those risks in an appropriate manner (Choo 2001).

Project risk management also provides an early warning system for impending problems that need to be addressed or resolved. Although risk has a certain negative connotation, project stakeholders should be vigilant in identifying opportunities. Although many associate uncertainty with threats, it is important to keep in mind that there is uncertainty when pursuing opportunities, as well.

It is unfortunate that many projects do not follow a formal risk management approach (Jones 1994). Because of their failure to plan for the unexpected, many organizations find themselves in a state of perpetual crisis characterized by an inability to make effective and timely decisions. Many people call this approach *crisis management* or *fire fighting* because the project stakeholders take a reactive approach or only address the project risks after they have become problems. Several common mistakes to managing project risk include:

- *Not Understanding the Benefits of Risk Management*—Often the project sponsor or client demands results. They may not care how the project team achieves its goal and objectives—just as long as it does! The project manager and project team may rely on aggressive risk taking with little understanding of the impact of their decisions (Lanza 2001). Conversely, project risks may also be optimistically ignored when, in reality, these risks may become real and significant threats to the success of the project. Unfortunately, risks are often schedule delays, quality issues, and budget overruns just waiting to happen (Wideman 1992). Risks can result in sub-par productivity and higher than average project failure rates (Kulik 2000).

- *Not Providing Adequate Time for Risk Management*—Risk management and the ensuing processes should not be viewed as an add-on to the project planning process, but should be integrated throughout the project life cycle (Lanza 2001). The best time to assess and plan for project risk, in fact, is at the earliest stages of the project when uncertainty for a project is the highest.

Catastrophic problems or surprises may arise that require more resources to correct than would have been spent earlier avoiding them (Choo 2001). It is better to reduce the likelihood of a risk or be capable of responding to a particular risk as soon as possible in order to limit the risk's impact on the project's schedule and budget.

- *Not Identifying and Assessing Risk Using a Standardized Approach*—Not having a standardized approach to risk management can overlook both threats and opportunities (Lanza 2001). Consequently, more time and resources will be expended on problems that could have been avoided; opportunities will be missed; decisions will be made without complete understanding or information; the overall likelihood of success is reduced; and catastrophic problems or surprises may occur without advanced warning (Choo 2001). Moreover, the project team may find itself in a perpetual crisis mode. Over time, crisis situations can have a detrimental effect on team morale and productivity.

Capers Jones (1994) suggests that effective and successful project risk management requires:

- *Commitment by all stakeholders*—To be successful, project risk management requires a commitment by all project stakeholders. In particular, the project sponsor or client, senior management, the project manager, and the project team must all be committed. For many organizations, a new environment and commitment to following organizational and project processes may be required. For many managers, the first impulse may be to shortcut or sidestep many of these processes at the first sign that the project is in trouble. A firm commitment to a risk management approach will not allow these impulses to override the project management and risk management processes that the organization has in place.

- *Stakeholder Responsibility*—It is important that each risk have an owner. This owner is someone who will be involved in the project, who will take the responsibility to monitor the project in order to identify any new or increasing risks, and who will make regular reports to the project sponsor or client. The position may also require the risk owner to ensure that adequate resources be available for managing and responding to a particular project risk. Ultimately, however, the project manager is responsible for ensuring that appropriate risk processes and plans are in place.

- *Different Risks for Different Types of Projects*—In a study that looked at IT project risks, Jones (1994) found that patterns of risk are different across different types of IT projects. The results of this study are summarized in Table 8.1. The implication is that each project has its own unique risk considerations. To attempt to manage all projects and risks the same way may spell disaster.

The remainder of this chapter will incorporate many of the processes and concepts outlined in the Project Management Body of Knowledge (PMBOK) that define the processes of risk management. More specifically, these processes include:

- *Risk Management Planning*—Determining how to approach and plan the project risk management activities. An output of this process is the development of a risk management plan.

- *Risk Identification*—Deciding which risks can potentially impact the project. Risk identification generally includes many of the project stakeholders and requires an understanding of the project's goal, as well as the project's scope, schedule, budget, and quality objectives.

Table 8.1 Various Software Risks for IT Projects

MIS Software Risks		Systems Software Risks		Commercial Software Risks		Military Software Risks		Contract or Outsourced Software Risks		End-User Software Risks	
Creeping user requirements	80%	Long schedules	70%	Inadequate user documentation	70%	Excessive paper work	90%	High maintenance costs	60%	Non-transferable application	80%
Excessive schedule pressure	65%	Inadequate cost estimates	65%	Low user satisfaction	55%	Low productivity	85%	Friction between contractor & client personnel	50%	Hidden errors	65%
Low quality	60%	Excessive paper work	60%	Excessive time to market	50%	Long schedules	75%	Creeping user requirements	45%	Unmaintainable software	60%
Cost overruns	55%	Error-prone modules	50%	Harmful competitive actions	45%	Creeping user requirements	70%	Unanticipated acceptance criteria	30%	Redundant application	50%
Inadequate configuration control	50%	Canceled projects	25%	Litigation expense	30%	Unused or unusable software	45%	Legal ownership of software & deliverables	20%	Legal ownership of software & deliverables	20%

SOURCE: T.C. Jones, *Accessment and Control of Software Risks,* 1994.

- *Qualitative Risk Analysis*—Focusing on a qualitative analysis concerning the impact and likelihood of the risks that were identified.

- *Quantitative Risk Analysis*—Using a quantitative approach for developing a probabilistic model for understanding and responding to the risks identified.

- *Risk Response Planning*—Developing procedures and techniques to reduce the threats of risks, while enhancing the likelihood of opportunities.

- *Risk Monitoring and Control*—Providing an early warning system to monitor identified risks and any new risks. This system ensures that risk responses have been implemented as planned and had the effect as intended.

IT PROJECT RISK MANAGEMENT PLANNING PROCESS

To manage risk, we first need to have a definition of *risk*. Although *Webster's* dictionary defines risk as *"hazard; peril; or exposure to loss or injury,"* the PMBOK defines **project risk** as:

> An uncertain event or condition that, if it occurs, has a positive or negative effect on the project objectives. (127)

The PMBOK definition provides an important starting point for understanding risk. First, project risk arises from uncertainty. This uncertainty comes from our attempt to predict the future based on estimates, assumptions, and limited information. Although project risk has a downside resulting from unexpected problems or threats, project risk management must also focus on positive events or opportunities. Therefore, it is important that we understand what those events are and how they may impact the project beyond its objectives. It is also important that we understand not

A WILD FRONTIER

Very few companies have a fully integrated approach to managing their information technology and business risks together. The companies that do tend to manage and monitor their IT risks with a fragmented approach. A survey conducted by Arthur Andersen & Co. and The Economist Intelligence Unit found that more than two-thirds of the 150 chief executive offices, chief financial officers, and chief information officers admit that IT risks are not that well-understood in their companies. In fact, only one-third of the companies have methods to determine risk. A common problem cited was that few companies try to anticipate problems once systems are implemented. For example, security is a common threat to many electronic business systems; however, few companies can actually say what impact security problems and threats would have on their customers. As it turns out, crisis management is much more expensive and embarrassing than risk management.

SOURCE: Adapted from Thomas Hoffman, Risk Management Still a Wild Frontier, *Computerworld,* February 16, 1998. http://www.computerworld.com/news/1998/story/0,11280,29808,00.html

only the nature of project risks but also how those risks interact and impact other aspects of the project throughout the life of a project.

The PMBOK defines **project risk management** as:

> The systematic process of identifying, analyzing, and responding to project risk. It includes maximizing the probability and consequences of positive events and minimizing the probability and consequences of adverse events. (127)

This PMBOK definition of risk management suggests that a systematic process is needed to effectively manage the risk of a project. In this section, an approach for risk management planning is introduced. It is illustrated in Figure 8.1.

The framework presented in Figure 8.1 outlines seven steps for managing IT project risk. Each of these steps will be discussed in more detail throughout the chapter.

Risk Planning

Risk planning is the first step and begins with having a firm commitment to the entire risk management approach from all project stakeholders. This commitment ensures that adequate resources will be in place to properly plan for and manage the various risks of the IT project. These resources may include time, people, and technology. Stakeholders also must be committed to the process of identifying, analyzing, and responding to threats and opportunities. Too often plans are disregarded at the first sign of trouble, and instinctive reactions to situations can lead to perpetual crisis management. In addition to commitment, risk planning also focuses on preparation. It is important that resources, processes, and tools be in place to adequately plan the activities for project risk management. Systematic preparation and planning can help minimize adverse effects on the project while taking advantage of opportunities as they arise.

Risk Identification

Once commitment has been obtained and preparations have been made, the next step entails identifying the various risks to the project. Both threats and opportunities must be identified. When identifying threats to a project, they must be identified clearly so that the true problem, not just a symptom, is addressed. Moreover, the causes and effects of each risk must be understood so that effective strategies and responses can

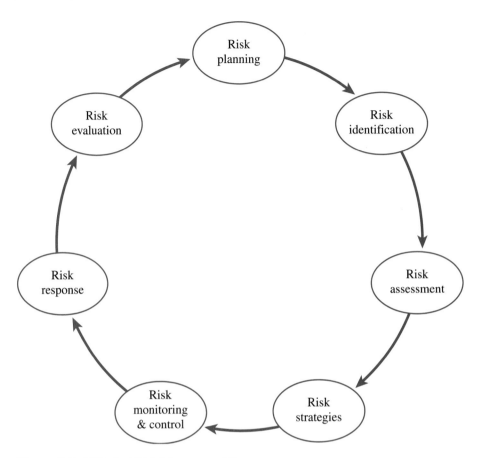

Figure 8.1 IT Project Risk Management Processes

be made. A framework for understanding the sources and nature of IT project risks will be introduced in the next section; however, it is important to keep in mind that project risks are rarely isolated. Risks tend to be interrelated and affect the project and its stakeholders differently.

Risk Assessment

Once the project risks have been identified and their causes and effects understood, the next step requires that we analyze these risks. Answers to two basic questions are required: What is the likelihood of a particular risk occurring? And, what is the impact on the project if it does occur? Risk assessment provides a basis for understanding how to deal with project risks. To answer the two questions, qualitative and quantitative approaches can be used. Several tools and techniques for each approach will be introduced later. Assessing these risks helps the project manager and other stakeholders prioritize and formulate responses to those risks that provide the greatest threat or opportunity to the project. Because there is a cost associated with responding to a particular risk, risk management must function within the constraints of the project's available resources.

Risk Strategies

The next step of the risk planning process is to determine how to deal with the various project risks. In addition to resource constraints, an appropriate strategy will be determined by the project stakeholders' perceptions of risk and their willingness to take on a particular risk. Essentially, a project risk strategy will focus on one of the following approaches:

- Accept or ignore the risk.
- Avoid the risk completely.
- Reduce the likelihood or impact of the risk (or both) if the risk occurs.
- Transfer the risk to someone else (i.e., insurance).

In addition, triggers or flags in the form of metrics should be identified to draw attention to a particular risk when it occurs. This system requires that each risk have an owner to monitor the risk and to ensure that resources are made available in order to respond to the risk appropriately. Once the risks, the risk triggers, and strategies or responses are documented, this document then becomes the **risk response plan.**

Risk Monitoring and Control

Once the salient project risks have been identified and appropriate responses formulated, the next step entails scanning the project environment so that both identified and unidentified threats and opportunities can be followed, much like a radar screen follows ships. Risk owners should monitor the various risk triggers so that well-informed decisions and appropriate actions can take place.

Risk Response

Risk monitoring and control provide a mechanism for scanning the project environment for risks, but the risk owner must commit resources and take action once a risk threat or opportunity is made known. This action normally follows the planned risk strategy.

Risk Evaluation

Responses to risks and the experience gained provide keys to learning. A formal and documented evaluation of a risk episode provides the basis for lessons learned and lays the foundation for identifying best practices. This evaluation should consider the entire risk management process from planning through evaluation. It should focus on the following questions:

- How did we do?
- What can we do better next time?
- What lessons did we learn?
- What best practices can be incorporated in the risk management process?

The risk planning process is cyclical because the evaluation of the risk responses and the risk planning process can influence how an organization will plan, prepare, and commit to IT risk management.

IDENTIFYING IT PROJECT RISKS

Risk identification deals with identifying and creating a list of threats and opportunities that may impact the project's goal and/or objectives. Each risk and its characteristics are documented to provide a basis for the overall risk management plan.

An IT Project Risk Management Framework

Identifying and understanding the risks that will impact a project is not always a straight-forward task. Many risks can affect a project in different ways and during different phases of the project life cycle. Therefore, the process and techniques used to identify risks must include a broad view of the project and attempt to understand a particular risk's cause and impact among the various project components. Figure 8.2 provides a framework for identifying and understanding the sources and impacts of IT project risks.

At the core of the IT project risk framework is the MOV, or measurable organizational value. The MOV is the goal of the project that defines the measurable value the organization expects from the project. It is both a measure and definition of project success.

The next layer of the framework includes the project objectives in terms of scope, quality, schedule, and budget. Although these objectives are not by themselves sufficient conditions for success, together they do play a critical role in supporting the MOV.

The third layer focuses on the sources of IT project risk. Risks can arise as a result of the various people or stakeholders associated with a project, legal considerations,

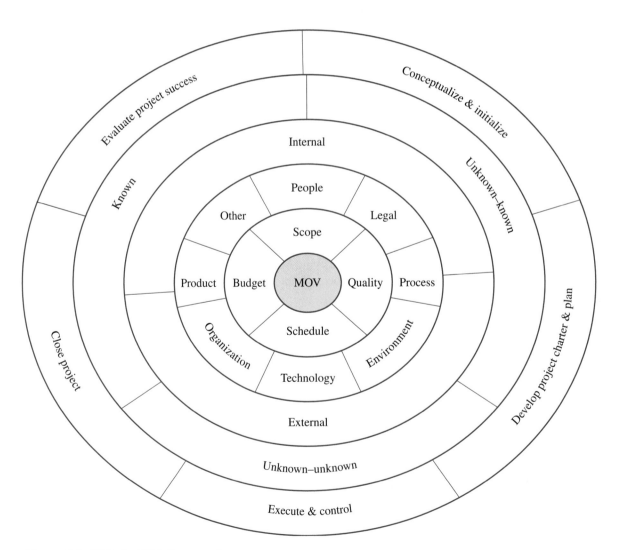

Figure 8.2 IT Project Risk Framework

the processes (project and product), the environment, the technology, the organization, the product, and a catchall category called *other*.

The next layer focuses on whether the sources of risk are internal or external to the project. It is important to make this distinction because a project manager is responsible and accountable for all project risks internal to the project. For example, if a project team member is not adequately trained to use a particular technology, then the project's objectives—scope, schedule, budget, and quality—may be impacted. In turn, this lack of training may inhibit the project from achieving its goal or MOV. Once this project risk has been identified along with its impact, the project manager can avoid or mitigate the risk by sending this particular project team member to training or by assigning certain critical tasks to a more experienced or skillful team member. On the other hand, a project manager may not be responsible for external risks. For example, a project manager would not be responsible or accountable if the project was cancelled because the organization sponsoring the project went bankrupt.

The distinction between internal and external risks is not always clear. For example, even though a particular hardware or software vendor may be external to the project, the project manager may still be responsible if that vendor is unable to deliver required technology resources. If the project manager chose that particular vendor, he or she would then be responsible or accountable for that risk. In short, a project manager will (or should) have control over internal risks, but not external risks. That distinction does not mean the project manager can ignore external risks. These risks can have a significant impact on the project, as well as the project manager's employment!

The fifth layer of the IT project risk management framework includes three different types of risks: **known risks, known-unknown risks,** and **unknown-unknown risks.** Wideman (1992) defines known risks as events that are going to occur. In short, these events are like death and taxes—they will happen and there is no uncertainty about it. On the other hand, known-unknowns are identifiable uncertainty. For example, if you own a home or rent an apartment, you know that you will receive a bill next month for the utilities you use. The precise amount you will owe the utility company will be unknown until you receive the actual bill. Unknown-unknown risks are residual risks or events that we cannot even imagine happening. For example, it was not too long ago that people had never even heard about the Internet. How could they comprehend the impact it would have on many of us? Unknown-unknown risks are really just a way to remind us that there may be a few risks remaining even after we may think we identified them all. In general, these are the risks that we identify after they have occurred.

The outer layer provides a time element in terms of the project life cycle. It may help us determine or identify when risks may occur, but also remind us that they may change over the life of the project. Although risk management is an important concern at the beginning of a project, the IT project risk management framework reminds us that we must be vigilant for opportunities and problems throughout the project life cycle.

Applying the IT Project Risk Management Framework

The GTS vignette at the beginning of the chapter can be analyzed using the process represented in Figure 8.1. For example, the risk faced by the GTS team could be defined as:

- A threat that occurred in the develop project charter and project plan phase.
- It was an unknown-unknown risk because it was identified after it occurred and, therefore, caught the GTS project team off guard.
- It was an external risk, and the project manager and project team should not be held responsible for the economic downturn experienced by Husky Air.

- The sources of risk to the GTS project include environment (economic), organizational (the client Husky Air) and people (if you would like to argue that Husky Air's management was lax in anticipating this problematic event).

- The impact on the GTS project was significant because it would affect the project's scope, schedule, and budget. Since Tim Williams was able to renegotiate the contract based on a trimmed scope, we can assume that quality would not be an issue. But if Husky Air's management insisted on maintaining the original scope, schedule, and budget, chances are good that quality would become an issue, especially if, for example, the scheduled testing time had to be shortened in order to meet the scheduled deadline.

- It is likely that the project's MOV would change as well because the project team would not complete the scope as originally planned. This, in turn, would determine the revised scope, schedule, and budget for the project.

This example shows how a risk can be understood after it occurs. The framework can also be used to proactively identify IT project risks. For example, a project team could begin with the project phases defined in the outer core of the framework. Using the project's work breakdown structure (WBS) and the individual work packages, the team could identify the risks for each of the work packages under the various project phases. Again, it is important that both threats and opportunities be identified. These risks could be classified as either known risks or known-unknown risks. The category of unknown-unknown risks should serve as a reminder to keep asking the question, What other threats or opportunities have we not thought about? Hopefully, the project team will do a more thorough job of identifying risks early in the project and reduce the likelihood of being surprised later.

The risks identified by the team can then be categorized as external or internal to the project. The internal risks are the direct responsibility of the project manager or team, while external risks may be outside their control. Regardless, both external and internal risks must be monitored and responses should be formulated.

The next step involves identifying the various sources of risk. Instead of trying to neatly categorize a particular risk, it may be more important to understand how the sources of risk are interrelated with each other. In addition, it may be a situation where precise definitions get in the way of progress. Instead of arguing or worrying about the exact source of a particular risk, it is more important the stakeholders understand the complex nature of a risk. Each risk-source category may mean different things to different stakeholders. Depending on the project, the stakeholders should be free to develop their own definitions and interpretations for each risk source category. They should also feel free to add categories, as needed.

After identifying the nature and characteristics of a particular risk, the project team can assess how a particular risk will impact the project. At this point, the team should focus on the project objectives that would be impacted if a particular risk occurred and, in turn, whether the project's MOV or goal would be impacted. Later on, these risks can be assessed to determine how the objectives will be impacted.

The above example shows how, working from the outside and then inward toward the center of the model, risks can be identified using the IT project risk framework. This procedure works well as a first pass and when using the project plan or WBS as a source of input. Many threats and opportunities may, however, be overlooked when relying only on the WBS.

The project team could start with the inner core of the IT risk framework and work outward. For example, the project team could identify how the MOV may be affected in terms of threats or opportunities that affect the project's scope, schedule, budget, or quality. Working away from the center, the team could identify possible sources of risk and then categorize whether the risk is internal or external, known, known-unknown, or unknown-unknown (i.e., did we miss something?), and when during the project life cycle this particular risk might occur.

Tools and Techniques

Identifying risks is not always easy. Risks tend to be interrelated and identifying each and every risk may not be possible or economically feasible. People may not want to admit that potential problems are possible for fear of appearing incompetent. As a result, stakeholders may deny or downplay a particular risk. Still, people and organizations have different tolerances for risk, and what may be considered a normal risk for one stakeholder or organization may be a real concern for another. So, the stakeholders may concentrate on a particular risk (that may or may not occur) at the expense of other risks that could have the same impact on the project.

It is, therefore, important that the project manager and team guide the risk management process. Risk identification should include the project team and other stakeholders who are familiar with the project's goal and objectives. Using one or more of the following tools, the IT project risk framework introduced earlier in this section can provide direction for identifying the threats and opportunities associated with the project:

- *Learning Cycles*—The concept of learning cycles was introduced in Chapter 4. The project team and stakeholders can use this technique, whereby they identify facts (what they know), assumptions (what they think they know), and research (things to find out), to identify various risks. Using these three categories, the group can create an action plan to test assumptions and conduct research about various risks. Based on the team's findings, both risks and lessons learned can then be documented.

- *Brainstorming*—Brainstorming is a less structured activity than learning cycles. Here the team could use the IT risk framework and the WBS to identify risks (i.e., threats and opportunities) starting with the phases of the project life cycle and working towards the framework's core or MOV or working from the MOV outward toward the project phases. The key to brainstorming is encouraging contributions from everyone in the group. Thus, initially ideas must be generated without being evaluated. Once ideas are generated by the group as a whole, they can be discussed and evaluated by the group.

- *Nominal Group Technique (NGT)*—The NGT is a structured technique for identifying risks that attempts to balance and increase participation (Delbecq and Van de Van 1971). Using the NGT:

  a. Each individual silently writes her or his ideas on a piece of paper.
  b. Each idea is then written on a board or flip chart one at a time in a round-robin fashion until each individual has listed all of his or her ideas.
  c. The group then discusses and clarifies each of the ideas.
  d. Each individual then silently ranks and prioritizes the ideas.
  e. The group then discusses the rankings and priorities of the ideas.
  f. Each individual ranks and prioritizes the ideas again.

g.   The rankings and prioritizations are then summarized for the group.

■ *Delphi Technique*—If the time and resources are available, a group of experts can be assembled—without ever having to meet face-to-face. Using the Delphi technique, a group of experts are asked to identify potential risks or discuss the impact of a particular risk. Initially, in order to reduce the potential for bias, the experts are not known to each other. Their responses are collected and made available anonymously to each other. The experts are then asked to provide another response based upon the previous round of responses. The process continues until a consensus exists. The advantage of using the Delphi technique is the potential for getting an insightful view into a threat or opportunity; but the process takes time and may consume a good portion of the project's resources.

■ *Interviewing*—Another useful technique for identifying and understanding the nature of IT project risks is to interview various project stakeholders. This technique can prove useful for determining alternative points of view; but the quality of the information derived depends heavily on the skills of the interviewer and the interviewees, as well as the interview process itself.

■ *Checklists*—Checklists provide a structured tool for identifying risks that have occurred in the past. They allow the current project team to learn from past mistakes or to identify risks that are known to a particular organization or industry. One problem with checklists is that they can lead to a false sense of security—i.e., if we check off each of the risks on the list, then we will have covered everything. Table 8.2 provides an example of items that may be included in a project risk checklist.

Table 8.2 Example of an IT Project Check List

Risk Checklist

✔ Funding for the project has been secured.
✔ Funding for the project is sufficient.
✔ Funding for the project has been approved by senior management.
✔ The project team has the requisite skills to complete the project.
✔ The project has adequate manpower to complete the project.
✔ The project charter and project plan have been approved by senior management or the project sponsor.
✔ The project's goal is realistic and achievable.
✔ The project's schedule is realistic and achievable.
✔ The project's scope has been clearly defined.
✔ Processes for scope changes have been clearly defined.

■ *SWOT Analysis*—SWOT stands for Strengths, Weaknesses, Opportunities, and Threats. Brainstorming, NGT, or the Delphi technique could be used to identify and understand the nature of IT project risks by categorizing risks using the framework illustrated in Figure 8.3. The usefulness of using SWOT analysis is that it allows the project team to identify threats and opportunities as well as their nature in terms of project or organizational strengths and weaknesses.

■ *Cause-and-Effect Diagrams*—The most widely known and used cause-and-effect diagram is the fishbone, or Ishikawa, diagram developed by Kaoru Ishikawa to analyze the causes of poor quality in manufacturing systems. The diagram can also be used for understanding the causes or factors of a particular risk, as well as its effects. An example of an Ishikawa diagram is illustrated in Figure 8.4. The diagram shows the possible causes and effects of a key member of the team leaving the project. This technique itself can be used individually or in groups by using the following steps:

a.   Identify the risk in terms of a threat or opportunity.

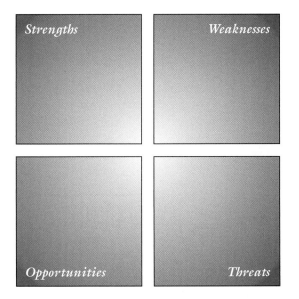

Figure 8.3 SWOT Analysis—Strengths, Weaknesses, Opportunities, and Threats

b. Identify the main factors that can cause the risk to occur.

c. Identify detailed factors for each of the main factors.

d. Continue refining the diagram until satisfied that the diagram is complete.

■ *Past Projects*—One of the themes in this text has been the integration of knowledge management to support the project management processes. Lessons learned from past projects can provide insight and best practices for identifying and understanding the nature of IT project risks. The usefulness of these lessons takes time and a commitment by the organization and project team to develop a base of knowledge from past projects. The value of this knowledge base will increase as the base does, allowing project teams to learn from the mistakes and successes of others.

RISK ANALYSIS AND ASSESSMENT

The framework introduced in the previous section provides tools for identifying and understanding the nature of risks to IT projects. The next step requires that those risks be analyzed to determine what threats or opportunities require attention or a response. Risk analysis and assessment provides a systematic approach for evaluating the risks that the project stakeholders identify. The purpose of **risk analysis** is to determine each identified risk's probability and impact on the project. **Risk assessment,** on the other hand, focuses on prioritizing risks so that an effective risk strategy can be formulated. In short, which risks require a response? To a great degree, this will be determined by the project stakeholders' tolerances to risk.

There are two basic approaches to analyzing and assessing project risk. The first approach is more qualitative in nature because it includes subjective assessments based on experience or intuition. Quantitative analysis, on the other hand, is based on mathematical and statistical techniques. Each approach has its own strengths and weaknesses when dealing with uncertainty, so a combination of qualitative and quantitative methods provides valuable insight when conducting risk analysis and assessment.

Qualitative Approaches

Qualitative risk analysis focuses on a subjective analysis of risks based upon a project stakeholder's experience or judgment. Although the techniques for analyzing project risk qualitatively can be conducted by individual stakeholders, it may be more effective if done by a group. This group process allows each stakeholder to hear other points of view and supports open communication among the various stakeholders. As a result, a broader view of the threats, opportunities, issues, and points of view can be discussed and understood.

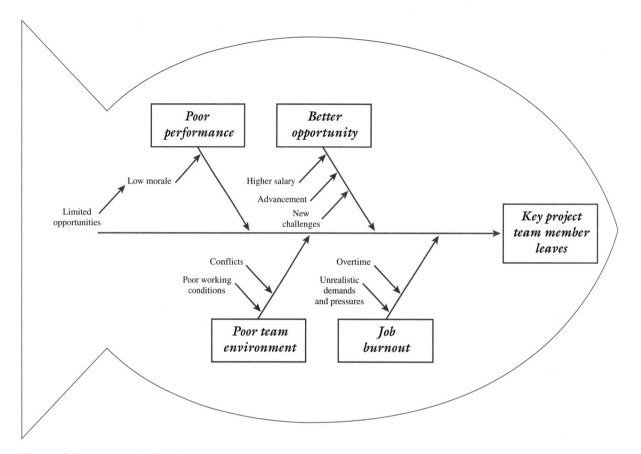

Figure 8.4 Cause and Effect Diagram

Expected Value   The concept of **expected value** provides the basis for both qualitative and quantitative risk analysis. Expected value is really an average, or mean, that takes into account both the probability and impact of various events or outcomes. For example, let's assume that a project manager of a consulting firm would like to determine the expected return or payoff associated with several possible outcomes or events. These outcomes or events, in terms of possible schedule scenarios, determine the return or profit the project will return to the consulting firm. The project manger believes each outcome has a probability of occurring and an associated payoff. The project manager's subjective beliefs are summarized in a **payoff table** in Table 8.3.

As you can see from Table 8.3, the project manager believes that the project has a small chance of finishing twenty days early or twenty days late. The payoff for finishing the project early is quite high, but there appears to be a penalty for completing the project late. As a result, the expected value or return to the consulting firm is $88,000. Since each event is mutually exclusive (i.e., only one of the five events can occur), the probabilities must sum to 100 percent.

Decision Trees   Similar to a payoff table, a **decision tree** provides a visual, or graphical, view of various decisions and outcomes. Let's assume that a project is going to overrun its schedule and budget. The project manager is contemplating reducing the time allocated to testing the application system as a way of bringing the project back within its original schedule and budget objectives.

Table 8.3 Expected Value of a Payoff Table

Schedule Risk	A Probability	B Payoff (in thousands)	A • B Prob • Payoff (in thousands)
Project completed 20 days early	5%	$ 200	$ 10
Project completed 10 days early	20%	$ 150	$ 30
Project completed on schedule	50%	$ 100	$ 50
Project completed 10 days late	20%	$ –	$ –
Project completed 20 days late	5%	$ (50)	$ (3)
	100%		$ 88

The project manager, then, is faced with a decision about whether the project team should conduct a full systems test as planned or shorten the time originally allocated to testing. The cost of a full test will be $10,000; but the project manager believes that there is a 95 percent chance the project will meet the quality standards set forth by the client. In this case, no additional rework will be required and no additional costs will be incurred. Since there is only a 5 percent chance the system will not meet the standards, the project manager believes that it would only require a small amount of rework to meet the quality standards. In this case, it will cost about $2,000 in resources to bring the system within standards.

On the other hand, the shortened test will cost less than the full test and bring the project back on track. But, if the project team limits the testing of the system, it will very likely lower the probability of the system meeting the quality standards. Moreover, a failure will require more rework and cost more to fix than if these problems were addressed during a full testing of the system. As you can see from Figure 8.5, a limited testing of the system will cost only $8,000, but the chances of the system failing to meet the quality standards increase. Moreover, the time and cost to complete the rework will be higher.

Even though the project manager still has a difficult decision to make, it now becomes a more informed decision. If the project team continues with the testing activities as planned, there is a very good chance that the system will not require a great deal of rework. On the other hand, reducing the time to test the system is more of a gamble. Although there is a 30 percent chance the limited testing will save both time and money, there is a high probability that the system will not pass or meet the quality standards. As a result, the required rework will make the project even later and more over its budget. If you were the project manager, what decision would you make?

Risk Impact Table We can create a **risk impact table** to analyze and prioritize various IT project risks. Let's use another example. Suppose a project manager has identified seven risks that could impact a particular project.

The left-hand column of Table 8.4 lists the possible risks that were identified using the IT project risk framework introduced in the last section. For simplicity, we will focus only on risks in terms of threats, but opportunities could be analyzed and assessed using the same technique.

The second column lists the subjective probabilities for each of the risks. In this case, the probabilities do not sum to 100 percent because the risks are not mutually exclusive. In other words, none, some, or all of the risk events could occur. A probability of zero indicates that a probability has absolutely no chance of occurring, while a probability of 100 percent indicates an absolute certainty that the event will occur. The next column provides the potential impact associated with the risk event occurring. This also is a subjective estimate based on a score from 0 to 10, with zero being no impact and ten having a very high or significant impact on the project.

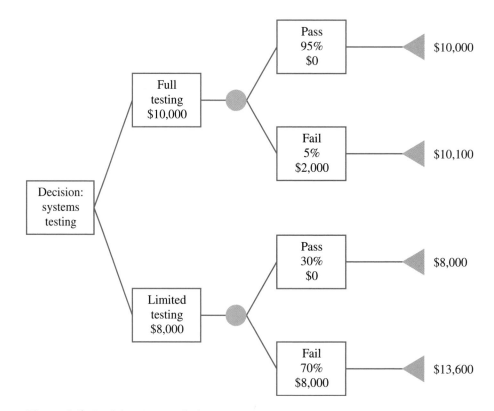

Figure 8.5 Decision Tree Analysis

Table 8.4 IT Project Risk Impact Analysis

Risk (Threats)	0–100% Probability	0–10 Impact	P • I Score
Key project team member leaves project	40%	4	1.6
Client unable to define scope and requirements	50%	6	3.0
Client experiences financial problems	10%	9	0.9
Response time not acceptable to users/client	80%	6	4.8
Technology does not integrate with existing application	60%	7	4.2
Functional manager deflects resources away from project	20%	3	0.6
Client unable to obtain licensing agreements	5%	7	0.4

Once a probability and an impact are assigned to each risk event, they are multiplied together to come up with a risk score. Although this score is based on the subjective opinions of the project stakeholders, it does provide mechanism for determining which risks should be monitored and which risks may require a response. Once a risk score is computed for each risk, the risks can be prioritized as in Table 8.5.

Table 8.5 shows that "Response time not acceptable to users/client" and "Technology does not integrate with existing application" are the two most significant risks to this project. The risk scores for all of the risks include the stakeholders risk tolerances and preferences since the subjective probabilities and impacts will reflect these tolerances and preferences.

The risk scores can be further analyzed using a risk classification scheme introduced by Robert Tusler (Tusler 1998). Figure 8.6 shows how the risk analysis can be used to classify the different risks.

As you can see in Figure 8.6, each risk from Table 8.4 is plotted against its probability and potential impact. Tusler suggests that risks can be classified according to the four quadrants:

- *Kittens*—Risks that have a low probability of occurring and a low impact on the project. These risks are rarely a source of trouble and, therefore, a great deal of time and resources should not be devoted to responding to these threats. Similarly, these types of opportunities are not worth pursuing since they offer little payback and have little chance of fruition.

- *Puppies*—Puppies are similar to kittens, but can become a source of problems very quickly because they have a high probability of occurring. Like the risks that they represent, puppies can grow into large troublesome dogs unless they are trained properly. Similarly, these types of risks must be watched so that corrective action can be taken before they get out of hand.

- *Tigers*—These types of risks have a high probability of occurring and a high impact. Similar to the dangerous animals they represent, they must be neutralized as soon as possible.

- *Alligators*—Alligators are not a problem if you know where they are, otherwise, they can be. These risks have a low probability of occurring, but a high impact if they do. These types of risks can be avoided with care.

Quantitative Approaches

Quantitative approaches to project risk analysis include mathematical or statistical techniques that allow us to model a particular risk situation. At the heart of many of these models is the probability distribution. Probability distributions can be continuous or discrete.

Discrete Probability Distributions **Discrete probability distributions** use only integer or whole numbers where fractional values are not allowed or do not make sense. For example, flipping a coin would allow for only two outcomes—heads or tails. If you wanted to find the

Table 8.5 Risk Rankings

Risk (Threats)	Score	Ranking
Response time not acceptable to users/client	4.8	1
Technology does not integrate with existing application	4.2	2
Client unable to define scope and requirements	3.0	3
Key project team member leaves project	1.6	4
Client experiences financial problems	0.9	5
Functional manager deflects resources away from project	0.6	6
Client unable to obtain licensing agreements	0.4	7

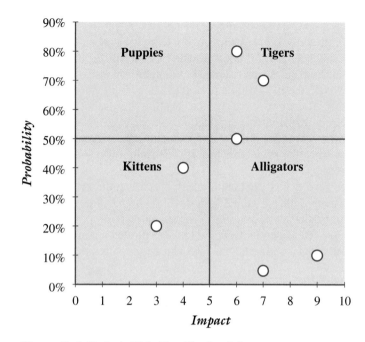

Figure 8.6 Tusler's Risk Classification Scheme

probability of flipping a fair coin into the air and having the outcome of the coin landing with the heads side up, just divide the number of favorable events (heads) by the number of total outcomes (heads or tails). This results in a ½ or 50 percent probability of the coin coming up heads. Since these events (heads or tails) are mutually exclusive and exhaustive (one and only one of these events will occur), the probability of tails is 50 percent (i.e., 100 percent − 50 percent = 50 percent). Probabilities must be positive and the sum of all of the event probabilities must sum to one.

If you were to flip a coin repeatedly a few hundred times and then record the outcomes, you would end up with a distribution similar to Figure 8.7.

Continuous Probability Distributions
Continuous probability distributions are useful for developing risk analysis models when an event has an infinite number of possible values within a stated range. Although in theory there are an infinite number of probability distributions, we will discuss three of the more common continuous probability distributions used in modeling risk. These include the **Normal Distribution, the PERT distribution,** and the **triangular distribution.** A quick overview shows how these distributions may be used to develop models for simulation or sensitivity analysis.

One of the most common continuous probability distributions is the normal distribution, or Bell Curve. Figure 8.8 provides an example of a normal distribution. The normal distribution has the following properties:

■ The distribution's shape is determined by its mean (μ) and standard deviation (σ). In Figure 8.8, this particular distribution has a mean of 0 and a standard deviation of 1. Other combinations of means and standard deviations will result in normal distributions with shapes that are either flatter or taller.

■ Probability is associated with area under the curve. Therefore, the total area under the curve and the baseline that extends from negative infinity ($-\infty$) to positive infinity ($+\infty$) is 100 percent. Subsequently, to find the probability of an event occurring between any two points on the baseline, just find the area between those two points under the curve. This is done by standardizing a given value for X using the formula: $z = (X - \mu) \div \sigma$ to obtain a z score. A table with the various z scores is then used to compute the probability for the area between any two z scores.

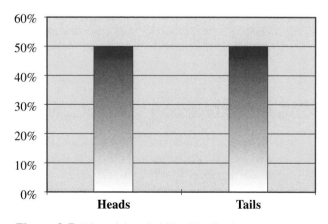

Figure 8.7 Binomial Probability Distribution

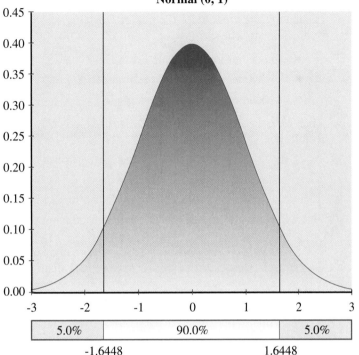

Figure 8.8 Normal Distribution

- Since the normal distribution is symmetrical around the mean, an outcome that falls between $-\infty$ and the mean, μ, would have the same probability of falling between the mean, μ, and $+\infty$ (i.e., 50 percent).
- Since the distribution is symmetrical, the following probability rules of thumb apply
  - About 68 percent of all the values will fall between $\pm 1\sigma$ of the mean
  - About 95 percent of all the values will fall between $\pm 2\sigma$ of the mean
  - About 99 percent of all the values will fall between $\pm 3\sigma$ of the mean

Therefore, if we know or assume that the probability of a risk event follows a normal distribution, we can predict an outcome with some confidence. For example, let's say that a particular project task has a mean duration of ten days. Moreover, over time we have been able to determine that this particular task has a standard deviation of two days. The mean tells us that if we were to complete this particular task over and over again, we would expect to complete this task, on average, in ten days. If we always completed the task in ten days, there would be no variability and the standard deviation would be zero. If, however, the task sometimes took anywhere between six and fifteen days to complete, we would have some variability, and the standard deviation would be a value greater than zero. The more variability we have, the larger is the computed standard deviation.

Using the rules of thumb described above, we could estimate, for example, that we would be about 95 percent certain that the project's task would be complete within six to fourteen days ($\mu \pm 2\sigma = 10 \pm 2 \times 2$). In addition, we could also say that we would be about 99 percent confident that the task would be completed between four and sixteen days ($\mu \pm 3\sigma = 10 \pm 3 \times 2$).

PERT Distribution   Using the PERT distribution, one can find a probability by calculating the area under the curve. However, the PERT distribution uses a three-point estimate where:

- *a* denotes an optimistic estimate
- *b* denotes a most likely estimate
- *c* denotes a pessimistic estimate

Therefore, the mean for the PERT distribution is computed using a weighted average as follow:

$$\text{PERT Mean} = (a + 4m + b) \div 6$$

And the standard deviation is computed:

$$\text{PERT Standard Deviation} = (b - a) \div 6$$

Figure 8.9 provides an example of a PERT distribution where $a = 2$, $m = 4$, and $b = 8$.

Triangular Distribution   Lastly, the triangular distribution, or TRIANG, also uses a three-point estimate similar to the PERT distribution where:

- *a* denotes an optimistic estimate
- *b* denotes a most likely estimate
- *c* denotes a pessimistic estimate

However, the weighting for the mean and standard deviation are different.

$$\text{TRIANG Mean} = (a + m + b) \div 3$$

$$\text{TRAING Standard Deviation} = [((b - a)^2 + (m - a)(m - b)) \div 18]^{1/2}$$

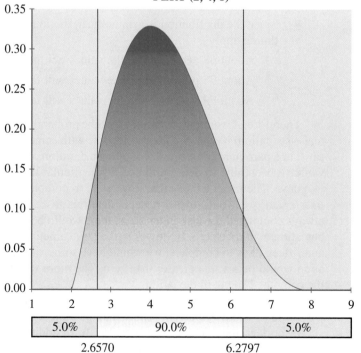

PERT (2, 4, 8)

5.0%	90.0%	5.0%

2.6570   6.2797

Figure 8.9   Example of a PERT Distribution

Figure 8.10 provides an example of a triangular distribution where $a = 4$, $m = 6$, and $b = 10$.

Simulations   In general, when people want to study a particular phenomenon, they pick a random sample. For example, if you wanted to know more about customer satisfaction or consumer tastes, you could survey a certain number of randomly selected customers and then analyze their responses. On the other hand, if you wanted to study projects, you might randomly select a certain number of projects and then collect data about certain attributes in order to make comparisons. This same approach can be used to analyze and understand how different input variables (e.g., task durations) can impact some output variable (e.g., project completion date).

   Monte Carlo simulation is a technique that randomly generates specific values for a variable with a specific probability distribution. The simulation goes through a specific number of iterations or trials and records the outcome. For example, instead of flipping a coin five hundred times and then recording the outcome to see whether we get about the same number of heads as we do tails, a Monte Carlo simulation can literally flip the coin five hundred times and record the outcome for us. We can perform a similar simulation using almost any continuous or discrete probability distribution.

   If we would like to apply our knowledge of probability distributions to risk analysis, there are a number of software tools available to model our project and develop simulations. One tool is an add-on to Microsoft Project called @Risk™, by Palisade Corporation. Let's say that a project manager has a project with five tasks (A through E) and has created a project plan using Microsoft Project. As you can see from Figure 8.11, the project is estimated to be completed in sixteen days. However, each task has a level of uncertainty in terms of each task's estimated duration. Therefore, we can create a Monte Carlo simulation that will tell us how likely it is that the project will

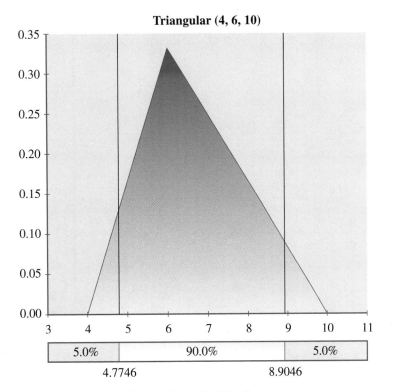

Figure 8.10   Example of a Triangular Distribution

be completed as planned. For example, Tasks A and D follow a PERT distribution, while Tasks B and C follow a triangular distribution. In addition, Task E follows a normal distribution. The distributions and values are listed in the @Risk Functions column created by the @Risk™ add-on.

The Monte Carlo simulation using @Risk™ was set to run five hundred iterations or trials. The output of this simulation is illustrated in Figure 8.12. Each bar in the histogram shows the frequency, or number of times, an iteration generated a particular completion date for the project based on the probability distributions for the five tasks.

Running the simulation using @Risk™, the project manager can assess the likelihood of the project finishing on September 26 (i.e., within the original sixteen-day estimate) by viewing a cumulative probability distribution (see Figure 8.13).

As you can see in Figure 8.13, the probability of completing the project on September 26—the end of the project manager's original sixteen-day estimate—is less than .200 or 20 percent.

In addition, the project manager can conduct a sensitivity analysis to determine the tasks that entail the greatest risk. Figure 8.14 illustrates a **tornado graph,** which summarizes the tasks with the most significant risks at the top. As the risks are ranked

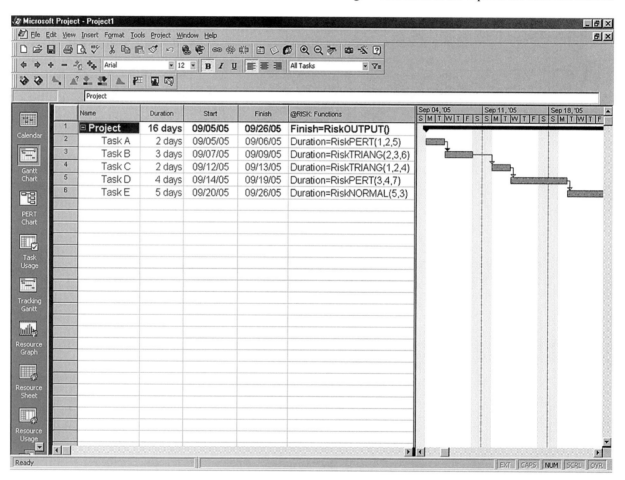

Figure 8.11 Risk Simulation Using @Risk™ for Microsoft Project

SOURCE: @Risk is used with permission of Palisade Corporation, Newfield, NY

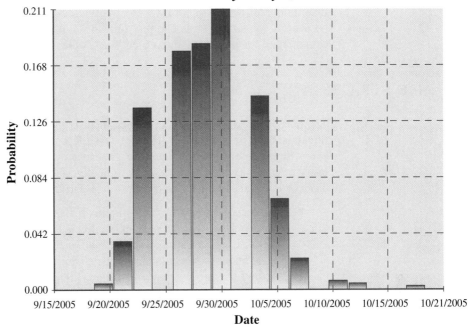

Figure 8.12 Output from Monte Carlo Simulation

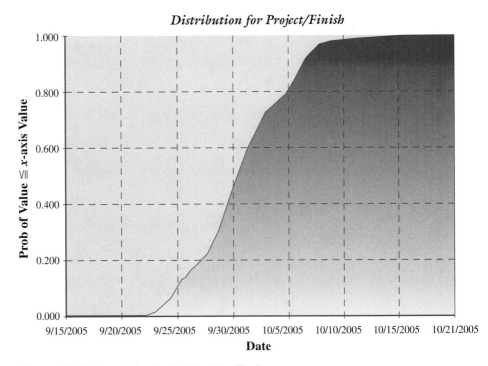

Figure 8.13 Cumulative Probability Distribution

from highest to lowest, the bars of the graph sometimes resemble a tornado. The tornado graph allows us to compare the magnitudes of impact for each of the tasks by comparing the size of each bar. As you can see in Figure 8.14, Task E has the greatest potential for impacting the project's schedule.

RISK STRATEGIES

The purpose of risk analysis and assessment is to determine what opportunities and threats should be addressed. It is not feasible or advisable to respond to each and every threat or opportunity identified because avoiding all threats or chasing after every opportunity requires resources to be diverted away from the real project work. Therefore, the risk strategy or response to a particular risk depends on:

- *The nature of the risk itself*—Is this really a threat to or opportunity for the project? How will the project be affected? At what points during the project life cycle will the project be affected? What are the triggers that would determine if a particular risk is occurring? Why should the risk be taken?

- *The impact of the risk on the project's MOV and objectives*—A risk has a probability and an impact on the project if it occurs. What is the likelihood of this occurring? And if this risk occurs, how will the project be affected? What can be gained? What could be lost? What are the chances of success or failure?

- *The project's constraints in terms of scope, schedule, budget, and quality requirements*—Can a response to a particular threat or opportunity be made within the available resources and constraints of the project? Will additional

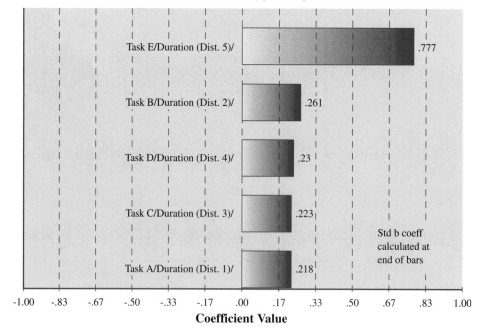

Figure 8.14 Sensitivity Analysis Using a Tornado Graph

resources be made available if a particular risk occurs? Can certain contractual obligations be waived or modified? What will happen if the desired result is not achieved?

- *Risk tolerances or preferences of the various project stakeholders*—Is a risk for one stakeholder a risk for another? How much risk is each stakeholder willing to tolerate? How committed is each stakeholder to the risk management process? Is the potential reward worth the effort?

A response to a particular risk may follow one of the following strategies:

- *Accept or Ignore*—Choosing to accept or ignore a particular risk is a more passive approach to risk response. The project stakeholders can either be hopeful that the risk will not occur or just not worry about it unless it does. This can make sense for risks that have a low probability of occurring or a low impact. However, reserves and contingency plans can be active approaches for risks that may have a low probability of occurring but with a high impact.

    - *Management Reserves*—These are reserves that are controlled and released by senior management at its discretion. These reserves are not usually included in the project's budget, but provide a cushion for dealing with the unexpected.

    - *Contingency Reserves*—A contingency reserve is usually controlled and released within specific guidelines by the project manager when a particular risk occurs. This reserve is usually included in the project's budget.

    - *Contingency plans*—Sometimes called an alternative plan, or *Plan B,* this plan can be initiated in the event a particular risk occurs. Although these types of plans are viewed as plans of last resort, they can be useful in a variety of ways. For example, a project team should have a disaster recovery plan in place should a natural disaster, such as a hurricane or earthquake, occur. This plan may have procedures and processes in place that would allow the project team to continue to work should its present workplace become unusable or unavailable. This type of disaster recovery plan is only useful if it is up-to-date and communicated to the various project stakeholders.

- *Avoidance*—The avoidance strategy focuses on taking steps to avoid the risk altogether. In this case, an active approach is made to eliminate or prevent the possibility of the threat occurring.

- *Mitigate*—The term *mitigate* means to lessen. Therefore, a mitigation risk strategy focuses on lessening the probability and/or the impact of threat if it does occur.

- *Transfer*—A transfer strategy focuses on transferring ownership of the risk to someone else. This transfer could be in the form of purchasing insurance against a particular risk or subcontracting a portion of the project work to someone who may have more knowledge or expertise in the particular area. As a result, this strategy may result in a premium, or added cost, to managing and responding to the risk.

Once the project risks and strategies are identified, they can be documented as part of the **risk response plan.** This plan should include the following:

- The project risk

- The trigger which flags that the risk has occurred
- The owner of the risk (i.e., the person or group responsible for monitoring the risk and ensuring that the appropriate risk response is carried out)
- The risk response based on one of the four basic risk strategies

The risk response plan can be developed using a template, such as the one illustrated in Figure 8.15.

RISK MONITORING AND CONTROL

Once the risk response plan is created, the various risk triggers must be continually monitored to keep track of the various IT project risks. In addition, new threats and opportunities may present themselves over the course of the project, so it is important that the project stakeholders be vigilant.

Risk monitoring and control should be part of the overall monitoring and control of the project. Monitoring and control focus on metrics to help identify when a risk occurs, and also on communication. The next chapter addresses how important it is to have a good monitoring and control system that supports communication among the various stakeholders and provides information essential to making timely and effective decisions.

Risk monitoring and control are analogous to a radarscope, as Figure 8.16 shows. Threats and opportunities present themselves at different times. Some are on the horizon, while others are closer to affecting the project's MOV and objectives.

Various tools exist for monitoring and controlling project risk. These include:

- *Risk Audits*—A knowledgeable manager or group can be useful for auditing the project team from time to time. The audit should focus on ensuring that the project manager and team have done a good job of identifying and analyzing project risks and on ensuring that proper procedures and processes are in place. Risk audits should be conducted by people outside the project team. Using outsiders provides a fresh perspective; the project team may be too close to the project and miss significant threats or opportunities.
- *Risk Reviews*—Risk audits should be conducted by individuals outside the project team; but risk reviews can be conducted internally. Throughout the project life cycle, the project stakeholders should hold scheduled, periodic risk reviews. These reviews should be part of each team meeting and part of the project team's learning cycles.
- *Risk Status Meetings and Reports*—Similar to risk reviews, a monitoring and control system should provide a formal communication system for monitoring and controlling project risks.

Risk	Trigger	Owner	Response	Resources required

Figure 8.15 Template for a Risk Response Plan

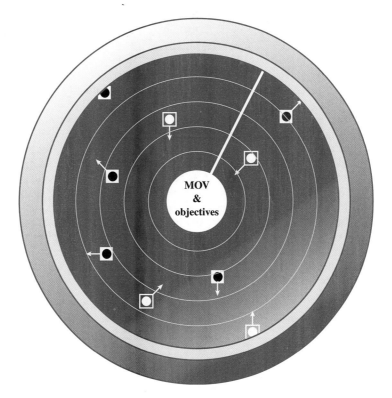

Figure 8.16 Project Risk Radar

RISK RESPONSE AND EVALUATION

The risk triggers defined in the risk response plan provide risk metrics for determining whether a particular threat or opportunity has occurred. A system for monitoring and controlling risk provides a mechanism for monitoring these triggers and for supporting communication among the various risk owners. The risk owners must be vigilant in watching for these triggers.

When a trigger occurs, the project risk owner must take appropriate action. In general, the action is responding to the risk as outlined in the risk response plan. Adequate resources must be available and used to respond to the risk.

The outcome of the risk response will either be favorable or unfavorable. Therefore, a great deal can be learned about the entire process of risk management (i.e., the preparedness of risk planning, identifying risks, analyzing and assessing risks, risk responses, and so forth). Lessons learned can lead to the identification of best practices that can be shared throughout the project organization. In summary, lessons learned and best practices help us to:

- Increase our understanding of IT project risk in general.

- Understand what information was available to managing risks and for making risk-related decisions.

- Understand how and why a particular decision was made.

- Understand the implications not only of the risks but also the decisions that were made.

- Learn from our experience so that others may not have to repeat our mistakes.

CHAPTER SUMMARY

This chapter introduced the processes and concepts of project risk management. Risk is an inherent component of IT projects because the project plan is based on a number of estimates that reflect our understanding of the current situation, the information available, and the assumptions that must be made. But, events seldom go according to plan, so the project must adapt to an ever-changing environment. Our inability to predict the future with 100 percent accuracy coupled with a dynamic environment create degrees of uncertainty or risk that must be addressed and managed throughout the project life cycle.

Although risk implies a negative connotation, project stakeholders must be vigilant in identifying opportunities presented by risk. The Project Management Body of Knowledge (PMBOK) points out that project risk management provides a systematic process for identifying, analyzing, and responding to project risks. A project risk management approach should focus on maximizing the probability and impacts of positive events while minimizing the probability and impacts of negative events.

In this chapter, two IT risk management frameworks were introduced. The first framework focused on the IT project risk management processes. These seven steps or processes include risk planning, risk identification, risk assessment, risk strategies, risk monitoring and controlling, risk response, and risk evaluation.

Risk planning begins with a firm commitment by all the project stakeholders to a risk management approach. A great deal of this commitment should be in terms of commitments to following the processes and to provide adequate resources when responding to risk events.

Risk identification should include identifying both threats and opportunities. Since most risks are interrelated and can affect the project in different ways, the project stakeholders should take a broad view of project risks. A second framework was introduced in this section to help understand the nature and influence of various IT project risks. This IT project risk framework is illustrated in Figure 8.2. It aids the project stakeholders in identifying and understanding the nature and influence of various risks.

Risk assessment allows the project stakeholders to determine what risks require a response. The goal of project risk management is not to avoid each and every risk at all costs, but to make well-informed decisions as to which risks are worth taking and which risks require a response. A well-informed decision requires an analysis of the probability of a particular risk occurring and its likely impact. Several qualitative and quantitative approaches were introduced to help in analysis. It is, however, important to keep in mind that there is a cost associated with responding to a particular risk, so risk management must function within the project's available resources.

Risk strategies define how the project stakeholders will respond to risk. In general, risk strategies include (1) accepting or ignoring the risk, (2) avoiding the risk, (3) mitigating or reducing the likelihood and/or impact of the risk, and (4) transferring the risk to someone else. A set of risk metrics should be defined to act as triggers, or flags, when a particular risk event occurs. The risks, the risk triggers, risk owners, and strategies should be formalized in a risk response plan.

Once the risk response plan has been completed and the project is underway, the various risks identified must be monitored and controlled. This process should include vigilance on the identified and unidentified threats and/or opportunities. As these risks present themselves, project risk owners should make resources available and respond to risk (Risk Response) in an appropriate manner, as outlined in the risk response plan.

Risk evaluation provides a key to learning and identifying best practices. A formal and documented evaluation of a risk response or episode can help an organization evaluate its entire risk management approach and provide insight for future project teams that may have to deal with a similar risk in the future.

WEB SITES TO VISIT

- **www.palisade.com:** Palisade Corp. provides many project risk management software tools. Free trial versions can be downloaded and evaluated.
- **www.decisioneering.com:** Decisioneering provides a risk management tool called Crystalball™. Free trial versions of several of its products can be downloaded and evaluated.
- **http://perso.wanadoo.fr/courtot.herve/links.htm:** Project Risk Management Sites of Interest.

- You can download a copy of this tool without cost from two Web sites, **www.iceincUSA.com** (Integrated Computer Engineering) and **www.spmn.com** (Software Program Managers Network): Integrated Computer Engineering, Inc. (ICE) provides Risk Radar™ (Version 2.02) as a free software product.

REVIEW QUESTIONS

1. What leads to uncertainty in an IT project?
2. How does a project risk management approach provide an early warning signal for impending problems or issues?
3. What is meant by crisis management? And why do many organizations find themselves in this mode?
4. Describe some of the common mistakes in project risk management.
5. Briefly describe what is required for effective and successful project risk management.
6. What is project risk?
7. What is project risk management?
8. What are the seven IT project risk management processes?
9. What types of commitment are necessary for risk planning?
10. Why can identifying IT project risks be difficult?
11. What is a "known" risk? Give an example of one.
12. What is a "known-unknown" risk? Give an example of one.
13. What is an "unknown-unknown" risk? Give an example of one.
14. What is the difference between an internal and external risk? Give an example of each.
15. Describe some of the tools and techniques that can be used to identify IT project risks.
16. Describe the nominal group technique and how it can be applied to identifying IT project risks.
17. Describe how learning cycles can be used to identify IT project risks.
18. What is the Delphi Technique? How can this technique be used to identify IT project risks?
19. How can interviewing be used as a technique for identifying IT project risks? What are some of the advantages and disadvantages of using this technique?

20. How do checklists help in identifying IT project risk? Discuss the pros and cons of using this technique.
21. What is SWOT analysis? How can this technique be used to identify IT project risks?
22. What is a fishbone (Ishikawa) diagram? How can this tool be used to identify IT project risks?
23. What is the purpose of risk analysis and assessment?
24. What is the difference between qualitative and quantitative risk analysis?
25. Describe the concept of expected value.
26. What is the purpose of a decision tree? What are the advantages and disadvantages of using a decision tree?
27. What is the purpose of a risk impact table?
28. What is the difference between a discrete probability distribution and a continuous probability distribution?
29. What are the rules of thumb that can be applied to a normal distribution?
30. Compare and contrast the normal distribution, the PERT distribution, and the triangular distribution.

31. What is a simulation? What value do simulations provide when analyzing and assessing IT project risks?
32. What is a Monte Carlo simulation? Describe a situation (other than the one used in this chapter) that could make good use of a Monte Carlo simulation.
33. Define and discuss the four risk strategies described in this chapter.
34. What is the difference between a management reserve and a contingency reserve?
35. What is a contingency plan?
36. Why can't a project team respond to all project risks?
37. What is a risk response plan? What should be included?
38. What are risk triggers or flags?
39. Why is having a risk owner a good idea? What role does a risk owner play?
40. What is risk monitoring and control?
41. Describe the three risk monitoring tools that were discussed in this chapter.
42. What is the purpose of evaluating a response to a particular risk?

EXTEND YOUR KNOWLEDGE

1. Using the Internet or the library, find an article about an IT project that failed. Using the IT project risk framework (Figure 8.2), identify the explicit or implicit risks that may have impacted this project.

2. Plan a trip to a show or a sporting event in another city. Define how you will get there and estimate how long it will take. Then define the risks that you might encounter and then construct a risk impact table. Afterwards, rank the risks and come up with a risk strategy for the three most significant risks.

BIBLIOGRAPHY

Choo, G. 2001. It's A Risky Business. www.systemcorp.com/frame-site/downloads/choo_p.html

Delbecq, A. and A. H. Van de Van. 1971. A Group Process Model for Identification and Program Planning. *Journal of Applied Behavioral Sciences* 7: 466–492.

Jones, T. C. 1994. *Assessment and Control of Software Risks.* Upper Saddle River, N.J.: Yourdon Press/Prentice Hall.

Kulik, P. 2000. What is Software Risk Management (And Why Should I Care?). www.klci.com

Lanza, R. B. 2001. Reviewing a Project Risk Management System. www.auditsoftware.net/infoarchive/articles/projmgmt/files/riskmgmt.htm

Tusler, R. 1998. An Overview of Project Risk Management. www.netcomuk.co.uk/~rtusler/project/elements.html

Wideman, R. M. 1992. *Project and Program Risk Management: A Guide to Managing Project Risks and Opportunities.* Newtown Square, Pa.: Project Management Institute.

Project Communication, Tracking, and Reporting

CHAPTER OVERVIEW

In this chapter, you will learn about developing an effective communications plan to better track, monitor, and report the project's progress. After studying this chapter, you should understand and be able to:

- Identify and describe the processes associated with the Project Management Body of Knowledge (PMBOK) area called project communications management, which includes project communications planning, information distribution, performance reporting, and administrative closure.

- Describe several types of reporting tools that support the communications plan.

- Apply the concept of earned value and discuss how earned value provides a means of tracking and monitoring a project's scope, schedule, and budget.

- Describe how information may be distributed to the project stakeholders and the role information technology plays to support the project communications.

GLOBAL TECHNOLOGY SOLUTIONS

Tim Williams stood in the doorway of Kellie Matthews' office. Kellie looked up from her notebook computer just as Tim was about to knock. "Hi, Tim. Come in and have a seat while I send off this e-mail," Kellie said.

Tim took a seat at the small, round conference table next to the window. Kellie clicked the send button, then got up from her desk and took a seat at the table across from Tim.

"So how are things going?" Kellie asked.

Tim leaned back in his chair. "So far, I think we're doing fine," he said. "We still have to make a few more changes to our revised project plan, but the changes are minor and we should get the final approval from Husky Air's management later this week. Then we can start on the real work."

Kellie smiled, "That's great news, Tim! So what do we have to do before we start development?"

Tim chuckled. "I'm glad you asked. I remember working on a project a few years ago. Everything was going well—the project was achieving its goal and was right on schedule and budget. The problem was that the project sponsor didn't know it. In fact, he thought the project was in trouble and that no one wanted to deliver the bad news."

Kellie sat back in her chair. "I see how one could assume that no news is bad news. So what happened?" she asked.

Tim gazed out the window and said, "It took several meetings with the client to smooth things over. I remember we had to stop in the middle of development to gather all kinds of project information to document what was done, what we were working on currently, and what we had left to finish. It really slowed the project down and we almost missed an important milestone."

Kellie thought for a moment. Then she said, "It sounds like a communication problem—or rather a lack of communication that created a problem. Is there anything I can do to help?"

Tim gave Kellie a sly smile. "It's funny you should ask. I was just going to ask for your help in devising a way for tracking and reporting the progress of the project. Besides, you're great with numbers!"

Kellie laughed, "I just knew you were up to something the minute I saw you standing at my door. I would say the first thing we need to do is develop some kind of communications plan that outlines how we'll communicate with the client. The plan should include a list of the stakeholders and outline what information they will need and when they will need it."

Tim started writing the ideas in his PDA. "That's a great idea," he said. "The project management software package I'm using to create the plan will allow me to benchmark our actual progress to our baseline plan. In fact, there are several *canned* reports that I can create and give to the client and to the team. Perhaps we can even schedule some face-to-face meetings or reviews with the client to let them know not only how things are going, but to address any issues or problems that need to be resolved as well."

Kellie leaned forward to get a better look at what Tim was entering into his PDA. "I think we'll also have to set up some way for the team to communicate with each other and with us. I've been playing around with a couple of software collaboration tools. Maybe I can set something up for the team members to use. They will be able to have online discussions and share documents with each other. They can even use the collaboration tool as a repository to store their learning cycles and lessons learned."

Tim looked up from his PDA and said, "That sounds terrific. I can keep an updated copy of the project plan in the repository. In fact, team members can even put their status and progress reports in the repository so we'll all know how things are going at any given time. Everyone will have access to the same information. Thanks, Kellie, you've been a big help as always."

Kellie smiled and answered, "Why don't you get started on the communications plan, while I start putting together our collaboration and reporting system. I think it would be a good idea to get the team member's input since they're the ones who will be making the most use of this system."

Tim got up from his chair, still entering thoughts in his PDA. "Okay," he said, as he walked to the door. "Why don't we plan on meeting again tomorrow with the team to polish these ideas?"

Both Tim and Kellie said quick good-byes. Kellie returned to her computer.

Things to Think About:

1. Why is communication among project stakeholders so important?
2. What kinds of information will the various stakeholders need?
3. What role does information technology play in supporting a communications plan?
4. When is face-to-face communication more appropriate than communication through e-mail?

INTRODUCTION

Information technology projects historically have demonstrated a poor track record for a variety of reasons. Often unrealistic project plans are created from inaccurate estimates, and, as a result, projects have little chance of achieving their objectives. As you saw earlier, various tools and techniques for estimating IT projects exist; but consistently developing accurate and realistic estimates remains a challenge. Much of an organization's capability to consistently and accurately estimate IT projects lies with well-defined processes, experience, and an information base of past projects.

Still, developing a realistic and effective project plan is only part of the solution. The project manager must also have a clear picture of how the actual progress or work compares to the original baseline plan. Seldom do things go according to plan, so the project manager must have the means to monitor and manage the project. This will allow him or her to make well-informed decisions, take appropriate actions when necessary, or make adjustments to the project plan.

Communication is important for successful project management. The PMBOK area called project communications management includes:

- *Communications Planning*—Communications planning attempts to answer the following questions:
  - How will information be stored?
  - How will knowledge be stored?
  - What information goes to whom, when, and how?
  - Who can access what information?
  - Who will update the information and knowledge?
  - What media of communication is best?

- *Information Distribution*—Focuses on getting the right information to the right people in the right format. Moreover, information distribution should also include organizing minutes from meetings and other project-related documents.

- *Performance Reporting*—Focuses on the collection and dissemination of project information to the various project stakeholders. This should include status reports, progress reports, and forecast reports.
- *Administrative Closure*—Focuses on verifying and documenting the project's progress. This includes organizing and archiving project records and lessons learned.

A project communications plan should include not only the information content for each stakeholder, but also the delivery of this information. Although a great deal of information can be obtained or distributed informally, the communications plan should detail the way data will be collected and the form in which information will be provided. Although an opportunity exists for capturing and disseminating data and information, an IT-based solution may not be practical or effective in all situations. For example, e-mail is a powerful tool for communication; however, richer forms of communication, such as face-to-face meetings, may be more appropriate or effective in certain situations.

Various stakeholders have different roles and interests in the project. For example, the project client or sponsor may be interested in the overall performance of the project. More specifically, is the work defined in the project scope being completed on time and within budget? And what is the likelihood of the project achieving its MOV? On the other hand, members of the project team may be interested in knowing what tasks or activities they should be working on and how their work relates to the activities and tasks being performed by other members of the project team. It is important that the people doing the actual work be empowered to take corrective action so that problems and issues can be resolved sooner rather than later.

Therefore, it is important that everyone associated with the project know what is going on. A project manager can develop an accurate and realistic project plan, but that plan is useless unless it is executed effectively. And, because no project plan is perfect, communication allows timely and intelligent adjustments to be made so it can be executed effectively.

When it comes to projects, no one likes surprises. Nothing can diminish a project manager's credibility faster than the surfacing of unexpected situations that should have been identified some time before. The unexpected does, however, happen, and no one can anticipate every conceivable contingency in a project plan. Senior management or the client will feel much more comfortable with a project manager who identifies unexpected problems, challenges, or issues early on and then suggests various alternatives. The project manager's credibility will rise if the project sponsor is confident that someone knows what the problem is and knows how to fix it. Conversely, confidence will diminish if problems surface that should have been identified earlier.

MONITORING AND CONTROLLING THE PROJECT

Let's begin with a story about a project manager. This particular project manager developed a detailed project plan and had several experienced and skillful members on the project team. The estimates were realistic and reasonably accurate. About two months into the project, one of the key team members left the project to play lead guitar in a country-western band. Although the team member/lead guitarist gave the usual two weeks notice, the project manager could only recruit and hire a less experienced replacement. The learning curve was steep. The other team members were asked to help this new person (in addition to doing their other work). As a result, many of the tasks and activities defined in the project plan took longer than expected. The schedule was in trouble. With a deadline looming in the near distance, the team began to take short cuts in an attempt to keep the project on track. The original project plan, for example, called for one month of testing. That seemed like a lot of time, so maybe the system could be tested in two weeks. As more and more tasks began to slip, testing was cut to one week, and then two days—okay, maybe the team could test the programs as they write them. Then they would just have to keep their fingers crossed and hope everything worked when the system was implemented!

On the day the system was supposed to be delivered, the project manager had to confess to senior management that the system was "not quite ready." Senior management then asked when the system *would* be ready. The project manager then sheepishly explained that there were a few *minor* setbacks due to unforeseen circumstances out of the project manager's control. Senior management once again asked when the system *would* be ready. After some hemming and hawing, the project manager explained that the project would take twice as long and cost twice as much to complete if the originally agreed upon scope was maintained. Needless to say, the *new* project manager kept senior management informed about the project's progress.

The moral of this story is that project sponsors do not like surprises. Regardless of how well a project is planned, unexpected situations will arise. These unexpected events will require adjustments to the project schedule and budget. In fact, many cost overruns and schedule slippages can be attributed to poorly monitored projects (Van Genuchten 1991). The project plan gets thrown out the window as slippage in one task or activity causes a chain reaction among the other interdependent tasks. If that task is on the critical path, the problem can be especially serious. You know you're in trouble if a project sponsor asks, Why didn't you tell me about this earlier?

The problem may gain strength and momentum as the project manager attempts to react to these unexpected events. For example, resources may be reassigned to different tasks or processes and standards may be overlooked. The wiser project manager, on the other hand, will try to be more proactive and recognize the impact of these unexpected situations in order to plan and act in a definite and timely manner. As our story points out, many times things happen on projects that are out of our control. If the project manager had identified this problem earlier and analyzed its impact, he or she could have apprised senior management of the situation and then laid out several alternative courses of action and their estimated impact on the project's schedule and budget. Although senior management may not like the news, they probably would respect the project manager for providing an early warning. Moreover, having a feeling that someone is in control will give them a sense of security.

A project manager *will not* lose credibility because an unexpected event or situation arises. He or she *will,* however, lose (or gain) credibility in terms of how they handle a particular situation. By addressing the problem early, the chain reaction and impact on other project activities can be minimized. There will be less impact on the projects' schedule and budget.

Therefore, planning and estimating are not sufficient. A project needs an early warning system to keep things on track. This early warning system allows the project manager to control and monitor the project's progress, identify problems early, and take appropriate corrective action.

The baseline plan acts as an anchor, allowing the project manager to gauge the project's performance against planned expectations. Once the baseline plan is approved, actual progress can be benchmarked to what was planned. This process is often referred to as comparing *actual to plan* performance, and the comparison is relatively easy and straightforward when using a project management software package.

Project control ensures that processes and resources are in place to help the project manager monitor the project. Although one might believe control has a negative connotation, it provides the capability to measure performance, alerts the project manager to problem situations, and holds people accountable. Controls also ensure that resources are being utilized efficiently and effectively while guiding the project toward its MOV. Controls can be either internal to the project (i.e., set by the project organization or methodology) or external (i.e., set by government or military standards). The control and monitoring activities of a project must be clearly communicated to all stakeholders. Everyone must be clear as to what controls will be in place and how data will be collected and information distributed.

THE PROJECT COMMUNICATIONS PLAN

The project communications plan can be formal or informal, depending on the needs of the project stakeholders and the size of the project. Regardless, communication is vital for a successful project. It is important that all of the project stakeholders know how their interests stand in relation to the project's progress.

Developing a communications plan starts with identifying the various stakeholders of the project and their information needs. Recall that stakeholder analysis helps the project manager and project team determine the different interests and roles of each of the stakeholders. Although some of the information contained in the stakeholder analysis may not be suitable for general dissemination, it provides a starting point for identifying who needs what information and when. Keep in mind that even stakeholders who may have a vested interest in the project *not* succeeding must be kept informed. Otherwise, a lack of communication and information can result in an attitude that "no news must be bad news," or speculation and frivolous assumptions that the project is in trouble.

The project communications plan can be in a table format similar to Figure 9.1. The idea behind this analysis is to determine:

- Who has specific information needs?
- What are those information needs?
- How will a particular stakeholder's information needs be met?
- When can a stakeholder expect to receive this information?
- How will this information be received?

This format helps clarify what all of the stakeholders know and what they still need to know. The following describes each of the areas for developing the communications plan:

Stakeholder	Information Requirements	Type of Report/Metric	Timing/ Availability	Medium or Format

Figure 9.1 The Project Communications Plan

- *Stakeholders*—Communication requires a sender, a message, and a receiver; however, we often focus mainly on the first two (Neuendorf 2002). Stakeholders are individuals or groups who have a "stake" or claim in the project's outcome and, therefore, are the receivers of the project information we send. In general, this group would include the project sponsor or client, the project manager, and the project team because each would have a specific interest in the project's performance and progress. Other people, such as senior managers, financial and accounting people, customers, and suppliers, may have a special interest in the project as well. Therefore, it is important that we keep these special interests informed.

- *Information Requirements*—A diverse group of stakeholders will result in diverse information requirements. Identifying the information requirements of the various stakeholders allows the project manager and project team to better determine the information reporting mechanisms, timings, and delivery medium for each stakeholder. Instead of a single report that may or may not meet the needs of each stakeholder, a particular report or metric can be designed to meet an individual stakeholder's needs and, therefore, improve communication with that stakeholder. In general, these information requirements will focus on scope, schedule, budget, quality, and risk. Depending on the needs of the stakeholder, the requirements and level of detail may be different.

- *Type of Report or Metric*—Depending on the information needs of a particular stakeholder, a specific report or reporting mechanism can be identified. These may include specific *canned,* or template, reports that are provided by a project management software tool or a custom report with specific metrics. In addition, reporting mechanisms may include formal or informal reviews of deliverables, milestones, or phases. Other reporting mechanisms, such as newsletters and other public relations tools, can serve a general population of stakeholders.

- *Timings/Availabilities*—The timing and availability of the reports sets expectations for the stakeholder. Some stakeholders may feel they need up-to-the-minute or real time access to the project's performance and progress. Other stakeholders may have an almost casual interest. Set timing and availability let people know when they will know. They also allow the project manager and team to stay focused by minimizing demands for ad hoc reports and status updates by powerful stakeholders.

- *Medium or Format*—The medium or format defines how the information will be provided. Possible formats include paper reports, face-to-face, electronic files, e-mail, or some other electronic format, such as the Web. Defining the format also sets expectations and allows the project manager to plan the resources needed to support the communications plan.

PROJECT METRICS

The communications plan described in the previous section is the output of the communications planning process. However, a project metric system must be in place to support the information requirements for all of the stakeholders. In general, project metrics should focus on the following key areas:

FYI (FOR YOUR INFORMATION)

Although the project budget, schedule, and resource assignments are in place, you can still have angered and frustrated stakeholders unless a comprehensive communications plan is in place. Rob Hennelly, a senior manager of financial processes and systems at Sears, Roebuck and Co. in Hoffman Estates, Illinois, points out that "communication goes to the heart of a lot of IT projects because it can ease the pain of change for end users." An effective communications plan should contain these principles:

1. *Identify your audience and their communication needs.* It is important to talk to the project's stakeholders and ask them what they need to know and how often they need to know it. For example, senior managers may want detailed reports, while end users may only want short messages.

2. *Determine the most effective means for communicating with this audience.* The basic question is how do the project stakeholders want to receive this information. In general, the most effective way to communicate is face-to-face, followed by

phone conversations. Although talk is fine, a project's official mode of communication should be in written form.

3. *Decide who should deliver the message.* It is important to assess how well, or how poorly, the IT project team members communicate with the business people. Business people tend to listen better to their own, while technical people tend to focus more on the technology. Getting the corporate communications people involved may be a good idea, especially when stakeholders outside the organization (i.e., customers, suppliers, unions, or stockholders) must be kept informed. In addition, timing is critical. It's a good idea to make important announcements, such as letting users know when their workstations will be replaced, before the impact.

SOURCE: Adapted from Rick Saia, One Project, One Voice, *Computerworld,* February 8, 1999. http://www.computerworld.com /news/1999/story/0,11280,33846,00.html

---

- Scope
- Schedule
- Budget
- Resources
- Quality
- Risk

Data to support these metric categories can be collected in a number of ways. For example, project team members may be asked to submit periodic reports or even time cards that describe what tasks they worked on, the time spent working on those tasks, and any other resources that they may have used on those tasks. In addition, the project team could report lines of code, function points, or even feature points. Data can be collected using expense reports, invoices, purchase orders, and so forth. Moreover, information can be provided informally through day-to-day contacts with various individuals or groups.

Collection of this data allows the project manager to compile a set of metrics that can be used to create the various reports for the stakeholders defined in the communications plan. A **project metric** may be defined as a qualitative measurement of some attribute of the project. This metric should be obtained from observable, quantifiable data (Edberg 1997). In addition, these metrics can be useful for developing a measurement program that allows the team and other stakeholders to gauge the efficiency and effectiveness of the work being done. Edberg suggests that a good project metric must be:

- *Understandable*—A metric should be intuitive and easy to understand; otherwise, the metric will be of little value and will most likely not be used.

- *Quantifiable*—A quantifiable metric is objective. A metric should have very little bias as a result of personal influence or subjectivity.

- *Cost Effective*—Data must be collected in order to produce a metric. Subsequently, a metric should be relatively easy and inexpensive to create and should not be viewed as a major disruption.

- *Proven*—A metric should be meaningful, accurate, and have a high degree of validity in order to be useful. The metric must measure exactly what one wants to measure. "What gets measured gets done!"

- *High Impact*—Although the efficiency of computing a metric is important, the metric must be effective. Why measure something that has little impact on the project?

Meyer (1994) suggests that trying to run a team without a good measurement system is like trying to drive a car without a dashboard. He suggests the following principles as a guide (Meyer 1994):

- *A measurement system should allow the team to gauge its progress.* The project metrics should let the team know when to take corrective action rather than waiting for the project manager to intervene. Instead of using a measurement system to control a team, it should be used to empower the team to solve problems on its own.

- *The team should design its own measurement system.* The people actually doing the work know what metrics are best suited. However, a team should not develop project metrics or a measurement system without the aid of the project manager or other members of the organization because independent action could result in inconsistencies and parochial interests being served.

- *Adopt only a handful of measures.* The old saying, "what gets measured gets done," can be an opportunity if the right metrics and measurement system are in place. Adding more and more measures as a means of encouraging team members to work harder can have the opposite effect. Collecting data to support a measurement system takes time and can interfere with the planned work. Having a few key measures keeps the team focused and creates minimal interference. In addition, these measures create a common language among team members and the other project stakeholders.

- *Measures should track results and progress.* Using the metaphor of a car's dashboard, Meyer suggests an array of graphic indicators and easy-to-read gauges can be useful in helping a project team measure and track its own progress and in letting it know when to take corrective action. For example, a relative measure could be used to track the remaining project budget, as illustrated in Figure 9.2. As you can see, Figure 9.2 vividly shows that the project is consuming its budget faster than planned.

Earned Value

Suppose that you hired the infamous consulting firm Dewey, Cheatem, and Howe to develop an information system for your organization. The project is expected to cost $40,000 and take four months to complete. To keep things simple, let's also assume that the project requires twenty activities or tasks that are evenly divided over the four-month schedule. Since each task is expected to take the same amount of time, the expected cost per task is $2,000. By the way, the contract that you just signed also stipulates that four payments must be made at the end of each month. Therefore, your planned payments each month would be $10,000. This $10,000 a month that you plan to spend is called the **budgeted cost of work scheduled (BCWS)**. If we were to graph the BCWS expenditures, the planned budget of cumulative cash flows would look like Figure 9.3.

At the end of the first month, let's say that you receive the following invoice for $8,000.

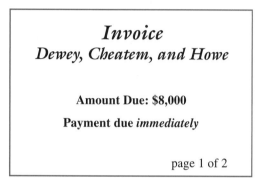

This actually sounds like good news! If you take a look at Figure 9.4, you planned to spend $10,000 at the end of the first month, but the invoice you just received states that you only have to pay $8,000. It would appear that you are spending less money than you originally had planned. The $8,000 you must pay to Dewey, Cheatem, and Howe has another fancy name and is referred to as the **actual cost of work performed (ACWP).** That must mean your project is ahead of budget by $2,000, right?

Actually, all we are doing is staying within our budgeted or planned outlays of funds. To understand what's really happening, we need to take a look at the second page of the invoice.

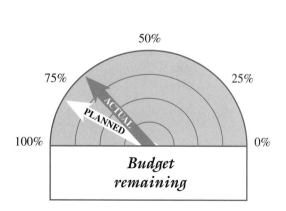

Figure 9.2 Dashboard Metric

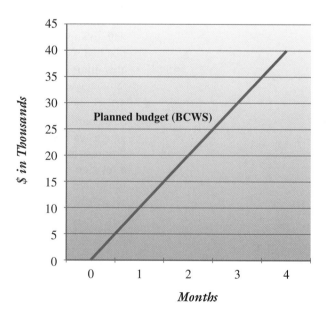

Figure 9.3 Planned Budget—Budgeted Cost of Work Scheduled (BCWS)

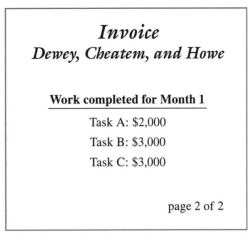

Invoice
Dewey, Cheatem, and Howe

Work completed for Month 1

Task A: $2,000

Task B: $3,000

Task C: $3,000

page 2 of 2

It looks like the consultants from Dewey, Cheatem, and Howe are only charging us $8,000, but they only completed three out of the five tasks that were expected to be completed by the end of the first month. In fact, since we estimated that each task would cost $2,000, we have really spent $8,000 in actual costs to achieve only $6,000 of actual work. This $6,000 is called the **earned value** and tells us how much of the budget we really should have been spent for the amount of work completed so far. Earned value is often referred to as budgeted **cost of work performed (BCWP),** and Figure 9.5 shows the relationship of earned value to budgeted and actual costs.

Using these basic values, we can extend our analysis and see how the earned value metric incorporates scope, budget, and schedule. For example, we can determine a true **cost variance,** which is the difference between a task's estimated cost and its actual cost.

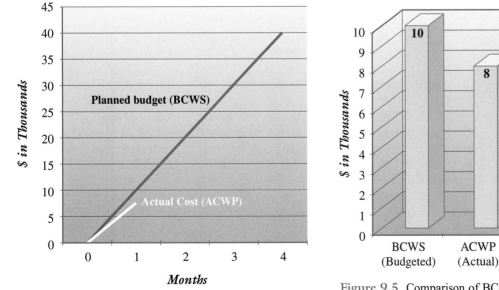

Figure 9.4 BCWS Versus ACWP

Figure 9.5 Comparison of BCWS, ACWP and Budgeted Cost of Work Performed (BCWP)

$$\text{Cost Variance (CV)} = \text{BCWP} - \text{ACWP}$$
$$= \$6,000 - \$8,000$$
$$= (\$2,000)$$

The negative $2,000 CV is an important metric because it tells us that we have spent $8,000 in order to achieve $6,000 worth of work. Earned value indicators, such as cost variance, can be either positive or negative. As you can see from above, a negative variance indicates that the project is over budget and/or behind schedule. Unless appropriate action is taken to get the project on track, you might have to increase the budget or reduce the project's scope. Conversely, a positive variance indicates that the project is ahead of schedule and/or under budget.

Often these cost overruns do not correct themselves and actually get worse as the project proceeds (Fleming and Koppelman 1996). In fact, if things continue as they are in our example, we can determine how much the project will really end up costing. You planned on spending $40,000, but given how things are going, is this still realistic? To answer this question, we compute a **cost performance index (CPI)** as follows:

$$\text{Cost Performance Index (CPI)} = \text{BCWP} \div \text{ACWP}$$
$$= \$6,000 \div \$8,000$$
$$= .75$$

A CPI of .75 tells us that for every dollar we spent, only $0.75 was really completed. In addition, we can also see the impact on the project's schedule by taking a look at the **schedule variance,** which shows the difference, in terms of cost, between the current progress and our originally scheduled progress.

$$\text{Schedule Variance (SV)} = \text{BCWP} - \text{BCWS}$$
$$= \$6,000 - \$10,000$$
$$= (\$4,000)$$

Using this information, we can create a schedule efficiency metric. A **schedule performance index (SPI)** can be computed as follows:

$$\text{Schedule Performance Index (SPI)} = \text{BCWP} \div \text{BCWS}$$
$$= \$6,000 \div \$10,000$$
$$= .6$$

The SPI provides a ratio of the work performed to the work scheduled. Therefore, for every $1.00 of work that was expected to be completed, only $0.60 was accomplished. These earned value metrics, such as the cost performance index (CPI) and the schedule performance index (SPI), can be greater than 1 or less than 1. A CPI or SPI ratio greater than 1 indicates that the project is ahead of schedule and/or under budget. On the other hand, a CPI or SPI that is less than 1 indicates that the project is behind schedule and/or over budget.

We can determine the minimum cost for this project by dividing the total budget by the CPI.

$$\text{Minimum Funds Needed} = \text{Original Total Budget} \div \text{CPI}$$
$$= \$40,000 \div .75$$
$$= \$53,333.33$$

If nothing changes (i.e., the project's performance does not get any better or any worse), it appears that the project will end up costing over $13,000 more than expected. However, the minimum funds needed value of \$53,333.33 assumes that everything will go according to plan after the first month. What if things do not get better? What if the schedule and cost variances continue? We can estimate this scenario by including the SPI in our estimate.

$$\text{Funds needed if things continue to get worse} = \text{Original Total Budget} \div (\text{CPI} \times \text{SPI})$$
$$= \$40,000 \div (.75 \times .60)$$
$$= \$40,000 \div .45$$
$$= \$88,889$$

As you can see, if this project continues to experience the same level of cost and schedule slippage, you will end up paying almost \$89,000. That's 125 percent over your original budget! No wonder the study by the Standish Group described in Chapter 1 is called *Chaos.* Hopefully, you can see how important it is to plan a project well and also how important controls and a monitoring system are to a project.

REPORTING PERFORMANCE AND PROGRESS

Once the project data have been collected, the project manager can use it to update the project plan. An example of an updated project plan using Microsoft Project 2000 is illustrated in Figure 9.6.

The project manager has a wide variety of software tools at his or her disposal, and these include project management software, spreadsheets, databases, and so forth.

In addition, project reporting tends to fall under one of the following categories:

- *Reviews*—Project reviews may be formal or informal meetings that include various project stakeholders. These reviews may focus on specific deliverables, milestones, or phases. The purpose of a review is to not only show evidence that the project work has been completed, but also that the work has been completed according to certain standards or agreed upon requirements. For example, the project team may present the project plan to the project sponsor. If the scope, schedule, and budget are agreed upon, then the project plan is accepted and the project may proceed to the next phase. In addition, review meetings provide a forum for surfacing issues, problems, and even opportunities that may require stakeholders to negotiate or make decisions.

- *Status Reporting*—A status report describes the present state of the project. In general, a status report compares the project's actual progress to the baseline plan. Analogous to a balance sheet used by accountants, a status report may include, for example, a variance analysis that compares actual schedule and cost information to the baseline schedule and budget.

- *Progress Reporting*—A progress report tells us what the project team has accomplished. This report may compare the activities or tasks that were completed to the activities or tasks outlined in the original project network.

- *Forecast Reporting*—A forecast report focuses on predicting the future status or progress of the project. For example, it may include a trend analysis that tells us when the project is most likely to finish and how much it will cost.

Many project management software tools, such as Microsoft Project 2000, provide a variety of *canned* reports or templates. The categories of reports found in Microsoft Project 2000 are illustrated in Figure 9.7.

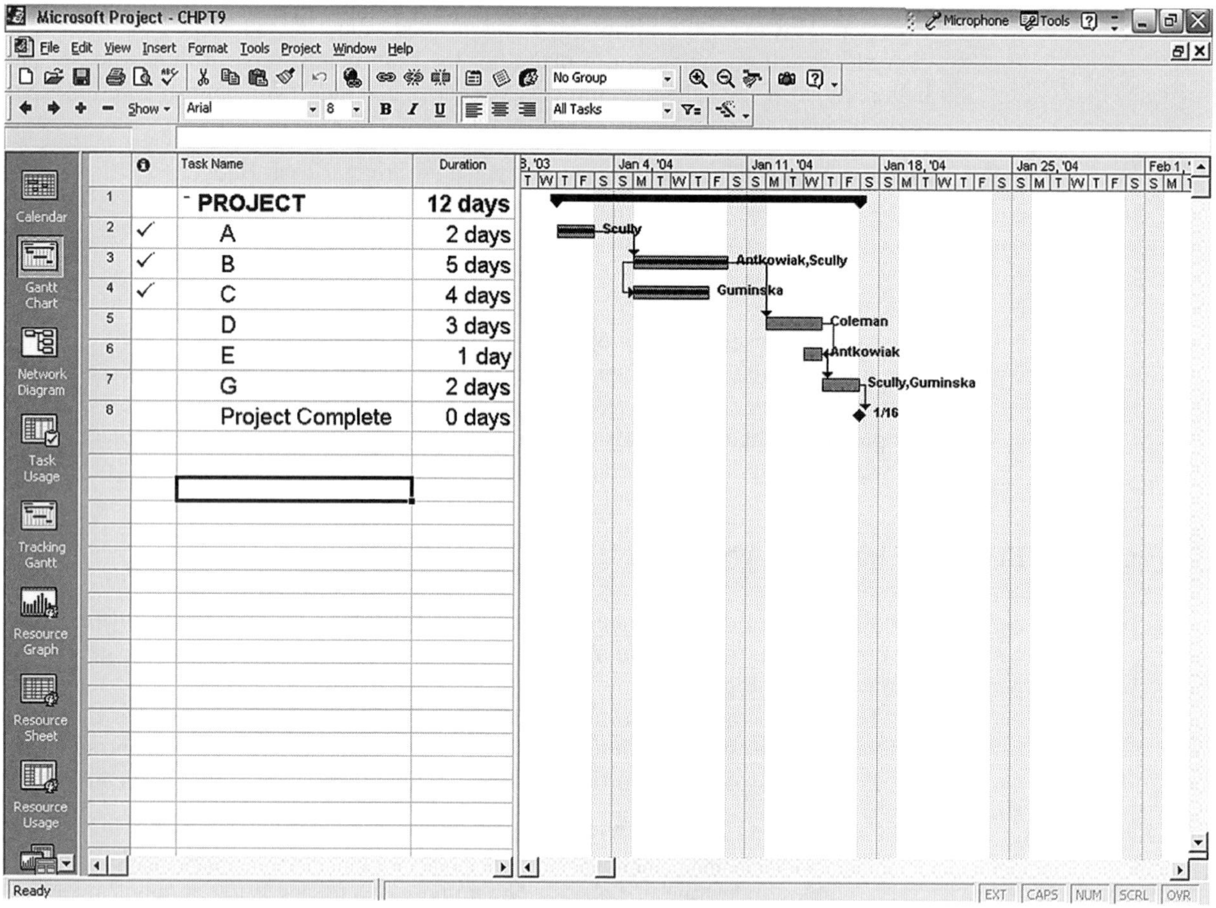

Figure 9.6 Updated Project Plan

INFORMATION DISTRIBUTION

To complete the project communications plan, the project manager and team must determine how and when the required information will be provided to the various stakeholders. Although a variety of media exist, most communication will involve:

- *Face-to-Face Meetings*—A great deal can be learned from face-to-face meetings. Such meetings may range from informal conversations to more formal meetings and presentations. The advantage of face-to-face meetings is that one can see other people's expressions and body language. Sometimes the way someone says something can be more expressive than what they say. On the other hand, face-to-face meetings require arranging schedules and additional costs if travel is involved. Certain issues and problems, of course, require people to meet face-to-face. For example, firing (or dehiring?) a person should only be done face-to-face. There are a number of war stories in the business world about people who found out they were let go by e-mail. The general consensus is that this is an insensitive and tactless way to treat people.

- *Telephone, Electronic Mail, and other Wireless Devices*—It appears that we are in the midst of a wireless and mobile revolution. Cellular phones,

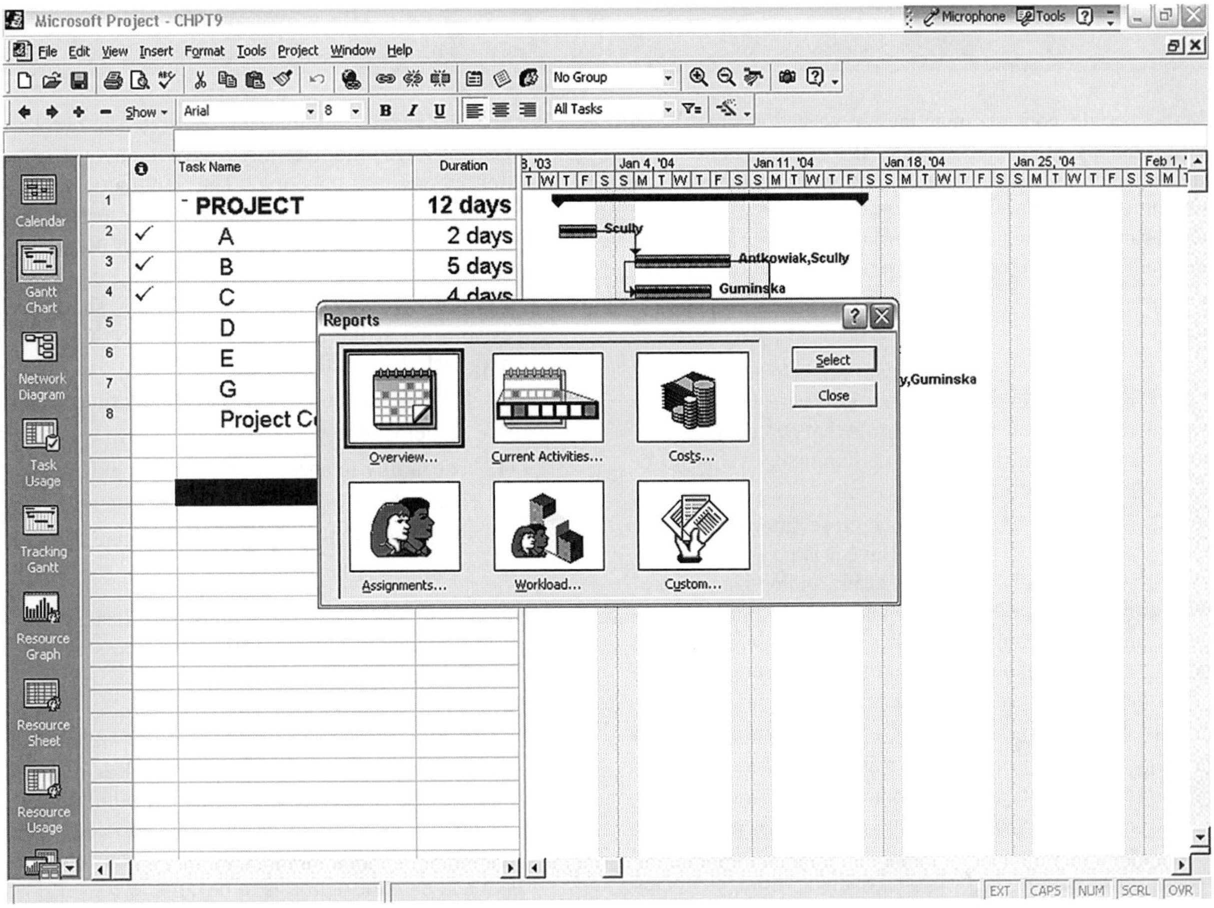

Figure 9.7 Project Report Categories

pagers, and other wireless devices are commonplace and have increased our mobility and accessibility. Although these communication devices are not as personal as face-to-face meetings, they certainly make communication possible when people cannot be at the same place at the same time. The communications plan (and project budget) should also include electronic means for the project team and other stakeholders to communicate.

- *Collaboration Technology*—There are a variety of information technology tools to support communication and collaboration. For example, a project team could use Internet or Web-based technologies to develop an Internet, intranet, or extranet application. The difference between Internet, intranet, or extranet really depends on who has access to the information stored on the server. For example, an Internet application would be available to anyone who has access to the World Wide Web or Internet. An intranet, on the other hand, may be developed using the same technology, but access is limited to the project team by means of passwords or firewalls. An extranet may include others outside the immediate project team or organization, such as the project sponsor or client. Similar to an intranet, access may be limited through the use of passwords or firewalls. Figure 9.8 provides an example of an extranet application developed by several

HOW TO RUN AN EFFECTIVE MEETING

Many people consider meetings a waste of time. And, unfortunately, many meetings are. Too often we are trapped in meetings that seem pointless and have no direction or outcome. Ken Johnson, a vice president at San Jose-based RJ Associates, offers the following advice for improving the quality and effectiveness of meetings.

1. *Plan in Advance*—Determine what specific results or outcomes you want to achieve from the meeting. Invite only those people who can help achieve those results. This procedure can also help you plan the meeting's agenda in terms of what percentage of the meeting will be used to disseminate, exchange, or receive information.

2. *Cover the Logistics*—Pay close attention to the meeting's environment. Have a large enough room with the right number of seats, audio/visual equipment, pens and paper, and handouts. If you are running the meeting, it is always a good idea to arrive early to make sure such things as room temperature and lighting are appropriate.

3. *Set a Clear Agenda*—A meeting should have a clear, concise agenda that is provided to the meeting's participants beforehand. This agenda may include the specific topics to be covered and the people who will be responsible for presenting the information. If possible, realistic time estimates allocated to the various items on the agenda should be provided. One may even indicate whether the specific items on the agenda require discussion, need a decision, or are just simply supplying information.

4. *Select a Facilitator*—A facilitator should be selected before the meeting to keep the meeting focused and moving along. The facilitator should be knowledgeable, credible, and respected in order to be objective and tactfully prevent anyone from dominating the meeting. The facilitator should ensure that everyone has an opportunity to share his or her ideas, concerns, or opinions in a nonhostile environment.

5. *Establish Ground Rules*—Ground rules should be established at the beginning of the meeting. They may include such things as:
   - Starting and ending the meeting on time
   - Participation by everyone
   - The ability to speak freely without judgment
   - The right to speak without being interrupted
   - Competition of assigned tasks on time
   - Confidentially

6. *Reinforce with Visual Aids*—Use overheads, computer presentation software, or flip charts to summarize important ideas.

7. *Keep a Meeting Record*—Every meeting should have someone assigned to take notes or minutes of the meeting and to record important ideas or summarize discussion on key items. In addition, the meeting record should include any decisions, outcomes, or actions, along with the responsible person and date the action is to be completed.

8. *Evaluate*—Each meeting should be evaluated to provide feedback to the facilitator. This evaluation should focus on the efficiency of the meeting and its effectiveness in meeting the planned objectives.

SOURCE: Ken Johnson, Running Effective Meetings, *High Technology Careers Magazine,* 1998. http://www.hightechcareers.com/docs/effective.html

project teams under the Business Information Technology Transfer Center (BITTC) at Northern Illinois University[1] to support communication, collaboration, and the sharing of knowledge.

Using this application, project teams can store, check out, and archive all project documents, as well as link to other resources. In addition, a search capability allows stakeholders to search for specific documents and lessons learned. Figure 9.9 provides an example of a learning cycle that is stored in the repository.

[1] The project was called the BITTC Knowledge Management Project. Three teams of students each developed a component of the KMS application over three semesters. The application now supports all of the project teams and the various stakeholders under the Center.

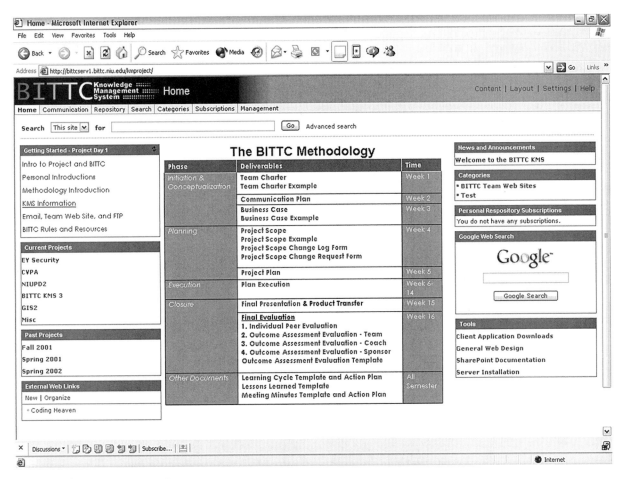

Figure 9.8 The BITTC KMS Extranet

In summary, the sharing of information includes support for communication, collaboration, and the sharing of knowledge among the various project stakeholders. Then, the project communications plan must focus on supporting communication for people working in different places and at different times. Figure 9.10 provides an example of how people communicate and interact today and some examples of how they may be supported.

CHAPTER SUMMARY

Project planning and estimation are critical processes. To be useful, the project plan must be accurate and realistic. But, even the best plans will fall short if the project manager and team do not follow the plan or know when to take corrective action. It is almost impossible to plan for all contingencies that may arise during a project, so the project plan should be revised and updated on an as-needed basis. For example, estimates made early in the project life cycle may be based on limited information. As new information comes to light, the project

manager should revise his or her estimates and project schedule and budget to ensure that the project plan is accurate and realistic. In addition, a project manager must be in control of the project and identify problems, issues, and situations that will impact the project schedule and budget. A measuring and reporting system allows the project manager to identify these situations early so that various alternative courses of action can be assessed and recommended. Although project sponsors may not like bad news, it is better for a project manager

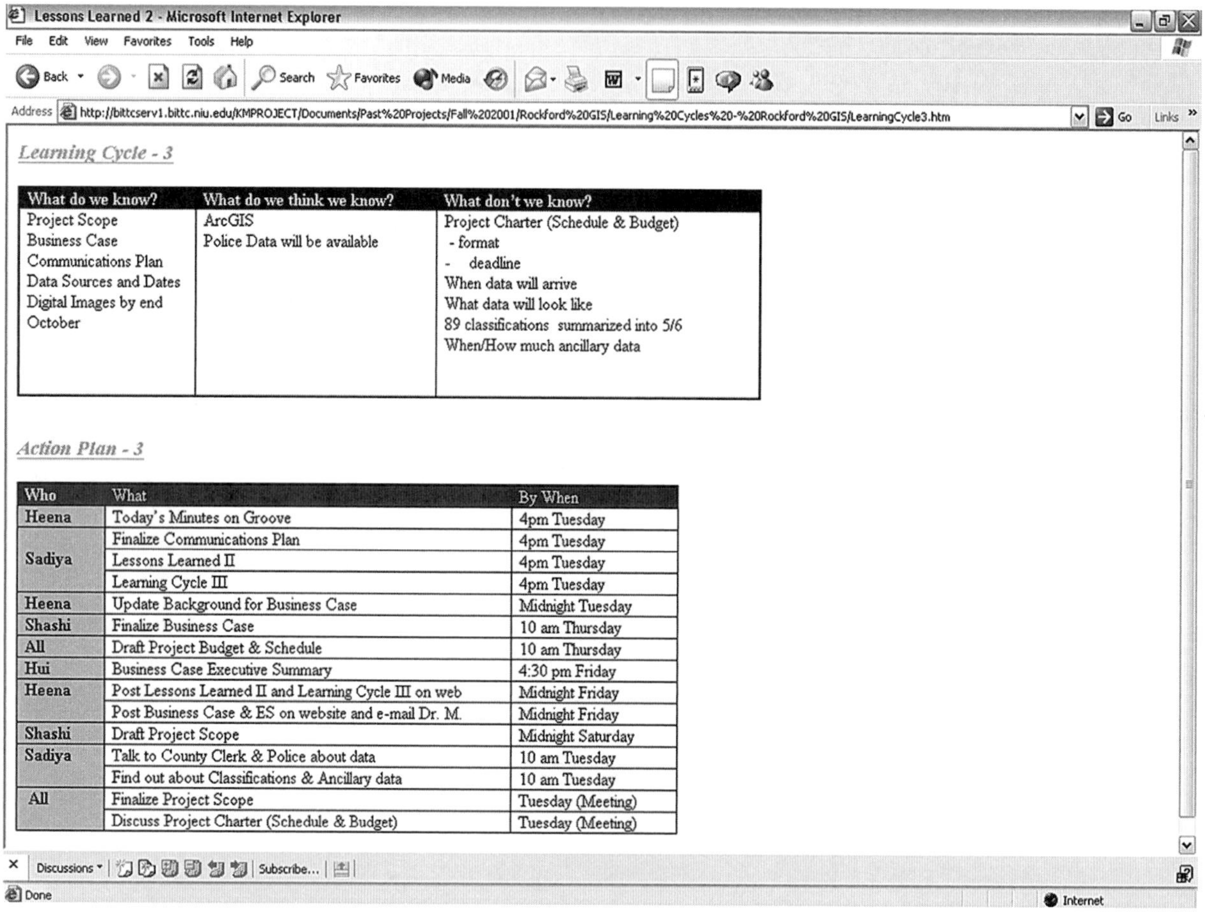

Learning Cycle - 3

What do we know?	What do we think we know?	What don't we know?
Project Scope Business Case Communications Plan Data Sources and Dates Digital Images by end October	ArcGIS Police Data will be available	Project Charter (Schedule & Budget) - format - deadline When data will arrive What data will look like 89 classifications summarized into 5/6 When/How much ancillary data

Action Plan - 3

Who	What	By When
Heena	Today's Minutes on Groove	4pm Tuesday
Sadiya	Finalize Communications Plan	4pm Tuesday
	Lessons Learned II	4pm Tuesday
	Learning Cycle III	4pm Tuesday
Heena	Update Background for Business Case	Midnight Tuesday
Shashi	Finalize Business Case	10 am Thursday
All	Draft Project Budget & Schedule	10 am Thursday
Hui	Business Case Executive Summary	4:30 pm Friday
Heena	Post Lessons Learned II and Learning Cycle III on web	Midnight Friday
	Post Business Case & ES on website and e-mail Dr. M.	Midnight Friday
Shashi	Draft Project Scope	Midnight Saturday
Sadiya	Talk to County Clerk & Police about data	10 am Tuesday
	Find out about Classifications & Ancillary data	10 am Tuesday
All	Finalize Project Scope	Tuesday (Meeting)
	Discuss Project Charter (Schedule & Budget)	Tuesday (Meeting)

Figure 9.9 BITTC Project Team's Learning Cycle

to deliver problematic news early than to have upper management unaware of the situation. Hoping that the problem will go away is not an effective action.

The Project Management Body of Knowledge defines a set of processes to support project communications management. This area of knowledge includes communications planning, information distribution, performance reporting, and administrative closure. The output of these processes is to develop a project communications plan. This plan may be formal or informal, depending on the size of the project and number of project stakeholders, but it must support an effective and efficient means of communication among the various project stakeholders. The development of this plan focuses on identifying the various stakeholders and their information requirements. In addition, the plan also sets expectations in terms of how and when this information will be made available.

The project communications plan must include a variety of ways for project stakeholders to communicate. More specifically, project stakeholders should be able to communicate:

- Same time–Same place
- Same time–Different places
- Different times–Same place
- Different times–Different places

Today, a number of IT-based tools and technologies are available to support the different needs of the project stakeholders; however, richer forms of communication, such as face-to-face meetings, are important and more appropriate in certain situations.

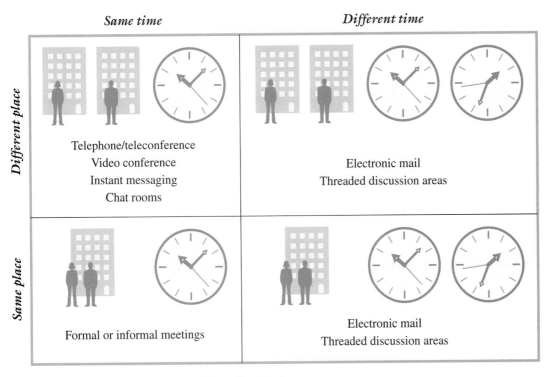

Figure 9.10 Communication and Collaboration Matrix

REVIEW QUESTIONS

1. Why should a project manager be concerned with monitoring a project's progress?
2. Describe the PMBOK area called communications planning.
3. Compare the information requirements of a project sponsor to those of a project team member. How are they similar? How are they different?
4. What kinds of contingencies would be difficult for a project manager to anticipate when developing the project plan?
5. What is the purpose of a project communications plan? What kinds of things should this plan address?
6. Why is effective and efficient communication vital to a project?
7. What are project metrics?
8. Describe the qualities of a good project metric.
9. Why should a project have a good measurement system in place?
10. Discuss why a good measuring system should guide the progress of the project team rather than management alone.
11. What are the advantages of having the project team design its own metrics and measuring system?
12. If "what gets measured gets done," why should a project team not be accountable to numerous project metrics?
13. Describe the concept of earned value.
14. What is BWCP?
15. What is ACWP?
16. What is BCWS?
17. Describe how the SPI and CPI can be used to forecast the final cost of a project.
18. What is a project review and what purpose does it serve?
19. What is a status report?
20. What is a progress report?

21. What is a forecast report?

22. When are face-to-face meetings more appropriate than phone calls or e-mail?

23. Describe the role IT can play in supporting the project communications plan.

24. When are Internet, intranet, and extranet applications appropriate in supporting the project communications plan?

25. Give an example of a type of meeting project stakeholders may have under the following circumstances. Describe how IT might support their communication needs
    a. Same time–same place
    b. Same time–different places
    c. Different times–same place
    d. Different times–different places

EXTEND YOUR KNOWLEDGE

1. Using the WWW, visit each of the following Web sites:
   ■ www.lotus.com
   ■ www.microsoft.com/exchange
   ■ www.groove.net

   Write a report that compares each specific tool. Be sure that the answers to the following questions are included:
   a. What technology platforms does each product require?
   b. Describe the functionality of each particular tool.
   c. Can you download and try each product before buying it?
   d. How well would each particular tool support communication and collaboration among project stakeholders?

   e. If you were a project manager interested in supporting communication and collaboration among the project's various stakeholders, which one of these tools might you choose? Why?

2. Given the following information, is this project in trouble? Explain.

Task	BCWS	BCWP	ACWP
A	$ 384.62	$ 384.62	$ 384.62
B	$ 576.92	$ 576.92	$ 576.92
C	$1,461.54	$1,461.54	$1,096.15
Total	$2,423.08	$2,423.08	$2,057.69

BIBLIOGRAPHY

Edberg, D. T. 1997. Creating a Balanced Measurement Program. *Information Systems Management* (Spring): 32–40.

Fleming, Q. W. and J. M. Koppelman. 1996. *Earned Value Project Management.* Newtown Square, Pa.: Project Management Institute.

Meyer, C. 1994. How the Right Measures Help Teams Excel. *Harvard Business Review* (May–June): 95–103.

Neuendorf, S. 2002. *Project Measurement.* Vienna, Va.: Management Concepts.

Van Genuchten, M. 1991. Why is Software Late? An Empirical Study of Reasons for Delay in Software Development. *IEEE Transactions on Software Engineering* 17(6).

10

IT Project Quality Management

CHAPTER OVERVIEW

The focus of this chapter will be on several concepts and philosophies of quality management. By learning about the people who founded the quality movement over the last fifty years, we can better understand how to apply these philosophies and teachings to develop a project quality management plan. After studying this chapter, you should understand and be able to:

- Describe the Project Management Body of Knowledge (PMBOK) area called project quality management (PQM) and how it supports quality planning, quality assurance, quality control, and continuous improvement of the project's products and supporting processes.

- Identify several quality gurus, or founders of the quality movement, and their role in shaping quality philosophies worldwide.

- Describe some of the more common quality initiatives and management systems that include ISO certification, Six Sigma, and the Capability Maturity Model (CMM) for software engineering.

- Distinguish between validation and verification activities and how these activities support IT project quality management.

- Describe the software engineering discipline called configuration management and how it is used to manage the changes associated with all of the project's deliverables and work products.

- Apply the quality concepts, methods, and tools introduced in this chapter to develop a project quality plan.

GLOBAL TECHNOLOGY SOLUTIONS

It was mid-afternoon when Tim Williams walked into the GTS conference room. Two of the Husky Air team members, Sitaraman and Yan, were already seated at the

217

conference table. Tim took his usual seat, and asked "So how did the demonstration of the user interface go this morning?"

Sitaraman glanced at Yan and then focused his attention on Tim's question. He replied, "Well, I guess we have some good news and some bad news. The good news is that our client was pleased with the work we've completed so far. The bad news, however, is that our prototype did not include several required management reports."

Yan looked at Tim and added, "It was a bit embarrassing because the CEO of the company pointed out our omission. It appears that those reports were specifically requested by him."

Tim looked a bit perplexed and asked, "So how did the client react?"

Sitaraman thought for a moment. "They were really expecting to see those reports," he replied, "but we promised that we would have them ready by next week. The CEO wasn't too happy to hear that it would take another week before we could add the reports and demonstrate the prototype again. However, everyone seemed pleased with what we were able to show them so far, and I think that helped buy us some time."

Tim took out his PDA and studied the calendar for a few minutes. Looking up, he asked, "So how will this impact our schedule?"

Yan opened the folder in front of her and found a copy of the project plan. She answered, "I wondered the same thing myself, and so I took a look at the original baseline project plan. The developers can begin working on what we've finished so far, but it looks like Sitaraman and I will have to work a few late nights this week and probably the weekend. That should get us back on track with minimal impact on the schedule."

Sitaraman sighed and said, "So much for going to the concert this evening. Do you know of anyone who would be interested in two tickets?" That brought a chuckle from the three team members.

Tim smiled and replied, "I'm glad to see that you both handled the situation fairly well and that you thought of a way to keep the project on track, even if it means some overtime for the two of you. However, I think we need to talk about why this problem occurred in the first place and what we can do to reduce the likelihood of similar problems happening again in the future."

Yan gave Tim's words a few seconds to sink in. "After our meeting with the client I talked to a few of the other members of the team," she said. "It turns out that the reports Husky Air's management wanted to see were defined in the requirements document. Unfortunately, several people were working on the same document, and we were given an earlier version of the document that didn't contain the entire specifications for the reports. As a result, we didn't even know the reports were part of the requirements and, therefore, didn't include them in the user interface prototype. I guess we should have checked with the other team members, but we were too busy just trying to get the prototype to work properly."

Tim stood up and walked over to the white board. He then wrote Quality, Verification/Validation, and Change Control on the board. Yan and Sitaraman gave Tim their full attention as he explained, "It seems that having several people work on the same documents, programs, or database files is a common problem. Often two people work on the same document or file at the same time without knowledge of what the other is doing. For example, let's say that person A is working on one section of a document or file, while person B is working on another. If person A saves the document or file to the server and then person B saves her or his document or file to the server afterwards, the changes to Person A's document or file are lost."

"That appears to be exactly what happened to the requirements document we used to develop the prototype!" exclaimed Yan.

"In fact," Sitaraman added, "Yan and I ran into a similar problem when we were working on the prototype. We had several versions of a program that we were developing, but it became confusing as to which version was the latest."

Tim turned to the two team members and said, "As I said before, this seems to be a common problem whenever several team members are working with the same files. What we need is a tool and a method for checking documents out and back in so that we reduce the likelihood of the errors we talked about."

Both Sitaraman and Yan agreed that this was a good idea. Sitaraman then interjected, "Tim, you have 'Verification and Validation' written on the board. Can you expand upon your idea?"

Tim glanced at the board and then turned his attention back to Sitaraman and said, "Sure. We often think of testing as being one of the last activities in software development. But catching problems and errors earlier in the project life cycle are easier and less expensive to fix. Moreover, by the time those problems or errors reach the client, it's too late and can be somewhat embarrassing, as the two of you found out this morning. We need to ask two important questions with respect to each project deliverable, Are we building the right product? And are we building the product the right way? These two questions are the foundation for verification and validation and should be part of an overall quality plan for the project."

Yan thought for a moment and said, "I remember learning about total quality management when I was in school. From what I recall, a lot of this quality stuff really focuses on the customer. But I think we need to rethink our idea of who exactly is our customer."

Both Sitaraman and Tim looked confused. Sitaraman was the first to speak. "But isn't Husky Air *our* customer?"

Yan knew she would have to explain. "Yes, they are, but they are our *end* customer. The team members who carried out the requirements definition and wrote the requirements document didn't realize that you and I were *their* customers because we needed a complete and accurate set of requirements in order to develop the prototype. In turn, the prototype that we develop will be handed off to several other team members who will use it to develop the application system. Subsequently, they will be our customers. I guess we can view the whole project as a customer chain that includes all of the project stakeholders"

"That is a very interesting idea, Yan!" said Tim. "We can build the concepts of quality, verification/validation, and change control into each of the project activities as part of an overall quality plan." The three members of the team felt they had discovered something important that should be documented and shared with the other members of GTS.

Tim replaced the cap on the dry erase pen and said, "It looks like we all have our work cut out for us this next week. While the two of you are busy working on the prototype for your presentation next week, I'll be working late developing a project quality management plan. By the way, do you know of anyone who would be interested in two tickets to a hockey game?"

Things to Think About:

1. What role does quality play in the IT project methodology?
2. How does verification/validation and change control support quality in an IT project?
3. Why should the project team focus on both internal and external customers?

INTRODUCTION

What is quality? Before answering that question, keep in mind that quality can mean different things to different people. For example, if we were comparing the quality of two cars—an expensive luxury car with leather seats and every possible option to a lower-priced economy car that basically gets you where you want to go—many people may be inclined to say that the more expensive car has higher quality. Although the more expensive car has more features, you may not consider it a bargain if you have to keep bringing it back to the shop for expensive repairs. The less-expensive car may start looking much better to you if it were more dependable or met higher safety standards. On the other hand, why do car manufacturers build different models of cars with different price ranges? If everyone could afford luxury cars, then quality comparisons among different manufacturers' cars would be much easier. Although you may have your eyes on a luxury car, your current financial situation (and subsequent logic) may be a constraint. You may have to buy a car you can afford.

Therefore, it is important not to define quality only in terms of features or functionality. Other attributes such as dependability or safety may be just as important to the customer. Similarly in software development, we can build systems that have a great deal of functionality, but perform poorly. On the other hand, we can develop systems that have few features or limited functionality, but also fewer defects.

However, we still need a working definition of quality. The dictionary defines quality as "an inherent or distinguishing characteristic; a property," or as something "having a high degree of excellence." In business, quality has been defined in terms of "fitness for use" and "conformance to requirements." "Fitness for use" concentrates on delivering a system that meets the customer's needs, while "conformance to requirements" centers more on meeting some predefined set of standards. Therefore, quality depends on the needs or expectations of the customer. It is up to the project manager and project team to accurately define those needs or expectations, while allowing the customer to remain within his or her resource constraints.

Although the concepts and philosophies of quality have received a great deal of attention over the last fifty years in the manufacturing and service sectors, many of these same ideas have been integrated into a relatively new discipline or knowledge area called project quality management (PQM). The Project Management Body of Knowledge defines PQM as:

> The processes required to ensure that the project will satisfy the needs for which it was undertaken. It includes all activities of the overall management function that determine the quality policy, objectives, and responsibility and implements them by means of quality planning, quality assurance, quality control, and quality improvement, within the quality system. (95)

Moreover, PMBOK defines the major quality management processes as:

- *Quality Planning*—Determining which quality standards are important to the project and deciding how these standards will be met.

- *Quality Assurance*—Evaluating overall project performance regularly to ensure that the project team is meeting the specified quality standards.

- *Quality Control*—Monitoring the activities and results of the project to ensure that the project complies with the quality standards. In addition, the project organization as a whole should use this information to eliminate causes of unsatisfactory performance and implement new processes and techniques to improve project quality throughout the project organization.

Therefore, PQM should focus on both the *product* and **process** of the project. From our point of view, the project's most important product is the information system solution that the project team must deliver. The system must be "fit for use" and "conform to specified requirements" outlined in both the project's scope and requirements definition. More importantly, the IT product must add measurable value to the sponsoring organization and meet the scope, schedule, and budget objectives. Quality can, however, also be built into the project management and software development processes. A process refers to the activities, methods, materials, and measurements used to produce the product or service. We can also view these processes as part of a quality chain where outputs of one process serve as inputs to other project management processes (Besterfield, Besterfield-Michna et al. 1999).

By focusing on both the product and chain of project processes, the project organization can use its resources more efficiently and effectively, minimize errors, and meet or exceed project stakeholder expectations. The cost of quality, however, can be viewed as the cost of conforming to standards (i.e., building quality into the product and processes) as well as the cost of not conforming to the standards (i.e., rework). Substandard levels of quality can be viewed as waste, errors, or the failure to meet the project sponsor's or client's needs, expectations, or system requirements (Kloppenborg and Petrick 2002).

Failing to meet the quality requirements or standards can have negative consequences for all project stakeholders and impact the other project objectives. More specifically, adding additional work or repeating project activities will probably extend the project schedule and expand the project budget. According to Barry Boehm (Boehm 1981), a software defect that takes one hour to fix when the systems requirements are being defined will end up taking one hundred hours to correct if not discovered until the system is in production. Moreover, poor quality can be an embarrassment for the project manager, the project team, and the project organization. For example, one of the most widely publicized software defect stories was the faulty baggage-handling software at the Denver International Airport. Bugs in the software delayed the opening of the airport from October 1993 to February 1995 at an estimated cost of $1,000,000 a day! Newspaper accounts reported that bags were literally chewed up and contents of bags were flying through the air (Williamson 1997).

The concepts and philosophies of quality management have received a great deal of attention over the years. Although popularized by the Japanese, many organizations in different countries have initiated quality improvement programs. Such programs include ISO certification, six steps to Six Sigma initiatives, or awards such as the Deming Prize or the Malcolm Baldridge National Quality Award. More recently, the Capability Maturity Model (CMM) has provided a framework for software quality that focuses on assessing the process maturity of software development within an organization. Based on writings and teachings of such quality gurus as Shewhart, Deming, Juran, Ishikawa, and Crosby, the core values of these quality programs have a central theme that includes a focus on the customer, incremental or continuous improvement, problem detection and correction, measurement, and the notion that prevention is less expensive than inspection. A commitment to these quality initiatives, however, often requires a substantial cultural change throughout the organization.

In this chapter, you will learn how the concepts of quality management can be applied to IT project management. We will also extend these concepts to include a broader view of PQM in order to support the overall project goal and objectives. As illustrated in Figure 10.1, PQM will not only include the concepts, teachings, tools, and methods of quality management, but also validation/verification and change control.

Verification and validation (V&V) activities within PQM should be carried out throughout the project life cycle. They require the project team to continually ask, Are

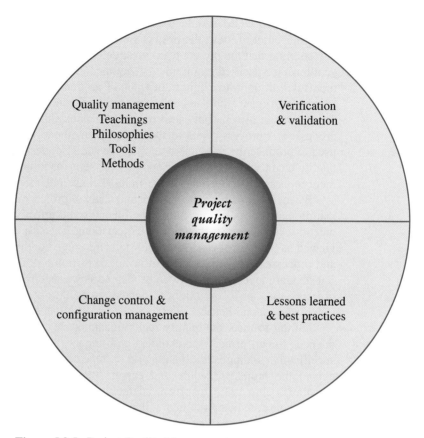

Figure 10.1 Project Quality Management

we building the right product? Are we building the product the right way? Therefore, the project quality plan should not only focus on final testing of the system at the end of the project life cycle, but also on all project deliverables. Finding and fixing problems earlier in the project life cycle is less costly than having to deal with them in the later stages of the project. Finding problems early not only leads to less rework later, but also saves the project manager and project team from having to deal with embarrassing issues and problems once the project's product is in the hands of the project sponsor or end-customer.

In addition, software development often requires a number of people to work on multi-versions of documents, programs, and database files that are shared and distributed among various project stakeholders. Change control in the form of configuration management, therefore, is a method of code and document management to track and organize the different versions of documents and files. It keeps the project team more focused and reduces the likelihood of errors.

In addition, knowledge management and the lessons learned can be implemented as best practices and incorporated in projects throughout the organization. Such changes lead to both continuous improvement and to a maturing of IT project management processes. Taken together, the concepts of quality management, V&V activities, change control, and knowledge management support the overall PQM plan. The plan not only helps improve the overall quality of the project's product and processes, but can also lead to a competitive advantage for the project organization because the project will have a greater likelihood of achieving its expected organizational value and support the scope, schedule, and budget objectives.

QUALITY?

Many experts believe that the quality of software is poor and only getting worse. In fact, the IS manager may give quality low priority because of budget cuts, increasing user demands, competitive pressures, and fast-changing technology. Too often the emphasis is on testing at the end of the development process, while ignoring cost-effective ways to detect and prevent defects earlier in the project. Although testing is important, a true quality practitioner is also interested in process improvement. An emphasis on process improvement is lacking at many organizations that produce poor software. These organizations tend to believe that the right people or right technology will deliver high quality software, but it is technology, people, and process that bring success. The key, therefore, is strong leadership and a commitment to quality throughout the organization. Ignorance and schedule pressure are enemies of quality. Many IS managers have been brainwashed into believing that meeting deadlines is preferable to getting it right the first time. Software defects are acceptable because they can always be fixed later during maintenance.

Compounding the problem, IS managers often resist quality improvement programs because they fear failure and see the benefits as intangible. Many vendors' claims of *silver bullet* tools confuse things even more. To overcome these problems, IS managers should get formal training in quality methods and hire one or two trained quality experts. Just having trained quality experts on board, however, does not guarantee success. These people must be given the respect and authority to do their jobs effectively. IS managers should not be intimidated by the effort to develop a comprehensive quality improvement program. They should choose a problem area that will result in the most benefit and be the most likely to result in success. In the end, it is important that the quality concepts be sold to management by showing them how quality improvements provide direct savings to the bottom line.

SOURCE: Adapted from Gary H. Anthes, Quality?! What's That?, *Computerworld,* October 13, 1997. http://www.computerworld.com/news/1997/story/0,11280,9974,00.html

The remainder of this chapter will focus on introducing and delving into several PQM concepts. It includes an overview of the quality movement and a brief history of the people who provided the cornerstones for quality initiatives. It also provides an overview of several quality systems. Finally, it gives a framework to support PQM that integrates the concepts and philosophies of quality, as well as the concepts of software testing, configuration management, and knowledge management.

THE QUALITY MOVEMENT

In this section, we will focus on the concepts associated with quality management, and the history and people who helped shape this important area. This knowledge may help us to better understand how to apply these concepts, ideas, and tools to IT projects.

Craftsmanship

Since the dawn of early humankind, quality was synonymous with craftsmanship. For the earliest Homo sapiens, the quality of the tools and weapons often determined one's survival. Parts could be interchanged to a limited degree, but people generally built things their own way and the products of their labor were highly customized.

This idea was formalized in the Middle Ages when the quality of products and the process to produce those products were held in high esteem. Guilds were created by merchants and artisans for each trade or craft. These unions of the past regulated who could sell goods or practice a trade in a particular town. Members of a guild charged similar prices for products of similar quality and ensured that there were never more craftsmen of a particular trade in a town than could make a decent living. If a worker became ill or too old to work, the guild supported him and his family.

Guilds also ensured the quality of a particular good by regulating the forms of labor. Members of the guild were classified as masters, apprentices, and journeymen. The masters owned the shops and trained the apprentices. An apprentice was bound to a master craftsman, but conditions of control were set by the guild. Training for apprentices required several years, and those who wanted to become master craftsmen had to demonstrate the quality of their work. The number of masters was also limited by the guild. Journeymen were those who had completed their apprenticeship training but were waiting to become masters.

The Industrial Revolution

Eli Whitney (1765–1825) is widely remembered as the inventor of the cotton gin—a machine that could clean the seed from cotton. Whitney's greatest contribution, however, may be the concept of mass producing interchangeable parts. In 1798, Whitney received a contract for $134,000 from the U. S. government to deliver ten thousand rifles within two years. At that time, guns were crafted by gunsmiths, and each gunsmith crafted the pieces differently from other gunsmiths. A lack of gunsmiths and the time required to build a rifle made it impossible to meet the terms of the contract. Time was critical because the United States was anticipating a war with France.

Faced with this problem, Whitney came up with the idea of a new production method in which individual machines could produce each part. Men could then be trained to operate the machines, and the guns could be assembled with parts that met certain tolerance limits. The men operating the machines would, therefore, not be required to have the highly specialized skills of a gunsmith. Whitney called this new production system and division of labor a *manufactory.*

Fortunately, the war between the United States and France never happened. It took Whitney almost a year to develop the manufactory, and then the weather, yellow fever epidemics, delays in obtaining raw materials, and ongoing cotton gin patent lawsuits delayed the implementation of the new production system (Woodall, Rebuck et al. 1997). However, Whitney was able to convince President John Adams of the importance of this innovative approach and subsequently obtained the government's investment and support. Although it took more than ten years to deliver the last rifle, Whitney demonstrated the feasibility of his system and established the seed for the modern assembly line.

Frederic W. Taylor (1856–1915)

As a young man, Frederic W. Taylor worked as an apprentice at the Enterprise Hydraulics Shop. Supposedly, he was told by the older workers how much he should produce each day—no more, no less (Woodall, Rebuck et al. 1997). The workers were paid on a piece rate basis, and if they worked harder or smarter, management would change the production rates and the amount a worker would be paid. These arbitrary rates, or *rules of thumb,* restricted output, and workers produced well below their potential.

Later, as an engineer, Taylor became one of the first to systematically study the relationships between people and tasks. He believed that the production process could become more efficient by increasing the specialization and the division of labor. Using an approach called **scientific management,** Taylor believed that a task could be broken down into smaller tasks and studied to identify the best and most efficient way of doing each subtask. In turn, a supervisor could then teach the worker and ensure that the worker did only those actions essential for completing the tasks, in order to remove human variability or errors. At that time, most workers in U. S. factories were immigrants, and language barriers created communication problems among the workers,

SIXTY-THREE THOUSAND KNOWN BUGS IN WINDOWS 2000?

In February 2000, a Microsoft Corp. memo caused quite a stir when it was leaked to the public. The memo was written by Marc Lucovsky, a Microsoft development manager, and an excerpt from that memo reads:

> Our customers do not want us to sell them products with over sixty-three thousand potential defects. They want those defects corrected. How many of you would spend $500 on a piece of software with over sixty-three thousand potential known defects?

Although it is virtually impossible to produce a piece of software of any size and complexity bug free, Microsoft received its share of bad press, especially as the leak coincided with a proposal in the State of Virginia's General Assembly to pass the Uniform Computer Information Transactions Act (UCITA). The Microsoft memo served as an example of how this act could benefit software vendors to the detriment of the customer. Many consumer and professional organizations opposed this legislation on the grounds that (1) a software vendor could legally disclaim any obligation to sell products that work, (2) in the event of a dispute, a software vendor could disable a customer's software remotely—even if it totally disrupted the customer's business, (3) security experts would be prohibited from reverse engineering software in order to examine it for defects and viruses, and (4) a software vendor could

legally stop a user from making public comments on the quality or performance of a product.

Microsoft insisted that the memo was intended to motivate the Windows development team after the source code was scanned using a tool called Prefix. According to Ken White, director of Windows marketing at Microsoft, Prefix flagged code that could be made more efficient in the next release, detected false positives, and analyzed 10 million lines of test code that was not even part of the release. Moreover, White used an analogy of running a grammar-check tool on F. Scott Fitzgerald's classic *The Great Gatsby*—although the tool may highlight unfamiliar words, it doesn't change the content of the novel. With over 750,000 beta testers and security analysts testing Windows 2000, White insisted that the product was "rock solid" and that "the claims are taken out of context and completely inaccurate."

SOURCE: Adapted from Ann Harrison, Microsoft Disputes Reports of 63,000 Bugs in Windows 2000, *Computerworld*, February 16, 2000, http://www.computerworld.com/news/2000/story/0,11280,43022,00.html; Frankly Speaking, Win 2K or Win 63K, *Computerworld*, February 21, 2000, http://www.computerworld.com/news/2000/story/0,11280,41418,00.html; Ann Harrison and Dominique Deckmyn, Win 2K Bug Memo Causes Brief Uproar, *Computerworld*, February 21, 2000, http://www.computerworld.com/news/2000/story/0,11280,41419,00.html; Dan Gillmor, UCITA Is Going to Hurt You If You Don't Watch Out, *Computerworld*, July 26, 1999, http://www.computerworld.com/news/1999/story/0,11280,36469,00.html.

their supervisors, and even with many coworkers. The use of a stopwatch as a basis for time-motion studies provided a more scientific approach. Workers could produce at their full potential, and arbitrary rates set by management would be removed. To be successful, Taylor also believed that the scientific management approach would require a spirit of cooperation between the workers and management.

Although the scientific management approach became quite popular, it was not without controversy. Many so-called efficiency experts ignored the human factors and tended to believe that profits could be increased by speeding up the workers. Dehumanizing the workers led to conflict between labor and management that eventually laid the foundation for labor unions. Just three years before Taylor died, he acknowledged that the motivation of a person can affect output more than just engineered improvements (Woodall, Rebuck et al. 1997).

Walter A. Shewhart (1891–1967)

In 1918, Walter Shewhart went to work at the Western Electric Company, a manufacturer of telephone equipment for Bell Telephone. At the time, engineers were working to improve the reliability of telephone equipment because it was expensive to repair amplifiers and other equipment after they were buried underground. Shewhart believed that efforts to control production processes were impeded by a lack of information.

Shewhart also believed that statistical theory could be used to help engineers and management control variation of processes. He also reasoned that the use of tolerance limits for judging quality was short-sighted because it provided a method of judging quality for products only after they were produced (Woodall, Rebuck et al. 1997). In 1924, Shewhart introduced the **control chart** as a tool to better understand variation and to allow management to shift its focus away from inspection and more toward the prevention of problems and the improvement of processes.

A control chart provides a picture of how a particular process is behaving over time. All control charts have a center line and control limits on either side of the center line. The center line represents the observed average, while the control limits on either side provide a measure of variability. In general, control limits are set at $\pm 3\sigma$ (i.e., ± 3 sigma) or $\pm 3s$, where σ represents the population standard deviation and s represents the sample standard deviation. If a process is normally distributed, control limits based on three standard deviations provides .001 probability limits.

Variation attributed to common causes is considered normal variation and exists as a result of normal interactions among the various components of the process—i.e., chance causes. These components include people, machines, material, environment, and methods. As a result, common cause variation will remain stable and exhibit a consistent pattern over time. This type of variation will be random and vary within predictable bounds.

If chance causes are only present, the probability of an observation falling above the upper control limit would be one out of a thousand, and the probability of an observation falling below the lower control limit would be one out of a thousand as well. Since the probability is so small that an observation would fall outside either of the control limits by chance, we may assume that any observation that does fall outside of the control limits could be attributed to an **assignable cause.** Figure 10.2 provides an example of a control chart where a process is said to be stable or in **statistical control.**

Variations attributed to assignable causes can create significant changes in the variation patterns because they are due to phenomenon not considered part of the normal process. An example of assignable cause variation can be seen by the pattern in Figure 10.3. This type of variation can arise because of changes in raw materials, poorly trained people, changes to the work environment, machine failures, inadequate methods, and so forth (Florac, Park et al. 1997). Therefore, if all assignable causes are removed, the process will be stable because only chance factors remain.

To detect or test whether a process is not in a state of statistical control, one can examine the control chart for patterns that suggest nonrandom behavior. Florac and his colleagues suggest several tests that are useful for detecting these patterns:

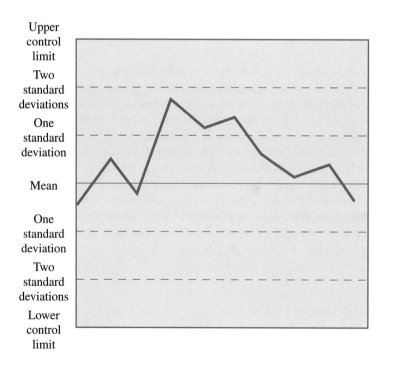

Figure 10.2 Control Chart for a Process within Statistical Control

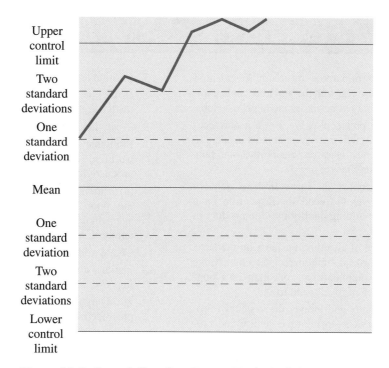

Figure 10.3 Control Chart for a Process Not in Statistical Control

- A single point falls outside the 3σ control limits.
- Although we won't get too bogged down in statistics, we can look for patterns that suggest that the observed data are not statistically independent. A process may not be in control if we observe:
  - At least two of three successive values that fall on the same side of and more than two standard deviations from the centerline.
  - At least four out of five successive values that fall on the same side of and more than one standard deviation away from the centerline.
  - At least eight successive values that fall on the same side of the centerline.

Control charts are a valuable tool for monitoring quality; however, it is important to keep in mind that one can see patterns where patterns may not exist (Florac, Park et al. 1997).

W. Edwards Deming (1900–1993)

While working at the Western Electric Hawthorne plant in Chicago, Illinois, during the 1920s, Deming became aware of the extensive division of labor. Management tended to treat the workers as just another cog in the machinery. Moreover, the workers were not directly responsible for the quality of the products they produced. Final inspection was used as a means to control quality and reductions in the per piece rate reflected scrap and rework.

Deming met Shewhart while working at Bell Laboratories in New Jersey in the 1930s and became interested in Shewhart's application of statistical theory. Deming realized that costly inspections could be eliminated if workers were properly trained and empowered to monitor and control the quality of the items they produced.

FOURTEEN POINTS FOR QUALITY

1. Create constancy of purpose toward improvement of products and services, with the aim to become competitive, and to stay in business, and to provide jobs.

2. Adopt the new philosophy. We are in a new economic arena. Western management must awaken to the challenge, must learn responsibilities, and take on leadership for change.

3. Cease dependencies on inspection to achieve quality. Eliminate the need for inspection on a mass basis by building quality into the product in the first place.

4. End the practice of awarding business on the basis of price tag. Instead, minimize total cost. Move toward a single supplier for any one item, on a long-term relationship of loyalty and trust.

5. Improve constantly and forever the system of production and service—to improve quality and productivity, and thus constantly decrease costs.

6. Institute training on the job.

7. Institute leadership.

8. Drive out fear, so that everyone may work effectively for the company.

9. Break down barriers between departments.

10. Eliminate slogans, exhortations, and targets for the workforce asking for zero defects and new levels of productivity.

11. (a) Eliminate work standards (quotas) on the factory floor. Substitute leadership. (b) Eliminate management by objective. Eliminate management by numbers, numerical goals. Substitute leadership.

12. Create pride in the job being done.

13. Institute a vigorous program of education and self-improvement.

14. Put everybody in the company to work to accomplish the transformation.

SOURCE: W. Edwards Deming, *Out of the Crisis,* Cambridge, MA: The MIT Press, 1982.

Deming and his teachings were relatively unnoticed in the United States. Soon after World War II, Japan was a country faced with the challenge of rebuilding itself after devastation and military defeat. Moreover, Japan had few natural resources so the export of manufactured goods was essential. Unfortunately, the goods that it produced were considered inferior in many world markets.

To help Japan rebuild, a group called the Union of Japanese Scientists and Engineers (JUSE) was formed to work with U. S. and allied experts to improve the quality of the products Japan produced. As part of this effort, in the 1950s Deming was invited to provide a series of day-long lectures to Japanese managers. The focus of these lectures was statistical control and quality. The Japanese embraced these principles, and the quality movement acquired a strong foothold in Japan. In tribute to Deming, the Japanese even named their most prestigious quality award the Deming Prize.

Until the 1970s, Deming was virtually unknown in the West. In 1980, an NBC documentary entitled "If Japan Can, Why Can't We" introduced him and his ideas to his own country and the rest of the world. Many of Deming's philosophies and teachings are summarized in his famous fourteen points for quality that are outlined and discussed in his book *Out of the Crisis* (Deming 1982).

Joseph Juran (1904–)

Joseph Juran's philosophies and teachings have also had an important and significant impact on many organizations worldwide. Like Deming, Juran started out as an engineer in the 1920s. In 1951 he published the *Quality Control Handbook,* which viewed quality as "fitness for use" as perceived by the customer. Like Deming, Juran was invited to Japan by JUSE in the early 1950s to conduct seminars and lectures on quality.

Juran's message on quality focuses on his belief that quality does not happen by accident—it must be planned. In addition, Juran distinguishes external customers from internal customers. Juran's view of quality consists of a quality trilogy—quality planning, quality control, and quality improvement—that can be combined with the steps that make up Juran's Quality Planning Road Map.

Quality Planning

1. Identify who are the customers.
2. Determine the needs of those customers.
3. Translate those needs into our language.
4. Develop a product that can respond to those needs.
5. Optimize the product features so as to meet our needs as well as customer needs.

Quality Improvement

6. Develop a process that is able to produce the product.
7. Optimize the process.

Quality Control

8. Prove that the process can produce the product under operating conditions.
9. Transfer the process to Operations.

Kaoru Ishikawa (1915–)

Kaoru Ishikawa studied under Deming and believes that quality improvement is a continuous process that depends heavily on all levels of the organization—from top management down to every worker performing the work. In Japan this belief led to the use of quality circles that engaged all members of the organization. In addition to the use of statistical methods for quality control, Ishikawa advocated the use of easy-to-use analytical tools that included cause-and-effect diagrams (called the Ishikawa diagram, or fishbone diagram, because it resembles the skeleton of a fish), the Pareto Chart, and flow charts.

Although the Ishikawa, or fishbone, diagram was introduced in an earlier chapter, it can be used in a variety of situations to help understand various relationships between causes and effects. An example of an Ishikawa diagram is illustrated in Figure 10.4. The effect is the rightmost box and represents the problem or characteristic that requires improvement. A project team could begin by identifying the major causes, such as people, materials, management, equipment, measurements, and environment, that may influence the problem or quality characteristic in question. Each major cause can then be subdivided in potential sub-causes. For example, causes associated with people may be lack of training or responsibility in identifying and correcting a particular problem. An Ishikawa diagram can be best developed by brainstorming or by using a learning cycle approach. Once the diagram is complete, the project team can investigate the possible causes and recommend solutions to correct the problems and improve the process.

Another useful tool is a **Pareto diagram,** which was developed by Alfred Pareto (1848–1923). Pareto studied the distribution of wealth in Europe and found that about 80 percent of the wealth was owned by 20 percent of the population. This idea has held in many different settings and has become known as the 80/20 rule. For example, 80 percent of the problems can be attributed to 20 percent of the causes.

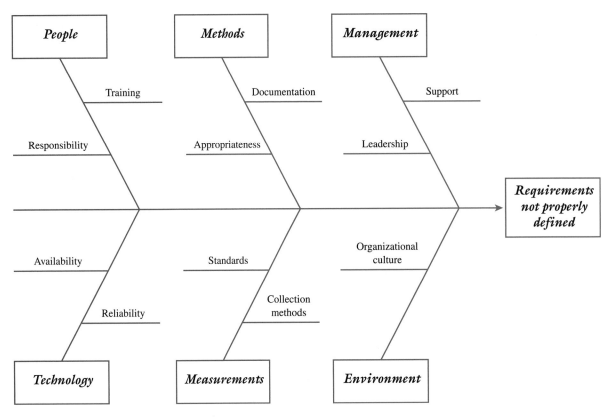

Figure 10.4 Ishikawa, or Fishbone, Diagram

Pareto diagrams can be constructed by (Besterfield, Besterfield-Michna et al. 1999):

1. Determining how the data will be classified. It can be done by the nature of the problem, the cause, non-conformity, or defect or bug.

2. Determining whether frequency, dollar amount, or both should be used to rank the classifications.

3. Collecting the data for an appropriate time period.

4. Summarizing the data by rank order of the classifications from largest to smallest, from left to right.

Pareto diagrams are useful for identifying and investigating the most important problems by ranking problems in descending order from left to right. For example, let's say that we have tracked all the calls to a call center over a period of one week. If we were to classify the different types of problems and graph the frequency of each type of call, we would end up with a chart similar to Figure 10.5.

As you can see, the most frequent type of problem had to do with documentation questions. In terms of quality improvement, it may suggest that the user documentation needs to be updated.

In addition, **flow charts** can be useful for documenting a specific process in order to understand how products or services move through various functions or operations. A flow chart can help visualize a particular process and identify potential problems or bottlenecks. Standardized symbols can be used, but are not necessary. It is more important to be able to identify problems or bottlenecks, reduce complexity, and determine who is the next customer (Besterfield, Besterfield-Michna et al. 1999).

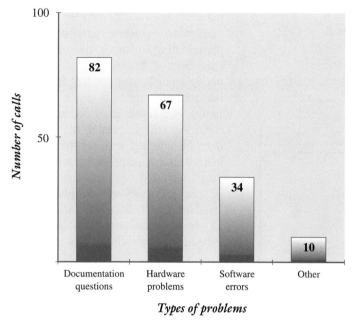

Figure 10.5   A Pareto Chart

Figure 10.6, for example, documents the project management process for verifying a project's scope. The original customer who initiates the original project request might be the project's client or sponsor. The customer who receives the output of the scope verification process might be a specific member of the project team.

Phillip Crosby (1926–2001)

Like F.W. Taylor, Philip Crosby developed many of his ideas from his experiences working on an assembly line. After serving in the Navy during the Korean War, he worked his way up in a variety of quality control positions until he held the position of corporate vice president and director of quality for ITT. In 1979, he published a best-selling book, *Quality is Free,* and eventually left ITT to start his own consulting firm that focused on teaching other organizations how to manage quality.

Crosby defined quality as conformance to requirements based on the customer's needs and advocated a top-down approach to quality in which it is management's responsibility to set a quality example for workers to follow. Crosby also advocated "doing it right the first time" and "zero defects", which translate into the notions that quality is free and that non-conformance costs organizations money.

QUALITY SYSTEMS

Although guilds were the first organizations to ensure quality standards, there are a number of different organizations and approaches for defining and implementing quality standards in organizations. **Standards** are documented agreements, protocols, or rules that outline the technical specifications or criteria to be used to ensure that products, services, processes, and materials meet their intended purpose. Standards also provide a basis for measurement because they provide criterion, or basis, for comparison.

International Organization for Standardization (ISO)

One of the most widely known standards organizations is the International Organizations for Standardization (ISO). Although you may think the acronym should be IOS, the name for the organization is ISO and was derived from the Greek word *isos,* which means *equal.* The name avoids having different acronyms that would result from International Organization for Standardization being translated in different languages.

ISO was officially formed in 1947 after delegates from twenty-five countries met in London the previous year with the intention of creating an international organization whose mission would be "to facilitate the international coordination and unification of industrial standards." ISO is not owned or managed by any national government, and

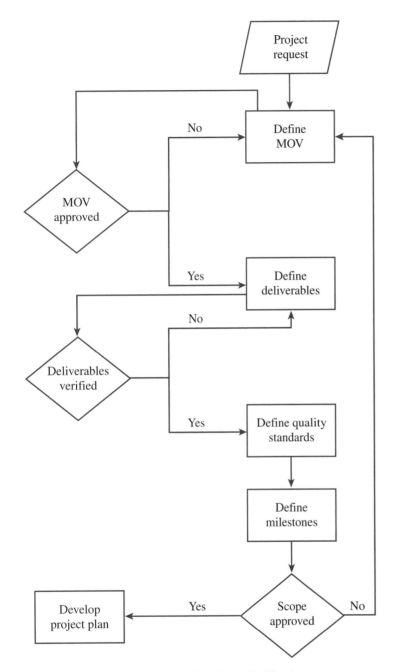

Figure 10.6 Flow Chart for Project Scope Verification

today it has over 130 member organizations, with one member per country. Each participating member has one vote, regardless of its country's size or economic strength, to ensure that each member country's interests are represented fairly. As a result, each country has an equal say with respect to the standards that are adopted and published. Each member is then responsible for informing other interested organizations in his or her country of any relevant international standard opportunities and initiatives.

International standards are established for many technologies and industries. Countries that do business with each other need to have an agreed upon set of standards to make the process of trade more logical and because a lack of standardization can create trade barriers. For example, credit cards adhere to a standard size and thickness so that they can be used worldwide.

Although most of the ISO standards are specific to a particular product, material, or process, a set of standards make up the ISO 9000 and ISO 14000 families. These are known as "generic management system standards" in which the same standards can be applied to any size or type of organization in any industry. The term **management system** refers to the processes and activities that the organization performs. ISO 9000 was originally initiated in 1987 and focuses on quality management with respect to improved customer satisfaction and the continuous improvement of an organization's performance and processes. On the other hand, standards that fall under the ISO 14000 came about in 1997 and are concerned primarily with environmental management—that is, how an organization can minimize any harmful effects on the environment that may be caused by its activities and operations.

The ISO 9000 standards were revised in 2000 (and are now called ISO 9000:2000) and focus on eight quality management principles that provide a framework for organizations:

1. *Customer Focus*—The customer is key for all organizations. Therefore, organizations should strive to meet and exceed the current and future needs of their customers.

2. *Leadership*—Strong leaders create a sense of purpose and direction for an organization by establishing and communicating a vision and mission for the organization. In addition, leaders inspire and provide their people with adequate resources, training, and empowerment to act within a set of well-defined responsibilities.

3. *Involvement of People*—To be successful, an organization must involve people at all levels so that individuals accept ownership for problems and the responsibility for solving them. This involvement requires the sharing of knowledge and experiences freely, while supporting and encouraging the open discussion of problems and issues.

4. *Process Approach*—In order to achieve a desired result, activities and related resources should be managed as a process, which allows for lower costs, improved cycle times, predictable results, and a focused approach for identifying opportunities for improvement.

5. *System Approach to Management*—To achieve its objectives, an organization must identify, understand, and manage its interrelated processes as a system. This system provides a more structured and integrated approach that recognizes the interdependencies among processes and reduces cross-functional barriers.

6. *Continual Improvement*—Continuous improvement of the organization's products, processes, and systems should be a permanent objective. It should entail an organizationwide approach with established goals to guide and measure progress.

7. *Factual Approach to Decision Making*—Decision making should be based on data and facts. Data and information should be accurate and reliable, and should be analyzed using valid methods. However, informed decision making should be balanced between analysis based on facts or data and experience and intuition.

8. *Mutually beneficial supplier relationships*—An interdependent relationship exists between an organization and its suppliers. This relationship can be mutually beneficial if it increases the ability to create value for both parties. This value can support a long-term relationship that allows for pooling expertise and resources, while improving flexibility and speed in jointly responding to changing markets or customer needs. This relationship requires trust, open communication, and the sharing of information that will support joint activities between an organization and its suppliers.

To show that a product, service, or system meets the relevant standards, an organization may receive a certificate as proof. For example, many organizations have been issued ISO 9000 certificates as testaments that they have quality management systems in place and that their processes conform to the ISO 9000 standards. Keep in mind that these standards focus on processes not products. An organization can be certified in one of three quality systems under ISO 9000:

- *ISO 9001*—For organizations whose business processes range from design through development, as well as production, installation, and service. ISO 9001 contains twenty standards, or requirements, that must be met for a quality system to be in compliance. Although ISO 9001 can be applied to all engineering disciplines, it is the one most relevant to software development.

- *ISO 9002*—For organizations that do not design and develop products. With the exception of design control requirements, the requirements are similar to ISO 9001.

- *ISO 9003*—For organizations whose business processes do not include design control, process control, purchasing, or service. The focus is on inspection and testing of final products and services in order to meet specified requirements.

If an organization decides that it would like to be ISO certified as meeting the ISO standards, it usually begins by studying the ISO guidelines and requirements. The organization then conducts an internal audit to make sure that every ISO requirement is met. After deficiencies or gaps are identified and corrected, the organization then has a third party called a **registrar** audit its quality management system. If the registrar finds that the organization meets the specified ISO standards and requirements, it will issue a certificate as a testament that the organization's products and services are managed and controlled by a quality management system that meets the requirements of ISO 9000. ISO does not conduct the audits or issue certificates. In addition, an organization does not have to have a formal registration or certificate to be in compliance with the ISO standards; however, customers may be more likely to believe that an organization has a quality system if an independent third party attests to it.

TickIT

The TickIT initiative began in 1991 following a report on software quality published by the British Department of Trade and Industry. The report reviewed the state of software quality and suggested that many software organizations were reluctant to adopt the ISO 9000 standards because they believed them to be too general or difficult to interpret.

The British government then asked the British Computer Society (BCS) to take on a project called TickIT, which would provide a method for registering software development systems under the ISO 9000 standards. TickIT guides a company through certification of software quality under the ISO 9001 framework. This certification is applicable to all types of information systems that include software development processes—from software houses that produce software as an end product or service to in-house software development supported by an internal IS function.

TickIT certification relates directly to ISO 9001:2000. More than 1,400 ISO 9001/TickIT certificates have been issued worldwide by twelve certification bodies accredited in Britain and Sweden. Certification is conducted by an independent external auditor who has been specially trained under the International Register of Certified Auditors (IRCO), which is supported by the British Computer Society. After being successfully audited by a TickIT certified auditor, an organization receives a certificate that it is in compliance with ISO 9001:2000 and it is endorsed with a TickIT logo. Subsequently, TickIT gives software developers an accredited quality certification specialized to software organizations and, hopefully, increases the confidence of customers and suppliers.

Six Sigma (6σ)

The term *Six Sigma* was originated by Motorola (Schaumburg, Illinois) in the mid-1980s. The concept of Six Sigma came about as a result of competitive pressures by foreign firms that were able to produce higher quality products at a lower cost than Motorola. Even Motorola's own management at that time admitted that "our quality stinks" (Pyzdek 1999).

Sigma (σ) is a Greek letter and in statistics represents the standard deviation to measure variability from the mean or average. In organizations, variation is often the cause of defects or out-of-control processes and translates into products or services that do not meet customer needs or expectations. If a manufacturing process follows a normal distribution, then the mean or average and the standard deviation can be used to provide probabilities for how the process can or should perform.

Six Sigma focuses on defects per opportunities (DPO) as a basis for measuring the quality of a process rather than products it produces, because products may vary in complexity. A defect may be thought of as anything that results in customer dissatisfaction. The sigma value, therefore, tells us how often defects are likely to occur. The higher the value of sigma, the lower the probability of a defect occurring. As illustrated in Table 10.1, a value of six sigma indicates that there will only be 3.4 defects per million, while three sigma quality translates to 66,807 defects per million. Table 10.2 provides several real-world examples that compare the differences between three sigma and six sigma quality.

Therefore, Six Sigma can be viewed as a quality objective whereby customer satisfaction will increase as a result of reducing defects; however, it is also a business-driven approach for improving processes, reducing costs, and increasing profits. The key steps in the Six Sigma improvement framework are the **D-M-A-I-C** cycle:

- *Define*—The first step is to define customer satisfaction goals and subgoals—for example, reduce cycle time, costs, or defects. These goals then provide a baseline or benchmark for the process improvement.

- *Measure*—The Six Sigma team is responsible for identifying a set of relevant metrics.

- *Analyze*—With data in hand, the team can analyze the data for trends, patterns, or relationships. Statistical analysis allows for testing hypotheses, modeling, or conducting experiments.

- *Improve*—Based on solid evidence, improvements can be proposed and implemented. The *Measure – Analyze – Improve* steps are generally iterative to achieve target levels of performance.

- *Control*—Once target levels of performance are achieved, control methods and tools are put into place in order to maintain performance.

To carry out a Six Sigma program in an organization, a significant investment in training and infrastructure may be required. Motorola adopted the following martial arts terminology to describe these various roles and responsibilities (Pyzdek 1999):

Table 10.1 Sigma and Defects per Million

Sigma	Defects Per Million
1 σ	690,000
2 σ	308,537
3 σ	66,807
4 σ	6,210
5 σ	233
6 σ	3.4

Table 10.2 Comparison of Three Sigma and Six Sigma

3 σ	6 σ
Five short or long landings at any major airport	One short or long landing in 10 years at all airports in the U.S.
Approximately 1,350 poorly performed surgical operations in one week	One incorrect surgical operation in 20 years
Over 40,500 newborn babies dropped by doctors or nurses each year	Three newborn babies dropped by doctors or nurses in 100 years
Drinking water unsafe to drink for about 2 hours each month	Water unsafe to drink for one second every six years

- *Master Black Belts*—Master black belts are people within the organization who have the highest level of technical and organizational experience and expertise. Master black belts train black belts and, therefore, must know everything a black belt knows. Subsequently, a maser black belt must have technical competence, a solid foundation in statistical methods and tools, and the ability to teach and communicate.

- *Black Belts*—Although black belts may come from various disciplines, they should be technically competent and held in high esteem by their peers. Black belts are actively involved in the Six Sigma change process.

- *Green Belts*—Green belts are Six Sigma team leaders or project managers. Black belts generally help green belts choose their projects, attend training with them, and then assist them with their projects once the project begins.

- *Champions*—Many organizations have added the role of a Six Sigma champion. Champions are leaders who are committed to the success of the Six Sigma project and can ensure that barriers to the Six Sigma project are removed. Therefore, a champion is usually a high-level manager who can remove obstacles that may involve funding, support, bureaucracy, or other issues that black belts are unable to solve on their own

Although the concept of Six Sigma was initially used in a manufacturing environment, many of the techniques can be applied directly to software projects (Siviy 2001). The usefulness of Six Sigma lies in the conscious and methodical way of achieving customer satisfaction through the improvement of current processes and products and their design.

The Capability Maturity Model (CMM)

In 1986, the Software Engineering Institute (SEI), a federally funded research development center at Carnegie Mellon University, set out to help organizations improve their software development processes. With the help of the Mitre Corporation and Watts Humphrey, a framework was developed to assess and evaluate the capability of software processes and their maturity, and the work of the SEI evolved into the Capability Maturity Model (CMM) (Humphrey 1988). The CMM provides a set of recommended practices for a set of key process areas specific to software development. The objective of the CMM is to provide guidance as to how an organization can best control its processes for developing and maintaining software. In addition, the CMM provides a path for helping organizations evolve their current software processes toward software engineering and management excellence (Paulk, Curtis et al. 1993).

To understand how the CMM may support an organization, several concepts must first be defined:

- *Software Process*—A set of activities, methods, or practices and transformations used by people to develop and maintain software and the deliverables associated with software projects. Included are such things as project plans, design documents, code, test cases, user manuals, and so forth.

- *Software Process Capability*—The *expected* results that can be achieved by following a particular software process. More specifically, the capability of an organization's software processes provides a way of predicting the outcomes that can be expected if the same software processes are used from one software project to the next.

- *Software Process Performance*—The *actual* results that are achieved by following a particular software process. Therefore, the actual results achieved through software process performance can be compared to the expected results achieved through software process capability.

- *Software Process Maturity*—The extent to which a particular software process is explicitly and consistently defined, managed, measured, controlled, and effectively used throughout the organization.

One of the keys to the CMM is using the idea of software process maturity to describe the difference between immature and mature software organizations. In an immature software organization, software processes are improvised or developed ad hoc. For example, a software project team may be faced with the task of defining user requirements. When it comes time to complete this task, the various members of the team may have different ideas concerning how to accomplish it. Several of the members may approach the task differently and, subsequently achieve different results. Even if a well-defined process that specifies the steps, tools, resources, and deliverables required is in place, the team may not follow the specified process very closely or at all.

The immature software organization is characterized as being reactive; the project manager and project team spend a great deal of their time reacting to crises or find themselves in a perpetual state of *fire fighting*. Schedules and budgets are usually exceeded. As a result, the quality and functionality of the software system and the associated project deliverables are often compromised. Project success is determined largely by who is (or who is not) part of the project team. In addition, immature software organizations generally do not have a way of judging or predicting quality. Since these organizations operate in a perpetual crisis mode, there never seems to be enough time to address problem issues or improve the current processes.

Mature software organizations, on the other hand, provide a stark contrast to the immature software organization. More specifically, software processes and the roles of individuals are defined explicitly and communicated throughout the organization. The software processes are consistent throughout the organization and continually improved based on experimentation or experiences. The quality of each software process is monitored so that the products and processes are predictable across different projects. Budgets and schedules are based on past projects so they are more realistic and the project goals and objectives are more likely to be achieved. Mature software organizations are proactive and they are able to follow a set of disciplined processes throughout the software project.

The CMM defines five levels of process maturity, each requiring many small steps as a path of incremental and continuous process improvement. These stages are based on many of the quality concepts and philosophies of Shewhart, Deming, Juran, and Crosby (Paulk, Curtis et al. 1993). Figure 10.7 illustrates the CMM framework for software process maturity. These levels allow an organization to assess its current level of software process maturity and then help it prioritize the improvement efforts it needs to reach the next higher level (Caputo 1998).

Maturity levels provide a well-defined, evolutionary path for achieving a mature software process organization. With the exception of Level 1, each maturity level encompasses several key process areas that an organization must have in place in order to achieve a particular level of maturity. There are five levels of software process maturity.

Level 1: Initial   The initial level generally provides a starting point for many software organizations. This level is characterized by an immature software organization in which the software process is ad hoc and often reactive to crises. Few, if any, processes for developing and maintaining software are defined. The Level 1 software organization does not have a stable environment for software projects, and success of a project rests

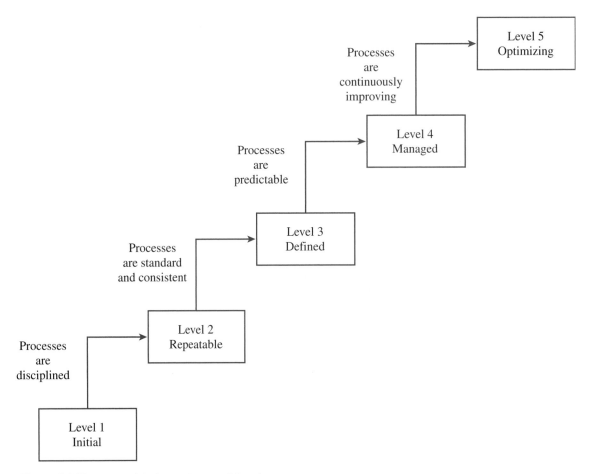

Figure 10.7 Levels of Software Process Maturity

largely with the people on the project and not the processes that they follow. As a result, success is difficult to repeat across different projects throughout the organization.

Key Process Areas

■ No key process areas are in place.

Level 2: Repeatable   At this level, basic policies, processes, and controls for managing a software project are in place. Project schedules and budgets are more realistic because planning and managing new projects is based upon past experiences with similar projects. Although software processes between projects may be different at this level, the process capability of Level 2 organizations is more disciplined because software processes are more documented, enforced, and improving. As a result, many previous project successes can be repeated by other project teams on other projects.

Key Process Areas

■ Software Configuration Management—Supports the controlling and managing of changes to the various project deliverables and software products throughout the project and software life cycles.

■ Software Quality Assurance—Provides project stakeholders with an understanding of the processes and standards used to support the project quality plan.

- Software Subcontract Management—Supports the selection and management of qualified software subcontractors.

- Software Project Tracking and Oversight—Ensures that adequate controls are in place to oversee and manage the software project so that effective decisions can be made and actions taken when the project's actual performance deviates from the project plan.

- Software Project Planning—Establishes realistic plans for software development and managing the project.

- Requirements Management—Ensures that a common understanding of the user's requirements is established and becomes an agreement and basis for planning.

Level 3: Defined   At Level 3, software engineering and management processes are documented and standardized throughout the organization and become the organization's standard process. And, a group is established to oversee the organization's software processes and an organizationwide training program to support the standard process is implemented. Thus, activities, roles, and responsibilities are well defined and understood throughout the organization. The software process capability of this level is characterized as being standard, consistent, stable, and repeatable. However, this standard software process may be tailored to suit the individual characteristics or needs of an individual project.

Key Process Areas

- Peer Reviews—Promotes the prevention and removal of software defects as early as possible and is implemented through code inspections, structured walkthroughs, and so forth.

- Intergroup Coordination—Allows for an interdisciplinary approach where the software engineering group participates actively with other project groups in order to produce a more effective and efficient software product.

- Software Product Engineering—Defines a consistent and effective set of integrated software engineering activities and processes in order to produce a software product that meets the users' requirements.

- Integrated Software Management—Supports the integration of software engineering and management activities into a set of well-defined and understood software processes that are tailored to the organization.

- Training Programs—Facilitates the development of individuals' skills and knowledge so that they may perform their roles and duties more effectively and efficiently.

- Organization Process Definition—Supports the identification and development of a usable set of software processes that improve the capability of the organization across all software projects.

- Organization Process Focus—Establishes organizational responsibility for implementing software processes that improve the organization's overall software process capability.

Level 4: Managed   At this level, quantitative metrics for measuring and assessing productivity and quality are established for both software products and processes. This information is collected and stored in an organizationwide repository that can be used to analyze and evaluate software processes and products. Control over projects is achieved by reducing the variability of project performance so that it falls within acceptable control boundaries. The software processes of software organizations at this level are characterized as being quantifiable and predictable because quantitative controls are in place to determine whether the process performs within operational limits. Moreover, these controls allow for predicting trends and identifying when assignable causes occur that require immediate attention.

Key Process Areas

- Software Quality Management—Establishes a set of processes to support the project's quality objectives and project quality management activities.
- Quantitative Process Management—Provides a set of quantitative or statistical control processes to manage and control the performance of the software project by identifying assignable cause variation.

Level 5: Optimizing   At the highest level of software process maturity, the whole organization is focused on continuous process improvement. These improvements come about as a result of innovations using new technology and methods and incremental process improvement. Moreover, the organization has the ability to identify its areas of strengths and weaknesses. Innovations and best practices based on lessons learned are identified and disseminated throughout the organization.

Key Process Areas

- Process Change Management—Supports the continual and incremental improvement of the software processes used by the organization in order to improve quality, increase productivity, and decrease the cycle time of software development.
- Technology Change Management—Supports the identification of new technologies (i.e., processes, methods, tools, best practices) that would be beneficial to the organization and ensures that they are integrated effectively and efficiently throughout the organization.
- Defect Prevention—Supports a proactive approach to identifying and preventing software defects.

As an organization's software process maturity increases, the difference between expected results and actual results narrows. In addition, performance can be expected to improve when maturity levels increase because costs and development time will decrease, while quality and productivity increase.

According to the SEI, skipping maturity levels is counter-productive. If an organization was evaluated at Level 1, for example, and wanted to skip to Level 3 or Level 4, it may be difficult because the CMM identifies levels through which an organization must evolve in order to establish a culture and experiences.

Both the CMM and ISO 9001 series of standards focus on quality and process improvement. A technical paper by Mark C. Paulk (1994) compares the similarities and differences between the CMM and ISO 9001. His analysis indicates an ISO 9001-compliant organization would satisfy most of the Level 2 and Level 3 goals. Although Level 1 organizations could be ISO 9001 compliant, it may be difficult for these organizations to remain compliant. In turn, there are many practices in the CMM that are not addressed by ISO 9001, and it is, therefore, possible for a Level 1 organization to be ISO 9001 compliant. A Level 2 organization should have little difficulty in receiving ISO 9001 certification.

After reading this section, you may be wondering which quality system is best. Should an organization focus on ISO certification? Or, should it concentrate its efforts on the CMM? Although the market may dictate a particular certification, an

THE COST OF NOT FOLLOWING DIRECTIONS

Most IT groups have formal guidelines for developing software. Unfortunately, these guidelines are in a thick binder that ends up collecting dust or hidden in someone's desk drawer. According to Software Productivity Research (SPR), a regular inspection of the application design and code can reduce software defects by 50 percent. The difficult part, however, is getting the development team to follow step-by-step instructions for reviews, inspections, or meetings with users. According to Roger Pressman, a software consultant from Orange, Connecticut, many developers view a process as an extraneous activity that one must endure before getting to the cooler part of development using a hot, new technology. But according to Pressman, "the problem is that without a process, you get screwed up just writing code." The problem becomes how to get developers to stick to the processes. One answer is to have them help write it—because people are more likely to follow the process if they are part of developing it. Therefore, the project team should be invited to add to the process any time they come up with a proven, effective technique. The goal of developing a process is not to create binders filled with paper that no one ever looks at, but to deliver projects or software on time, within budget, and that meet or exceed expectations. Although SPR has estimated that a company can save $17 in maintenance costs for every $1 invested up-front on requirements reviews, design and code inspections, and other development processes, the problem is that most developers are rewarded for getting the project done and not for following a process. As a result, developers get the project done any way they can get it done fast.

SOURCE: Adapted from Julia King, Ignoring Development Guidelines Raises Costs, *Computerworld,* May18, 1998, http://www.computerworld.com/news/1998/story/0,11280,30906,00.html.

organization should be focused on continuous improvement that leads to competitive advantage and not necessarily on a certificate or maturity level (Paulk 1994).

THE IT PROJECT QUALITY PLAN

All project stakeholders want quality; unfortunately, there is no commonly accepted approach for PQM so many project managers approach it differently (Lewis 2000). Therefore, a basic framework will be introduced here to guide and integrate the knowledge areas of quality planning, quality assurance, quality control, and quality improvement. This framework provides a basic foundation for developing an IT project quality plan to support the project's quality objectives. This plan may be formal or informal, depending on the size of the project; however, the underlying philosophies, standards, and methods for defining and achieving quality should be well-understood and communicated to all project stakeholders. Moreover, the project quality plan should support the project organization, regardless of whether it is attempting to meet ISO or CMM requirements or self-imposed quality initiatives and objectives.

PQM also becomes a strategy for risk management. The objectives of PQM are achieved through a quality plan that outlines the goals, methods, standards, reviews, and documentation to ensure that all steps have been taken to ensure customer satisfaction by assuring them that a quality approach has been taken (Lewis 2000). Figure 10.8 provides a representation of the IT project quality plan discussed in this section.

Quality Philosophies and Principles

Before setting out to develop an IT project quality plan, the project and project organization should define the direction and overall purpose for developing the project quality plan. This purpose should be grounded upon the quality philosophies, teachings, and principles that have evolved over the years. Although several different quality gurus and their

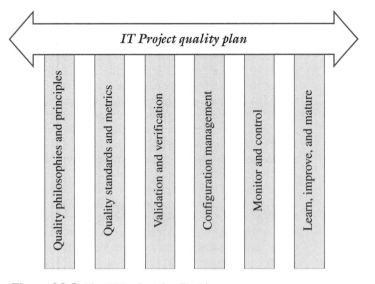

Figure 10.8 The IT Project Quality Plan

teachings were introduced in this chapter, several common themes can provide the backbone for any organization's plan for ensuring quality of the project's processes and product. These ideas include: a focus on customer satisfaction, prevention of mistakes, improving the process to improve the product, making quality everyone's responsibility, and fact-based management.

Focus on Customer Satisfaction Customer satisfaction is the foundation of quality philosophies and concepts. Customers have expectations and are the best judge of quality. Meeting or exceeding those expectations can lead to improved customer satisfaction. In addition, it is important to keep in mind that customers may be either internal or external. The external customer is the ultimate customer—that is, the project sponsor or client. However, internal customers are just as important and may be thought of as an individual or group who are the receivers of some project deliverable or an output of a process.

For example, project team members may be assigned the task of defining the detailed user requirements for an application system. These requirements may be handed off to one or several systems analysts who will develop the design models and then hand these models off to the programmers. The quality of the requirements specifications, in terms of accuracy, completeness, and understandability, for example, will have a direct bearing on the quality of the models developed by the systems analysts. In turn, the quality of the models will impact the quality of the programs developed. Therefore, we can view the series of project and software development processes as a customer chain made up of both internal and external customers.

As you might expect, a chain is only as strong as its weakest link, and any quality problems that occur can impact the quality of the project's product downstream. The primary focus of the project team should be to meet or exceed the expectations and needs of their customer because the customer is the ultimate judge of quality (Ginac 1998).

Prevention not Inspection One of Deming's most salient ideas is that quality cannot be inspected into a product. Quality is either built into the product or it is not. Therefore, the total cost of quality is equal to the sum of four components—prevention, inspection, internal failure, and external failure. The cost associated with prevention consists of all the actions a project team may take to prevent defects, mistakes, bugs, and so forth from occurring in the first place. The cost of inspection entails the costs associated with measuring, evaluating, and auditing the project processes and deliverables to ensure conformance to standards or requirement specifications. Costs of internal failure can be attributed to rework or fixing a defective product before it is delivered to the customer. These types of problems are, hopefully, found before the product is released. External failure costs entail the costs to fix problems or defects discovered after the product has been released. External failure costs can create the most damage for an organization because the customer's views and attitudes toward the organization may keep the customer from doing repeat business with the organization in the future. Thus, prevention is the least expensive cost and can reduce the likelihood of a defect or bug reaching the customer undetected. In turn, this will reduce the cost of developing the system and improve the overall quality of the product (Lewis 2000).

Improve the Process to Improve the Product   Processes are needed to create all of the project's deliverables and the final product—the information system. Subsequently, improving the process will improve the quality of the product. Project processes must be activities that add value to the overall customer chain. In addition, processes can be broken down into subprocesses and must be repeatable and measurable so that they can be controlled and improved. Improving any process, however, takes time because process improvement is often incremental.

Quality Is Everyone's Responsibility   Quality improvement requires time and resources. As many of the quality gurus point out, quality has to be more than just a slogan. It requires a commitment from management and the people who will do the work. Management must not only provide resources, but also remove organizational barriers and provide leadership. On the other hand, those individuals who perform the work usually know their job better than their managers. These people are often the ones who have direct contact with the end customer. Therefore, they should be responsible and empowered for ensuring quality and encouraged to take pride in their work. Quality improvement may not be all that easy to achieve because it may require an organization to change its culture and focus on long-term gains at the expense and pressure to deliver short-term results.

Fact-Based Management   It is also important that a quality program and project quality plan be based on hard evidence. As Kloopenborg and Petrick (2002) point out, managing by facts requires that the organization (1) capture data and analyze trends that determine what is actually true about its process performance, (2) structure itself in such a way that it is more responsive to all stakeholders, and (3) collect and analyze data and trends that will provide a key foundation for evaluating and improving processes.

Quality Standards and Metrics

Standards provide the foundation for any quality plan; however, standards must be meaningful and clearly defined in order to be relevant and useful. As illustrated in Figure 10.9, the project's goal, defined in terms of the measurable organizational value or MOV, provides the basis for defining the project's standards. The MOV defines the project's ultimate goal in terms of the explicit value the project will bring to the organization. In turn, the MOV provides a basis for defining and managing the project's scope, which defines the high-level deliverables of the project as well as the general features and functionality to be provided by the IT solution. However, the scope of the project, in terms of the features and functionality of the information system, are often defined in greater detail as part of the requirements definition.

As Figure 10.9 illustrates, the project's standards can be defined in terms of the project's deliverables and, most importantly, by the IT solution to be delivered. Once the features, functionality, or requirements are defined, the next step is to identify specific quality attributes or dimensions associated with each project deliverable. A customer-driven quality assurance plan first identifies each customer's requirements, represents them as quality attributes or dimensions, and then translates those dimensions into metrics (Ginac 1998). For example, Kan (1995) suggests several dimensions that can serve as quality standards for the software product. These include the application's features, reliability, usability, performance,

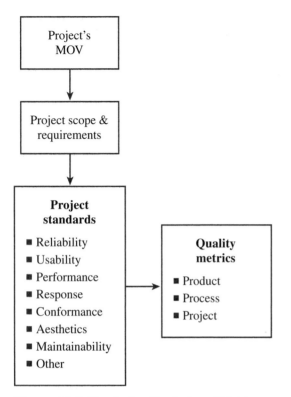

Figure 10.9 Developing Standards and Metrics

response, conformance, aesthetics, and maintainability. Although these dimensions focus on the application system, other dimensions can be identified for each of the project deliverables (e.g., business case, project charter and baseline project plan, project reporting, user documentation, etc.).

Metrics are vital for gauging quality by establishing tolerance limits and identifying defects. A **defect** is an undesirable behavior associated with the product or process (Ginac 1998). It is a failure to comply with a requirement (Lewis 2000). In software development, defects are often referred to as bugs.[1]

Once the quality dimensions are identified, the next step is to define a set of metrics that allow the project manager and team to monitor each of the project standards. There are two parts to a metric—the metric itself and an acceptable value or range of values for that metric (Ginac 1998). Metrics should focus on three categories (Kan 1995):

■   *Process*—The control of defects introduced by the processes required to develop or create the project deliverables. Process metrics can be used to improve software development or maintenance processes. Process metrics should focus on the effectiveness of identifying and removing defects or bugs.

■   *Product*—The intrinsic quality of the deliverables and the satisfaction of the customer with these deliverables. These metrics should attempt to describe the characteristics of the project's deliverables and final product. Examples of product metrics may focus on customer satisfaction, performance, reliability, and design features.

■   *Project*—The control of the project management processes to ensure that the project meets its overall goal as well as its scope, schedule, and budget.

Metrics can be used to determine whether the software product and project deliverables meet requirements for "fitness for use" and "conformance to requirements" as defined by the internal or external customers. Many technical people, however, often feel that standards are restricting and only serve to stifle creativity. Although too many standards that are rigidly followed can lend support to that argument, well-defined standards and procedures are necessary for ensuring quality. A quality approach can also decrease development costs because the sooner a defect or bug is found and corrected, the less costly it will be down the road (Lewis 2000). Table 10.3 provides a summary of some common process, product, and project metrics.

---

[1] The term *bug* was introduced to the computer field by Dr. Grace Murray Hopper (1906–1992)—an extraordinary woman who retired as a Rear Admiral in the U. S. Navy. In 1946, while working on the Mark II and Mark III computers, she found that one of the computers crashed as a result of a moth that had became trapped in one of the computer's relays. The moth was carefully removed and taped to the logbook where an inscription was made that the computer was *debugged*. For some reason the term stuck, and errors, or *glitches*, in a program or computer system are called *bugs*.

Table 10.3 Examples of Process, Product, and Project Metrics

Type	Metric	Description
Process	Defect arrival rate	The number of defects found over a specific period of time
	Defects by phase	The number of defects found during each phase of the project
	Defect backlog	The number of defects waiting to be fixed
	Fix response time	The average time it takes to fix a defect
	Defective fixes	The number of fixes that created new defects
Product	Mean time to failure	Average or mean time elapsed until a product fails
	Defect density	The number of defects per lines of code (LOC) or function points
	Customer found defects	The number of defects found by the customer
	Customer satisfaction	An index to measure customer satisfaction—e.g., scale from 1 (very unsatisfied) to 5 (very satisfied)
Project	Scope change requests	The number of scope changes requested by the client or sponsor
	Scope change approvals	The number of scope changes that were approved
	Overdue tasks	The number of tasks that were started but not finished by the expected date or time
	Tasks that should have started	The number of tasks that should have started but have been delayed
	Over budgeted tasks	The number of tasks (and dollar amount) of tasks that have cost more to complete than expected
	Earned value	Budgeted Cost of Work Performed (BCWP)
	Over allocated resources	The number of resources assigned to more than one task
	Turnover	The number of project team members who quit or terminated
	Training hours	The number of training hours per project team member

Verification and Validation

Verification and validation (V&V) are becoming increasingly important concepts in software engineering (Jarvis and Crandall 1997). V&V activities continually prompt us to ask whether we will deliver an IT solution that meets or exceeds our project sponsor's expectations.

The concept of **verification** emerged about twenty years ago in the aerospace industry, where it is important that software perform all of its intended functions correctly and reliably because any error in a software program could result in an expensive or disastrous mission failure (Lewis 2000). Verification focuses on the process-related activities of the project to ensure that the product or deliverable meets its specified requirements before final testing of the system begins.

Verification requires that the standards and metrics be defined clearly. Moreover, verification activities focus on asking the question of whether we followed the right procedures and processes. In general, verification includes three types of reviews (Ginac 1998):

- *Technical Reviews*—A technical review ensures that the IT solution will conform to the specified requirements. This review may include conformance to graphical user interface (GUI) standards, programming and documentation standards, naming conventions, and so forth. Two common approaches to technical reviews include structured walkthroughs and inspections. A **walkthrough** is a review process in which the programmer or designer leads a group of programmers or designers through a program or technical design.

The participants may ask questions, make comments, or point out errors or violations of standards (Ginac 1998). Similarly, **inspections** are peer reviews in which the key feature is the use of a checklist to help identify errors. The checklists are updated after data is collected and may suggest that certain types of errors are occurring more or less frequently than in the past (Lewis 2000). Although walkthroughs and inspections have generally focused on the development of programs, they can be used as a verification of all project deliverables throughout the project life cycle.

- *Business Reviews*—A business review is designed to ensure that the IT solution provides the required functionality specified in the project scope and requirements definition. However, business reviews can include all project deliverables to ensure that each deliverable (1) is complete, (2) provides the necessary information required for the next phase or process, (3) meets predefined standards, and (4) conforms to the project methodology.

- *Management Reviews*—A management review basically compares the project's actual progress against the baseline project plan. In general, the project manager is responsible for presenting the project's progress to provide a clear idea of the project's current status. Issues may need to be resolved, resources adjusted, or decisions made to either stay or alter the project's course. In addition, management may review the project to determine if it meets the scope, schedule, budget, and quality objectives.

Validation, on the other hand, is a product-oriented activity that attempts to determine if the system or project deliverable meets the customer or client's expectations and ensures that the system performs as specified. Unlike verification, validation activities occur toward the end of the project or after the information system has been developed. Therefore, testing makes up the majority of validation activities. Table 10.4 provides a summary of the various types of tests that can be conducted for a software engineering project. Volumes and courses can be devoted to software testing, so just an overview (or refresher) can be provided in this text. However, understanding what needs to be tested and how is an important consideration for developing a quality strategy and plan for the IT project.

Testing provides a basis for ensuring that the system functions as intended and has all the capabilities and features that were defined in project's scope and requirements. In addition, testing provides a formal, structured, and traceable process that gives management and the project

Table 10.4 Testing Approaches

Test	Description
Unit testing	Unit testing is done at the module, program, or object level and focuses on whether specific functions work properly. Unit testing can be accomplished via: ■ *Black box testing*—Tests the program code against specified requirements (i.e., functionality) ■ *White box testing*—Examines paths of logic inside the program (i.e., structure) ■ *Gray box testing*—Study the requirements and communicate with the developer to understand internal structure of the program (i.e., functionality and structure)
Integration testing	Tests whether a set of logically related units (e.g., functions, modules, programs, objects, etc.) work together properly after unit testing is complete
Systems testing	The system is tested as a whole in an operating environment to verify functionality and fitness for use. May include tests to verify usability, performance, stress, compatibility, and documentation
Acceptance testing	To certify that the system satisfies the end customer's scope and detailed requirement specifications after systems testing is complete. The end user or client is responsible for assuring that all specified functionality is included and will provide value to the organization as defined by the project's goal or MOV.

sponsor confidence in the quality of the system (Lewis 2000). In addition, Lewis (2000) provides several suggestions for making software testing more effective:

- Testing should be conducted by someone who does not have a personal stake in the project. In other words, programmers should not test their own programs because it is difficult for people to be objective about their own work.

- Testing should be continuous and conducted throughout all the development phases.

- In order to determine whether the test met its objectives correctly, a test plan should outline what is to be tested, how it will be tested, when it will be tested, who will do the testing, and the expected results.

- A test plan should act as a service level agreement among the various project stakeholders and should encourage "quality before design and coding."

- A key to testing is having the right attitude. Testers should not be out to "break the code" or embarrass a project team member. A tester should evaluate a software product with the intent of helping the developers meet the customer's requirements and make the product even better.

Change Control and Configuration Management

Suppose you were developing a database application system for a client. After several weeks, you would undoubtedly make a number changes to the tables, attributes, user interface, and reports as part of a natural evolution of the project. This evolution is both normal and expected as you learn more about the technology and the requirements. In addition, the user/client may suggest changes or enhancements if the organizational environment changes.

If you are working alone, you may store all the products of the software development (i.e., reports, plans, design models, program and database files) on your computer. Change control may be nothing more than just keeping your documents and files organized. If, however, you need to share these files and documents with even one other person, controlling these changes becomes more problematic. You could all keep the files and documents being worked on at everyone's stand-alone workstation. Unfortunately, if you need to share or work on the same documents or files, this sharing can lead to several different versions of the same document or file distributed among several different computers. On the other hand, you may store all the work in a shared directory on a server. This solution would certainly allow everyone to share and use the same documents or files, but problems could occur if two or more people work on the same document or file at the same time. The changes one makes would be lost if someone else were to save a file after the first person saved it, thus replacing new file with a different new file. There could be a great deal of confusion and wasted time.

Change is inevitable throughout the life of the project. On any given project, each deliverable will progress through a series of stages from an initial conception through a final release. As the deliverable develops, changes will be made informally until it gets to a state of completeness, whereupon revision control is needed. At some point informal changes should be no longer permitted. After final acceptance, the deliverable should be frozen until it is released. An informal change control allows changes that can be traced and captured sequentially to be made to an evolving project deliverable. It provides for rapid development while allowing for backup and some measures of control. On the other hand, formal change control is a procedure in which changes to an accepted work are formally proposed and assessed and decisions to accept or reject proposed changes are documented to provide an element of stability beyond the informal change controls.

Configuration management is an important aspect of PQM that helps control and manage document and software product change (Jarvis and Crandall 1997). It provides the project team with an environment for efficiently accessing different versions of past documents or files. Its basic purpose is to establish and maintain the integrity of the various project work products and deliverables throughout the project life cycle. In short, configuration management attempts to answer the following basic questions (Ginac 1998):

- What changes were made?
- Who made the changes?
- When were the changes made?
- Why were the changes made?

Configuration management tools allow different project team members to work on a specific section of a document or file. The document or file can be checked out and checked back into a repository or library in order to maintain control. Software and the supporting project deliverables often go through an evolution of successive temporary states called versions (Lewis 2000). Configuration management, therefore, includes a set of processes and tools that allows the project team to manage its various documents and files as various configurations of IT solutions and project deliverables are derived. It may include specifying and enforcing various policies that restrict access to specific individuals or preventing two people from changing the same document or file at the same time (Ginac 1998).

According to Lewis (2000), software configuration management includes four elements—component identification, version control, configuration building, and change control.

Component Identification   This first element focuses on the processes or activities for defining or describing the various software configuration items or work products that make up a specific project deliverable. Guidelines are established and followed for identifying and naming the various baselines, software components, and configurations. As these elements go through changes, a numbering and/or naming scheme is used to uniquely identify each of the various versions or revisions as they evolve and change over time. The various components are often stored in a library or repository, where a list of all the components can be cataloged.

Version Control   As the project deliverables and work products evolve and change over time, many different versions are created. Errors may be corrected and enhancements are made until the work product becomes stable. Each evolutionary change results in a new version. It is essential that these components be organized so that different versions can be distinguished from one another. With the exception of the first version, each subsequent version will have a predecessor and the ability to trace each version becomes the component's history. Allowing the project team to go back to any single version provides an important backup and allows for specific ideas to be saved and made available for reuse later on.

Configuration Building   Configuration building entails identifying the correct component versions and then being able to execute the build procedures. A **build** includes all the software components, such as data files, programs, and so forth that are needed to implement one or more software functions (Pressman 2001). A software product must be built in order for it to run. For example, if you have a single program, building the application may require compiling and linking the program file in order to create an executable program. However, a larger application system may require hundreds or even thousands of files to be compiled, linked, and combined to create an executable system. This process can become time-consuming and complicated (McConnell 1996). Therefore, configuration building ensures that the derived software components are correctly associated and put together with each other in order to create an accurate build.

Change Control   Once a software component becomes stable and accepted, a decision process must be in place to control any proposed changes. Moreover, a simple change will often involve several other components, so it is important that the impact of any change requests be assessed. The change control activities ensure that any modification to a software component is proposed, evaluated, approved or rejected, scheduled, and tracked. It provides the basis for reporting and auditing processes. If a change is made, the component should be checked back into the library or repository where it becomes a new component version and the previous version is retained.

Monitor and Control

Quality control focuses on monitoring the activities and results of the project to ensure that the project complies with the quality standards. Once the project's standards are in place, it is important to monitor them to ensure that the project quality objective is achieved. Moreover, control is essential for identifying problems in order to take corrective action and also to make improvements once a process is under control.

Similar to the quality assurance activities, quality control should be ongoing throughout the life cycle of the project and only end when the customer or project sponsor accepts the final IT solution (Kloppenborg and Petrick 2002). Moreover, quality control includes monitoring and controlling activities concerning the product, processes, and project. Using the system concept as illustrated in Figure 10.10, quality control activities must focus on the inputs and outputs of each process. If inputs to a process are of poor quality, then the output of a particular process will be of poor quality as well because, in general, the process may not be capable of changing the inherent quality of the input. Moreover, even if the input to a process is of high quality, the process itself may create an output of lower quality. Finally, the input and process may not produce a quality output or product if the requirements are not properly defined.

To support the quality control activities, several tools and techniques were introduced in this chapter. Figure 10.11 provides a summary of those tools. As Besterfield, et al (1999) point out, these tools can be used to monitor the process, product, and product metrics in order to:

Learn, Mature, and Improve

A central theme of this text has been the application of knowledge management as a tool for team learning and identifying best practices. Monitoring and controlling activities and tools can help point out problem areas, but the project team must solve these problems. Therefore, it is important that the lessons

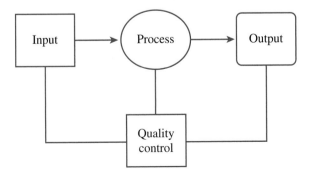

Figure 10.10 Quality Control Activities

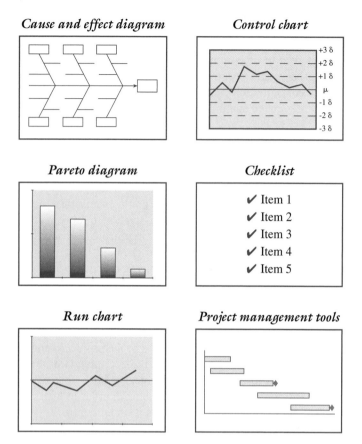

Cause and effect diagram

Control chart

Pareto diagram

Checklist

✔ Item 1
✔ Item 2
✔ Item 3
✔ Item 4
✔ Item 5

Run chart

Project management tools

Figure 10.11 Quality Control Tools

learned from a project team's experiences be documented so that best practices be identified and disseminated to other project teams. Continual, incremental improvements can make a process more efficient, effective, stable, mature, and adaptable (Besterfield, Besterfield-Michna et al. 1999). A project quality plan should be more than an attempt to build a better IT solution, it should also support the organization in searching for ways to build a better product (Woodall, Rebuck et al. 1997).

▮ CHAPTER SUMMARY

Project quality management (PQM) is a knowledge area defined by the Project Management Body of Knowledge. It is defined as:

> the processes to ensure that the project will satisfy the needs for which it was undertaken. It includes all activities of the overall management function that determine the quality policy, objectives, and responsibility and implements them by means of quality planning, quality assurance, quality control, and quality improvement, within the quality system.

In this text, PQM has been expanded to include not only the quality management concepts, but also verification and validation activities and change control to manage the various configurations of the project products throughout the project life cycle.

Although quality can mean different things to different people, quality in organizational settings has been traditionally defined as "fitness for use" and "conformance to requirements." Before the focus on interchangeable parts, quality was controlled by guilds that regulated membership, pricing, and trade in a particular town. With Eli Whitney's concept of mass producing interchangeable parts as part of a *manufactory,* the seed for the modern assembly line was born. Instead of training people to perform skilled work, they could instead be trained to operate machines to do the work, as long as the parts produced by the machines remained within certain tolerances.

The scientific method put forth by F.W. Taylor attempted to define the best way for workers to perform tasks—allowing them to produce at their full potential while removing management's proclivity to set arbitrary production rates. Although the scientific method had the best of intentions, many managers used it as a way to speed up workers and increase profits. The work of Walter A. Shewhart and W. Edwards Deming attempted to change management's mindset by advocating leadership, prevention over inspection, and statistical control to improve productivity and quality. Because Japan faced the daunting task of rebuilding its economy after World War II with few natural resources and a reputation for inferior goods, a group called the Union of Japanese Scientists and Engineers (JUSE) was formed with the help of Japan's allies to help transform the nation. As part of this effort, Deming and Joseph Juran were invited to give lectures on statistical quality control. Japanese managers embraced these principles and ideas, and the quality movement was officially born. Many others, such as Kaoru Ishikawa and Philip Crosby, contributed to this worldwide movement, and proprietary and nonproprietary quality management systems have gained increasing popularity in many organizations.

As part of the quality movement, standards in the form of documented agreements, protocols, or rules that outline specific criteria for quality became the backbone for ensuring quality. Several organizations and quality initiatives have gained fame over the years. ISO, probably the most widely known standards organization, was formed in 1947 with the intention of creating and coordinating a set of international standards. While the ISO 14000 focus on environmental management, the ISO 9000 focus on eight quality management principles that provide a framework for different organizations. A third party, called a registrar, can audit an organization and issue a certification that the organization's processes conform to the ISO standards.

Other quality initiatives, such as Six Sigma, focus on variations in processes that may translate into products or services that do not meet customer needs and expectations. By improving the quality of its processes, an organization can achieve its Six Sigma goal of only producing 3.4 defects per million. More recently, the Software Engineering Institute at Carnegie Mellon University introduced the Capability Maturity Model (CMM) that provides a set of recommended practices for a set of key process areas specific to software development. The CMM also provides a path of five levels to help organizations determine their current maturity level and then take steps toward software engineering and management excellence. Although the competitive environment may dictate that an organization achieve or hold a particular certificate or level of maturity, an organization should be focused on continuous improvement. Continuous improvement leads to competitive advantage by incorporating the lessons learned from their experiences and then translating those experiences into best practices that can be repeated throughout the organization.

The concepts, tools, methods, and philosophies of the quality movement provide a foundation for developing the IT project quality plan. The plan should be based on the following:

- *Quality Philosophies and Principles*—To guide the plan's objective and mission.

- *Quality Standards and Metrics*—To define the quality objectives and expectations and to provide a baseline for benchmarking improvements.

- *Validation and Verification Activities*—To ensure a quality approach throughout the project. Verification activities, such as technical, business, and management reviews, determine whether the project team is building the system or producing project deliverables according to specified standards or requirements; validation activities, such as software testing, tend to focus on whether the project's products will meet customer expectations.

- *Change Control and Configuration Management*—To support the natural evolution of the project's products. As these products evolve, change is inevitable. It is important that this change is managed effectively in order to reduce confusion and wasted effort. It includes a document repository library where files or documents can be checked out and checked in as needed. This process allows for versioning, backup, and safeguarding so that documents or files are not accidentally replaced by other project team members. Configuration building also allows for identifying the correct component versions needed to execute build procedures. Configuration management also provides formal change control to ensure that changes to accepted work are formally proposed and assessed and any decisions to make the changes are documented.

- *Monitor and Control*—To focus on monitoring the project activities to ensure that the project meets its quality standards. Once the project work begins, it is important that these activities be monitored and assessed so that appropriate corrective action can be taken when necessary. Quality control tools and techniques can be used to monitor each project or software development process and the inputs and outputs of the process, as well.

- *Learn, Mature, and Improve*—To focus on continuous quality improvement. As a project progresses, lessons learned can be documented from the project team's experiences. Recommendations, issues, challenges, and opportunities can be identified and shared with other project teams; and many of these experiences can provide the basis for best practices that can be implemented throughout the organization.

▮ WEB SITES TO VISIT

Quality Gurus

http://www.juran.com/

http://www.deming.org/

http://www.philipcrosby.com/

UCITA

http://www.infoworld.com/ucita/

ISO

http://www.iso.ch/iso/en/ISOOnline.frontpage

Software Engineering Institute/ CMM

http://www.sei.cmu.edu/

Configuration Management

http://www.cmtoday.com/

▮ REVIEW QUESTIONS

1. Define quality in your own words. How would you define quality in a word processing, spreadsheet, or presentation software package?

2. Why is the number of features of a software system not necessarily the best measure of that system's quality?

3. How does "conformance to requirements" or "fitness for use" provide a definition of quality for an information system or software product?

4. What is PQM?

5. Define the following: (a) Quality Planning; (b) Quality Assurance; (c) Quality Control

6. Why should quality management include both the products and processes of a project?

7. What is scientific management? Why was it so popular? Why was it so controversial?

8. What is a control chart? When is a process said to be in statistical control? How would you know if it was not?

9. Why did the teachings of Deming and Juran have such an important impact on Japan just after World War II?

10. What is an Ishikawa diagram? How can it be used as a quality control tool for an IT project?

11. What is a Pareto diagram? How can it be used as a quality control tool for an IT project?

12. What is a flow chart? How can it be used as a quality control tool for an IT project?

13. What is a standard? What role do standards play in developing an information system?

14. What is ISO? Why would an organization wish to be ISO certified?

15. What is the difference between ISO 9000 and ISO 14000?

16. Can an organization be ISO compliant but not certified?

17. What is TickIT?

18. Briefly describe Six Sigma and its objectives.

19. How does achieving a Six Sigma objective improve quality?

20. What is process capability?

21. What is process maturity?

22. Describe an immature software organization.

23. Describe a mature software organization.

24. What is the relationship between standards and metrics?

25. What is a process metric? Give an example.

26. What is a product metric? Give an example.

27. What is a project metric? Give an example.

28. What is a defect? Give an example of a software defect.

29. Describe verification. What activities support verification?

30. Describe validation. What activities support validation?

31. Describe how technical, management, and business reviews are different.

32. What is the purpose of change control?

33. Why should some changes be allowed to be made informally, while other changes should be made formally?

34. What is configuration management? How does it support change control?

35. What role does knowledge management play in continuous quality improvement?

EXTEND YOUR KNOWLEDGE

1. Interview two or three people who regularly use an application software package. Examples of an application software package include an Internet browser, electronic spreadsheet package, or a word processing package. Summarize each interview in one or two pages based upon the following questions:

   a. What application software package do you use the most?

   b. How often do you use this particular software package?

   c. Which features or functions do use the most? The least?

   d. How would you rate the overall quality of the software package on a scale from one to ten, where one indicates very low quality and ten indicates very high quality?

   e. Why did you give the software package this score?

   f. In your opinion, what are the three most important attributes of a high quality software package?

2. Contact someone in an organization who is willing to talk to you about her experiences implementing a quality program such as Six Sigma, ISO, TickIt, or the CMM. If this is not feasible, use the Internet or library to find an article. Prepare a short report that answers the following:

   a. What were the compelling reasons for initiating a quality program?

   b. What was the biggest challenge that the organization faced when trying to implement the quality program?

   c. How long did it take to implement the program? Or how far along are they?

   d. What lessons did the organization learn from its experience?

3. You and two other students have been hired by a local swim team to develop a Web site that will provide information about the team. The information on the Web site will be used to recruit new swimmers and will provide information to current members about upcoming meets and practices. In addition, team and individual statistics will be posted after each swim meet. Before you begin, you need to develop a quality plan. The plan should include:

   a. Your own quality philosophy.

   b. Two metrics for ensuring that reliability standards are met.

   c. Two metrics for ensuring that performance standards are met.

   d. A means for validating and verifying that your client's needs and expectations will be met.

BIBLIOGRAPHY

Besterfield, D. H., C. Besterfield-Michna, et al. 1999. *Total Quality Management.* Upper Saddle River, N.J.: Prentice Hall.

Boehm, B. W. 1981. *Software Engineering Economics.* Englewood Cliffs, N.J.: Prentice Hall.

Caputo, K. 1998. *CMM Implementation Guide: Choreographing Software Process Development.* Reading, Mass.: Addison-Wesley.

Deming, W. E. 1982. *Out of the Crisis.* Cambridge, Mass.: The MIT Press.

Florac, W. A., R. E. T. Park, et al. 1997. *Practical Software Measurement: Measuring for Process Management and Improvement.* Pittsburgh, Pa.: Software Engineering Institute.

Ginac, F. P. 1998. *Customer Oriented Software Quality Assurance.* Upper Saddle River, N.J.: Prentice Hall.

Humphrey, W. 1988. Characterizing the Software Process: A Maturity Framework. *IEEE Software* 5(3): 73–79.

Jarvis, A. and V. Crandall. 1997. *Inroads to Software Quality: How to Guide and Toolkit.* Upper Saddle River, N.J.: Prentice Hall PTR.

Kan, S. H. 1995. *Metrics and Models in Software Quality Engineering.* Boston, MA: Addison-Wesley.

Kloppenborg, T. J. and J. A. Petrick. 2002. *Managing Project Quality.* Vienna, VA: Management Concepts.

Lewis, W. E. 2000. *Software Testing and Continuous Quality Improvement.* Boca Raton, FL: Auerbach.

McConnell, S. 1996. *Rapid Development: Taming Wild Software Schedules.* Redmond, WA: Microsoft Press.

Paulk, M. C. 1994. A Comparison of ISO 9001 and the Capability Maturity Model for Software. *Software Engineering Institute* CMU/SEI-94-TR-12.

Paulk, M. C., B. Curtis, et al. 1993. The Capability Maturity Model for Software. *IEEE Software* 10(4): 18-27.

Pressman, R. S. 2001. *Software Engineering: A Practitioner's Approach.* Boston, MA, McGraw-Hill.

Pyzdek, T. 1999. *The Complete Guide to Six Sigma.* Quality Publishing.

Siviy, J. 2001. *Six Sigma.* The Software Engineering Institute (SEI).

Williamson, M. 1997. Quality Pays. *Computerworld* (August 18).

Woodall, J., D. K. Rebuck, et al. 1997. *Total Quality in Information Systems and Technology.* Delray Beach, FL: St. Lucie Press.

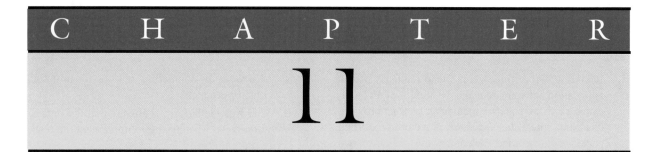

11

Managing Organizational Change, Resistance, and Conflict

CHAPTER OVERVIEW

This chapter will focus on preparing the organization for change. After studying this chapter, you should understand and be able to:

- Describe the discipline of organizational change management and its role in assessing the organization's readiness and capability to support and assimilate a change initiative.

- Describe how change can be viewed a process and identify the emotional responses people might have when faced with change.

- Describe the framework for managing change that will be introduced in this chapter.

- Apply the concepts and ideas in this chapter in order to develop a change management plan. This plan should focus on assessing the organization's willingness and ability to change, developing a change strategy, implementing and tracking the progress toward achieving the change and then evaluating whether the change was successful, and documenting the lessons learned from those experiences.

- Discuss the nature of resistance and conflict and apply several techniques for dealing with conflict and resistance in an efficient and effective way.

▌ GLOBAL TECHNOLOGY SOLUTIONS

Tim Williams could hear the drone of a single engine airplane as it flew overhead. He was sitting in the office of L.T. Scully, president and CEO of Husky Air. No one was really sure what the initials "L.T." represented; everyone just referred to Husky Air's top manager as "L.T." Tim could see by the pictures on the office walls that L.T. had begun his flying career in the military and then worked his way up to captain of a major airline. Five years ago L.T. left the airline and, along with several other investors, purchased Husky Air. Behind L.T.'s desk was a large window overlooking the ramp area and hangers where Husky Air's planes were kept. Tim watched as one of the service people towed a business charter jet from its hanger.

L.T. folded his hands on his tidy desk. "Tim, thanks for coming in on such short notice, but I think we might have a little problem."

Tim was a bit perplexed. The testing of the system was going forward as planned. Tim began, "L.T., testing is going as expected. Sure we found a few problems, but the team is confident that the bugs will be fixed and implementation will go according to plan."

"No, no," L.T. responded. "I'm very happy with the work you all have done so far. In fact, I have every bit of confidence in you and your team. My degree was in engineering, so I understand that finding problems and fixing them is all part of the process. Heck, I'm just glad that you're finding them instead of us! No, it seems that the problem is one that I may have created."

Tim was intrigued, but confused, and urged L.T. to explain.

"I may have underestimated how the change of introducing a new system will affect my employees," L.T. said. "My vice president of operations, Richard Woodjack, told me that several of our employees are not happy about the new system. A few of them have even threatened to quit. I almost told those employees that they have a choice—they can like it or leave—even if it would mean a large disruption to our business. But then I calmed down and recalled how I grumbled along with my coworkers at the airline when management would try to get us to do something new. It became sort of a joke because management would make a big deal of some new way of doing things and then expect everyone to just jump on board. Things would change for awhile but then people would revert to the old way of doing things. Soon, nobody took these announcements very seriously. It seemed that the more things changed, the more things stayed the same. I guess I thought my employees would see this new system as a positive change and that they would be open and welcome to it. I guess I was wrong."

Tim was impressed by L.T.'s candor. "I know what you mean. In fact, I've been on projects where the system ended up being a technical success, but an organizational failure. The system worked fine, but the people in the organization didn't accept it. It means missed opportunities because the system is never fully used as intended."

L.T. let out a deep sigh. "Ok, you're my consultant. How should we handle this? We really need the new system, but it's important that we have everyone on board."

Tim thought for a moment. "The reason the employees are resistant to the new system is because they may be feeling that they have no control over the situation," he said. "Also, they may not understand the benefits of the new system or how they will fit into the new picture. We need to come up with a plan and strategy that communicates the benefits of the new system and why the company has to replace the old system."

"That's a good idea, Tim," reflected L.T. "However, I think it's important that we not only tell the employees, but listen to them and engage them in the process so that they become part of the change." L.T. sat back in his executive chair. "Would you be willing to work with Richard Woodjack on this, but keep me informed about your progress?" he asked. Before Tim could respond, L.T. smiled and said "I know what you're going to say. This is definitely scope creep. Why don't you get back to me as soon as you can with the schedule and budget increases so I know what my little mistake is going to cost?"

Tim laughed and said, "L.T., if you ever get tired of flying planes and running a company, you should get a job as a mind reader."

L.T. picked up his phone. "I'll let Richard know that you'll stop by and see him and explain to him what's going on. I know he'll be relieved."

Tim and L.T. shook hands, and Tim headed out the door and down the hallway to Richard Woodjack's office.

Things to Think About:

1. Why shouldn't managers expect people to just accept a new information system?
2. What impacts can implementing a new information system have on the people in an organization?
3. Why might people be resistant to a new information system?
4. How might people demonstrate this resistance?
5. What can the project team and organization do to help people adjust and accept the new information system?

INTRODUCTION

Most technical people tend to enjoy the challenges of setting up a network, writing snazzy code using the latest and hottest technology, or designing a solution to solve some organizational problem. After all, that is what they're trained to do, and most people who enter the IT profession enjoy new challenges and learning new things. Indeed, many IT professionals believe that given enough time, training, and resources just about any technical problem can be solved. Being stuck in a boring job with obsolete skills is not a condition for career longevity—people will either leave to find new challenges or find themselves looking for new jobs. It is important to keep pace with technological changes, and many of these changes are welcome.

As you may recall from Chapter 1, IT projects are planned organizational change. And, an IT project has an impact on the organization, and the organization has an impact on the IT project. Organizations are made up of people, and the implementation of the IT project's product can change the way people work, affect the way they share information, and alter their relationships. Whether you are an outside consultant or work for an internal IS department within the organization, your mere presence will often be met with suspicion and hostility because you will be viewed as a person who has the potential to disrupt their stability. You are an agent of change. As an old saying goes, the only people who like change are wet babies!

It is easy to concentrate on the hard side of IT project management. Dealing with the people issues, or soft side of technology, is an area that most technical people do not enjoy. It is human nature to focus on what we can accomplish with minimal conflict or on what we can control. Implementing a network of computers that communicate with each other or getting a program to work properly may be much easier and less stressful than dealing with resistance and conflict during systems development.

In addition, many technical people and managers naively believe that the users within the organization will gladly embrace a new system if it is built properly. Although a system may include the required features and functionality and perform as intended, this "build a better mousetrap and the world will beat a path to your door" mentality can still lead to a system that is a technical success but an organizational failure.

Implementation of the new system is a technical challenge. The system must be moved from the development environment to a production environment and properly tested before *going live*. The people within the organization, however, must be

MANAGING CHANGE

According to Leslie Jaye Goff, change management really boils down to getting users to accept a new business process and the technology that enables it. Although the topic of change management may seem abstract for many people, it is an important area that project leaders, business analysts, applications developers, help desk staffers, trainers, managers, and executives should know about and understand. Gabriel Cooper, a consultant in Santa Rosa, California, believes, "It is human beings that make companies work, not technology. Technology is just a tool, and users have to be excited about it, believe in it, (be) trained in it, and supported in it. And change management is about making sure all of those things are included from the beginning as part of a project." In fact, International Data Corp., a research firm in Framingham, Massachusetts, estimates that services for change management in the U.S. will exceed $6 billion by 2003.

Not every IT project requires a formal change management approach. For example, upgrading an operating system or installing a new voice mail system would probably not create a great deal of stress among users. On the other hand, new applications that fundamentally change the way people work and their relationships with others may create a great deal of anxiety. For example, implementing a new ERP or e-commerce site will drastically alter a person's job. While some people are invigorated by new technology, others may be frightened by such changes. Often people become frustrated, feel powerless, or rebel against rapid change.

Change management is about helping people deal with their emotions. IT professionals should be willing to put themselves in their users' shoes in order to understand how change will affect them. To reduce anxiety and help people accept change, consultants suggest finding a business champion for the project, including line workers in the design and development activities, communicating constantly about the project's progress, reiterating the business reasons for taking on the project, and providing adequate education and training. In addition, it is important to remember that you cannot separate people, processes, and technology. Many projects have failed because of someone's inattention to the abstract, touchy-feely things.

SOURCE: Adapted from Leslie Jaye Goff, Change Management, *Computerworld*, February 14, 2000, http://www.computerworld.com /news/2000/story/0,11280,41308,00.html.

---

prepared for the impact that the new system will have on them. It is easy to underestimate this impact and, given human nature, downplay the response people will have. Managers and technical people may be given to false beliefs:

- "People want this change."
- "Monday morning we'll turn on the new system and they'll use it."
- "A good training program will answer all of their questions and then they'll love it."
- "Our people have been through a lot of change—what's one more change going to matter?"
- "We see the need for helping our people adjust, but we had to cut something…"
- "They have two choices: they can change or they can leave."

The above statements reflect the view that it is easier to gain compliance than it is to gain acceptance. This supposition is faulty because it assumes that everyone will comply and that compliance will be long-lasting. The results may be quite different:

- The change may not occur.
- People will comply for a time and then do things to get around the change.
- Users will accept only a portion of the change.

The full benefits of the project are never realized or are realized only after a great deal of time and resources have been expended.

The central theme of this text has been the concept of measurable organization value. The MOV is not only the overall goal of the project, but is also a measure of the project's success. It is how we define the value our project will bring to the organization after the project is implemented as originally envisioned. It provides a means for determining which projects should be funded and drives many of the decisions associated with the project throughout its life cycle. If the project's MOV is not realized in its entirety, then only a portion of the project's value to the organization is realized. Organizations today cannot afford to mismanage change initiatives. Competitive pressures provide little room for error. There is also the potential for lawsuits arising from stress-related disabilities and wrongful discharge (Bridges 1991). Therefore, while it is important that we manage the development of our project well, we also need to ensure that the project's product is transferred successfully and accepted by the organization with minimal adverse impact.

Acceptance by the users of the system is much more powerful and longer-lasting than compliance, which means we need to ensure that the people within the organization are prepared properly *before* the system is implemented. The discipline called **change management** is the area of IT project management that helps smooth the transition and implementation of the new IT solution. The Gartner Group defines change management as:

> The transforming of the organization so it is aligned with the execution of a chosen corporate business strategy. It is the management of the human element in a large-scale change project.

The remainder of this chapter will focus on how change may be viewed as a process and on the emotional aspects normally associated with change. A framework for developing a change management plan and several techniques for dealing with the resistance and conflict that are a natural part of the change initiative will be introduced. Although this chapter deals will the soft side of IT project management, it is an important foundation for planning the implementation of the IT solution that will be discussed in the next chapter.

THE NATURE OF CHANGE

In this section, we will focus on how change affects both individuals and organizations. Change tends to unfold in fairly predictable patterns (Conner 1995). In order to effectively plan and manage organizational change, it is important to understand the impact of change, how change may be viewed as a process, and the emotional behavioral patterns of change.

The Impact of Change

At any given time we must deal with changes that affect us. These changes may result from world or local events, the organizations we are part of, or personal decisions and relationships (Conner, 1995). Think about the changes that are going on in your life right now. You may be graduating soon, seeking employment, moving to a new residence, or scheduling root canal work with your dentist the day after tomorrow. The point is that there are a number of changes going on in our lives at any given moment. We may view these changes as being either positive or negative. As Jeanie Duck (2001) observes, nearly all change in our lives entails some amount of anxiety. Anxiety combined with hope is anticipation, while anxiety combined with apprehension is dread.

Whether we view change as positive (anticipation) or negative (dread), there is a certain amount of stress that accompanies each change. For example, let's say that you will graduate this semester and start a new job that requires you to move to a distant city. Although you may be looking forward to leaving school and earning some real money, you may still feel some apprehension. After all, you will have to leave your circle of family and/or friends and the familiarity of your present environment. Once you arrive in your new city, you will need to find a new place to live, make new friends, and become familiar with your new job, the company, and its people. Moving to a new city is relatively easy compared to the other transitions. The move itself is a change that will occur fairly quickly; the transition required to adjust to the change takes longer.

In *Managing at the Speed of Change,* Daryl Conner (1995) points out that an individual must deal with a variety of changes in his or her life and that we must assimilate these changes over time. **Assimilation** is the process of adapting to change and determines our ability to handle current and future change (Davidson 2002). For example, you may be dreading that root canal work next Wednesday, but once it's over you won't have the same level of anxiety that you are feeling right now. Or, you may be in the midst of planning a wedding. Most people view weddings as happy occasions, but anyone who has planned and gone through a wedding knows it can be a stressful. The stress and anxiety felt before the ceremony, however, become a distant memory once the happy couple celebrates their first anniversary. It simply takes time to assimilate change because we must adjust to the transition. Major changes, whether positive or negative, will require more time to assimilate than small ones. But once change is assimilated, it no longer creates the same level of anxiety or stress.

According to Conner, the problem occurs when we cannot assimilate change fast enough. Unfortunately, change tends to have a cumulative effect, and we can only assimilate change at a given pace. Different people will assimilate change at a different pace, and this ability to assimilate change becomes our resiliency to handle change. Figure 11.1 illustrates the cumulative effect of assimilating change over time.

Problems occur when we have to deal with too many changes or when we cannot assimilate change fast enough. When an individual passes a certain threshold, he or she may become stressed out and exhibit dysfunctional behaviors. The behaviors depend largely on the person and may range from mild irritability to depression or dependence on alcohol or drugs. Therefore, it is important to manage the assimilation of change to keep things below the change threshold. In order to do this, an individual may try various tactics, such as exercising more regularly or postponing major life changes so as to deal more effectively with the present changes.

Conner (1995) points out that organizations are made up of people and these people have any number of personal changes going on in their lives. Changes proposed by an organization (e.g., reorganization, downsizing, implementing a new information system) will certainly affect the way people work and the relationships that have become established. Although these organizational changes will have to be assimilated by each person, the organization must assimilate

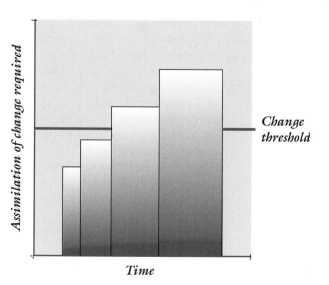

Figure 11.1 Assimilating Change

SOURCE: D. Conner, *Managing at the Change of Speed* (New York: Villard Books, 1995).

change similar to an individual. After all, organizations are made up of people! Therefore, each change adopted by an organization must be assimilated and managed within the change threshold. Just like people, organizations can exhibit dysfunctional behaviors. These behaviors may include an inability to take advantage of new opportunities or solve current problems. Eventually, an organization's inability to assimilate change will be reflected in the organization's ability to make a profit. Like an individual who cannot effectively deal with change and the associated stress, the long-term health and sustainability of the organization becomes questionable.

Change as a Process

Although a great deal has been written about change management, one of the most useful models for understanding change was developed by Kurt Lewin. Lewin developed the concept of Force Field Analysis or change theory to help analyze and understand the forces for and against a particular plan or change initiative (Lewin 1951). A Force Field Analysis is a technique for developing a big picture that involves all the forces in favor of or against a particular change. Forces that are viewed as facilitating the change are viewed as driving forces, while the forces that act as barriers or that work against the change are called restraining forces. By understanding all of the forces that act as aids or barriers to the change, one may enact strategies or decisions that take into account all of the various interests.

Lewin's basic model includes three concepts: unfreezing, changing, and refreezing as illustrated in Figure 11.2. The present state represents an equilibrium or status quo. To change from the current state, there must be driving forces both to initiate and to motivate the change. This requires an unfreezing, or an altering of the current state's habits, perceptions, and stability.

Figure 11.2 also depicts a transition from the present state to the desired state. This state is sometimes referred to as the neutral zone and can be a limbo or emotional wilderness for many individuals (Bridges 1991). Problems arise when managers do not understand, expect, or acknowledge the neutral zone. Those in the organization who act and support the driving forces for the change may be likely to rush individuals through the transition. This rushing often results in confusion on the part of those in the neutral zone, and the resisting forces (i.e., the emotional and psychological barriers) tend to push those individuals back to their present state. People do not like being caught in the neutral zone. They may try to revert back to the original status quo or escape. Escape may mean leaving the organization or resistance to the change initiative altogether. In addition, individuals who find themselves in the neutral zone too long may attempt to create a compromise in which only a portion of the change is implemented. This compromise will only result in missed opportunities and sets a bad precedence for the next change initiative—if this one did not work, why should anyone believe the next one will?

People do not necessarily resist change. They resist losses and endings. Unfreezing, or moving from the current state, means letting go of something. Therefore, viewing change from

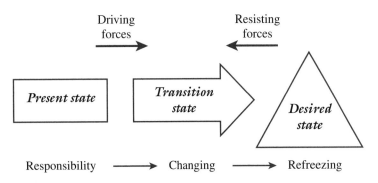

Figure 11.2 Change Process

SOURCE: Based on K. Lewin, Field Theory in Social Science (New York: Harper and Row, 1951).

Lewin's model suggests that beginning a change starts with an ending of the present state. Transition through the neutral zone also means a loss of equilibrium until an individual or organization moves to the desired state. Once there, it is important that the attitudes, behaviors, and perceptions be refrozen so that the desired state becomes the new status quo and equilibrium for the individuals involved.

Emotional Responses to Change

Until now, we have looked at change as a process and how change affects different areas of the organization. Change can also bring out emotional responses. An individual may have an emotional response to a change when the change is perceived as a significant loss or upsets a familiar or well-established equilibrium. In her book *On Death and Dying,* Elizabeth Kübler-Ross (Kübler-Ross 1969) provides insight into the range of emotions one may experience from the loss of a loved one. These same emotional responses can be applied to managing change whenever people experience the loss of something that matters to them.

The original model included five stages that we go through as part of a grieving process that leads to eventual healing. If people are not allowed to grieve and go through the first four stages, it becomes difficult to reach the last stage—acceptance. A person may have a number of emotions, such as sorrow, loneliness, guilt, and so forth, but the inability to work through these five stages can create more stress and difficulties than working through the stages. Although Kübler-Ross's model has been widely accepted, it has also been criticized as being oversimplified. However, it still provides some valuable insight for understanding how people may react to significant changes that affect their lives. The five stages include:

- *Denial*—The first stage is characterized by shock and denial. It is a common reaction when a person is given first notice of a change that will have significant impact. For example, when a person is informed that he or she is being fired by an organization, the initial response may be, Are you serious? This can't be true! The reality may be too overwhelming. Disbelief may be the immediate defense mechanism. The initial news, however, provides a beginning for understanding the full impact of the change that is about to take place.

- *Anger*—Once a person gets over the initial shock of the announcement, he or she may become angry toward others, or even the messenger. The reaction is to blame whoever is responsible for creating the change. Although anger is a more active emotional response, it can be a cathartic expression when people are allowed to vent their emotions. Keep in mind that there is a difference between feeling anger and acting out in anger. While having feelings is always acceptable, the latter never is.

- *Bargaining*—In the third stage, the person is no longer angry. In fact, he or she may be quite cooperative and may try to make deals in order to avoid the change. For example, the person who lost her job may begin making promises that she will "double my productivity" or "take a cut in pay" in order to avoid being let go. A person may look for ways to extend the status quo, or the present equilibrium, by trying to "work things out."

- *Depression*—Once a person admits that the change is inevitable, he or she may understand the full impact of the change and may enter the fourth stage—depression. This stage generally occurs when there is an overwhelming sense of the loss of the status quo. Although losing a job involves losing income, most people become depressed because they also lose the identity associated with their job.

- *Acceptance*—The last stage is when a person comes to grips with the change. A person does not have to like the change in order to accept it. This fifth stage has more to do with one's resolve that the change is inevitable and must be dealt with. Acceptance is an important part of ending the status quo and getting on with a new state.

These emotional responses can help us understand why people react the way they do when faced with organizational change. Because of these emotions, people may be drained and productivity in the organization will suffer. It is also important to understand that people will have different perceptions of change. But, to them, their perception is their reality. Often management and the project team will have known about and have had the time to prepare for an upcoming change. While they may be impatient for the change to occur, others in the organization will lag behind. Management and the project team may want to "get on with it," while the others are still dealing with their emotions during the transition. Instead of trying to suppress these individuals and their emotions, the leaders of change should accept them as a normal part of the change process and address them in the change management plan (Duck 2001).

THE CHANGE MANAGEMENT PLAN

The key to any organizational change is to plan for and manage the change and the associated transition effectively. This entails developing a change management plan that addresses the human side of change. The mere existence of such a plan can send an important message throughout the organization that management cares about the people in the organization and will listen and take their needs and issues seriously (Bridges 1991). Depending on the size and impact of the change initiative, the change management plan can be an informal or formal document; however, the project team and sponsor should address and be clear on several important areas. These areas are summarized in Figure 11.3, and provide a framework for the developing a change management plan discussed in this section.

Assess Willingness, Readiness, and Ability to Change

The first step to developing a change management plan is to assess the organization's willingness, readiness, and ability to change. This assessment entails defining who the players or stakeholders involved in the change will be, their roles, and how they will interact with each other (Davidson 2002). Conner (1995) defines several roles or players involved in a change initiative: the sponsor, change agents, and targets.

Sponsor The sponsor can be an individual or group that has the willingness and power, in terms of authority and making resources available, to support the project. Although this person or group is often the project sponsor, an **initiating sponsor** may hand off the project to a **sustaining sponsor.** More specifically, after making the decision to fund and support the project, the initiating sponsor may become completely removed from the project. Without the support of a sustaining sponsor, the project will eventually lose steam and direction. Therefore, the sustaining sponsor must become the primary sponsor for the project. A major portion of the organization's ability and willingness to support the change rests with the sponsor's commitment to the project and

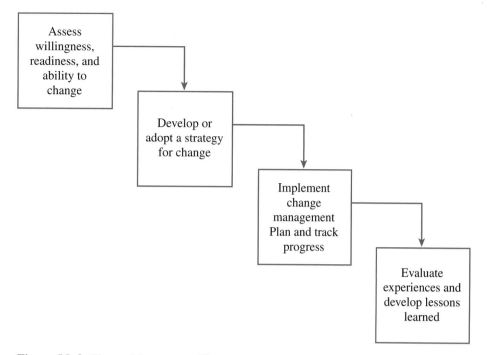

Figure 11.3 Change Management Plan

the associated change that will impact the organization. This commitment may be in terms of how they communicate with the rest of the organization, how they deal with challenges and issues, and the amount and quality of resources made available. In addition, sponsors must be effective leaders. If the project fails because the organization cannot adapt to the change, the project's envisioned value to the organization is lost and the sponsor's credibility is diminished. As Conner points out, "they lose twice."

Change Agents   In the most basic terms, the change agents will be the project manager and team; however, others from inside or outside the organization may be involved as well. An agent may be an individual or group responsible for making the change happen in order to achieve the project's goal and objectives. Change agents report directly to the sponsor and must be able to diagnose problems, plan to deal with these issues and challenges effectively, and act as a conduit of communication between the sponsor and the targets of change. The ability to sustain the change associated with the IT project rests largely with the change agents. They must be ready and properly prepared to meet the challenges they face.

Targets   The target is the individual or group that must change. In general, these may be the users of the new system or those who will use or be directly involved with final product of the project. Conner uses the term "target" because these are the people who are the focus of the change effort and who play a critical role in the ultimate success of the project.

Although the project sponsors and change agents play important roles in supporting and carrying out the change effort, the dynamics associated with the targets of change become the most critical. Therefore, the willingness, ability, and readiness to change also rest largely with the change targets. This may require: (1) clarifying the real impacts of the change, (2) understanding the breadth of change, (3) defining what's over and what's not, and (4) determining whether the rules for success have changed.

The project team and sponsor often do not think about how the planned change and transition will really affect people within the organization. As described in the previous section, change often brings about endings and a sense of loss of control. The project team and sponsor should take the time to think about what various individuals or groups stand to lose. For example, perceptions of loss may include power, relationships with other people, stability, or even control. As a result, people may become confused and disoriented.

Change within an organization can affect different things in different ways. Leavitt's model, as illustrated in Figure 11.4, suggests that changes in people, technology, task, or organizational structure can influence or impact the other areas (Leavitt 1964). These four components are interdependent where a change in one can result in a change in the others For example, a change in the organization's technology (e.g., implementing a new information system) can impact the people within the organization (e.g., new roles, responsibilities, etc.) as well as the tasks the individual's perform (i.e., the work they perform), and the organization's structure (i.e., formal or informal).

As a result of the planned change, people will go through a variety of emotions. On first learning of the impending change, people may feel shock, anger, and even denial. Later on, they may try to bargain or negotiate as a way of maintaining stability. This time is difficult because compromise, or appeasement, may seem to be a good alternative for avoiding conflict and resistance. Unfortunately, this tactic will only undermine the effectiveness of the change initiative. Therefore, it is important that a boundary be defined in a way that allows the change to happen as planned, but also allows individuals to "take something with them" by giving them something familiar to hold on to so as to ease the transition. This allows the past to be remembered with reverence and can also mark the end and the new beginning.

People become confused and disoriented when the rules for success change or are no longer clearly defined. Let's say that you have been working at a company for several years. Over that time, you have come to understand and become part of that culture. You know from your own experience and from those around you that promotion is based solely on seniority. As long as you meet the minimum performance requirements of your job, you know that promotions and the pay raises that follow will come after working a specific amount of time in a particular job. If the company ever has to layoff employees, you know that layoffs will begin with the employees with the least seniority. But what if the company you work for has been acquired by a larger organization? The acquiring company has decided to "make a few changes" and starts by downsizing the workforce in your company. But now each employee's performance will be reviewed and only the top performers will be invited to stay. You can only begin to imagine peoples' reactions. The rules for success have changed.

Develop or Adopt a Strategy for Change

Once the organization's capability to change is assessed, the next step involves developing or

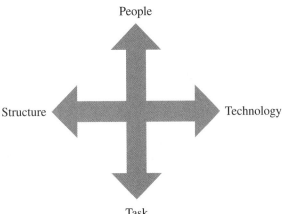

Figure 11.4 Leavitt's Model of Organizational Change

adopting a strategy for change. Davidson (2002) provides four approaches to change management.

Rational–Empirical Approach   The rational-empirical approach to change management is based on the idea that people follow predictable patterns of behavior and that people will follow their own self-interests. Therefore, a change agent must be persuasive in convincing, explaining, and demonstrating how a particular change will benefit a particular person or group identified as a target of the change.

It is important that the individuals affected by the change be provided with consistent and timely information. Consistent information means that the project team and sponsor send the same message to all individuals and groups throughout the organization. Mixed messages can lead to confusion and suspicion. Credibility should not become suspect. In addition, each message must be accurate and timely. Often the excuse is, "It may be better to wait until we have all the details." But, saying nothing at all can send the wrong message.

When people are not given enough information, they tend to seek information from other sources. Often these sources rely on innuendos, misinformation, and opinions, which become gossip that spreads through the informal organization. Stress levels rise until a point is reached where the organization becomes dysfunctional. It is better to be honest and tell people that there is no news before the rumor mill goes into warp drive.

Many managers believe that it is better to spare people bad news until the very last moment. However, it may be better to give people enough advanced warning to allow them to prepare for any upcoming changes. Then they can deal effectively with the gamut of emotions that will be brought on by the change.

The change management plan based on this strategy should provide each individual with the purpose, a picture, and a part to play. Purpose is the reason for the change. Often individuals within the organization have a narrow view of their job and its relationship to the rest of the organization. It may be useful to provide people with a chance to see or experience the problem or opportunity first-hand. For example, a person may be given the chance to witness how the current level of poor service is affecting the organization's customers. Then, it should be clear to that person that unless the organization does something (i.e., implement a new information system), it will continue losing customers to its competition. In time, the company will have to reduce its workforce or inevitably face bankruptcy.

A picture, on the other hand, provides a vision or a picture in the individual's mind as to how the organization will look or operate like in the future. If done effectively, this procedure can help the individual buy into the proposed change.

A part to play can be very effective in helping the individual become involved in the proposed change. Although purpose and a picture of the proposed change are important, it is also important for the individual to understand and visualize the part he or she will play once the change is instituted. Having a part may provide the needed WIIFM (or what's in it for me?) to help them through the transition.

Normative-Reeducation Approach   The normative-reeducation strategy for change management is based on the work of Kurt Lewin. This approach takes the basic view that people are social beings and that human behavior can be changed by changing the social norms of a group. Instead of trying to change an individual, one must focus on the core values, beliefs, and established relationships that make up the culture of the group. For example, you may hear, "That's the way things are done

HOW *NOT* TO MANAGE CHANGE

Sheila Smith and Mary Silva Doctor offer some sure-fire ways to disrupt a change initiative:

- *Communicate by Vulcan Mind Meld*—Although being able to learn another person's thoughts and feeling like Mr. Spock in the old *Star Trek* TV series has its advantages, many managers seem to believe that as soon as they think something is a good idea, everyone else in the organization will know it, too. Unfortunately, this type of communication does not work very well.

- *The Rational Person View of Change*—Often organizational leaders and managers believe that people will support an idea if it makes sense. Unfortunately, change can be emotional and unsettling for many people, and, therefore, people may not always act rationally.

- *Cuckoo Clock Leadership*—Ineffective change leaders tend to isolate themselves from the rest of the organization and communicate through their staff. A company whose leaders only pop out of their offices occasionally to champion a particular cause soon became known as cuckoo clock sponsors.

- *Sponsoring the Concept, Not the Implementation*—Sponsoring the recommended solution for a change initiative is an important, but not sole, ingredient for success. An effective change leader must also sponsor the implementation as well. Championing a concept is relatively easy compared to its actual implementation.

- *The Best-Laid Plans*—Although a transition plan is important, it cannot be the only plan to make the change successful. Moreover, a carefully constructed, detailed plan may not be all that useful when much of the real change is opportunity-driven, and the opportunities can occur in the day-to-day, informal interactions among the people in the organization.

SOURCE: Adapted from Sheila Smith and Mary Silva Doctor, Sure-Fire Ways to Derail Change Efforts, *CIO.COM,* September 1, 1997, http://www.cio.com/archive/090197/change.html.

---

around here." The targets of change in this case may be highly resistant to new ideas or new ways of doing things.

This approach can be very difficult and time-consuming because the change agents and sponsor must study the existing values and beliefs of a group. It requires unfreezing the current norms so that the change can take place and so that a new set of norms can be refrozen in order to solidify the acceptance of the new way of doing things by the group. As a result, change becomes more effective when each person adopts the beliefs and values of the group. The focus for managing change under this strategy becomes helping people redefine their existing social norms into a new set that supports the change effort. Some key principles include:

- Capacity for change is directly related to a person's participation in a group. When we become part of a group, our views and beliefs and those of the group become interwoven with each other.

- Effective change requires changing something not only about the individual's values and beliefs, but also the values and beliefs that make up the existing group's culture.

- Bias and prejudice toward guarding one's closely held beliefs and values diminishes one's ability to think rationally. Even when presented with the facts, many people may not act upon them in a rational way.

Power-Coercive Approach   The power-coercive approach to change management attempts to gain compliance from the change targets through the exercise of power, authority, rewards, or threat of punishment for non-conformance. Many managers may be lured into using this deceptively easy and straightforward approach, but there is a real risk when used in the wrong situation. People may comply (or at least go through the motions of compliance), but an approach based solely on rewards or punishment may have only short-term effect. For example, a person may comply for the time being, until they can find new employment. On the other hand, a person may view the change as temporary and just "wait out the storm" until it is convenient or safe to go back to the old way of doing things.

There are, however, situations where the power-coercive approach is useful and effective. In such cases, the targets of change recognize the legitimate power or expertise of the change agent. For example, a person may not change his indolent lifestyle until the doctor cautions him that certain health problems will get worse unless he changes his diet and begins an exercise program. Similarly, an organization may be faced with a situation that requires immediate attention—i.e., any inaction or time lost trying to get "everyone onboard" would spell disaster for the company. In this case, the use of rewards and threats would be a rational approach. As Davidson observes,

> People's dependency on an organization largely dictates how effective the power-coercive approach and the use of sanctions can be. If people are highly dependent on the organization; live paycheck to paycheck; have few job alternatives; and are not financially, mentally, or emotionally prepared to walk, you are on relatively safe ground using the power-coercive approach judiciously. (90–91)

The objective is to change the behaviors of the targets so that their new behavior supports the change effort. Davidson points out that sanctions should be imposed on an individual level and should focus on what an individual values and what they dread losing—perhaps a bonus, a paycheck, or a position within the organization. Sanctions can be imposed in ascending order to demonstrate a point in the beginning and to keep any target's losses at a minimum. A change agent or sponsor can lose credibility, however, if they issue a warning or sanction that they do not fully intend to carry out. Finally, the change agent or sponsor should never be abrasive or disrespectful and should not impose sanctions in a cruel or vindictive manner.

Environmental-Adaptive Approach   Like a pair of old, comfortable shoes, people often become attached to and comfortable with a certain way of doing things, perhaps an older system or established processes that have become part of the group's culture and norms. The premise of the environmental-adaptive approach is that although people avoid disruption and loss, they can still adapt to change.

Following this approach, the change agent attempts to make the change permanent by abolishing the old ways and instituting the new structure as soon as possible. Cortez, the explorer, probably displayed the most drastic form of this approach. After landing in the New World, many of his men began to grumble about the conditions and what lay ahead. In response, Cortez burned the boats so that there was no option other than pressing on. A much less drastic example would be upgrading everyone's word processing software over the weekend so that when everyone returned to work on Monday morning, they would have no choice but using the new software package. In both examples, the targets of change were given no choice but to change.

Although this approach may be effective in certain situations, it is still important that the targets of change assimilate the change as quickly as possible in order to adapt to the change as soon as possible. Some ways may include helping the targets of change see the benefits and showing them how the new way is similar to their old, familiar way of doing things.

The change management strategies introduced here are typical for many change initiatives. A single strategy or approach, however, may not be effective in every situation. A more useful approach may be to combine the different strategies, depending on the impact of the change and the organization.

Implement the Change Management Plan and Track Progress

Once the players and the strategy for the change management plan have been defined, the next step entails implementing the change management plan and tracking its progress. Although tracking progress should be integrated into the overall project plan and monitored using the various project tools, such as the Gantt chart, PERT chart, and so forth, introduced in an earlier chapter, milestones and other significant events should be identified and used to gauge how well the organization is adapting to the change.

In addition, one of the most critical issues for ensuring that the change takes place as planned is the establishment of effective lines of communication. At the very outset of any change initiative, gossip, rumors, and people's perceptions will find their way in both the formal and informal organizations. It is important that the project team and project sponsor create and open channels of communication.

The communication media can be important, especially when delivering certain types of news. For example, a richer media, such as face-to-face communication, is generally preferable when delivering important or bad news. There are a number of stories about people who realized that they were being let go when they found their phone line and network connections disconnected and security guards standing by their desk waiting to escort them out of the building. Delivering bad news is something that no one really enjoys, but must be done nonetheless. The point is that management can handle difficult situations with class or with very little class.

Finally, open channels of communication should be both ways. The project team and sponsor must communicate effectively with the various groups within the organization affected by the change, and these groups, in turn, must be able to communicate effectively with the project team and sponsor. In addition, Web sites, e-mails, memos, and newsletters can all be mediums for effective communication.

Evaluate Experience and Develop Lessons Learned

As the project team carries out the change management plan, they will, no doubt, learn from their experiences. These experiences should be documented and made available to other team members and other projects so that experiences can be shared and best practices can be identified. At the end of the project, it is important that the overall success of the change management plan be evaluated. This evaluation may help determine the effectiveness of the different players or a particular change management strategy. The important thing is to learn from experience and to share those experiences with others while adding new form and functionality to the project organization's IT project methodology.

DEALING WITH RESISTANCE AND CONFLICT

Resistance and conflict are a natural part of change (Davidson 2002). In this section, we will look at the nature of resistance and conflict and several approaches for dealing with these two issues. Keep in mind that the concept of conflict presented in this section can be applied to conflicts within the project team as well as external conflicts brought about by the change effort.

Resistance

Resistance should be anticipated from the outset of the project. Rumors and gossip will add fuel to the fire, and the change effort can easily run out of steam if those affected by the change begin to resist. Resistance can be either overt, in the form of memos, meetings, etc., or covert, in the form of sabotage, foot dragging, politicking, etc. Once the change is compromised, management and the project team will lose credibility, and the organization may become resistant to all future changes.

Resistance can arise for many valid reasons. For example, someone may resist an information system because the response time is too slow or because it does not provide the features or functionality that were originally specified as part of the requirements. On the other hand, resistance due to cultural or behavioral reasons is harder to rationalize, but still can keep a project from reaching its intended goal. People may resist change even though they understand that the change will be beneficial (Davidson 2002). For example:

- Some people perceive the change as requiring more time and energy than they are willing to invest.

- Sometimes people feel that that a change will mean giving up something that is familiar, comfortable, and predictable.

- People may be annoyed with the disruption caused by the change, even if they know that it will be beneficial in the long run.

- People may believe that the change is being imposed on them externally, and their egos will not tolerate being told what to do.

- In addition, people may resist because of the way the decision to change was announced or because it was forced upon them.

Resistance is human nature and a natural part of any change process. Understanding what an individual or group perceives as a loss is the first step to dealing with resistance effectively. Because the project team and sponsor are the agents of change, it is easy to see those who resist as overreacting or not being logical. As the proponents of change, the project team and sponsor have had the luxury of knowing about the change early and, therefore, have had the time to become used to it. The rest of the organization, however, may learn about the change much later and, therefore, may not be at the same place for digesting the change. Subsequently, it is important that the project team and sponsor listen to what the rest of the organization is saying. Instead of arguing and trying to reason, it is better to allow people to vent their anger and frustration. Again, having defined a boundary of what is and what is not part of the change can help deal with stressful conflict situations. Keep in mind that empathizing or sympathizing with an individual is not the same as agreeing with them.

Conflict

Closely associated with resistance is the concept of conflict. Conflicts arise when people perceive that their interests and values are challenged or not being met. **Conflict management** focuses on preventing, managing, or resolving conflicts. Therefore, it is important to identify potential conflicts as early as possible so that the conflict can be addressed. Although conflict can be positive and help form new ideas and establish commitment, negative conflict left unresolved can lead to damaged relationships, mistrust, unresolved issues, continued stress, dysfunctional behavior, and low productivity and morale (Davidson 2002). As Verma (1998) suggests:

> Although conflict is one of the things most of us dislike intensely, it is inevitable. Most often when we try to avoid conflict, it will nevertheless seek us out. Some people wrongly hope that conflict will go away if it is ignored. In fact, conflict ignored is more likely to get worse, which can significantly reduce project performance. The best way to reduce conflict is to confront it. (367)

RESISTANCE (TO CHANGE) IS FUTILE

According to David Foote, resistance to change can be one of the "nastiest, most debilitating workplace cancers." It is difficult to understand why even successful companies fail to carry out well-conceived solutions to problems, discourage innovative and creative ideas, lose valued employees, or watch their successes from the past evaporate. Often the reason is resistance to change. Foote provides several success factors based on the experiences of companies that have managed resistance well.

- *Manage the transition, not the change*—Resistance is more deeply rooted in the transition rather than the change itself. Transition is more psychological in nature, whereas change is more situational. Transitions are more internally felt and focus on endings. Therefore, it is important to think through who will have to let go of what.

- *Fear is real when pursuing change*—When fear fuels resistance, it is important to determine who is losing what, anticipate overreaction, acknowledge the losses, and give something back. It is important to look for signs of grieving and allow people to vent their emotions. In addition, treat the past with respect (symbolically and literally), and let people take a piece of the past with them.

- *Keep change teams small*—Empirical evidence suggests that small, empowered teams comprised of six to eight people have the greatest impact on change initiatives. Smaller teams are better at following the rules and improvising creative solutions when faced with obstacles.

- *Anticipate and embrace failure*—Progress toward the project goal counts. But, learning can be difficult, and relapses are a normal part of the change process.

- *Use metrics*—Metrics are important for measuring progress and for rewarding performance being made toward the change objective.

- *Be in agreement*—An organization's leaders must be in agreement so that a clear, consistent message is being sent throughout the organization. This message should focus on the compelling reasons for the change. Dissension can fuel resistance.

- *Invite broad participation*—For a change initiative to succeed, at least 15 percent of the people who are affected by the change must be actively engaged and committed to the change.

- *Over-educate*—Management and the change agents should manage expectations and resistance through effective and timely communication. Communication should focus on the mission, vision, philosophy, process, choices, and details about the impending change.

- *It takes time*—Change does not happen overnight. Often organizations take years to prepare, practice, and build their capabilities to manage change.

SOURCE: Adapted from David Foote, The Futility of Resistance (to Change), *Computerworld,* January 15, 2001, http://www.computerworld.com/managementtopics/management/story/0,10801,56246,00.html.

There are three different views of conflict that have evolved from the late nineteenth century to today (Verma 1998). These views are (1) the traditional view (mid-nineteenth century to mid-1940s), (2) the contemporary view (mid-1940s to 1970s), and (3) the interactionist view (1970s to present).

- *Traditional View*—The traditional view considers conflict in a negative light and feels conflict should be avoided. Conflict, according to this view, leads to poor performance, aggression, and devastation if left to escalate. Therefore, it is important to manage conflict by suppressing it before it occurs or eliminating it as soon as possible. Harmony can be achieved through authoritarian means, but the root causes of the conflict may not be adequately addressed.

- *Contemporary View*—The contemporary view, on the other hand, suggests that conflict is inevitable and natural. Depending on how conflict is handled, conflict can be either positive or negative. Positive conflict among people can stimulate ideas and creativity; however, negative conflict can have damaging effects if left unresolved. Therefore, positive conflict should be encouraged, while keeping negative conflict in check.

■ *Interactionist View*—Today, the interactionist view holds that conflict is an important and necessary ingredient for performance. Although the contemporary view accepts conflict, the interactionist view embraces it because teams can become stagnant and complacent if too harmonious or tranquil (Verma 1998). Subsequently, the project manager should occasionally stir the pot in order to encourage conflict to an appropriate level so that people engage in positive conflict. This may, however, be a fine line to walk for many project managers. Although someone who plays the role of the devil's advocate can be effective in many situations, people may become annoyed when it is used in every situation or used ineffectively.

To better understand the nature of conflict, Verma (1998) points out that conflict within projects can fit one, or a combination, of three categories:

1. Conflicts associated with the goals, objectives, or specifications of the project.
2. Conflicts associated with the administration, management structures, or underlying philosophies of the project.
3. Conflicts associated with the interpersonal relationships among people based on work ethics, styles, egos, or personalities.

According to a study conducted by Thomas and Schmidt (Thomas and Schmidt 1976), a typical middle or top-level manager spends about 20 percent of her or his time dealing with conflict! For the project manager and project team, the seeds of resistance can easily lead to negative conflicts. Subsequently, it is important to understand how to deal with conflict. Blake and Mouton (Blake and Mouton 1964) and Verma (1998) describe five approaches for dealing with conflict. A project team member or project manager should choose an appropriate approach for managing conflict based on the situation.

■ *Avoidance*—Avoiding conflict focuses on retreating, withdrawing or ignoring conflict. Sometimes, a cooling-off period may be a wise choice, especially when emotions and tempers are high. Avoidance may be appropriate when you can't win, the stakes are low, or gaining time is important. However, it may not be useful when the immediate, successful resolution of an issue is required.

■ *Accommodation*—Accommodation, or smoothing, is an approach for appeasing the various parties in conflict. This approach may be useful when trying to reach an overall goal when the goal is more important than the personal interests of the parties involved. Smoothing may also be effective when dealing with an issue that has low risk and low return or when in a no-win situation. Because accommodation tends to work only in the short run, conflict may reappear in another form later on.

■ *Forcing*—When using this approach, a person uses his or her dominant authority to resolve the conflict. This approach often results in a one-sided or win-lose situation in which one party gains at the other's expense. This approach may be effective when no common ground exists, when you are sure you are right, when an emergency situation exists, or when time is of the essence. Forcing resolution may, however, cause the conflict to redevelop later because people dislike having a decision or someone else's views imposed upon them.

- *Compromise*—Compromise includes aspects of both forcing and accommodation; it gives up more than forcing and less than accommodation. Compromise is essentially bargaining—one person or group gives up something in exchange for gaining something else. In this case, no party actually wins and none actually loses, so that some satisfaction is gained from resolution of the conflict. This approach may be useful when attempting to resolve complex problems that must be settled in a short time and when the risks and rewards are moderately high. Unfortunately, important aspects of a project may be compromised as a means of achieving short-term results—for example, quality standards may be compromised in order to meet the project's schedule.

- *Collaboration*—When the risks and benefits are high, collaboration may be the best approach for dealing with conflict. This approach requires confronting and attempting to solve the problem by incorporating different ideas, viewpoints, and perspectives. The focus of collaboration is learning from others and gaining commitment, trust, respect, and confidence from the various parties involved (Verma 1998). Collaboration takes time and requires a sincere desire to work out a mutually acceptable solution. In addition, it requires a willingness to engage in a good-faith problem-solving process that facilitates open and honest communication.

According to Verma (1998), each conflict situation is unique and the choice of an approach to resolve conflict depends on:

- Type of conflict and its relative importance to the project.
- Time pressure to resolve the conflict.
- Position of power or authority of the parties involved.
- Whether the emphasis is on maintaining the goals or objectives of the project or maintaining relationships.

Polarity Management

Often the project manager or project team is faced with a conflict situation that appears to have no solution. For example, the agents of change (i.e., the project team) may be faced with conflict and resistance from the targets of change (i.e., the users). Often one side finds itself advocating a change (e.g., a new system), while the other side is trying to maintain the status quo. The problem is that both sides end up in a polarity where each side can only see the upsides or advantages of their pole and the downsides or disadvantages of the other. For many, this is a difficult dilemma that can create even more resistance and conflict.

In his book, *Polarity Management: Identifying and Managing Unsolvable Problems,* Barry Johnson (Johnson 1996), advocates a technique that can help people see the whole picture and then structure the process of change to bring about an effective method for collaboration.

According to Johnson, the problem is that we often frame a problem or dilemma as something that can be solved by choosing one side over another. Crusaders are those who want to change the status quo and are the supporters of change. Tradition Bearers are those at the opposite end of the pole and wish to preserve the best of the past and present. Using a tool called **polarity mapping,** we can see the upsides and

HOW TO HANDLE CONFLICT

Kenneth Cloke is the director of the Center for Dispute Resolution, and Joan Goldsmith is an organizational consultant and educator. Together they provide a number of ideas to help make the most of conflict. The following steps can help you to think about yourself, your opponent, and your conflict:

1. *Look inward*—The first thing to do is to focus on yourself by making a decision to approach and engage in conflict constructively. Being open to learning during the process and being committed to resolving the conflict constructively are required.

2. *Set the stage for dialog*—The next step is to find a neutral environment, perhaps by inviting your opponent to lunch or some other locale away from the office. It is important to be open, honest, and friendly rather than hostile or suspicious.

3. *Listen carefully*—Now is the time to disengage from your fight-or-flight response and be open to listening empathically to your opponent. Conflict is fundamentally a communication problem, and to be an effective listener you need to control your emotions. Control your anger and refuse to take comments personally.

4. *Speak carefully*—Your needs and self-interests should be stated clearly and without emotion. Becoming angry yourself can escalate the conflict and diminish your integrity and credibility.

5. *Dig deeper*—Look beyond the words spoken to the real meaning of what is being said. This can help you to understand the underlying reasons for the conflict. Often the conflict is not about the issue you are arguing about, but about issues that lie beneath the surface.

6. *Don't get personal*—People often think that they are right and that the other person is reason for the conflict. Conflict can present opportunities when you separate the person from the problem, focus on the future and not the past, and stop arguing about what you want and instead talk about why you want something. Positions that focus on what you want limit thinking, perceptions, and imagination, while interests that focus on why you want something can broaden choices and focus on the future.

7. *Think creatively*—It helps to work with the other person to brainstorm potential solutions. When in conflict, it is easy to spend a great deal of time trying to get the other person to accept your solution while poking holes in theirs. Brainstorming allows for expanding the range of solutions and seeing the big picture.

8. *Collaborate*—It is better to negotiate collaboratively than aggressively. Negotiating can help both parties to shift from anger to problem solving.

9. *Use the right tools*—Appropriate problem-solving techniques, mediation, and so forth can help overcome an impasse, find common ground, and reach a resolution to the conflict.

10. *Be forgiving*—Letting go of your judgments and perceptions about the other party can help you to improve your own skills at handing his or her difficult behaviors. Sometimes you have to admit to yourself that you do not know how to respond effectively to his or her behaviors. You may have to learn to let go of your conflicts so that your future is not overshadowed by what has happened in the past. Your lessons learned from your experiences should help you to "remember and forgive" rather than "forgive and forget."

11. *Don't surrender*—You cannot always avoid conflict, but you can turn conflicts into collaboration and opportunity. Resolving a conflict does not mean losing or giving in because both parties cheat themselves out of the chance to learn from what the conflict has to teach.

12. *Look outward*—It is important to recognize that larger organizational and social issues are expressed as a result of conflict. Conflict can lead to change that offers the promise of a better world. Your role in this change can allow you to grow and feel connected with others.

13. *Search for completion*—Conflicts will continue if you do not feel that you have been heard or have communicated completely what you think. You can help the other party by summarizing what the other person has said, asking them to summarize what you have said, and ensuring that the person (or you) has not held anything back. Only then can you feel as though something has changed.

SOURCE: Adapted from Kenneth Cloke and Joan Goldsmith, Making the Most of Conflict, *CIO.COM,* http://www.cio.com/leadership/edit /020100_conflict.html.

downsides that each side is advocating. Figure 11.5 provides an example of a polarity map for implementing a new word processing application.

The polarity map illustrated in Figure 11.5 shows how the two polarities can be mapped. In the upper left quadrant, the Tradition Bearers' (TB+) view of the upsides for keeping the current word processing software package are listed, while the Crusaders' (C+) view of the upsides for upgrading to a new word processing package are listed in the upper right quadrant. Often the conflicts occur in the lower two quadrants or on the diagonals. For example, people who advocate upgrading to a new word processing package may focus on the upsides of the upper right quadrant (C+) and the downsides of the lower left quadrant (C-). Similarly, those in favor of maintaining the status quo will focus on the quadrants TB+ and TB-. Often the upside of one quadrant (e.g. "familiarity" in TB+) becomes a downside in the opposite quadrant (e.g., "will take time to learn" in TB-). Subsequently, resistance and conflict only escalate unless both sides see the entire picture.

Brainstorming is a useful technique for having both the Tradition Bearers and the Crusaders list the upside and downsides for both polarities. Starting in any quadrant is fine, and either side can add to the upsides or downsides of any quadrant. It is important to see the big picture and for both sides to communicate a particular perception. Johnson suggests that before using polarity management, both sides should:

1. Clarify what you value and what you do not want to lose.

2. Let the other side know that you are aware of the downsides of the pole you favor.

3. Assure the other side that you want to maintain the upsides of their pole.

The effective use of polarity mapping helps people *get away* from seeing their initiative as the only solution to the problem and from believing a decision must choose one pole over the other. In fact, both Crusaders and Tradition Bearers make important contributions to the process. For example, Crusaders contribute by identifying the downsides of the current pole and provide the energy to move away from the current pole. Similarly, Tradition Bearers, by identifying the upsides of the current pole, help identify things that should be preserved. Tradition Bearers also identify downsides of the opposite pole. Everyone's concerns are valid and important in coming up with a

	Keep current word processing software package	Upgrade to a different word processing software package
Upsides	■ Familiarity ■ Does what I need it to do ■ No additional training needed *TB+*	■ Faster than current software ■ Expanded functionality ■ Most popular WP software used—easy to find & hire people who have the skills *C+*
Downsides	■ Slow ■ Limited functionality ■ No longer supported by vendor *C-*	■ Will take time to learn ■ Too many features & functions ■ Training will be required *TB-*

Figure 11.5 Polarity Mapping

SOURCE: From *Polarity Management: Identifying and Managing Unsolvable Problems,* copyright © 1996, Barry Johnson. Amherst, MA: HRD Press, Inc. Used with permission.

mutually agreeable solution. Those advocating the change are forced to recognize that an initiative can only be successful if the old system's upsides are carried forward in the new environment.

The key to polarity management is recognizing that both polarities must be managed simultaneously. The goal of the Tradition Bearers and Crusaders then becomes coming up with ways of pursuing the upsides, while attempting to avoid the downsides. Following our word processing example, it seems that the Tradition Bearers feel that learning a new system may create a distraction or interruption. If upgrading to a new word processing package, both groups may try to come up with training plan flexible enough so that both groups get what they want. For example, training could be phased in over time, with the early training phases covering only the basic features and functionality of the new system.

CHAPTER SUMMARY

Understanding organizational change is an important area for IT project management. IT professionals may concentrate exclusively on the technical, or hard, side of the project at the expense of the people, or soft, side. Unfortunately, this position often results in the implementation of information systems that are technical successes, but organizational failures. The system performs efficiently, but the people or users do not accept the system because of what the system represents.

Therefore, it is important the project sponsor, the IT project manager, and the project team help prepare the users, or targets of the intended change, before the system is implemented. Preparation requires that we first understand the nature of change when a change is introduced into the organization. Often change and peoples' reaction to change unfold in predictable patterns or behaviors.

In this chapter, we first looked at change as a process. Kurt Lewin introduced the concept of Force Field Analysis, in which we try to first understand the driving and resisting forces that push and repel the change. In addition, Lewin's model of change helps us to understand that we must unfreeze the current state, or status quo, and then move through a transitional state until the new or desired state is reached. Then, these new behaviors must be refrozen so that they become ingrained as the new status quo. It is important that those who sponsor and are responsible for implementing the change acknowledge and understand the transition state. Sometime referred to as the neutral zone, the transition state can be frightening and frustrating for people who find themselves in a state of limbo. While the change is relatively easy, the transition can be a difficult time in which people may try to escape, or revert back to the more comfortable and familiar previous state. Moreover, initiating a change begins with an ending of the current equilibrium and may bring out a number of

emotional responses as a result of a perceived loss. Since both people and organizations can only assimilate or process change at a given rate, the cumulative effect of change can result in stress and dysfunctional behavior if an individual's or organization's threshold for change is exceeded.

Understanding the effects of change on the organization allow us to develop a change management plan. This plan should first focus on assessing the organization's willingness, readiness, and ability to change. This assessment should focus on the change sponsor's commitment to supporting the change and associated transition and on the change agents' ability to facilitate the change. In addition, the sponsors and change agents should determine the impact the change will have on the targets. This assessment includes (1) clarifying the real impacts of the change, (2) understanding the breadth of change, (3) defining what's over and what's not, and (4) determining whether the rules for success have changed.

The next step of the change management plan should focus on adopting a strategy to support the change. Four approaches were outlined in the chapter: (1) rational-empirical approach, (2) normative-reeducation approach, (3) power-coercive approach, and (4) environmental-adaptive approach. A change management plan could include one or a combination of approaches, depending on the situation.

The third component of the change management plan should center on implementing the plan and tracking its progress. Although several tools for tracking the project's progress were introduced in an earlier chapter (e.g., Gantt chart, PERT chart, etc.), several milestones and other significant events should be used to mark the organization's progress toward adapting and adopting the change.

The change management plan should also include the evaluation and documentation of lessons learned. It is important that the effectiveness of a given strategy be assessed and experiences be documented so that they may be shared and so that best practices can be identified.

Although a change management plan may send an important message to the organization that management cares about its people, resistance and conflict can still arise. Both resistance and conflict are a natural part of the change process and should be anticipated from the outset of the project. Resistance can arise for many reasons and take many forms. Although the traditional view of conflict suggests that all conflict is bad and should be avoided or resolved as soon as possible, the contemporary and inter-actionist views of conflict support the idea that positive conflict can stimulate new ideas and improve creativity.

In addition, several approaches to managing or dealing with conflict were introduced. These approaches include (1) avoidance, (2) accommodation, (3) forcing, (4) compromise, and (5) collaboration. Each approach has its advantages and disadvantages, and a project stakeholder should choose an appropriate approach based on the situation.

Finally, polarity management was introduced as a tool that provides a collaborative approach for dealing with conflict and resistance. Using this technique, Crusaders (those who are proponents for a particular change) work together with the Tradition Bearers (those to wish to maintain the status quo) to develop a polarity map. This map defines the upsides and downsides of each pole that the Crusaders and Tradition Bearers advocate. Polarity mapping allows each side to see the big picture and to discuss their concerns in order to work together to develop a solution for maintaining the upsides of each pole while minimizing the downsides.

While this chapter focuses on the soft side of IT project management, it will provide an important foundation for understanding and supporting the operational objective of implementing the IT project's final product.

▮ REVIEW QUESTIONS

1. As an IT professional, why does your mere existence in an organization suggest change?

2. Why is it just as important to deal with the people issues of an IT project as it is to deal with the technical issues?

3. Why do many IT professionals shy away from dealing with the people issues, the soft side of IT projects?

4. How can a system be a technical success, but an organizational failure?

5. How does change management fit with IT project management?

6. What is wrong with the idea of just expecting people to adapt to a new system by compliance?

7. Why is acceptance more powerful than compliance?

8. What are some down sides if an organization does not accept the project's final product as originally envisioned?

9. In your own words, define change management.

10. What is the difference between positive change and negative change? Do positive changes create stress for an individual? Why or why not?

11. Define assimilation and its importance to understanding how people deal with change.

12. What happens when an individual cannot assimilate change fast enough?

13. What happens when an organization cannot assimilate change fast enough?

14. Describe Force Field Analysis.

15. Describe the three stages of Lewin's model for change.

16. Why is the transition state often referred to as the neutral zone?

17. What might happen if the project manager and sponsor do not understand, expect, or acknowledge the neutral zone?

18. What is the difference between a change and a transition? Give an example of each.

19. Why would a person have emotional responses when faced with doing her or his job differently or being forced to use and learn new technology?

20. Describe the emotional responses a person might go through when given the news that her job has been eliminated as a result of the implementation of a new accounts payable system.

21. Why is having a change management plan important?

22. Why should the project manager assess the willingness, readiness, and ability of the organization to change?

23. What is a change sponsor? What is the difference between an initiating sponsor and a sustaining sponsor?

24. What important criteria should be used to determine whether a sponsor can help the organization through the planned change?

25. What is a change agent? What role does a change agent play?

26. What is a target? Why are targets important to a change initiative?

27. Why should the real impacts of change be clarified in the change management plan?

28. Using Leavitt's model, provide an example of how an electronic commerce application would affect the organization's people, technology, task, and structure.

29. Why should the project team and sponsor be clear on defining what is over and what is not before a new system is implemented?

30. What are rules for success? Why is it important to determine whether the rules for success have changed in an organization before a new system is implemented?

31. Describe the rational-empirical approach to change. What things would a change management plan address under this approach?

32. Describe the normative-reeducation approach to change. What things would a change management plan address under this approach?

33. Describe the power-coercive approach to change. What things would a change management plan address under this approach?

34. Describe the environmental-adaptive approach to change. What things would a change management plan address under this approach?

35. How can you track the progress of your change management plan?

36. Why is it important to evaluate your change management experiences and document them as lessons learned?

37. What is resistance? How might an individual or group resist the implementation of a new information system?

38. Why would people resist change even if it was beneficial to them?

39. Why would a manager think that an individual or group is overacting to a planned change?

40. What is conflict? Why should you anticipate conflict over the course of your project?

41. In your own words, define conflict management.

42. Why is it worse to try to ignore conflict than to deal with it.

43. Describe the traditional view of conflict.

44. Describe the contemporary view of conflict

45. Describe the interactionist view of conflict.

46. What is the avoidance approach to dealing with conflict? When is it most useful? When is it not appropriate?

47. What is the accommodation approach to dealing with conflict? When is it most useful? When is it not appropriate?

48. What is the forcing approach to dealing with conflict? When is it most useful? When is it not appropriate?

49. What is the compromise approach to dealing with conflict? When is it most useful? When is it not appropriate?

50. What is the collaboration approach to dealing with conflict? When is it most useful? When is it not appropriate?

51. In your own words, describe polarity management?

52. What is a crusader? What role does a crusader play?

53. What is a tradition bearer? What role does a tradition bearer play?

54. How can developing a polarity map help overcome conflict?

▪ EXTEND YOUR KNOWLEDGE

1. Interview someone who has faced a major change. The change could be either positive or negative. Examples include someone moving to a new country, a new city, losing a job, or any major life event. Your questions should include, but should not be limited, to the following:
   a. Describe the change.
   b. What was the reason for the change?
   c. Describe the transition.
   d. How difficult was the transition?
   e. How did you adjust?
   f. What feelings or emotions did you feel over the course of the change?
   g. How long did it take before you finally accepted the change?

2. Suppose you were a project manager of an IT project and you hired a new college graduate. This person just graduated and has moved from a distant

city to work for your firm. You are not only providing a decent salary and benefits package, but have paid for moving expenses and four weeks of IT boot camp training.

    a. What feelings or emotions might this person have?

    b. What could you do to help this person adjust and become a valued member of your team?

3. As a systems analyst, you have been assigned to interview a department supervisor. This supervisor has been with the company for almost 30 years and is known to be difficult to work with. However, his department's productivity and profitability have always been a model for the rest of the organization. Your task is to write up a report detailing the requirements and specifications for a new system. You arrive at this person's office on time for your meeting. You say hello in your most friendly voice, but he gruffly says, "What do you want? I'm really busy and don't have a lot of time for you right now.

Besides, I can't understand why the company wants to throw away good money fixing something that isn't broke." How would you handle this situation?

4. Assume that three months ago you were hired as a project manager for a medium-size consulting firm. Shortly after arriving, you find out that one of your star network specialists and a senior manager of the company that hired your firm deeply dislike one another. Your network specialist is extremely knowledgeable and good at what she does, but, unfortunately, not a really good people person. On the other hand, the manager thinks he knows everything, but he really doesn't know much about technology. That has never stopped him from giving out advice and trying to impress everyone with his limited knowledge—especially about networks. This behavior only makes the network specialist more resentful. How would you handle this conflict so that the project can continue as planned?

BIBLIOGRAPHY

Blake, R. R. and J. S. Mouton. 1964. *The Managerial Grid.* Houston, Tex.: Gulf Publishing.

Bridges, W. 1991. *Managing Transitions: Making the Most of Change.* Cambridge, Mass.: Perseus Books.

Conner, D. 1995. *Managing at the Change of Speed.* New York: Villard Books.

Davidson, J. 2002. *Change Management.* Indianapolis, Ind.: Alpha.

Duck, J. D. 2001. *The Change Monster: The Human Forces That Fuel or Foil Corporate Transformation and Change.* New York: Crown Business.

Johnson, B. 1996. *Polarity Management: Identifying and Managing Unsolvable Problems.* Amherst, Mass.: HRD Press.

Kübler-Ross, E. 1969. *On Death and Dying.* New York: Macmillian.

Leavitt, H. J. 1964. Applied Organizational Change in Industry: Structural, Technical and Human Approaches. In *New Perspectives in Organizational Research,* edited by H. J. Leavitt. Chichester: John Wiley: 55–71.

Lewin, K. 1951. *Field Theory in Social Science.* New York: Harper and Row.

Thomas, K. W. and W. H. Schmidt. 1976. A Survey of Managerial Interests with Respect to Conflict. *Academy of Management Journal:* 315–318.

Verma, V. K. 1998. Conflict Management. In *Project Management Handbook,* edited by J. K. Pinto. San Francisco: Jossey-Bass.

12

Project Implementation, Closure, and Evaluation

CHAPTER OVERVIEW

In this chapter, we will focus on three important areas: project implementation, closure, and evaluation. After studying this chapter, you should understand and be able to:

- Describe the three tactical approaches to information system implementation and installation: (1) direct cutover, (2) parallel, and (3) phased, as well as compare the advantages and disadvantages of each approach.

- Describe the processes associated with project closure to ensure that the project is closed in an orderly manner.

- Identify the four different project evaluations or reviews: (1) individual performance review, (2) postmortem review, (3) project audit, and (4) evaluation of the project's MOV.

▌ GLOBAL TECHNOLOGY SOLUTIONS

The party was winding down as Tim Williams and Kellie Matthews sat alone at a table and watched the band pack up its instruments and sound system. It was getting late and only a few other GTS employees and their guests remained. The company had rented a stylish banquet room in a local hotel to mark the conclusion of the Husky Air project. The event allowed Tim and Kellie the opportunity to formally recognize and thank each member of the team for the hard work over the last several months. During a ceremony before dinner, Tim gave each member of the project team a small gift to commemorate Global Technology Solutions' first successful project. In addition, several humorous certificates were given out to keep the occasion fun and lively. The dinner and the band were excellent, and everyone had a great time.

As Tim and Kellie sat at the table, Kellie raised her glass in the air, "Well, here's to the first of many successful projects."

Tim raised his glass as well, "And here's to a great party."

GTS was growing. The company had successfully completed its first project and now two new projects were scheduled to start in a few weeks. Moreover, one of the Husky Air team members, Yan, had been promoted to project manager for one of the upcoming projects. To support this growth, three new employees had been hired and were scheduled to start the next week.

The glasses clinked, then both Kellie and Tim sipped from their glasses. "It was a lot of work, but a lot of fun," reflected Tim.

Kellie smiled, "Don't forget we still have a few things to wrap up before it's really over. I have to meet with each member of the team next week to make sure that all of the project documents and deliverables are organized and archived. You'll be pretty busy finishing up each team member's evaluation. Then there are these two new projects that we have to start thinking about. And, don't forget, we still have to meet with Husky Air's management in a couple of weeks to assess how well the project met its MOV."

"Okay, okay!" laughed Tim. "I didn't want to turn this into a business meeting. For once, let's leave work at the office."

"You're right," laughed Kellie. "Let's leave it at the office. However, I think our little party was a success. We may have even started a new tradition for GTS."

Tim smiled, "I could get used to this. It was kind of stressful at times, especially towards the end, but completing the project and having this party has helped everyone feel good about themselves and the work they did."

By this time the band carried away the last amplifier, and one could sense that the wait staff wanted to clear the last of the remaining tables and go home. It was clearly time to leave. Kellie and Tim stood and started walking towards the door. As they put their coats on, Kellie turned to Tim and gave him a quick hug. "It has been a real pleasure starting this company and working so closely with you," she said. "No one in our family would have thought when we were kids that we'd work this well together."

Tim returned the hug. "I never thought that I'd ever get along with my sister this well either."

As they headed toward the elevator, Kellie reminded Tim, "Don't forget about dinner at Mom and Dad's house tomorrow night. Mom expects us around six, so don't be late again."

Tim shook his head as the elevator door opened. "Geez, do you always have to act like my older sister?"

Things to Think About:

1. What is the purpose of bringing closure to a project?
2. Why is it important to evaluate the project and the team's performance?
3. Why should the project's MOV be evaluated some time after the project is implemented and some time has passed?

▌ INTRODUCTION

The topic of change management was introduced in the previous chapter and focused on preparing the people within the organization for the upcoming change and, more importantly, the transition that will occur as a result of the change. Understanding the human element or the "soft side" of IT project management is critical for ensuring that the individuals or groups within the organization will accept and adapt to the new information system implemented by the project team.

In this final chapter we will concentrate on three important areas—project implementation, closure, and evaluation. **Project implementation** focuses on installing or delivering the project's major deliverable in the organization—the information system that was built or purchased. The implementation of the information system requires a tactical plan that allows the project team to move the IT solution from a development and test environment to the day-to-day operations of the organization.

In general, implementing the product of an IT project can follow one of three approaches. These approaches are (1) direct cutover, (2) parallel, or (3) phased. Each approach has unique advantages and disadvantages that make a particular approach appropriate for a given situation. Subsequently, understanding and choosing an appropriate approach can have a profound impact on the success or failure of the project.

As discussed in Chapter 1, a project is a temporary endeavor undertaken to accomplish a unique purpose. This means that a project has a definite beginning and a definite end. Once the information system is implemented, the project manager and team must prepare for terminating, or closing, the project. Closing a project includes organizing and archiving project documents and deliverables, performing an audit and assessment of the project, documenting lessons learned, evaluating the performance of the project manager and team, releasing project resources, and closing all project-related accounts.

For a project to be closed successfully, the product of the project must be formally accepted by the project sponsor or customer. Not all projects, of course, are successful; however, a number of administrative tasks must still be completed. In such cases, it is necessary to assess whether any salvage value exists, and, more importantly, to understand the nature and reasons why the project was not successful.

Once the project is closed, the project manager should evaluate each project team member individually in order to assess and provide feedback to the individual about his or her performance on the project. In addition, the project manager and project team should meet to conduct a postmortem review of the project. The outcome of this review should be a set of documented lessons learned and best practices that can be shared throughout the organization.

In addition, the project should be reviewed by an impartial outside party. An audit or outside review can provide valuable insight on how well the project was managed and on how well the project members functioned as a team. The auditor or audit team should also determine whether the project manager and team acted professionally and ethically.

The project's real success will be determined by the project sponsor or customer. In this text, the project's overall goal was defined as the MOV, or measurable organizational value. The MOV must be clearly defined and agreed upon in the early stages of the project. Unfortunately, the project's true value to the organization may not be discernable immediately following implementation. It may take weeks or even months after the information system is implemented, but an evaluation must be made to determine whether the project was successful, as defined by its MOV.

The remainder of this chapter has three sections. In the next section, we will look at three approaches for implementation. This section will be followed by one that describes the processes required to formally close a process. Finally, the last section will look at evaluating the project team and the project as a whole.

PROJECT IMPLEMENTATION

At some point, testing is complete and the project team and project manager then become responsible for ensuring that the information system is transferred successfully

---

ERP IMPLEMENTATION IN 10 EASY STEPS?

1. Ask the board of directors for an arbitrary but large sum of money ($300 million should suffice).
2. Give half of the money to consultants. Ask them to select an appropriate ERP package for your company. Consultants will audit your business processes for six months and then select SAP, which they happen to sell.
3. Form cross-functional implementation teams. Hold meetings.
4. Reengineer all your business processes to match the software model.

5. Give the other half of the money to the consultants.
6. Install the software.
7. Train end users repeatedly.
8. Cross your fingers.
9. Turn on the software.
10. If you're still in business, immediately return to Step 1 because it's time for an upgrade.

SOURCE: From Derek Slater, ERP Implementation in 10 Easy Steps, *CIO.COM*, April 1, 2001, http://www.cio.com/archive/040101/tl_erp.html.

---

from the development and test environment to the operational environment of the sponsor or customer's organization. This transfer requires a tactical approach, and it can be a stressful time for all the stakeholders involved. Choosing an inappropriate implementation approach can negatively impact the project's remaining schedule and budget. In general, the project team can take one of three approaches for implementing the information system. These approaches include (1) direct cutover, (2) parallel, and (3) phased.

Direct Cutover

The direct cutover approach, as illustrated in Figure 12.1, is an approach where the old system is shut down and the new system is turned on. In general, a target, or *go live,* date is agreed upon, and the new system simply replaces the old.

This approach can be effective when quick delivery of the new system is critical or when the existing system is so poor that it must be replaced as soon as possible. Direct cutover may also be appropriate when the system is not mission critical—i.e., the system's failure will not have a major impact on the organization. It is important, however, that the new system be thoroughly tested so everyone is confident that few, if any, major problems will arise.

Although there are some advantages to using the direct cutover approach, there are also a number of risks involved that generally make this the least favored approach except in a few, carefully planned situations. Although the direct cutover approach can be quick, it may not always be painless. You might think of this approach as walking a tightrope without a safety net. You may get from one end of the tightrope to other quickly, but not without a great deal of risk. Subsequently, there may be no going back once the old system is turned off and the new system is turned on. As a result, the organization could experience major delays, frustrated users and customers, lost revenues, and missed deadlines. The pressure of ensuring that everything is right or having to deal with problems and irate users or project stakeholders can create a great deal of stress for the project team.

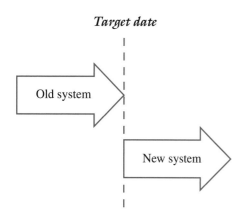

Figure 12.1 Direct Cutover

Parallel

As Figure 12.2 illustrates, the parallel approach to implementation allows the old and the new systems to run concurrently for a time. At some point, the organization switches entirely from the old system to the new.

The parallel approach is appropriate when problems or the failure of the system can have a major impact on the organization. For example, an organization may be implementing a new accounts receivable package. Before switching over completely to the new system, the organization may run both systems concurrently in order to compare the outputs of both systems. This approach provides confidence that the new system is functioning and performing properly before relying on it entirely.

Although the parallel approach may not be as stressful for the project team as the direct cutover approach, it can create more stress for the users of the system. The users will probably have to enter data into both systems and even be responsible for comparing the outputs. If the new system performs as expected, they may be willing to put up with the extra workload until the scheduled target date when the new system stands alone. If, however, unexpected problems are encountered, the target date for switching from the old to the new system may be pushed back. The extra workload and overtime hours may begin to take their toll and pressure for the project team to "get on with it" may create a stressful environment for everyone involved.

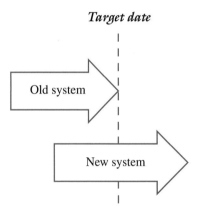

Figure 12.2 Parallel

Phased

Following the phased approach, the system is introduced in modules or in different parts of the organization incrementally as illustrated in Figure 12.3. For example, an organization may implement an accounting information system package by first implementing the general ledger component, then accounts payable and accounts receivable, and finally payroll.

The phased approach may be appropriate when introducing a software system to different areas of the organization. When upgrading an operating system, for example, the IT department may perform the upgrade on a department-by-department basis according to a published schedule. In this case, a target date for each department would be set to allow each department to plan for the upgrade accordingly. A phased approach may also allow the project team to learn from its experiences during the initial implementation so that later implementations run more smoothly.

Although the phased approach may take more time than the direct cutover approach, it may be less risky and much more manageable. Also, overly optimistic target dates or problems experienced during the early phases of implementation may create a chain reaction that pushes back the scheduled dates of the remaining planned implementations.

Table 12.1 provides a summary of each of the three implementation approaches discussed.

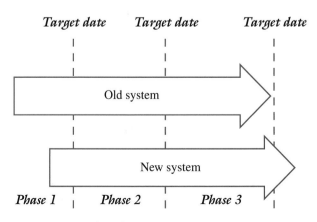

Figure 12.3 Phased

IMPLEMENTATION PROBLEMS CONTRIBUTE TO FEDEX PILOT'S STRIKE

A new scheduling system at Federal Express got its pilots so riled up that it may have been a major reason for them to go on strike. Although the packaged software was installed successfully at several other airlines, the problem appears to have been the up-front planning process. Tony Hauserman, communications chairman for the 3,200-member Pilot Associate Union, said, "The system was extremely disruptive, we weren't consulted before it was implemented and they said they'd run parallel tests on it before it went live—but they didn't." In fact, the poorly implemented system has helped to bring the union members closer together as the company and union were in the midst of contract negotiations. A spokesperson for FedEx explained that the system didn't "roll out the way we wanted to," but added that the company was addressing the problems pointed out by the pilots. Interestingly, TWA uses the same system but tested the system for a year before it was turned on. Moreover, TWA engaged representatives from the pilots' union from the beginning and performed parallel testing as well. The problem at FedEx, however, was that the system utilized a flight schedule optimizer that could string together the most efficient routes and schedules that would allow the pilots to get out of and then back into their home airport. Unfortunately, the FedEx pilots were caught off guard because the past union contracts were not written with strict enough rules about layovers, route preferences, and time away from home. As a result, high-tech software can make negotiations between employees and their companies more complex.

SOURCE: Adapted from Stewart Deck, System Implementation may Contribute to Pilots' Strike at FedEx, *Computerworld,* October 26, 1998, http://www.computerworld.com/news/1998/story/0,11280, 33157,00.html.

Table 12.1 Comparison of Implementation Approaches

Direct Cutover	*Parallel*	*Phased*
▪ Implementation can be quick ▪ Can be risky if system is not fully tested ▪ Places more pressure on the project team	▪ Provides a safety net or backup in case problems are encountered with the implementation of the new system ▪ Can increase confidence in the new system when output of old system and new system is compared ▪ Takes longer and may cost more than direct cutover approach ▪ Places more pressure on the users of the system	▪ Allows for an organized and managed approach for implementing system modules or a system/upgrades in different departments or geographical locations ▪ Experience with early implementation can guide and make later implementations go more smoothly ▪ Takes longer and may cost more than the direct cutover approach ▪ Problems encountered during early phases can impact the overall implementation schedule

As the end of the project draws near, everyone may become anxious to finish the project and move onto other things. Unfortunately, there is often a great deal of work that still needs to be completed. Delays or unanticipated problems may require additional time and unbudgeted resources, leading to cost and schedule overruns or extra unpaid effort, especially if an implied warranty exists (Rosenau 1998).

During the final stages of the project, the project team may be faced with both time and performance pressures as the project's deadline looms in the near future. On the other hand, the sponsor or client may become more concerned about whether the time and money spent on the project will reap the envisioned benefits. The project manager is often caught in the middle attempting to keep the project team happy and on track, while assuring the project sponsor that all is well.

ADMINISTRATIVE CLOSURE

Although all projects must come to an end, a project can be terminated for any number of reasons. Gray and Larson (2000) define five circumstances for ending a project: normal, premature, perpetual, failed, and changed priorities.

- *Normal*—A project that ends normally is one that is completed as planned. The project scope is achieved within the cost, quality, and schedule objectives, although there probably was some variation and modification along the way. The project is transferred to the project sponsor, and the end of the project is marked with a celebration, awards, and recognition for a good job well done by those involved. As you might suspect, this is an ideal situation.

- *Premature*—Occasionally, a project team may be pushed to complete a project early even though the system may not include all of the envisioned features or functionality. For example, an organization may need to have a new system operational—with only a core set of original requirements— to respond to a competitor's actions, to enter a new market early, or as a result of a legal or governmental requirement. Although there is pressure to finish the project early, the risks of this decision should be carefully thought through by all the project stakeholders.

- *Perpetual*—Some projects seem to take on a "life of their own" and are known as runaway, or perpetual, projects. These projects never seem to end. Perpetual projects may result from delays or a scope or MOV that was never clearly defined or agreed upon. Then, the project sponsor (or even the team) may attempt to add on various features or functionality to the system, which results in added time and resources that increase the project schedule and drain the project budget. Some runaway projects result from an organization not making the appropriate decision to "pull the plug" on an unsuccessful project. The decision to terminate a project is not an easy one if egos and perhaps even careers or jobs are on the line. This phenomenon may also occur when the project has a high payoff to the organization and when admitting to failure is strongly against the corporate culture (Keil 1995). No matter what the cause, project resources are eventually drained to a point where a potentially successful project becomes unsuccessful (Nicholas 1990). Attention to defining and agreeing to the project's MOV, the project scope processes, and timely project reviews can reduce the risk of perpetual projects.

- *Failed*—Sometimes projects are just unsuccessful. In general, an IT project fails if insufficient attention is paid to the people, processes, or technology. Even though the project's MOV may define the project's value to the organization, cost and schedule overruns may drain the project's value to a point where the costs of completing the project outweigh the benefits.

- *Changed Priority*—In some circumstances, a project may be terminated as a result of a change in priorities. Financial or economic reasons may dictate that resources are no longer available to the project. Or, management may decide to divert resources to higher priority projects. This change can happen when the original importance or value of the project was misjudged or misrepresented or when organizational needs or technology change over the course of a long-term project. Some projects are "terminated by starvation." As Meredith and Mantel (2000) describe it, successive budget cuts over time can slowly starve a project budget to the point where it is ended but the termination is masked. Senior management may not want to admit that it had

KNOW WHEN TO SAY WHEN

Identifying the lost-cause IT project is not an easy task. Constant attention to project metrics and an intuitive understanding of the business are required. But, once a lost-cause project is identified, it is important for the organization to shut it down quickly and efficiently. Terminating a project should be an option at each stage or phase of the project. For example, Petrotin, a former subsidiary of Texaco, has about twenty-five IT projects underway that it scrutinizes closely. In the last two years, the company shut down two projects for different reasons. Pulling the plug on these projects before implementation saved the company money and the IT department's credibility. Raj Kapur, vice president of the Center for Project Management in San Ramon, CA, believes that once the decision to kill a project is made, the next set of steps is critical. The company should first put together a cancellation plan that carefully considers all of the project stakeholders and budget implications. For instance, there may be legal ramifications if the project involves contracts with vendors, suppliers, or even customers. The human resources department should also be consulted as soon as possible if terminating the project means letting people go. The next step, according to Kapur, is to inform all the key people associated with the doomed project, especially the project champion and the project manager, before a public announcement is made. Afterwards, the project team should try to salvage as much work as possible. For example, code and testing methodologies may be saved. It is also helpful to debrief the team and have new assignments ready for them. Robert Wourms, an IT consultant, suggests that a report about the failed project should be written to document the lessons learned from both a business and technology perspective. IT mangers should also be trained on how to detect a failing project as early as possible. Often project managers take their projects to heart and want to see them through to the end. But, it is better that the IT manager be able to make the call before the CFO tells him or her to kill the project.

SOURCE: Adapted from Mark Hall, Dead in Its Tracks, *Computerworld,* March 18, 2002, http://www.computerworld.com /managementtopics/management/story/0,10801,69115,00.html.

championed a failed project or that a project will be unsuccessful in meeting its goals. The project budget receives a large cut or a series of smaller cuts. The result is that the project will eventually die and the project resources will be reassigned, even though the project is never officially closed.

Ideally, a project is closed or terminated under normal circumstances. The project achieves its desired goal and objectives. The project sponsor is delighted with the project's product and shows his or her delight by paying for the invoiced project work on time and contracts for more work in the future. Unfortunately, closing a project does not often happen this way. As J. Davidson Frame (1998) points out, the project manager and team should be prepared to deal with the following realities:

- *Team members are concerned about future jobs.* Often the members of the project team are borrowed from different departments or functional areas of the organization. Once the project is finished, they will return to their previous jobs. For consulting firms, the project team members will move from one project to the next as part of their career path. Regardless, as the project nears its end, these project team members may begin to wonder what they will do next. For some, there will be a rewarding life after the project—for others it may mean looking for new jobs. For many it may mean disrupting a close-knit relationship with other members of the project team (Meredith and Mantel 2000). Therefore, project team members may become preoccupied with moving on with their lives and the project at hand may become a lesser priority. As a result, the project team members may not focus on what has to be done to close the project, and wrapping up the project may be a challenge.

- *Bugs still exist.* Testing the information system is an important process of systems development. However, software quality testing may not find all the defects, and certain bugs may not become known until after the system has been implemented. The appearance of these problems can be frustrating and stressful to all the project stakeholders. Unless these defects and bugs are promptly addressed and fixed, the project sponsor's satisfaction with the project team and the information system may become an issue.

- *Resources are running out.* Resources and the project schedule are consumed from the project's earliest inception. At the end of the project, both resources and time remaining are usually depleted. As unanticipated issues, problems, or challenges arise, the project manager may find that adequate resources to deal with these events effectively are not available. The project manager may find his or her situation aggravated if management decides to cut or control the project's budget.

- *Documentation attains paramount importance.* Information technology projects have numerous documentation requirements. They require project, system, training, and user documentation. Under ideal circumstances, the time to write documentation is built into the project plan and completed throughout the project. Many times, however, documentation is put off until the end of the project. As the end draws near, documentation becomes increasingly important. As a result, documentation may require more time and resources to complete, or shortcuts are taken to remain within the current project constraints.

- *Promised delivery dates may not be met.* Most projects experience schedule slippage. This slippage may be due to poor project management, implementation risks, competitive requirements, or overly optimistic estimates. A project will require a certain amount of resources and a certain amount of time to complete. Any misjudgment concerning what has to be done, what is needed to complete the job, and how long it will take will result in a variance between the planned and actual schedule and budget.

- *The players may possess a sense of panic.* As schedules begin to slip and project resources become depleted, various project stakeholders may experience a sense of alarm. The mangers or partners of a consulting firm may worry that the project will not be profitable or satisfactory to the customer. The sponsor or customer may worry that the information system will not be delivered on time and within budget or provide the expected value to the organization. Moreover, the project manager and team may also be worried that the project will not be successful and the blame will rest squarely on their shoulders. As the sense of panic increases, the chances for an orderly closeout grow dim.

Regardless of whether a project ends normally or prematurely, it is important that an orderly set of processes be followed in order to bring it to closure. A good closeout allows the team to wrap up the project in a neat, logical manner. From an administrative view, this procedure allows for all loose ends to be tied up. From a psychological perspective, it provides all of the project stakeholders with a sense that the project was under control from the beginning through to its end (Frame 1998).

Project Sponsor Acceptance

The most important requirement for closure under normal circumstances is obtaining the project sponsor's acceptance of the project. Delivery, installation, and implementation of the information system do not necessarily mean that the project sponsor or client will accept the project's product. Since acceptance depends heavily on the fulfillment of the project's scope, the project manager becomes responsible for demonstrating that all project deliverables have been completed according to specifications (Wysocki, Beck et al. 1995). Ancillary items, such as documentation, training, and ongoing support, should not be afterthoughts. These items should have been included in the original scope of the project. Any attempt to renegotiate what is and what is not part of the project work at this late stage of the project can create ill feelings or hold up payment by the client (Rosenau 1998).

Rosenau (1998) observes that there are two basic types of project sponsors. *Shortsighted* sponsors tend to view the project as a short-term buyer-seller relationship in which getting the most for their money is the most important criteria for accepting the project. This view often leads to an adversarial relationship if the sponsor attempts to renegotiate the project scope or price at the end of the project.

Knowledgeable sponsors realize that they have an important stake in the outcome of the project. As a result, they will be actively involved throughout the project in a constructive manner. As Rosenau points out, knowledgeable sponsors may ask tough questions during project reviews, but their objective is not to embarrass the project team or manager, but to ensure the success of the project. Instead of an adversary trying to get the most in a "win-lose" situation, the knowledgeable sponsor will negotiate intelligently and in good faith.

Regardless of whether the sponsor is short-sighted or knowledgeable, the project manager and team can improve the likelihood that the project will be accepted if they (1) clearly define the acceptance criteria for the project at the early stages of the project, and (2) document the completion of all project deliverables and milestones.

A clear definition of the project deliverables is an important concern for project scope management (discussed in an earlier chapter). Yet, defining and verifying that the project scope and system requirements are accurate and complete is only one component. Having scope change procedures in place that are understood by all the project stakeholders also ensures that everyone has the same expectations concerning what will and what won't be delivered at the end of the project.

The IT project methodology incorporated in this text also focused on managing the project based on phases that focus on specific deliverables. Project milestones ensure that the deliverables are not only complete, but completed right. Documenting each deliverable and milestone throughout the project provides confidence to the project sponsor that the project has been completed fully.

The Final Project Report

In general, the project manager and team should develop a final report and presentation for the project sponsor and other key stakeholders. The objective of the report and presentation should be to give the project sponsor confidence that the project has been completed as outlined in the business case, project charter, and project plan. By gaining this confidence, the sponsor or client will be more likely to formally accept the project that will allow for a smooth termination of the project.

The report may be circulated to key stakeholders before the presentation in order to get feedback and to identify any open or unfinished items that need to be scheduled for completion (Rosenau 1998; Buttrick 2000). Once finalized, the final project report provides a background and history of the project. The report should include and discuss the following areas at a minimum:

- Project Summary
  - Project Description
  - Project MOV
  - Scope, Schedule, Budget, and Quality Objectives
- Comparison of Planned versus Actual
  - Original Scope and history of any approved changes
  - Original scheduled deadline versus actual completion date
  - Original budget versus actual cost of completing the project
  - Test plans and test results
- Outstanding Issues
  - Itemized list and expected completion
  - Any ongoing support required and duration
- Project Documentation List
  - Systems Documentation
  - User Manuals
  - Training Materials
  - Maintenance Documentation

The Final Meeting and Presentation

If the project manager has been diligent in gaining the confidence of the project sponsor, the final meeting and presentation should be a simple, straightforward affair. Buttrick (2000) suggests that the final meeting is useful for:

- *Communicating that the project is over.* By inviting key stakeholders to the meeting, the project manager is formally announcing that the project is over. This action not only provides a sense of closure for those close to the project, but also for the organization, as well.
- *Transferring the information system from the project team to the organization.* Although the information system may have been implemented and is being used by the organization, the final meeting provides a formal exchange of the project's product from the project team to the organization. Unless some type of ongoing support is part of the contractual agreement, this transfer signals that the project team will not be at the client or sponsor's site much longer.
- *Acknowledging contributions.* The meeting provides a forum for the project manager to acknowledge the hard work and contributions of the project team and other key stakeholders.
- *Getting formal signoff.* Finally, the meeting can provide a ceremony for the sponsor or client to formally accept the information system by signing off on the project. A space for signatures could be part of the final project report or part of some other contractual document.

Closing the Project

Once the project is accepted by the sponsor or customer, a number of administrative closure processes remain. These last items can be difficult because the project manager or team may view these administrative items as boring or because they are already looking forward to and thinking about their next assignment (Gray and Larson 2000). Unfortunately, administrative closure is a necessity because once the project manager and team are officially released from the current project, getting them to wrap up the last of the details will be difficult. The requirements for administrative closure include:

1. Verifying that all deliverables and open items are complete.
2. Verifying the project sponsor or customer's formal acceptance of the project.
3. Organizing and archiving all project deliverables and documentation.
4. Planning for the release of all project resources (i.e., project team members, technology, equipment, facilities, etc.).
5. Planning for the evaluations and reviews of the project team members and the project itself.
6. Closing of all project accounts.
7. Planning a celebration to mark the end of a (successful) project.

PROJECT EVALUATION

The question on everyone's mind throughout the project is, Will this project be successful? However, different stakeholders will have different views of success. For the project team members, it may be gaining valuable experience and feeling that their work will have a positive impact on the organization. For the project manager, it may be leading a project that will be profitable to the firm or a promotion to a larger and more visible project. On the other hand, the client or sponsor may view project success in terms of organizational value received after the project is implemented.

Therefore, four types of project evaluations should be conducted. There should be (1) an individual review of each team member's performance, (2) a postmortem review by the project manager and project team, (3) an audit of the project by an objective and respected outside party, and (4) an evaluation sometime after the project is implemented to determine whether the project achieved its envisioned MOV.

Individual Performance Review

The project manager should conduct an individual performance review with each project team member. Although the project organization may have its own process and procedure for conducting reviews, the project manager should focus on the following points:

■ *Begin with the individual evaluating his/her performance.* Evaluating someone's performance can be an emotional experience. Even with the best intentions, being critical of someone can put her or him on the defensive. Instead of beginning an evaluation with a critique of the individual's performance, it is usually more effective to begin by asking how *that person* would evaluate her or his performance. Surprisingly, most people are more critical of themselves. This opening provides an opportunity for the person doing the evaluation either to agree or to disagree with the individual's self-evaluation and to point out several positive aspects of the person's performance. This system creates a useful dialog that provides the individual with more useful feedback.

- *Avoid "why can't you be more like....?"* It is easy to compare individuals. Unfortunately, comparisons can have a counter effect. First, the person that you exalt may not be the shining star you think they are. Second, others may become jealous and look for ways to discredit or disparage the individual. Keep in mind that people are different and should be evaluated as individuals.

- *Focus on specific behaviors, not the individual.* When discussing opportunities for improvement with a person, it is important to focus on specific behaviors. For example, if a project team member has a habit of consistently showing up late and disrupting team meetings, it is important not to focus on the individual (i.e., why are you so lazy and disrespectful?), but on how showing up late to team meetings is disruptive. Often people do not realize how their behaviors affect others.

- *Be consistent and fair.* Being consistent and fair to everyone is easier said than done. The person conducting the evaluation should be aware of how decisions concerning one person may affect the entire group. Also, be aware that people talk to one another and often compare notes. Therefore, making a decision concerning one person may set a precedent for others. Having policies and procedures in place and sticking to them can mitigate the potential for inconsistency and the perception that that the evaluator is not fair with everyone.

- *Reviews should provide a consensus on improving performance.* The purpose of conducting a review or evaluation with each project team member is to provide constructive feedback for individuals. No one is perfect, so understanding where an individual can improve and how they might go about improving is important. The individual and the evaluator should agree on what areas the individual needs to improve upon and how the organization can support this endeavor. For example, the individual and the evaluator may agree that the team member should improve his or her communication skills. The evaluator may then recommend and provide support for the person to attend a particular training class.

The meeting can serve to help prepare the individual to move on and accept the psychological fact that the project will end (Gray and Larson 2000). And, in most cases, the project manager could use this meeting to discuss the project team member's next assignment.

Postmortem Review

Shortly after the final project report and presentation are completed, the project manager and project team should conduct a postmortem review of the project. This should be done before the project team is released from the current project. It is more difficult to get people to participate once they are busy working on other projects or if they no longer work for the project organization. Moreover, memories tend to become clouded as time passes. Thoroughness and clarity are critical (Nicholas 1990). The formal project summary report should focus on the project's MOV and the project management knowledge areas. The focus of this review should include the following:

- *Review the initial project's MOV.* Was the project's MOV clearly defined and agreed upon? Did it change over the course of the project? What is the probability that it will be achieved?

- *Review the project scope, schedule, budget, and quality objectives.* How well was the scope defined? Did it change? How effective were the scope management processes? How close were the project schedule and budget estimates to the actual deadline and cost of the project? Were the quality objectives met? How well did the quality management processes and standards support the project processes?

- *Review each of the project deliverables.* How effective were the business case, the project charter, the project plan, and so forth? How could these deliverables be improved?

- *Review the various project plans and Project Management Body of Knowledge (PMBOK) areas.* The team should review its effectiveness in the following areas:
  - project integration management
  - project scope management
  - project time management
  - project cost management
  - project quality management
  - project human resources management
  - project communications management
  - project risk management
  - project procurement management
  - organizational change management
  - project implementation

- *How well did the project team perform?* Were conflicts handled effectively? Did the team suffer any morale problems? What main challenges did the team face? How well did they handle these challenges? How well did the members function as a cohesive team?

The discussion and recommendations from the postmortem review should be documented. In particular, the project manager and team should identify what they did right and what they could have done better. These lessons learned should be documented so that they can be shared with others in the organization. Moreover, best practices should be identified and become part of the organization's IT project methodology.

Project Audit

The individual performance and postmortem reviews provide an important view of the internal workings of the project. In general, these reviews are conducted between the project manager and the project team. To provide a more objective view of the project, an audit or review by an outside party may be beneficial for uncovering problems, issues, or opportunities for improvement. Similar to the postmortem review, the auditor or audit team should focus on how well the project was managed and executed. This may include the project plans and Project Management Body of Knowledge areas described in the previous section, as well as the underlying project management and systems development processes outlined in the organization's IT project methodology. In addition, the auditor or audit team should assess whether the project manager and team acted in a professional and ethical manner.

As Gray and Larson (2000) suggest, the depth of the audit depends on the organization's size, the importance and size of the project, the risks involved, and the problems encountered. The audit may involve the project manager and the project team, as well as the project sponsor and other key project stakeholders. In addition, the third party auditor or audit team should:

- Have no direct involvement or interest in project.
- Be respected and viewed as impartial and fair.
- Be willing to listen.
- Present no fear of recrimination from special interests.
- Act in the organization's best interest.
- Have broad base of project and/or industry experience.

The findings or results of the project audit should be documented, as well as any lessons learned and best practices.

Evaluating Project Success—The MOV

The MOV, or measurable organization value, was defined at the beginning of the project. It provided the basis for taking on the project and supported many of the decision points throughout the project life cycle. Often, the MOV cannot be readily determined at the close of the project. Many of the benefits envisioned by the implemented system may require weeks or even months before they are realized.

Although the different project stakeholders and players may have different views as to whether the project was a success, it is important to assess the value that the project provides the organization. This review may be conducted by several people from both the project sponsor or client's organization and the organization or area responsible for carrying out the project. In particular, this review should focus on answering and documenting the following questions:

- Did the project achieve its MOV?
- Was the sponsor/customer satisfied?
- Was the project managed well?
- Did the project manager and team act in a professional and ethical manner?
- What was done right?
- What can be done better next time?

Before conducting this evaluation, the consulting firm or individuals representing the project should be sure that the information system delivered has not been changed. Often when an information system is handed over to the project sponsor, the users or support staff may make changes. It is not uncommon for these changes to have unintended adverse affects. Care should be taken to ensure that the system being evaluated is the system that was delivered (Nicholas 1990).

The evaluation of the project's MOV may be intimidating—it can be the moment of truth as to whether the project was really a success. However, a successful IT project that brings measurable value to an organization provides a foundation for organizational success.

◼ CHAPTER SUMMARY

This chapter provides closure for both this text and for managing an IT project. Throughout the project life cycle, processes to support both the project and development of the project's product—the information system—have been discussed. These processes are important for managing the project from its inception right through to its conclusion.

Once the information system has been built or purchased, it must be adequately tested in order to make installation of the system go more smoothly. However, implementation requires a tactical approach for ensuring that the information system is transferred efficiently and effectively from the project environment to the day-to-day operations of the organization.

Three approaches to implementation were discussed in this chapter. The first approach, called direct cutover, provides the quickest means for implementing the system. In general, the old system is turned off and the new system is turned on. This approach can be risky if the system has not been thoroughly tested. As a result, it can put a great deal of pressure on the project team to "get it right" the first time, especially if the system supports a mission critical function of the organization.

The parallel and phased approaches are less risky alternatives, although implementation may take longer. The parallel approach requires that both the old system and new system run concurrently for a time until there is enough confidence that the new system is working properly. At some point, a switch is made from the old system to the new system. The parallel approach can be stressful for the users of the system because they may be required to provide input for both systems and then compare the outputs.

The phased approach may be appropriate when implementing an upgrade or modular system in different departments or at different geographical locations. Under this approach, implementation takes place over phases according to a published schedule. Experience gained from early implementations can make later implementations go more smoothly; on the other hand, any unanticipated problems can create a chain reaction that pushes back the entire implementation schedule. Choosing and implementing the correct implementation approach can have a significant impact on the project schedule and budget.

Once the information system has been implemented, the project manager and team must plan for an orderly end to the project. Projects can be terminated for a variety of reasons, but a project must be properly closed, regardless of whether the project ends successfully or unsuccessfully. Ideally, the project is closed under normal conditions—that is, the project scope is completed within reasonable modifications to the original schedule, budget, and quality objectives. Delivery or installation of the information system does not necessarily mean that the project's sponsor or customer will accept the project. Therefore, closure must focus on providing both proof and confidence that the project team has delivered everything according to the original business case, project charter, and project plan.

A useful way to gain acceptance is the development of a final project report. This report provides a history of the project and outlines how each deliverable was completed and meets the standards of the client or sponsor. The report should also address any open items or issues so that they can be completed within a reasonable time. This report can serve as a foundation for the project team's final meeting with and presentation to the key stakeholders of the project. This meeting not only provides closure for the project, but also serves as a communication tool for informing the stakeholders that the project has been formally accepted and, therefore, is coming to an end.

Several processes for closing a project were discussed in this chapter. They include closing the project accounts, releasing or transferring project resources, documenting lessons learned, and archiving all project documents and deliverables.

Before a project is completely terminated, it is important that several reviews or evaluations be conducted. These evaluations include a performance review between the project manager and each project team member. A postmortem review with the project manager and the entire team should include all of the project deliverables, project plans, and, in general, the various project management body of knowledge areas. Lessons learned should be documented and best practices identified.

The performance reviews and postmortem should provide preparation for the project audit. In this case, a respected and objective third party should review all of the project deliverables and processes to assess how well the project was managed. The auditor or audit team should also focus on the specific challenges the project manager and team faced and how well they addressed these challenges. The professional and ethical behavior of the project manager and project team should be examined, as well.

The concept of a project's measurable organization value (MOV) has been a central theme in this text. The MOV provided a basis for deciding whether to invest in the project and guided many of the project decisions throughout the project life cycle. Although different stakeholders may have different views of project success, the overall guiding mechanism for determining whether the project was a success is the project's MOV. Unfortunately, the organizational value that a project provides may not be readily discernable immediately after the information system is implemented. Even if it

takes place weeks or months after the project is officially closed, an evaluation as to whether the project has met its MOV must still be conducted. This evaluation should involve various key stakeholders. This moment of truth may make some people anxious, but it provides the necessary means for determining whether the project has brought any real value to the organization.

REVIEW QUESTIONS

1. What is implementation?
2. Describe the three approaches to implementing an information system.
3. What are the advantages and disadvantages of the direct cutover approach?
4. What are the advantages and disadvantages of the parallel approach?
5. What are the advantages and disadvantages of the phased approach?
6. Describe the various scenarios for project termination.
7. Why might an organization terminate a project prematurely? What are the risks?
8. What is a perpetual project? Why might an organization be reluctant to terminate a project that many would consider unsuccessful?
9. Why would senior management cut a project's budget without officially terminating the project?
10. Why might some project team members be reluctant to see the end of a project?
11. Why can the end of a project be stressful for many of the project stakeholders?
12. Why is the sponsor's acceptance of the project important to project closure?
13. How can the project manager and project team facilitate the project sponsor's acceptance of the project?

14. What is the difference between a *shortsighted* and a *knowledgeable* project sponsor? How can making this distinction help the project manager during project closure?
15. What is the purpose of the final project report?
16. What is the purpose of the final meeting and presentation?
17. Describe some of the steps for administrative closure.
18. What is the purpose of the project manager conducting a performance review with each member of the project team?
19. What is the purpose of conducting a postmortem review?
20. What is the purpose of a project audit?
21. What criteria should be used to choose a project auditor or auditing team?
22. What is the purpose of evaluating the project's MOV?
23. Why would it be difficult to evaluate whether or not a project achieved its MOV shortly after the information system is implemented?
24. Why should any lessons learned from project evaluations be documented?
25. Why would evaluating whether a project achieved its MOV make many project managers and teams anxious? Why should it still be done?

EXTEND YOUR KNOWLEDGE

1. Suppose you are the project manager for a midsized consulting firm. You have been leading a team of twelve consultants who have been working three months on a six-month project for your firm's largest client. You have managed two projects in the past for this client, and both of these projects were successful. In fact, the client has asked that you personally lead the current project. Your relationship with the client's Chief Information Officer (CIO)

has been excellent. Unfortunately, that CIO left the company two weeks ago to start a blues band. Her replacement has just been hired, and your meeting with the new CIO this morning did not go well at all. The new CIO figuratively shredded a status report that you had prepared. Moreover, the CIO seemed to have little understanding of the technology being used to develop the system and complained that the prototypes of the user interface that your team had developed were "too hard to understand and use." Just before leaving his office, the new CIO mentioned that this project was costing way too much money and taking too long to complete. Given the state of the economy, some cuts to project's budget and schedule may be forthcoming.

a. Given the situation, do you think this project will survive?

b. Terminating this project prematurely would have a major impact on the profitability of your firm. What could you do to save either the project or the long-term relationship with this client?

2. Suppose that a client has complained that your organization has allegedly acted in a manner both unprofessional and unethical. While investigating these allegations, senior management has asked you to draft a one-page statement to guide your organization's behavior. How could this code be monitored to ensure that all employees comply? You may use the World Wide Web (WWW) or any other resources as reference, but be sure to cite your references.

3. Using the WWW or any other resources (e.g., you could interview a project manager), write a summary of a company's experience implementing an Enterprise Resource Planning (ERP) system. Was this implementation successful? Why or why not? What were the major challenges? Did the implementation go according to plan? What lessons did the organization learn from this experience? Be sure to include your reference(s).

BIBLIOGRAPHY

Buttrick, R. 2000. *The Interactive Project Workout.* London: Prentice Hall/Financial Times.

Frame, J. D. 1998. Closing Out the Project. In *Project Management Handbook,* edited by J. K. Pinto. San Francisco, Calif.: Jossey-Bass: 237–246.

Gray, C. F. and E. W. Larson. 2000. *Project Management: The Managerial Process.* Boston: Irwin McGraw-Hill.

Keil, M. 1995. Pulling the Plug: Software Project Management and the Problem of Project Escalation. *MIS Quarterly* (December): 421–447.

Meredith, J. R. and S. J. Mantel, Jr. 2000. *Project Management: A Managerial Approach.* New York: John Wiley.

Nicholas, J. M. 1990. *Managing Business and Engineering Projects: Concepts and Implementation.* Upper Saddle River, N.J.: Prentice Hall.

Rosenau, M. D. J. 1998. *Successful Project Management.* New York: John Wiley.

Wysocki, R. K., R. J. Beck, et al. 1995. *Effective Project Management.* New York: John Wiley.

An Introduction to Function Point Analysis

This appendix provides more information about function point analysis. Keep in mind that even this discussion will provide you with only a basic understanding. Although function point analysis is not difficult, the rules for counting function points can be complex for the novice. Resources, such as books, Web sites, training, and certification, are widely available if you are interested in learning more.

BACKGROUND

Lines of code (LOC) or source lines of code (SLOC) have been the traditional way of estimating the size of an application. Although intuitively appealing, estimating or counting lines of code have several disadvantages. First, many organizations develop applications using different programming languages, platforms, tools, and so on. An IT project developed in Visual Basic and SQL Server will be difficult to compare to a mainframe-based COBOL application. Moreover, experienced and talented programmers tend to write more efficient code than novice programmers. As a result, experienced programmers may write fewer lines of code than novices and still accomplish the same thing. In addition, no set standard exists for determining what exactly should be counted. For example, should remarks or documentation lines be counted? What about the initialization of variables? Although counting lines of code seems fairly straightforward, the actual implementation becomes problematic.

To overcome many of the inherent problems with counting LOC, Allan Albrecht proposed the idea of function points at a conference sponsored by IBM in 1979. The basic concept behind function points is to focus on the *functionality* of the application. After all, the size and complexity of an application (and subsequently the number of lines of code to be written) are based upon what the application must do. Function points provide a synthetic metric, similar to hours, kilos, and degrees Celsius, for software engineering that gives consistent results, regardless of the technology or programming language used.

In the early 1980s, statistical analysis provided the means for refining the function point technique. Since 1986, function point analysis rules and guidelines have been overseen by a nonprofit organization called the International Function Point Users Group (IFPUG). The IFPUG maintains the *Counting Practices Manual* that contains all the current guidelines and certification for counting function points under the IFPUG standard. The material in this appendix will be based upon the latest counting practices by IFPUG.

You should know, however, that there is an alternative way of counting function points. In 1983, Charles Symons, working for Nolan, Norton, and Company (later acquired by KPMG Consulting) critiqued Albrecht's proposed function point technique and argued the existence of several flaws. As a result, Symons proposed an alternative function point technique called the Mark II approach. The Mark II technique has become popular primarily in the United Kingdom and is overseen by the United Kingdom Function Point Users Group (UFPUG).

WHAT PRECISELY IS A FUNCTION POINT?

Function point analysis is a structured technique for breaking up or modularizing an application by categories or classes based on functionality. A function point is a software metric. Similar to the many metrics you use each day, a function point provides an idea of the size and complexity of a particular application or module of that application. For example, it should be pretty straightforward that a 4,000-square-foot home is larger than a 2,000-square-foot home. But will a 4,000-square-foot house take twice as long and cost twice as much as a 2,000-square-foot house? It depends. What if the larger house uses stock material and includes only the basic amenities while the 2,000-square-foot house has many custom features? The custom features may include a handcrafted staircase, exotic wood, imported marble, and other very expensive items. As you can see, depending on the features or requirements of each house, the time to build and the cost for each house can differ radically (Dekker 1999).

Similarly, an application that has 4,000 LOC has twice as many lines of code as a 2,000 LOC application. But will a 4,000 LOC application take twice as long and cost twice as much to build as a 2,000 LOC application? Again, the answer is that it depends. In this case, it depends more on the features or required functionality of the system and the complexity of those required features. Function points provide a useful metric that combines both functionality and complexity. For example, a 4,000 function point application will, in fact, be larger, have more functionality, and be more complex than a 2,000 function point application. Since function points are independent of the technology, we can compare these two applications regardless of the fact that one application is written in Java and the other in COBOL. More specifically, the size of the application is based upon functionality in terms of:

- Inputs
- Outputs
- Inquiries
- Internal files
- External files
- The complexity of the general characteristics of the system

Therefore, the key to function point analysis is having a good understanding of the system's requirements. Often at the outset of a project, the requirements may not be clear. A function point analysis can still be conducted and then updated throughout the project life cycle as these requirements become more clearly defined. For example, a function point analysis can be conducted based upon the definition of the project's scope. This analysis will provide a solid definition of the application's boundary and will provide a starting point for defining and subsequently estimated the size and complexity of the application deliverable. A clearer picture of the features and functionality of the application will follow during the analysis and design phases of the project. Later on, a function point analysis can be conducted when the project application is delivered, in order to compare the agreed upon requirements to what was delivered. In general, function points can be useful for:

- *Managing Scope*—Scope changes will change an application's total function point count. As a result, the project manager and project sponsor/client use function point analysis to determine the impact of a proposed scope change in terms of the project's schedule and budget.

- *Benchmarking*—The value of function point analysis is that data can be collected and compared to other projects. For example, the true value of counting function points is to compare a project to past projects and to other projects throughout the organization. This comparison allows an organization to identify challenges and opportunities in order to take corrective action when necessary. In addition, estimation becomes more meaningful and accurate when similar methods, tools, and resources are part of the data analysis. An organization can inventory its application portfolio to understand cost structures and the impact of new best practices. Function points by themselves do not provide much information without the use of other metrics, such as time, cost, and quality.

- *Reliability*—Once knowledgeable and experienced in function point counting, different people can count function points for the same application and obtain the same measure within an acceptable margin of error.

HOW TO CONDUCT A FUNCTION POINT ANALYSIS

The process of conducting a function point analysis can be summarized in seven steps:

- Determine the function type count to be conducted.
- Define the boundary of the application.
- Define all data functions and their degree of complexity.
- Define all transactional functions and their complexity.
- Calculate the Unadjusted Function Point Count.
- Calculate the Value Adjustment Factor based on a set of General System Characteristics.
- Calculate the final Adjusted Function Point Count.

Step 1: Determine the Function Type Count to Be Conducted

The first step in conducting a function point analysis is to determine the type of function count to be conducted. Function points can be counted by an individual or a small team, and the type of function point count will help the counters plan their strategy and determine what documents and resources will be required. A function type count can be one of three types:

- *Development*—A development function type count would be made for a new project. These types of counts would be based initially on the scope definition of the project and would be updated throughout the project life cycle as requirements and functionality are more clearly defined. The basic purpose of development function type counts is estimating the size and effort of the application.

- *Enhancement*—Enhancement focuses more on maintenance projects, or projects that attempt to modify or enhance existing applications. These projects may include deleting, changing, or adding functionality to the existing application.

- *Application*—An application function type count may be viewed as an inventorying of an existing application in the IT project portfolio in order to create a baseline or benchmark. Combined with other metrics, a database can be created to support analysis and estimation.

Step 2: Define the Boundary of the Application

The application boundary defines the border for the user, the application itself, and any other external application. The boundary should be based upon the user's view of the domain and not technology partitions or platforms. Often applications today must interface or integrate with each other, so it is important that the boundary be defined clearly. Scope management is concerned with defining, managing, and controlling the project's scope. More specifically, tools such as data flow diagrams and use case diagrams are useful for defining the project's scope and the boundary for the application.

Step 3: Define All Data Functions and Their Degree of Complexity

Data function types may be thought of as data at rest; they are the logical data that can be updated and queried. The transactional functions, such as external inputs (EI), external outputs (EO), and external inquiries (EQ), are processes that set the data in motion. These processes act directly on the logical data to perform the updates and queries. In particular, data functions can be either internal logical files (ILF) or external interface files (EIF). As their names imply, ILFs are maintained within the application boundary and EIFs are maintained by an external application but available to the application being counted. For example, a sales application might keep track of customers and the products they purchase, but customer balances and other credit-related information may be maintained by a separate accounts receivable application.

Once the ILFs and EIFs are identified and counted, they are scored or rated based on their functional complexity in terms of their number of record type elements (RETs) and data element types (DETs). A record type element, or RET, is a recognizable subgroup of data elements contained within the ILF or EIF. These are one of the more difficult concepts in function point analysis, but you can think of them as representing a parent-child relationship. In object-oriented terms, you can think of this as a subclass and a superclass. On the other hand, a data element type, or DET, is defined as a unique, non-recursive field recognized by the user. For example, let's say that an entity called student has a student identification number, name, address, and a cumulative number of credit hours. In addition, there are two types of students—undergraduate and graduate. If the data about students were stored, updated, retrieved, and queried by our application, we would count this as 1 ILF with 6 DETs and 2 RETs as illustrated in Table A.1.

Once the ILFs and EIFs and their associated RETs and DETs have been identified and counted, their complexity can be determined using the matrix shown in Table A.2. For example, the Student ILF would have a complexity score of Low because the number of RETs is less than 2 and the number of DETs is between 1 and 19.

Step 4: Define all Transactional Functions and Their Complexity

Transactional functional types focus on the processing of data between the user and the application and between the application and any external applications. Therefore, transactional functions, called external inputs (EIs), external outputs (EOs), and external inquiries, (EQs) perform updates, retrievals, and queries on the data contained within the ILFs and EIFs.

An external input (EI) is defined as an elementary process that processes data or control information that originates from outside the application boundary. An elementary process is defined as the smallest unit of activity that is meaningful to the user. The elementary process must be viewed from the user's perspective (i.e., not a technical perspective) and must leave the application in a consistent state after performing its function. Data refers to the actual data processed by the transaction, while control information refers to such things as rules or parameters passed to application. An example of an EI would be an input screen to add new students to the student ILF. The elementary process would require that all required fields be filled before adding the new student's information to the student ILF in order to leave the application in a consistent state.

Once the EIs have been identified and counted, their complexity can be determined using the following matrix based on the file types referenced (FTR) and data element types. An FTR is just the number of ILF and EIF files referenced. For example, if an input screen to add new students only accessed the student ILF and included only 6 DETs, the complexity rating for this particular EI would be Low. See Table A.3.

Similarly, an external output (EO) is an elementary process that allows data or control information to exit the application boundary. Examples of EOs would include reports, receipts, confirmation messages, derived or calculated totals, and graphs or charts. Once the EOs are identified and counted, their relative functional complexity can be determined based on the FTRs and DETs. Continuing with our example, suppose that the student application printed two reports, one report listing all the students alphabetically and the other grouping by graduate and undergraduate. If all data fields were included in each report, the complexity rating for the application's EOs would be Low. See Table A.4.

An external inquiry (EQ) is defined as an elementary process that includes both a combination of inputs and outputs for retrieving data from one or more ILFs and/or EIFs. Unlike an EI, the EQ input process does not update any internal or external files, and the output of the EQ transaction does not calculate or derive any data. Once the EQs have been identified and counted, a relative complexity score can be made. For example, let's suppose our student application allows searching by student number. This query would count as one EQ. In addition, let's suppose that an error message is displayed if no matching student numbers are found. The number of DETs would include the 6 data fields plus an additional DET for the error

Table A.1 Data Function Count

	Count As
Superclass: Student	ILF
Student ID number	DET
Name	DET
Address	DET
Cumulative credit hours	DET
Subclass: Graduate	RET
Graduate assistantship	DET
Subclass: Undergraduate	RET
Class standing	DET

Table A.2 Complexity for ILFs and EIFs

RET: Record Element Type	DET: Data Element Type		
	1–19	*20–50*	*51 or More*
Less than 2	Low	Low	Average
2–5	Low	Average	High
More than 5	Average	High	High

Table A.3 Complexity for External Inputs (EI)

FTR: File Types Referenced	DET: Data Element Type		
	1–4	*5–15*	*16 or More*
Less than 2	Low	Low	Average
2	Low	Average	High
More than 2	Average	High	High

Table A.4 Complexity for External Outputs (EO)

FTR: File Types Referenced	DET: Data Element Type		
	1–5	*6–19*	*20 or More*
Less than 2	Low	Low	Average
2–3	Low	Average	High
More than 3	Average	High	High

message. Therefore, the complexity rating for the application's EQ would be Low. See Table A.5.

Step 5: Calculate the Unadjusted Function Point Count

Using the counts for each ILF, EIF, EI, EO, and EQ, an Unadjusted Function Point count can be computed using Table A.6.

To find the Total Unadjusted Function Point Total (UAF), multiply the number of low, average, and high ILFs, EIFs, EIs, EOs, and EQs by the appropriate number in each cell. These values are then summed across the rows for each function type. The grand total is just a summation of these row totals.

Step 6: Calculate the VAF Based on a Set of General System Characteristics

The Value Adjustment Factor (VAF) is multiplied by the Unadjusted Function Point (UAF) calculated in step 5 to come up with a Final Adjusted Function Point total. In identifying each ILF, EIF, EO, EI, and EQ, a complexity matrix was used to determine the complexity for each data and transactional function type in terms of low, average, or high complexity. However, at this time a set of fourteen General System Characteristics (GSC) are used to compute a Total Degree of Influence. This degree of influence will be used to compute the VAF.

To determine the Total Degree of Influence, each GSC is rated based on its degree of influence using the following 0 to 5 scale:

0. Not present or no influence
1. Incidental influence
2. Moderate influence
3. Average influence
4. Significant influence
5. Strong influence throughout

Table A.5 Complexity for External Inquiries (EQ)

FTR: File Types Referenced	DET: Data Element Type		
	1–5	*6–19*	*20 or More*
Less than 2	Low	Low	Average
2–3	Low	Average	High
More than 3	Average	High	High

Table A.6 Computing UAF

	Complexity			
	Low	Average	High	Total
Internal Logical Files (ILF)	__ × 7 = __	__ × 10 = __	__ × 15 = __	
External Interface Files (EIF)	__ × 5 = __	__ × 7 = __	__ × 10 = __	
External Input (EI)	__ × 3 = __	__ × 4 = __	__ × 6 = __	
External Output (EO)	__ × 4 = __	__ × 5 = __	__ × 7 = __	
External Inquiry (EQ)	__ × 3 = __	__ × 4 = __	__ × 6 = __	
Total Unadjusted Function Points (UAF)				

Following is information about each GSC that can be used to rate it.

1. *Data Communications*—A communication facility is required to send data and control information via teleprocessing (TP). These links require protocols that allow for the exchange of data between a sender and receiver. Examples include TCP/IP, Ethernet, AppleTalk, etc.

   Degree of Influence

   0. Pure batch or stand-alone PC

   1. Batch but with remote data entry or printing

   2. Batch but with remote data entry and remote printing

   3. Online data collection or TP on the front end to a batch processing or query system

   4. More than a front end, but only one type of TP protocol supported

   5. More than a front end with more than one type of TP protocol supported

2. *Distributed Data Processing*—Distributed data processing is a characteristic of the application.

   Degree of Influence

   0. Does not aid the transfer of data or processing function between components of the system

   1. Prepares data for end user processing or another component of the system (e.g., spreadsheet, DBMS, etc.)

   2. Data prepared for transfer, then transferred and processed by another component

   3. Distributed processing and data transfer are online but only in one direction

   4. Distributed processing and data transfer are online and in both directions

   5. Processing of functions is dynamic and performed by the most appropriate component of the system

3. *Performance*—Performance in terms of response time or throughput. It will greatly influence the design, development, implementation, support, and maintenance of the application.

   Degree of Influence

   0. No special performance requirements stated

   1. Performance and design requirements stated and reviewed, but no special attention needed

   2. Response time or throughput critical at peak times. No special design required and processing deadline is the next business day

   3. Response time and throughput are critical during all business hours. Although no special design for CPU utilization is required, the processing deadline requirements with interfacing systems pose constraints

   4. Stated user performance requirements are stringent and require a performance analysis in the design phase

   5. Performance analysis tools needed in the design, development, and/or implementation phases to meet stated user performance requirements

4. *Heavily Used Configuration*—The volume of data and transactions placed on a particular hardware platform.

   Degree of Influence

   0. No operational restrictions
   1. Operational restrictions exist, but are not overly restrictive and no special attention is needed
   2. Some security and timing considerations are needed
   3. Specific processor requirements for a specific component of the application exist
   4. Stated operational restrictions exist and require special attention
   5. There are special constraints with respect to the distributed components of the system

5. *Transaction Rate*—Similar to GSC 3, the number of transactions handled by the application will be a performance consideration with respect to the design, development, implementation, and maintenance of the system.

   Degree of Influence

   0. No peak transaction period is anticipated
   1. A single peak transaction period (i.e., daily, weekly, monthly, etc.) is anticipated
   2. A peak transaction period will occur weekly
   3. A peak transaction period will occur daily
   4. Transaction rates are high enough that a performance analysis is required during the design phase
   5. Transaction rates are high enough to require performance analysis and, in addition, the use of performance analysis tools during the design, development, and/or implementation phases

6. *Online Data Entry*—The amount of data entered online will influence the design development, implementation, and maintenance of the application. Note: these guidelines may not be realistic since they have not been updated to reflect most systems today.

   Degree of Influence

   0. All transactions are processed in batch mode
   1. 1–7 % of transactions are done interactively
   2. 8–15% of transactions are done interactively
   3. 16–23% of transactions are done interactively
   4. 24–30% of transactions are done interactively
   5. Over 30% of transactions are done interactively

7. *End User Efficiency*—The functions provided by the application may emphasize user efficiency. This may include

   ▪ Navigational aids
   ▪ Menus
   ▪ Online help/documentation
   ▪ Automated cursor movement

- Scrolling
- Remote printing
- Preassigned function keys
- Submission of batch jobs from online transactions
- Cursor selection of screen data
- Heavy use of reverse video, highlighting, colors, etc.
- Hard copy user documentation of online transactions
- Mouse interface
- Pop up windows
- As few screens as possible to accomplish a business function
- Bilingual support
- Multilingual support

Degree of Influence

0. None
1. 1–3
2. 4–5
3. Six or more but with no specific user requirements in terms of efficiency
4. Six or more and stated user requirements are strong enough to require design tasks for human factors to be included (e.g., minimize keystrokes)
5. Six or more and stated user requirements are strong enough to require special tools and processes to demonstrate that requirements have been achieved

8. *Online Update*—Related to the number of ILFs updated by the application.

Degree of Influence

0. None
1. Online update of one to three files, but volume of updating is low and recovery is easy
2. Online update of four or more files, but volume is low and recovery is easy
3. Online update of major internal files internal logical files (ILF)
4. In addition, protection from data loss is critical and must be specially designed and built into the system
5. In addition, high volumes lead to high recovery cost considerations, whereby recovery procedures must be automated and cause minimal operator intervention

9. *Complex Processing*—Complex processing is a characteristic of the application and includes:

- Sensitive control and/or application specific security processing
- Extensive logical processing
- Extensive mathematical processing
- A great deal of exception processing whereby incomplete transactions that may be caused by such things as TP interruption, missing data values, or failed edits must be processed again

■ Complex processing to handle multiple input/output possibilities (e.g., multimedia or device dependence)

Degree of Influence

0. None
1. Any one
2. Any two
3. Any three
4. Any four
5. All five

10. *Reusability*—The degree to which the application will usable in other applications.

Degree of Influence

0. There is no reusable code
1. Reusable code is used within the application
2. Less than 10% of the application considers more than one user's needs
3. 10% or more of the application considered more than one user's needs
4. The application was specially developed to ease reuse. The application is customizable to the user at the source code level
5. The application was specifically designed to ease reuse. The application is customizable to use at source code level by means of user parameter maintenance

11. *Installation Ease*—The ease or degree of difficulty during conversion and installation.

Degree of Influence

0. No special considerations stated by the user. No special setup required
1. No special considerations stated by the user. However, special setup required for installation
2. Conversion and installation requirements stated by the user. Conversion and installation guides provided and tested, but impact of conversion is not considered important
3. Conversion and installation requirements stated by the user. Conversion and installation guides provided and tested, but impact of conversion is considered important
4. In addition to 2., automated conversion and installation tools were provided and tested
5. In addition to 3., automated conversion tools were provided and tested

12. *Operational Ease*—The efficiency and effectiveness of startup, backup, and recovery procedures that were provided and tested during the system testing phase.

Degree of Influence

0. No special considerations were stated by the user other than normal backup procedures

1–4. Select the following items that apply to the application. Each item has a value of one unless noted otherwise:

- Effective startup, backup, and recovery processes were provided, but operator intervention is required.

- Effective startup, backup, and recovery processes were provided, but no operator intervention is required (count as 2 items).

- The application minimizes the need for tape mounts.

- The application minimizes the need for paper handling.

5. The application is designed for unattended operation—that is, no operator intervention is needed other than to start or shut down the application. Automatic error recovery is a feature of the application.

13. *Multiple Sites*—The degree to which the application has been designed specifically to be installed and operated at multiple sites and/or for multiple organizations.

Degree of Influence

0. Only one user/installation site is required

1. Needs of multiple sites were considered and the application is designed to operate only under identical hardware and software environments.

2. Needs of multiple sites were considered and the application is designed to operate only under similar hardware and software environments.

3. Needs of multiple sites were considered and the application is designed to operate only under different hardware and software environments.

4. Documentation and a support plan are provided and tested to support the application at multiple sites as described in 1. or 2.

5. Documentation and a support plan are provided and tested to support the application at multiple sites as described in 3.

14. *Facilitate Change*—The degree to which the application was developed to facilitate change.

Degree of Influence

0. No special user requirements were stated to minimize or facilitate change

1–5. Select the items that apply to the application:

- Flexible query/report facility is provided to handle simple requests—i.e., and/or logic is applied to only one ILF (count as 1)

- Flexible query/report facility is provided that can handle requests of average complexity—i.e., and/or logic applied to more than one ILF (count as 2 items)

- Flexible query/report facility is provide that can handle complex requests—i.e., and/or logic combinations on one or more ILFs (count as 3 items)

- Control data is kept in tables and maintained by the user online. Changes take effect next business day

- Control data kept in tables and maintained by the user online. Changes take effect immediately (count as 2 items)

Once each of the fourteen General Systems Characteristics (GSCs) is evaluated on a scale of one to five, the fourteen scores are summed to compute the Total Degrees of Influence.

$$\text{TDI} = \sum_{i=1}^{14} \text{Degrees of Influence}$$

The TDI is then used to determine the Value Added Adjustment Factor (VAF) using the following equation:

$$\text{VAF} = (\text{TDI} \times 0.01) + .65$$

Note that if all the degrees of influence for each of the GSCs are scored as zero, the VAF will be equal to .65. On the other hand, if all of the GSCs are scored as five, the VAF will be equal to 1.35. Therefore, simpler systems will score closer to .65, while more complex systems will score closer to 1.35. Subsequently, an application of average complexity will score close to 1.00. Therefore, the VAF can be used as a reality check for assessing the overall complexity of the application.

Step 7: Calculate the Final Adjusted Function Point Count

The Final Adjusted Function Point Count is readily found by multiplying the Unadjusted Function Point (UAF) by the Value Added Adjustment Factor (VAF).

$$\text{FP} = \text{UAF} \times \text{VAF}$$

The project team should then review the function point analysis for completeness and accuracy. Errors usually are the result of forgetting or missing something; therefore, the person or small group in charge of the function point analysis should be certified and use the most current standards as published in the IFPUG *Counting Practices Manual.* As with most things in life, function point analysis becomes easier and more meaningful with experience. If a function point analysis is conducted for each application, the function point information can be married with other financial and non-financial metrics to improve estimating and understanding of the development process.

BIBLIOGRAPHY

Albrecht, Allan J. 1979. Measuring Application Development Productivity. Proceedings SHARE/GUIDE IBM Applications Development Symposium, Monterey, Calif., Oct 14–17, 1979.

Albrecht, A. J. and J. E. Gaffney. 1983. Software Function, Source Lines of Code and Development Effort Prediction: A Software Science Validation. *IEEE Transactions Software Engineering,* SE-9(6): 639–647.

Boehm, B. W. 1981. *Software Engineering Economics.* Englewood Cliffs, N.J.: Prentice Hall.

Dekker, C. A. 1999. Managing (the size of) your projects: A project management look at function points. *Crosstalk: The Journal of Defense Software Engineering,* February: 24–26.

Dennis, A. and W. B. Haley. 2000. *Systems Analysis and Design: An Applied Approach.* New York: John Wiley.

Garmus, D. and D. Herron. 1996. *Measuring the Software Process.* Upper Saddle River, N.J.: Prentice Hall.

Jones, T. C. 1998. *Estimating Software Costs.* New York: McGraw-Hill.

Longstreet, David. *Function Point Training and Analysis Manual.* Longstreet Consulting Inc, Revision Dates: Feb. 2001, 30 Aug. 2001, 1 March 2002. <http://www.SoftwareMetrics.Com/free-manual.htm>.

McConnell, S. 1996. *Rapid Development: Taming Wild Software Schedules.* Redmond, Wash.: Microsoft Press.

INDEX